BEST OF ALL HE LOVED THE FALL
THE LEAVES YELLOW ON THE COTTONWOODS
LEAVES FLOATING ON THE TROUT STREAMS
AND ABOVE THE HILLS
THE HIGH BLUE WINDLESS SKIES
NOW HE WILL BE A PART OF THEM FOREVER
ERNEST HEMINGWAY · IDAHO · 1939

"*and best
of all
he loved
the fall*"

High on the Wild
with
Hemingway

SAN FRANCISCO DE PAULA, CUBA, SUMMER OF 1940
A fine likeness of Papa Hemingway, who gave the negative to this writer. Photograph made by Toby Bruce with the novelist's battered old Graflex.

High on the Wild with Hemingway

By

LLOYD R. ARNOLD

ILLUSTRATED WITH PHOTOGRAPHS

The CAXTON PRINTERS, Ltd.
CALDWELL, IDAHO
1969

First printing November, 1968
Second printing January, 1969

Library of Congress Catalog Card No. 68-15029

Lithographed and bound in the United States of America by
The CAXTON PRINTERS, Ltd.
Caldwell, Idaho   83605
111666

To Tillie
and
In memory of my father, Bill

Acknowledgement

Acknowledgement is made to Ellis Chapin, to Lou Holliday, and to Ken Crabtree for photos made for this book in co-operation with the writer.

Foreword

The author was a good and true friend of Papa's over a span of twenty-two years. He has remained my friend and my family's for that long and more. Over the years of Hemingway peregrinations to Idaho, Lloyd's life was inextricably interwoven with ours, first as a photographer and fellow shooter, then increasingly, then permanently as a part of Hemingway life in Idaho.

This book is Lloyd's sympathetic and evocative testimony to an important facet of my father's life. He brings to it a well-founded understanding of the elements which go to make up a sportsman as well as a deep love and appreciation for a sportsman's country. Perhaps, most importantly, Lloyd's sense of humor and his Westerner's way of expression give to his book a very special quality of earthiness and of truthfulness.

HIGH ON THE WILD WITH HEMINGWAY will stand, and well, on its own merits without the added dividend of a profuse and well-chosen collection of Lloyd Arnold's own photographs. I am happy that a small group of old and close friends gathered after Papa's funeral in 1961 and were more than right when they agreed that, to tell the story of "the way it really was" in Idaho, Lloyd Arnold was the one.

John H. Hemingway

KETCHUM, IDAHO
March 21, 1968

Table of Contents

List of Illustrations

1.

On a Bright Morning . . .

1

On a bright morning in the last days of the summer of 1939, I rode a spirited horse across the path of a big darkly colored man and a tall attractive blonde girl on the grounds at Sun Valley, Idaho. At some fifty yards between us, my first glance at the strangers was a casual one, and necessarily brief; the horse I had coveted for some time and now intended to buy was in charge for a few seconds when I mounted up at the wrangler corral between the resort's hotels. I had stopped there to make a phone call, reporting in about a date within the hour. It was near nine o'clock, and at ten we were to ride up big Baldy Mountain, then being developed as one of the world's great ski hills, the work in progress at a rush pace for the winter opening in December. At that time the not quite three-year-old Sun Valley was almost as quiet as if closed; in fact its Lodge was closed for the fall, the sprawling Challenger Inn the hostelry open to the public for the off-season. But the couple who arrested my attention were walking briskly from the Lodge, obviously heading for a late breakfast at the Inn; besides that, the big man, dressed like a ranch hand slicked up for a night in town, had a familiar look about him. When I lifted my hand in a little "Howdy, strangers" salute he grinned broadly and returned it, snapping it off briskly as a sharp soldier would do. In a dozen paces of my horse we were out of sight, but by then my wits were putting together a few facts: the massive stranger in the neat but worn blue jeans, very flat-soled boots, wearing a fringed latigo leather hunting vest over a light shirt with rolled-up sleeves, was none other than Ernest Hemingway. The clues were so obvious that I would bet the horse under me; I gave him his head on the soft road to the stables a quarter mile down valley where one of the wranglers informed me that I was to meet my good friend and colleague, Gene Van Guilder, the publicity genius for Sun Valley, in the lobby of the Inn as quickly as I could make it there. That cinched it; I was the resort's chief photographer, in which capacity I was quite sure we would not be riding up the mountain that day.

I was right, and I knew that Gene Van Guilder, whose original idea it was to lure

Hemingway into coming for a look at Sun Valley, would be as surprised as I. For over two years and a few months we had worked as closely together as men can, in perfect harmony, at a business strange to both of us at the start. Gene was an Idahoan, I came in 1937, when the brand-new glittering resort, with a single winter season to its credit, was still in the building stage—a sprawling confusion, to say the least, an enormous investment to its builders, the Union Pacific Railroad, the fabulous brainchild of the company's board chairman, Averell Harriman.

But this narrative is concerned as much with country as with a great resort, and odd as it may seem, Ernest Hemingway was, by his own admission, a "publicity property" as the parlance of the trade would have it; and he was not the only one in those formative years of Sun Valley. His name and presence had value, the country had the same for him, a big land of great variance that was much like I expected, and more—which is the key to all that follows here.

It had happened to be my good fortune that the railroad's chief photographer selected me to spend the first summer with him at Sun Valley, exploiting with all pho-

With my hands full of *mucho caballo*, I gave him but a glance. . . .

tographic mediums the great fishing, the fantastic mountain scenery to the north of the resort via pack string; for though conceived as a skiing mecca in Averell Harriman's mind, Sun Valley was also blueprinted as a year-round Western playground second to none. Due to a sudden change of plans I had missed the first winter season. I did not mind at all, for I was no winter sports fan—not in my home country where snow was something to shovel off our sidewalks in Council Bluffs, Iowa, where I was born and raised. But when my boss, a genial but hardworking, hardheaded Scotsman named Vince Hunter, chose me from his small staff for the Idaho job I was ready, and somewhat prepared for it by previous experiences in other parts of the West.

When we got off the train at Shoshone on June 7 in 1937 I was not at all impressed with the incessant winds of the seemingly endless flat country of sagebrush. In the off-season the only way to get up to Ketchum, fifty-six miles north at the end of the rail's branch line, was to wait until the following morning and ride the caboose of the local daily freight train, or take a small privately-operated bus that met our train at a little past noon. We took the little bus, a stretched-out Model A Ford affair that we

. . . like a big ranch hand slicked up for a night on the town. (September 20, 1939.)

Gene Van Guilder, the first of a pair of real sharpies to think
of luring Hemingway to Idaho, a remote but successful idea
two years later.

RODEO MAJORDOMO
Sports Director Bob Miles, who seconded Gene's idea—in
Cooke City, Montana, in July, 1937.

and our load of gear almost filled to capacity; its driver was the owner of the line
and a fair talk-up man for the country. A short way north of town where Highway
93 crossed a narrow belt of low-crop agricultural land he remarked of it being as fine
pheasant hunting in the fall as a man could find. I point-blank asked him where
in hell was the tall corn, like we hunted in in South Dakota, for the gaudy king of
the upland birds? I must say that Idaho was not an advertiser of itself in those days,
and I had never heard of it as pheasant country, or for any game you hunted with a
shotgun. To me it was a state of big game. I took the man's word and put it out of
mind—we had no plans for beyond the summer.

Ahead of us for nearly thirty miles the monotonous sage rolled on and on, spring-
fresh and scented, leading toward the far horizon of snowcapped mountains. I didn't
mind the sage; I knew it well from a couple of successful Wyoming antelope hunts,
and from my kid days when our family spent three years on my maternal grandfather's sheep ranch in the Oklahoma Panhandle during World War I. The road, littered
with traffic-casualty jackrabbits, put me in a nostalgic mood, remembering sitting on
my pony, shooting them by the sackful with a .22 rifle, for the state paid a nickel
bounty on each pair of joined ears; the young were great eating, a welcome change
from the near constant fare of sheep, as were the countless mourning doves that we

shot in the war days whenever we felt like it—twenty miles from town and the law, if there was such a thing on them. That period in my youth was when, as a city-bred lad, I learned to ride, got a great deal of my training with guns at the hands of my father and my granddad. At twelve years of age I was upgraded to a saddle-handy Winchester .30-30 carbine which we carried when chasing sheep-killing coyotes on fast horses behind greyhounds. Back of all of that was the built-in hunting heritage of several generations; our father, born and raised on the Platte River in Nebraska; a market hunter as a boy, with his father—a memory that he abhorred. The first shot-gun that I shared with my older brother was a little 20-gauge double-barrel Ithaca that we earned ourselves, put it under our Christmas tree when I was but a few months past my eighth birthday. We were rigidly taught to use it with care and extreme respect.

But riding up the highway that day I didn't see much sign of any use for such a heritage. Then after skirting bleak endless-appearing fields of outcropping lava the little bus climbed a long easy slope, laboring like a pack mule to the top where a notch in the low line of rolling hills separated the low country from the high. A sign beside the road read: YOU ARE LEAVING MAGIC VALLEY OF THE SNAKE RIVER AND ENTERING THE VALLEY OF BIG WOOD RIVER. The former meant the vast belt of irrigated farmlands along the great river some miles south of Shoshone, of which I had only seen the fringe, and I was told to look for entirely different country now, once we got beyond the notch and down what was called Timmerman Hill. To cool his engine our driver stopped at the top of Timmerman, and indeed it was different.

I saw an immense triangular basin, its floor table-flat, with grazing cattle and the unmistakable signs of abundant water. Off to the left the bright green ribbon of cottonwoods traced the course of Big Wood River as far northward up the steadily narrowing valley as my eyes could see, then the high wall of mountain white. I was told that everything to the right of the highway was known as Silver Creek country. I was looking down on its subterranean source, a myriad of spring-fed streams that merged a few miles eastward to form Silver Creek itself—water reputed to be one of the finest dry-fly trout streams in the West, if not the whole nation. We would be on it in a few days, with Sun Valley's newly hired fishing guides doing their stuff for our still and motion-picture cameras, before heading for the mountain fishing. At the bottom of Timmerman Hill a sign read: KETCHUM 26 MILES. I looked for the inevitable bullet holes in the sign. There were none.

I was totally unprepared for my next surprise when crossing that big verdant basin to enter the valley itself. To put it mildly I saw it as headquarters for mourning doves—it was the first of the long mating and nesting season and I could scarcely believe my eyes. Was this number one upland game bird considered a songbird in Idaho, I asked the driver, or was he a game bird and was there an open season in the game laws? Oh, he guessed so, but would a man really shoot "them little things" when the same shell would bring down a nice big pheasant or a duck? His question told me a thing or two and I drooled for twelve miles or more up the road between fencerows, power and telephone wires, a party line loaded with the little wild pigeons, right into the town of Hailey, the seat of Blaine County, still a dozen miles from our destination. When our driver made a mail sack drop at the post office he brought back a folder on state game laws and seasons. It was quite revealing.

The river level didn't climb much in the miles up to Ketchum, but the country increasingly stood nearly on end; dense forests on the left, the jumbled east face of Baldy Mountain; open, high-rolling uplands on the right, small mountains in themselves. The narrow steel-arched bridge that spanned the Big Wood a couple of miles from town framed a spectacular mountain peak on the north horizon—one nudging twelve thousand feet. The population sign at the edge of town read: KETCHUM—206.

Ketchum was a dead ringer of the colorful old mining towns that I had tramped around so much with a camera in Colorado. Its few-blocks-long main drag was paved—the highway itself—but sidewalks were intermittent and few, of smooth-worn aged planks, the others of packed dirt right up to the establishment doors. The populace most evident at the midafternoon hour were shaggy dogs of various hues lying contentedly in the warm sun or sauntering across the nearly empty thoroughfare. For Ketchum, since the near-total decline in mining not so long past the turn of the century, was now the hub of a thriving high-country sheep-ranging industry, a major origin point for shipment to market by rail. I noted aloud:

"Sheep dogs, or their descendants."

"Yeah . . . and Heinz," the driver grinned. "Fifty-seven varieties."

His quip matched everything of the town that I could see at our crawling pace: a parked car of World War I vintage, a few spanning a generation of human age, a couple of current model Cadillacs; a log truck with a load a good forty feet long; a few saddled horses dozed at a hitchrack. The one liveliest-looking block was dominated by saloons, called "joints" because each sported a casino for the wide-open but illegal gambling. One, called the Alpine, had a restaurant. In jest, so I thought, I was told of the joints: "No hands on their clocks and the doors have no locks." It was more truth than jest. Excepting one, I judged not a building in sight less than half a century in age, looking twice as much in deterioration by the elements.

The building most imposing was an aging two-story brick cornering a main intersection, and to which was affixed a sign reading: SUN VALLEY—1¼ MILES; the letters perched on an arrow pointing right. You had to look twice to see it. Fronting the building was a low broad porch of weathered plank on which a small group of men slouched on a long bench, an old chair or two, and one teetered on a box. Sheepmen, obviously; I knew from Vince's tales of little Ketchum that this was Jack Lane's stockmen's supply store, Jack also being a leading operator in the production of lamb and wool. Too, as a shipper on the railroad, Jack's had been a voice when the traffic men had guided about the big Western snow country the young Austrian, Count Felix Schaffgotsch, a scout for Averell Harriman in search for the ideal dry powder snow, a must for the skiing mecca he envisioned. Jack Lane sent or took a party for

Father of Sun Valley—durable Averell Harriman, then board
chairman, Union Pacific Railroad.

a look at the Ketchum winter conditions. That did it: the beginning of the second
boom for the upper Big Wood River country.

A look at the genial group on that old porch gave no evidence of anything vaguely
indicating the roaring building boom going on up in the smaller spur valley of Trail
Creek; but a boom it was, just the same. In spite of it, Sun Valley was to feel its way
with a first summer operation to open July 1, with only the one hotel, Sun Valley
Lodge itself, for accommodations, and our headquarters for the summer. As soon as
we were set up there we'd return to town, for there were a few things we needed
from Jack's store. Vince asked our driver to slow it a bit; he stopped it dead in the
turn and Vince hollered at Jack, what time did he close? Mr. Lane was insulted at a
question on a little thing called time, but said he had a cowboy there who was way-
laying us. We sent the bus on with our gear and got out to ride with this cowboy
fella who was the long-legged one teetering on the box. He grinned handsomely and
started for the end of the porch to greet us. I knew who he was, had talked to him
on the phone a few times, but I was not prepared for a reasonable physical facsimile
of Gary Cooper. Well, nobody looked quite like Gary Cooper; for that matter, neither did anyone look quite like Gene Van Guilder. But from a short distance anyone
could take him at first glance as Cooper's double. Dressed in ordinary cowhand
clothes, Gene fooled me for a second, and many of his mannerisms were exactly
those that I'd noted in Gary Cooper's film image.

Gene was never a Union Pacific man, but was, in the parlance of the trade, the
Steve Hannagan "associate"—meaning in simple terms the press agent, or publicity
man. In his heyday the great and flamboyant Steve Hannagan himself was labelled

by a writer as the Prince of the Press Agents, and he pretty much proved it by his masterful handling that put Miami Beach, Florida, on the map for Carl G. Fisher. Averell Harriman selected Steve's organization to do the same for Sun Valley, with straight news, and other mediums aside from outright advertising. Always in his time, it was conceded that Gene Van Guilder took the circusy element out of the Hannagan effectiveness, applied it equally so in a disguised, more dignified and quiet, unblaring form. In short, a thirty-third degree press agent, a skilled feature writer, a good commercial artist, and, to cap it off, a likable, charming gentleman.

An Illinoisan by birth, Gene's mother died at an early age and he was raised in Twin Falls, Idaho, by an aunt and uncle; finished a formal education back in his home town of Decatur, at Millikin University; then worked in New York City for a number of years, rounding out his skill in advertising agencies and the like. But as he often put it, from a small boy he didn't remember anything but the West so, "Just call me a native, and I know it a hundred years too late, missed it when it was good." The expression of a born romantic, a self-developed Westerner from the core out. In his school days he'd spent the summers working in the mountains—in the forests, and once he did a little mining in a diggings still going good. He was, naturally, filings to the magnet when Sun Valley came into being; he returned West at once to free-lance for himself. For some time after its initial opening Sun Valley had nothing whatever with which to make ballyhoo—its slopes as bare of snow as your hat. When it finally arrived in a sufficiency for skiing the place was jam-packed with impatience, a first unit movie company from Hollywood waiting to film the winter sports sequences of *I Met Him in Paris*, starring Claudette Colbert, Robert Young, and Melvyn Douglas. From the East Coast the "400" set was well represented; all told a rich harvest of names-in-the-news, when Steve Hannagan swore that daily he prayed for snow, all-out on bended knee, until it chose to fall. At that critical moment there was a night in town for both his agent and cameraman; they weren't much good in the morning, and left on the night train. Steve knew Jack Lane from the discovery days. He asked him if he knew an available newspaper reporter he could lay hands on in a hurry. No, but Jack knew a man who might do, and he took Steve a half block to buy him a drink at the Stockmen's Saloon. Its interior was Gene's handiwork. For its Basque owner he had turned an ordinary bar into a perfect replica of an old-time Western saloon, authentic enough for duty as a movie set for a Zane Grey story. Leave it to Jack, Mr. Van Guilder was there. Steve liked his cut at once, so his problems were solved. Gene's performance caught Averell Harriman's attention that winter, so it might be said—he had no problems either.

His big job for the first summer was the promotional work on the true highlight— the hell-for-leather Sun Valley Rodeo. No corners were cut to put across the first of those annual mid-August events, the show's major domo was handed a blank check to do the job. Which brings us to a man who backed Gene to the hilt with his "idea." He was Bob Miles, former Paramount Pictures man from Hollywood, a "Western" expert, stunt man and what have you, and he knew his way around. His title was

A Trap Squad—Sun Valley Hotshots of the Old Days

Left to right: Friedl Pfeifer, hottest shot skier, partly responsible for bringing me to Idaho; Don Fraser, skier also; this reporter; Chief Guide Taylor Williams; and Ellis "Chape" Chapin, "lensman of brevity" in Hemingwayan.

Sports Director, which, if changed to promoter, spelled in capitals, would have fit him better. Gene spent the best part of the summer working hand-in-hand with Bob, and what a team they were! It was on one of their many "drumming" trips that Gene, as he put it, "came to with a jolt" and he told me about it at the rodeo itself.

The pair left Sun Valley at daylight one July morning, hoping to make Red Lodge, Montana, that night, by way of Yellowstone Park, out its northeast Silver Gate entrance, then over the spectacular Beartooth Pass to their destination. In Red Lodge lived the Greenoughs, top-name rodeo performers, Turk and his two sisters, Alice and Marge. Turk made headlines in that era by marrying the entertainment sensation of the thirties—fan dancer Sally Rand. Bob's purpose in their Red Lodge stop was to assure the Greenoughs' presence at his first show. They didn't make it there that night; darkness caught them leaving the Park and by a stroke of luck a service-station man in the little shoestring town of Cooke City, Montana, gave them the right tip for lodging. They left their car for servicing, had dinner, and when they returned they heard a tourist ask the man if Cooke City was the place where Ernest Hemingway came to fish and hunt big game in the falls. Yes, the man replied, he knew Hemingway very well; he stayed at a ranch a few miles east of town—had been coming there for years.

Gene said he knew that, had forgotten it—thought to himself: a fellow we should have doing that in Idaho. He spoke to Bob about it and they decided to find out all they could while in the district.

"And so?" I said.

"We both jumped onto Steve about it at dinner last night," Gene said. "Told him we learned a few things about Hemingway from some people over there, including the Greenough bunch who know him well. We know that he likes it there, and it *is* fantastically beautiful country."

I asked him for Steve's reaction, who agreed that it was a whale of an idea, but pointed out that Hemingway was wrapped up clear to his ears in the Spanish Civil War, but he did say that he had his good man in the Miami Beach office who might be able to make an approach some time when Hemingway was at home in Key West.

End of story so far as I was concerned, but with us that Sunday morning, railbirding on the rodeo arena fence, was a man who believed that anything could be done if the will existed. At that time he was a fishing guide—a good one, among other special qualities—but no ordinary man, by a long shot. Taylor Williams was a Kentuckian, come west to Idaho a long way back, in 1912, when the great irrigation development was under way in the lower country. By then I knew him well, had quickly become very fond of him on a couple of mountain fishing trips. At fifty years of age he was a bundle of steel-wire energy; a medium-small man with the face of a hawk; as an outdoorsman, atavism personified. In blunt terms I didn't care much for him at first; I thought him too caustic in humor, too critical—which he was, but justifiably, I'd learn, in most cases—but a man to reckon with in his capacity. In his driving way he got the ear of a couple of the "brass" that summer which started him on his way. A widower, some ten years before I knew him, he had two grown sons and a daughter in other parts of the West, but he was a thorough circulator, the best of company when his ways were learned—in short, when you fell for Taylor Williams you fell all the way.

A moderate drinking man himself, he built the most luscious mint juleps, started a mint bed—location secret—as one of his first acts when he joined the guide service in May of 1937. Those tall cold delights of his were to become an institution in Sun Valley's red carpet policies, which I understood quite well when I had my first one! Due to his great finesse in serving them up he was given the name of Colonel by a little redheaded camp cook we had on pack trips with us. To that handle Red added a prefix because Colonel Williams was credited with originating the great fish-killing dry fly called the Renegade. Whether he did or not is beside the point, but one that cannot be dodged is the fact that you were aware of the renegade colonel's presence every second. He had a hand in my permanent-as-glue nickname which I go by to

Three of Sun Valley's original "stinkin' fishin' guides"—John Bauman; Clayton "Stew" Stewart; and "Colonel" Taylor "Beartracks" Williams, John's successor. In those days, should you use Beartracks, you damn well better be running! The place: Idaho's Silver Creek, world-famed for rainbow trout.

this day, almost to the total exclusion of my right one. Vince Hunter called me "Pap" and Taylor dressed it on out to "Pappy." I remember him using it the first time on the coincidental occasion of my birthday on the thirty-first of July, which happened to be my thirty-first one—in 1937. We were in the mountains on a little jewel of a lake at the ten thousand foot level of altitude; it was loaded with pan-size cutthroat trout, truly great delicacies from the ice-cold water. I was behind in my fishin' so the colonel fixed me with a cold eye and ordered me to catch supper for the five of us. Miracle of miracles, I did, in no time! My birthday cake was a sourdough biscuit adorned with a single sliver of pine so full of pitch it sputtered like a Roman candle when lit. The biscuit tasted like hot turpentine, but as the colonel said, no one went thirsty on my "thirsty-first birthday."

Finished with our summer work, Vince and I came back to make an extensive big game hunting trip that fall. It was fully successful, in game bagged, and photographically. We missed on elk, but what I got from it was to pay off in the future. Tied up with other things Taylor did not go with us; Gene had hoped to go, but passed it up to marry a pretty blonde divorcée called "Nin" Davis. Oddly enough, Gene was not much on hunting, was a great shot with pistols, the only kind of guns that he owned. It was after our big game trip—in mid-November—that I got my eyes fully open as to what the shooting was in the lower country on upland birds, and ducks, plus the latter on Silver Creek. Suffice it to say that the aggregate would make a shotgun man drool. It was too late in the season, the weather stinking, for good upland shooting, but I remembered well indeed what the bus driver had said back in June. The potential was there and never had I seen so many ducks in agricultural country before. The lingering of water in the irrigation canals, laterals and feeder ditches was responsible. On Silver Creek, jump-shooting afoot, we filled up on big ducks, mallards, within an hour. This old webfoot from the Middle West was amazed with Silver Creek; we'd been barking up the wrong tree at our job helping promote the real hunting so close and handy. We did not know what we could ever do about it.

We were in Sun Valley all of the second winter, making ski movies and stills: Mr.

Clockwise from left: Dry-fly originator, Renegade Taylor Williams; "Big A" (Art) Wood; and Ray "Pop" Mark. "The Question's kid brother, but he catches fish where they ain't any."

Ernie Hemingway's "on-sight clincher" —hooked with our country. The locale is Silver Creek.

Harriman insisted we learn to ski so we could get around like cameramen are supposed to do. In the spring of 1938 Gary Cooper and his pretty wife Rocky came to Sun Valley for their first time. Rocky was bitten by the ski bug, Coop went nuts over the great varmint shooting with his hot little rifles in the lower country. He got a bobcat in the lava beds his first day out, shot countless of the crop-eating 'chucks—the western cousin of the eastern woodchuck and known as marmots, or rock 'chucks. The Fred MacMurrays were with the Coopers; we never got them back, but the Coopers were hooked. I was held over a short while that spring; Gene's camerman left him, Coop was interested in some Snake River property, came close to acquiring it and always wished that he had. It was Averell Harriman's work that lured the Coopers to Sun Valley, Rocky being a New Yorker—and a great shot at the popular game of skeet. In line with Taylor Williams' big moaning over the location of the skeet layout—'way over behind the hills where the "noise" would not disturb guests—Rocky crabbed too. Mr. Williams stepped into the breach and got something done about it, pronto.

Coop was the great easy-to-like guy that an admirer of his type would expect in the flesh, a wonderful shot with a rifle and only a fair one on targets with a shotgun. He "cottoned" to Gene and Taylor right off, and rather to my surprise I was included in. Probably because I was as big an all-around gun nut as he. When I left for home that spring there was nothing on the Sun Valley docket, but I remember with a bit of amusement Coop saying:

"Aw, Podner, ah'll bet you'll join us at a few pheasants and ducks come fall."

Everybody was Podner to Coop.

I was home two months and back in June of '38. I found Taylor a very sick man, flat on his back, and was told that he'd barely escaped cashing in for keeps. The head guide had purchased three light pleasure canoes, to be used on the little Sun Valley lake that was made by damming Trail Creek a few hundred yards from the hotels, and for car-topping to mountain lakes for fishing—if needed by guide service. I had been asked the fall before what kind to buy, and I did not recommend that type, but the more stable north-woods guide models, with flotation chambers for further safety. Around small boats all my life, I had owned a few canoes, had an old veteran of the type bought, back home in my garage. Anyway, when the tricky craft arrived, Gene and Taylor broke one out of its crate, launched it in Big Wood River at the peak of the spring runoff, following the record snowfall winter. The river was a raging torrent that would knock the feet from under a stout mountain horse only wanting to drink from it. They roared down a hundred or so yards and capsized. Taylor was afraid of nothing that moved, but could not swim a lick. He took a frightful beating. Gene got him out of the icy water, the canoe took care of itself without a scratch. Taylor was put to bed by the tiny medical department of an elderly doctor and one nurse, given something for exposure and shock. This occurred coincidentally with the department administering anti-Rocky Mountain fever serum shots, for spring was when the often fatal fever was carried by the prevalent wood

Merchant sheep rancher Jack Lane, of Ketchum, Idaho—a man with a good idea for Sun Valley's originator, Averell Harriman.

ticks. Something went wrong in Taylor's case—a mistake, obviously, it was said, probably a dosage for a horse instead of a man—and the medical department took full responsibility for it.

I brought a shotgun with me that summer, got in a couple of dove shoots with the colonel in early September—he perched on a stool near a water hole, with a cane to help his limited walking. Even with a stiff-fingered left hand, swinging a short open-bored shotgun, he was the fastest human I'd ever seen operate. Fair hand as I was with the little 20-gauge of my youth, he made me look like a tyro. Mr. Williams was the same sound-as-ever-investment for Sun Valley; he had just been made Chief Guide by the chairman of its board and the railroad's president.

Mr. Cooper's prediction for the fall proved true. I had some filming to do on the railroad in eastern Idaho in October, so juggled my work to linger long enough to get in a couple of pheasant hunts with the boys when Coop came. I must say that it beat all-hollow that "tall corn" kind of pheasant shooting I knew from the Midwest. What little corn was grown in Idaho was short and quite easy; the low-crop cover, one big picnic. I shot no ducks that fall but I took home a suitcase of grain-fed mallards that the bunch fixed me up with. That time I was sure that I was saying good-bye at last.

At Christmas back home I was greatly surprised, and touched, when a little gift from Coop arrived. I still wear the lovely old silver and gold buckle-and-keeper set with rubies, hardware that has worn out several belt leathers down the years since. I guess it was in appreciation of the good times we had in Idaho, and for a cute picture that I made of Coop shooting skeet. The focal plane shutter of my Leica camera actually "froze" the shotstring from his full choke shotgun, the head of the string just connecting with the clay target. Accidental, or lucky, timing was all I could lay it to, but I had a color print made from the transparency, sent it to Gene in Sun Valley, who sent it on to Coop from the "bunch." Coop's card read: "Good shootin', Podner, we'll do it again some time."

My New Year's gift was orders to leave January 2 for Sun Valley, do a single colorphoto job for future calendar purposes, and return home but be equipped for any eventuality. Mr. Harriman would be in Sun Valley much of the winter. He was —held me for all of it, making another general winter movie, mainly. At season's end he asked me to do the near-impossible: make a special film on a champion Austrian skier whom he made the head of the rapidly growing Ski School. Other material featuring the former head was as dead as yesterday's news. Friedl Pfeifer's was currently the hottest name in the sport; certainly he was worth a try; it was a challenge to me—a scary one. The valley floor and nearby slopes were devoid of snow, green with spring. No one knew the variables toward failure better than Mr. H.; we discussed it, then he went into action: big rotary snowplows opened thirty miles of gravelled highway to Galena Summit and the high snowfields, a road never open before June; he wished me luck and returned to New York in early April—after getting my opinion on the Sun Valley photographic situation. At month's end I telegraphed him that I had his film in the cans. Friedl's brilliance as a skier, and the good Lord's arm around my neck deserved the credit. I got home the first day of May.

When in Las Vegas in mid-May, making color on Hoover Dam and Lake Mead, I got a phone call to skip another job and come to Omaha—be prepared to transfer to the Sun Valley staff permanently, taking over all photographic operations—if I saw fit to accept. I was slated to spend most of the summer in Sun Valley due to the expansion program. In a word, there was no letup in sight of my absence from home a good four-fifths of the time. I phoned my wife to be thinking it over and caught the train—all mixed up as to what to do. We decided it quickly—we had an eleven-year investment in each other that we valued above all else.

On June 16 we arrived in Sun Valley, followed a day later by a red-balled freight

Our pack string—1937—in the exotic White Cloud Peaks of central Idaho. ". . . remind me so much of the Dolomites in north Italy," Ernest said of them, "but I never saw more than their cloud-blending white tips from a distance, and only once from the air." Years later I had his promise to go into them, but. . . .

My boss, Chief Photographer Vince Hunter, and this reporter on a successful big game/picture trip into Idaho's Middle Fork of the Salmon River Primitive Area. (October, 1937.)

car into Ketchum, loaded with the necessities of making a life of it in my usual big comfortable room smack in the center of the Inn. A competent businesswoman—a stickler for system—my wife took over management of the retail-guest service end of it, made order out of a mess left by the lessee operating it up to then. We ran it for the company—not for ourselves. Omaha's needs were my responsibility, as well as the resort's; Gene's headache had been a succession of cameramen—an intolerable situation. I had recommended a local man to him the year before who now was my "outside" crew, pretty much assigned to Gene. Thus, ours was a harmonious group from the outset. There was work to do; we got it done.

The resort was taking on the finished look, the summer business which lagged far behind the winter's, was catching on well. The flavor of the community as a whole was distinctly Western, due, of course, to Sun Valley's rodeo. The '39 show was a real corker, a two-day event itself, but for nearly a week you couldn't find stand-up sleeping room anywhere, and the joints in town threw away their rusty keys. I recall that wild time best from a night on the town when the Greenough girls from Red Lodge were with us, Gene joking them about nothing ever coming of his tired idea of luring a fellow named Hemingway away from Montana. They remarked that that particular time would be right down his alley. Aside from Taylor and Bob Miles occasionally pumping Gene as to whether he had ever heard of any contact with Hemingway via the Hannagan people (he hadn't), his name had come up once before that summer. *Field and Stream* magazine sent a filming crew to Sun Valley to make a fine fishing picture, the editor himself, Ray Holland, heading the group. The narrative writer, who seemed to know all about Hemingway's big game fishing in the Bimini and Gulf Stream waters, talked at length about him.

The funny thing was that Gene considered it a very tired idea and never had much faith in it. Steve Hannagan stayed on until early in September. Gene and I spent a lot of time with him; the subject was never mentioned.

The red-whiskered gent on the right gave Colonel Williams that handle of his because of his prowess as a skilled mint-julep builder, but the subject of this story publicly gets the credit. Messina, New Yorker, gone West, Red Anable didn't mind. A super big-game hunting guide, Sandy Brooks, at left, our first Idaho guide, in 1937.

By mid-September Sun Valley housed perhaps thirty lingering guests, mostly fishermen, out all day. We had a fair booking of fall hunting business, nothing to boast of, so we looked forward to a fairly easy time of it. I had an elk hunting trip all lined up, to the area which we missed in '37. Management was in the process of closing up the Lodge. The one significant event in the fall plans was an affair slated for Armistice Day, November 11, a promotional idea of Gene. It was set up as a potlatch dinner, wild game of all kinds, for sports and outdoor writers, newspapermen, sportsmen's clubs, all in cooperation with the State Fish and Game Department. Which brings us to the significant date of September 20, that day on which Gene and I were to ride up Baldy Mountain. It was Wednesday, and on Thursday morning Gene would make a two-day trip, firming up plans on his idea. Taylor Williams was in the White Cloud Peaks with a pair of outdoor writers prepared to take their own pictures, fishing my "birthday" lake and others. I took the early morning ride, when I waved at the stranger and the girl with long blonde hair and the long stride of a tomboy in her Western riding clothes.

"A roaring confusion." Sun Valley as I first knew it. (Rodeo time, August, 1937.)

2.

The Fall of 1939 . . .

1

Just two words more than adequately describe Gene Van Guilder's and my first talk with Ernest Hemingway: interestingly funny. To substantiate, I quote him verbatim—a later remark he made about it:

"Who was kiddin' who and nobody kidded nobody." Well salted with laughter.

Aside from his familiar look when I waved to him, a lone car parked in front of the Lodge—a very dusty, current model black Buick convertible—was a further clue to his identity. If the car had come from Montana by the most direct route, I was indeed familiar with a stretch of road that made it look so travel-weary. That was when I gave the horse his head for an all-out run to the stables.

I found Gene dressed for cocktails instead of his usual Westerns of quiet good taste, scolding himself a bit, for he said he had only a look at Hemingway—from his "hole" in the bell service desk in the lobby. Was I willing to go with him when the couple finished breakfast, and was I excited about meeting Hemingway? No, not too much, I said. Then why hadn't I taken off my stub-shank spurs, and how do you drive a car with 'em on and not know it? He was beaming from ear to ear, mentally rubbing his hands in glee; repeating his "But who'd ever believe it?" Gene had been off the premises when Hemingway and his lady arrived well after dark the night before; General Manager Pat Rogers happened to be in the Lodge lobby at the time; he knew of the old idea, vaguely, was surprised right out of his shoes, and put the pair in the best of the Lodge's deluxe suites of rooms. Gene got word of it early that morning. He called the Hannagan New York office, talked to Steve's next-in-charge, who seemed mildly surprised that Hemingway had shown up. But he did know that he was due in Montana roughly at that time and said he understood Hemingway had told whoever contacted him that if things worked out right he might take a couple of days and drive over for a look at Sun Valley. Point-blank I asked Gene if he'd been offered an on-the-cuff deal of some degree. He laughed, said, "What do you think?" Then with a rather sardonic grin on his handsome face he said that he'd been warned to handle the man with silk gloves—"he spooks easy." Did I remember anyone we had spooked? I couldn't remember that I had; certainly Gene's slate was clean in that department. We retired to the far end of the lobby to await a signal from the maitre d' that the people had finished their meal. A point that troubled Gene was this: There was nothing but fishing going on, so how did we expect to hold this man who, Gene had been advised, was interested mainly in hunting, and that he had a heavy writing program underway? A good question. For a quarter of an hour we schemed and planned to the laughing point. But I wanted to know who the girl was—she was not Mrs. Hemingway whose picture I'd seen a few times. No, she was Martha Gellhorn, the writer responsible for the book *The Trouble I've Seen*. Did I know that the Hemingway marriage was on the rocks? No, I did not—I was a follower of Hemingway mainly by reading him, not about him. My mind at the moment was on the hunt I had planned and I thought of Hemingway only as a big game hunter, from reading *Green Hills of Africa*, a favorite of mine.

Sun Valley's first hell-for-leather rodeo, August, 1937, a spectacular
feature that, sadly, was abandoned after one postwar show.

Little Stan and Don Atkinson
with a Silver Creek product.

When the maitre d' sauntered across the lobby, making little tents with his fingers and beaming his happy Bavarian grin, we knew that his lingual artistry was getting him by in fine style with Herr Hemingway; he called him a very funny man who talked anything you liked. Karl Geppert could fetch a laugh from a cigar store Indian. He said that Herr Hemingway had asked for the Hannagan man, but had fumbled in recalling his name.

"You go now, shentlemen," he grinned, but went on ahead so his absence was not so obvious.

Hemingway, at a window table-for-two far back in the otherwise empty room, glued his eyes on us, and did not unglue them for an instant. At Gene's greeting he rose hastily and said, "Yeah, sure," and apologized for their lateness, wondered if they were breaking the establishment rules—shyly, hesitantly soft-voiced, ill at ease. He introduced "Miss Gill" who was perfectly at ease, and who wore as infectiously pretty a smile as I'd seen in some time from a stranger. There was an awkward moment of word fumbling all around, then she reminded Mr. Hemingway to ask us to sit down. A good idea. He grinned. Around a table was the place to talk, easy on the feet and legs and something to lean on in support of your theories. He laughed heartily in support of his wit, finished it in a high treble "Hmph!" and sat down while Karl slid chairs under us.

To open things Gene asked him if they had driven in by the south route or from the east. Hemingway eyed us both suspiciously, hedged a bit, grinned like a cat about to pounce on a mouse, and let us have it—straight. They came from the east, he said, the Park he always enjoyed, and he liked what he saw of Idaho—very pretty country down the Snake River over east around Idaho Falls and west across the vastly big Arco desert. The gaunt mountains to the north of the plain reminded him of Spain— heavily stressed—then, at our knowing nods, yes, right at dusk when you don't know whether to turn on lights and can't tell if you have, they had climbed the long easy grade that burst them suddenly upon the bleak, forbidding lavas of the Craters of the Moon National Monument. He referred to them as Dante's Inferno gone to sleep, and Mr. Dante's country—and Mr. Dante could damn well have it—and if he could

have seen a place for a turnaround in that hell or purgatory they'd have headed back
to Idaho Falls, have a few stiff ones and say to hell with the great Sun Valley that
he'd heard so much about. A sheepish grin ended it, then I got a half startled glare
for laughing outright. I told of coming through the Craters the fall before, blowing
out a tire on the miserable gravel road, flattening a rear spring in the bargain, around
midnight when it was black as pitch with coyotes off in nowhere calling for the moon.
He howled gleefully and said, "Thanks ever so much."

Sun Valley, in the summer of 1939, was taking on the finished look. Bob Miles, a favorite
model of mine, rides in the center; and my wife is on a chunky gray "movie risk horse"
called Antelope, very much in the text.

In apologetic back off, he went on to say that going back would have been a hundred miles to a drink and bed, he didn't see as owls do, and was not a record holder
on any road. Besides, if a place like Sun Valley was so hard to get to there must be
something here. He waved an arm toward outside, said he was now quite sure of it
—a very pretty place, what little they'd seen.

Little formality was permitted from the outset—if any—most evident by his quick dispensing with the "Mr." stuff, subtly, referring to himself as "old Ernie." We went along with this name-conscious man who, of Gene's surname, shyly said, "Dutch money is always solid." He mistook the short of my nickname when Gene introduced us, got it straight this way:

"That was much horse you rode out there . . . *mucho caballo,* my . . . uh, ah . . . how do they call you? Did we hear it as Pat?"

No, it's Pap, or Pappy, either one. I had nothing in the flesh to justify it and didn't mind much what I was called so long as it's in time for meals. Sure, said he, humanity generally finds the right one on the way up. Mine sounded all right. Did I mind if they joined the club, though my handle was a mild infringement on one of his? Hemming and hawing at my question about that, he was cut off by Miss Gill who said that his sons called their father Papa and that some of his cronies had picked it up. He thought it old-fashioned, she added, but one would have to be pretty thick not to recognize that he liked it. He *almost* blushed and I stifled my laugh; I said all old-fashioned kids used Papa, as I had until grown, then called my father Bill, as everyone else did.

"I like that," he said. "Like huntin' pals do."

He edged his way out of the "Miss Gill" business by referring to her as "the Marty" which seemed perfectly natural, and accused us of being Midwesterners from our speech. Miss Gill asked where, and said she, too—from St. Louis—and laughed. That's all there was to that, so these people were Marty and Ernie to us.

A blind man could see that Ernest was impressed with Gene. He obviously knew he was in sheep country, which meant there were lots of Basque people, too—the original imported herdsmen—so the two got into both Spanish and the difficult Basque tongue. Obviously, most of it was unprintable. Listening to the guffaws, my impression was: This guy may be the great author Hemingway, but I like the big kid I see—a shrewd one, examining you subtly and carefully.

That, he did indeed, knew more about other things than he let on; quite cagey too, when it came to the business at hand, and then ever so slowly, he commenced to loosen up about it. Suddenly he gave it to us in a single package: He was not particularly interested in fishing—"too involving"—big game hunting, secondary, the time element; but he understood that a man could have a lot of fun with a shotgun in our parts. Up to that point I had been mostly the listener, then Gene said to Ernest, "Ask Pap about his surprises when he first saw it a couple of years ago." He grinned when in a half-question, half-statement, I said I might take him for an all-out shotgun man. I was fixed with his warm brown eyes while a forefinger bobbed in the general direction of his brow and he flatly said that of the few sports he truly liked he'd rather be a top wing shot than tops at any other. I said, "So would I," and that was all I said about it. He said he would like to see a little of our shotgun country at our convenience and if our time was short just give him a map—at reading maps, he was pretty good, he thought. Gene told him of his trip on the morrow, what it was for, and that he could easily put it off a few days. The old newspaperman responded instantly.

"Hell, no, don't put it off, Gene . . . wine 'em and dine 'em and they write the good stuff for you and it's more convincing from someone else, no matter how good you do it."

It was about nine-thirty when we'd sat down to talk, and the waitresses were checking their stations for lunch when Ernest broke it off, with apologies for taking so much of our time. Thanking us again, he said, "That's a pretty fancy wigwam that Mr. Rogers put us in over there . . . guess I'll have to do some stocking-up pretty soon."

After Gene got off a message to Hannagan about our questionable publicity property we sat down to talk it over, and in the notebook that he slept with he put it all down.

"What do you call that way-out talk, Gene?"

"I guess you just add an *an* to his name . . . Hemingwayan."

"Get enough of it . . . Hemingwayana, huh?"

I wondered if we would get very much, and had a feeling that we just might. I offered to bet Gene that the trunk of the convertible was packed full. I wished that I had driven past it coming up from the stables to look for signs of a load. He didn't take me up.

Late that afternoon I was called to the general manager's office. Pat Rogers, whom we all referred to as the "Old Man," was in a fine high mood, so I expected what I had heard many times in connection with special guests: "Feed 'em good, my boy, you never go wrong in that." My orders were to be available by phone from that moment on; when I showed Hemingway some country, see to it that an ample

General manager for Sun Valley—Pat "Old Man" Rogers.

pantry was aboard; the kitchen had been alerted and was at my command. Gene was there, quite bright-eyed, for he had spent an hour or so with Ernest in the Ram at a late lunch. He said iced tea laced with Scotch was a pretty fair drink, and that at sixteen ounces per, one was enough! He also threw me a curve.

"How would you like to take a fella named Hemingstein with you on your elk hunt?"

Who? Why, hell yes, I'd like to take him. Why not, he'd had lots of experience at it. I hadn't, only missed a long shot at one. The Old Man had okayed the trip—at company expense—and if Hemingway liked the sound of it I was to invite him as our guest. In those days there was no elk hunting very close by; the animals were in the Selway Forest country far to the north, about the best on the continent, and it so happened that I was the only staffer who had been there. Taylor Williams was going with me and aside from the need of pictures the Old Man wanted a pair of good heads to be mounted and hung on a pair of massive stone fireplaces in the new Trail Creek cabin—a party attraction, a mile up the valley. Ours was a big order. I asked Gene if he learned anything else. He said no, he knew little more—Ernest had talked almost entirely of the goings-on in Europe—World War II was then just twenty days old—and had told Gene he was working on a novel based on the Spanish Civil War. When he left the next morning Gene told me that Ernest would call me

Sun Valley Lodge in the "old days." Glamour House and its sun deck just under the fireplace flue second from the left. "Withering Heights" in Hemingwayan, but how he loved it as a place to work.

within the hour; I got it from Karl in the dining room, asking my wife's presence too, if convenient.

We stopped in the lobby to file a telegram and I waved to Ernest that we'd be right in. He was at some nonsense with Karl but suddenly his wide laugh froze, he actually stared in our direction, and spoke to Marty, who turned her head to look. Ernest did the introducing himself, hung onto Tillie's hand with both of his—embarrassing himself but rattling off things to keep my wife laughing. I can't begin to repeat it—it was like trying to count machine-gun fire. When we sat down I had not said a word. Then I wanted to kick Tillie's shins under the table; she burst out in hilarious laughter at Ernest's breakfast: a full-size dinner plate of rolled marinated herring, a stein of beer half gone and a full one in reserve!

"Sure, daughter, have some . . . good for the kidneys!"

He answered for her by calling for a plate and a glass. But I couldn't figure that other. A look from Marty said, "Just wait, you will." I did, almost at once.

"Now, Marty, shall we tell this girl she was a spook for a minute or so, that she spooked the hell outa me, anyway?"

"Why, of course we tell her . . . Tillie, you're like Pauline. Not exactly a twin, but close enough to be her young sister. You had me a little spooked too, in fact I gasped until I got a closer look at you."

She went on to say that Pauline was Mrs. Hemingway, the mother of Ernest's two youngest sons. I recalled the well-circulated news photo of Mrs. Hemingway leaning on a ship's rail with Ernest and saw little resemblance, but Ernest spoke pointedly of Tillie's coloring, her quite round cheeks, pointed to his own full-cheeked face, and said the little boys got theirs from both their parents.

"On them and their mother and you . . . very good. On me like a horse with a double shot of the mumps."

Tillie said she had only noticed the horse's sunburned and peeling nose. She had a fair remedy that worked well for hers.

"Yeah, daughter, old tenderhouse always raises hell with me. If you have the recipe I'll try it . . . I'm all out of the failures I've tried."

Where did the name Tillie come from, he wanted to know. Was it a short for Matilda? She did not mind telling how she got it. In the twenties when the gals took over our barbershops, had their hair shingled in back, very short, my father said she looked like the comic-strip Tillie the Toiler. She did, and the name banished her right one to all but her immediate family.

"I bet it fits you all the way, daughter . . . Tillie . . . now we're organizoots in the name department."

He elaborated on the resemblance, said if Tillie, in her tan saddle pants and shirt and a light chamois leather jacket, wore a broad-brimmed hat he could visualize her standing in a safari tent. She laughed and said, "You mean P. O. M.?"

Again he *almost* blushed. "Sure . . . but I wasn't trying to find out anything . . . truly I wasn't."

There was not the slightest evidence of embarrassment in any of this. Always much more critical of her few women friends than of men, Tillie liked Marty right off—it was mutual—and I saw Ernest watching for that sign from the outset. At thirty-four, one day younger than Gene Van, Tillie looked a youthful twenty-four. Ernest accused me of robbing the school when I married her in '28; learned her birthday was April 6, and he said, "Fine, diamonds are indestructible."

He switched the subject to our elk hunt so suddenly that I hadn't yet figured how to approach him. So I did it with the finesse of a pig in church—about like this:

"If you can spare the time, Ernie, well, old Uncle Peter is picking up the tab, you know." ("Uncle Peter" was railroad lingo for Union Pacific). I guess I couldn't have said it better.

"You mean, Chief, that you'd take along old inexperienced, non-native guide Ernie as a rifle?"

His laughter was quite a mixture, his appreciation as genuine as my red face. But he learned what I knew of the immense Selway-Bitteroot wilderness region in north-central Idaho—Lewis and Clark's Lolo Trail country—knew of its reputation of being as rough to hunt as they come. From our discussion mine was, I was sure, a very good look at a square shooter, quite humble and fumbling in making it clear that a trade was a trade. In a word, if he could help us in filling a very tough order, he'd do his best to work it into his time. Two remarks that I noted:

"Man's country where you're going . . . I hear it tries you on for fit on its terms."

When Marty reminded him that he'd told her he needed another elk like an extra tail on his shirt—what would he do with one:

"Work like horse to get him out of the bushes . . . and I'm told that they're going to smoke plenty of the meat for Gene's affair in November. . . . I would build the fire and keep it going under that myself . . . smoked elk and deer is man's meat, if a man can fight his way past the women once they get a taste of it."

Again it was nearly noon when we broke it up. Sauntering out, the girls ahead of us, Ernest suddenly put a hand on my shoulder, got in front of me like a line blocker, his voice low, as if he were passing on a confidential tip, telling me how sorry he was for calling Tillie a spook.

"But she was, and it came out before I could stop it . . . and she understood and was so damn good about it that I couldn't apologize . . . that would have made me out a fool. You're a lucky dog; she's fresh as a breeze." Then he moved out of my way, pulled a skeleton-crowned fishing cap with a six-inch-long green visor from a hip pocket. Out on the porch he laid a forefinger on his nose—he'd just thought up a remedy of his own. Would we be interested in trying some of it along late in the afternoon—or might they be outvoted by a horse?

"*Gracias,*" I said. "Does it ring true if we say he might be getting some new shoes about then?"

"I can't think of a better one," he said. "I'll come by and collect you."

He did, and spent the better part of an hour in the photo shop, going through a

When admiring his asked-for print of this shot of Tillie the Toiler, Ernest quipped in the vein of a true joke about it: "Yeah, a jewel in the tall grass, but you said that you courted her in a hearse! Me, I'd court her anyplace."

myriad of photographs, talking people and country, familiarizing himself on our rather complex operation. At the time I was preparing several dozen albums of specially selected pictures on fishing, hunting, and summer activities at the resort to be sent to railroad ticket offices throughout the country—a big task. The pictures impressed Ernest, and that was when he had his first look at Silver Creek—a fishing picture. He knew the great stream's reputation for fly fishing, but it had not been mentioned to him in any other vein. Nor was it then. In our big counter album of personalities he found a recent picture of a guest who had been in the Red Cross ambulance unit with him in World War I. He had not seen Freddie Spiegel in years, he said, but coming upon his picture 'way out in Idaho he called "a good spook, among the others we have discovered so far . . . the old saying 'it's a small world' we can depend on wherever we go." (We had discovered some spooks of that sort, but I can't expect you to believe them.)

Instead of the Ram Bar for testing his remedy, Ernest said it was much more cheerful and bright in the sitting room of their fancy wigwam in the Lodge, though at that stage they were not organizoots, his bar goods were sitting on the floor. Did I have influence with the housekeeping department? I pointed to a small table of no particular use in my workroom-office combination—would it do?

"Exactly right, if it's legit to steal it."

We stole it, plus a tablecloth from the dining room. Carrying it over between us, Ernest chuckled softly and said:

"I hope, kids, that you're on good terms with the gendarmes here, us carting the establishment's furniture around . . . but you know, ol' Ernie's never had it so good out West . . . and don't tell a soul that he's flat-ass broke, will you?"

Gene's and my guess about the load in the convertible proved out. There was enough outdoor gear piled in disarray in 206's sitting room to keep four men going all fall. Every window in the place was open—it reeked with the pungent odor of leather and cloth from the semitropics. A stack of full-length gun cases in a corner, two eiderdown sleeping bags—extra large size—a lightweight umbrella tent, a case of fly-rods, boots and chest waders—to name but a few. And books—hard-cover ones—at least a hundred, in cartons and piles on the furniture.

"How did you find room for yourselves in the car?" I laughed.

"Oh . . . there's a war on, you know . . . you just go prepared for anything that might rear up in front of you."

He said that rattling around all by themselves in that great big hotel gave them a very superior feeling of splendid isolation. Tillie tried a staffer's joke about the Lodge when it was closed.

"It's kind of prison looking, you know, cast of concrete, the landscaping not yet grown very much . . . a smart aleck said it reminded him of Wuthering Heights."

Ernest's expression was a classic in amusement.

"Then in our case we'll call it "Withering Heights" . . . reduces us to size . . . sorry about our mouldy smell . . . Pappy, if you steal us some ice somewhere in Withering, we'll drown it."

From the Redwood Room I borrowed a fancy card table to pile the books on. When I returned the bar was all prettied up, its undershelf stocked like the real commercial thing. There was much nonsense around Tillie's dissertation on the glamorous names that 206 had housed in its young life. Out of it came a quick naming—in succession: Hemingstein's Harry's Bar in the Harry Morgan Room of the House of Glamour. The latter quickly became just Glamour House, but the name Harry Morgan threw both of us. Tillie asked.

"Well, daughter, old Harry is a good son of a . . . 'scuse me . . . who did not do so good for himself in the piece I wrote about him, and that has not done very good for me either . . . but maybe it will before it ends up in the morgue of off-color literature that it is not. Harry's in the pile here from which you are welcome to anything you like."

Since we had a date to see shotgun country the following morning I went straight to the subject of how Ernest was gunned for it. His reaction was instant and amusing—for the next half hour. He said:

"Christ! . . . I'd better get all the guns out of those tight cases, sweat and rust, maybe, from sea level. . . ."

So out they all came: the lovely old Griffin & Howe Springfield of *Green Hills of Africa;* Pauline's little 6.5 Mannlicher, or that which literarily done in poor Francis Macomber; a couple of .22 plinking rifles; and two shotguns made to order for our country. His old Model 12 Winchester pump gun was a sight for sorry eyes, a weapon you wouldn't give ten dollars for if seen in a hock-shop window—that is, unless you were a lover of Model 12's. It rattled like a corn sheller in "loose as a goose action" and light oil spray flew out of it in a cloud when you slammed home the breech. The over-oiling had settled into the grip of the stock which was split where it butted the metal and was so loose it was about to fall off.

"Yeah, we gotta tighten 'er up, Chief . . . couldn't operate without this ol' stopper . . . bet your Model 12 doesn't look like this one."

But the other shotgun had a special significance for him, and he was bursting to tell me about it for he figured I might know the man from whom he'd won it in a live bird shoot in France. In the sporting circles of the Midwest, wealthy sportsman Ben Gallagher's name was synonymous with top shotgunning. I knew him but slightly through former employers of mine—good shots and hunters themselves. So I knew that Ben G was a great shot and told Ernest he'd have to have poured it on to win that cracking good Browning over-under double barrel 12 gauge—choked for short and medium ranges; a short, very handy piece.

"You're damn right I did." He laughed. "Ben made me go, over my head, maybe, and when it was over he said, 'And furthermore, now you can take the goddamn gun and. . . .'"

"And futhermore"—I thought—where have I heard that before? Ah, now I can find out, from the man who wrote it. So, on the spot I asked him what about the "furthermore" business in *Green Hills,* and Ernest chuckled and said, "You mean about taking the sleigh?"

"Yes," I said. "Always puzzled about that phrase, from a folk tale?"

He jumped at it like a trout at fly-hatch time: "I like the story for its moral value
. . . when I was learning my trade, broke, too damn proud to ask for help, some Yankee practicality straightened me out." His tale:

The Vermont farmer who in winter needed a sleigh to haul in his crop of maple sap
—a proud man who didn't particularly like his neighbor a mile up the road who had
one he knew was not in use. Desperate, he walked the mile in deep snow in argument with his pride. Maybe he *is* using his sleigh, maybe he wouldn't want to loan
it to *me* anyway. He found himself at the man's door, still debating if he should
knock, when the door opened; he shook his fist in the neighbor's face and shouted,
". . . and furthermore you can take your goddamn sleigh and. . . ."

Yes, we could take it from there all right, and so did its narrator, a few days hence
in drastically different circumstances. We had never heard of the writer who'd told
Ernest the moral-pointer, but I'm sure that the title of a later work by Elliot Paul—
The Last Time I Saw Paris—will endure for a very long time.

It all reminded me of the amusing episode in which Taylor Williams had won
himself a Browning just that summer, by the hard route. I couldn't pass it up, urged
by my audience who'd heard so much of the man he'd not met. At Sun Valley's first

Two favorite Hemingway Idaho
gals: Annie the Antelope and
Miss Till Arnold. ". . . you call
this—your work—a complex operation? Move over, and let me
take over." Fresh from the wild,
little Bucko looks on from safety.

major trap shoot he admired a Browning over-under trap grade owned by a gun
fancier with a trunkful of fine guns. Taylor tried to buy it on a name-your-price
basis—no deal. But the man made the mistake of offering it to the colonel to shoot
the doubles event. His position in our squad was next to me and he shot the gun like
he was born with it in his hands. That night a hundred shooters made for the night
life in bustling Ketchum and Taylor zeroed in on his man at the old Casino Bar. He
got him half loaded, a skinful himself—me, too—but it was a three-ring circus listening to the tobacco auctioneer chanting (from his young days in Kentucky), watching
the bourbon whiskey getting in its licks. The colonel started at a low figure, upped
his offers a dollar at a time. The good-natured man made his second mistake; he was
naïve enough to think a ridiculously low price would shame the colonel off. He
reached into nowhere, said he'd take not a penny less than eighty-five bright and
shining silver dollars for that gun—by God! Taylor whipped out a signed blank check,
filled in the do-re-mi, and stuffed it in the man's pocket.

"The house will convert that into bright and shining dollars, my friend," he cackled like a hen laying a double. "I thank you, sir."

"Good God," Ernest howled. "You don't mean to tell me that whiskey and an auctioneer chant laid him an egg like that?"

"Yes, I mean it; he shows off that cleared check as if it were on sheet gold, and you
should see him shoot that Browning."

"I believe it." Ernest laughed. "And I believe he was boozed up like a fox . . .
Marty . . . one character coming up."

"About tomorrow night, or some time Saturday morning he'll be out of the mountains," I said. "And I'll lay you five to two that he'll have cutthroat trout sticking
out of his ears."

"Thanks for the tip." Ernest laughed. So being a fair press agent for the colonel
I told him the little tale of his antics on my birthday in my first summer in Idaho. He
said:

"From your pictures I see his as a face a man could write about, and feel that you
know him before you do . . . and now I know your age, Pappy . . . in seven more years
and ten more days you'll be as old as me . . . but I'll bet you never catch me."

Learning his age was about all that we got from him, but like our morning's talk,
he went on looking over our credentials to the point of embarrassment to himself.
But who doesn't like an intense audience? We had great fun talking of Kansas City,
which I knew as well as he, a decade later, in the late twenties and early thirties, at
the peak bootlegging years of the Prohibition era. Under Boss Tom Pendergast's
thumb in those days—Tom's Town, the title of an eventual book that Ernest sent me
a copy of—Kansas City was truly a snorter. I learned it best in my several seasons
of boat racing, as one of a wild breed in pioneering the sport when outboard motors
grew up into snarling beasts pushing little saucers of boats at terrifying speeds. So,
of all the Midwest river towns on the circuit, other than my own, I knew old K.C.
the best. My audience told some dillies, too—what a storyteller! This all led to an

This writer's favorite sport in the late twenties and early thirties—a sport that made him wind up in the hospital. A narrow squeak, too. It was no good for my kidneys!

earlier time of my helter-skelter life and relating it I learned a side of Ernest of which I was not aware. Its humorous high point was one he never forgot.

Not long out of school I went to work for a thriving undertaking establishment and learned the business. Its owner, a friend of my father's family, was coroner of our big county, of which Council Bluffs was the seat, for more years than I can remember. This, coupled with the regular business, swelled the volume to around five hundred cases (funerals) a year—which means, counting the days in a year, that it was indeed a busy life, and one to remember. In those wild years anything might come up in the way of violence and death—shootings, suicides, "mysteries" pulled from the Missouri River; you name it, we got it. Never eager to talk about it, I was quite surprised at Ernest's open fascination, so I did, freely. Tillie came into the talk and brought it to a howling climax when she told of my coming back through the business district from a late afternoon funeral in a driving rain; I was courting her then, not getting anywhere, but I saw her at the door of the office building where she worked, without a raincoat and a couple of blocks to go for a streetcar home. I swung over and took her home in the hearse—an elegant Cadillac long as a freight car. The windows of the Harry Morgan Room nearly blew outward from the laughter.

"Good Christ! Did he win you in pulling off that great deed, Tillie?"

"No, but his boss heard about it and he very near got fired. But, you know, I saw Mr. Cutler not long before we left home this spring, he wished us good luck in our

Chuck Atkinson, a member of the original "tribe," on my right. (July, 1954.)

new life, said in his book I was still the only gal he knew who was courted in a hearse."

"By a guy with guts enough to try it." Ernest laughed.

"Not guts, Ernie," the guy said. "Just eager impulse."

The remedy that we went to try at around five o'clock grew into a dinner three hours long, and bed close to midnight.

2

We were barely out of bed the morning of September 22 when Ernest called about breakfast with us.

"Good morning, Chief. Wagh! What a beauty Indian summer day."

"Just what the doctor ordered," I said. "But Indian summer? You know better. . . ."

"Yeah, the haze she's smoke from sagebrush fire somewhere . . . even bad Indian no allow that. . . ."

His squaw still slept but he'd be right over, bring his pony, all loaded for the day's expedition. . . . Had I forgotten my promise to do the driving? "You can't look at new country with both hands full."

We looked for him in the lobby, but found him with a bellboy out by the big Village Square lagoon, helping him grain-feed the "wild" mallard ducks and a dozen-and-three family of Canada geese that fed from children's hands if their elders gave them a chance. Annie the antelope—the pretty lady that Taylor got from a rancher who'd found her as a tiny orphan—begged for a bite of grain. Ernest said that the ducks on the lagoon so close by the sun deck at Glamour House were his alarm clock that morning. "I came to, reaching for a gun." His exuberance was not the kind that rubbed off on you—he poured it on by the bucketful.

He'd gone to sleep on my *Idaho Encyclopedia* and had been absorbing it since first light, brought it back to me—"A hell of a lot of State, this Idaho, that I didn't know about." We waited for Marty, talking in our room, me wondering when Ernest would ask where I planned to take them. My gear was in our huge closet and when I got it out, with hip waders included, he said: "I had a hunch, it smells of duck . . . I put ours in too." Browsing in our modest but good-quality library he said he'd be honored with a loan card—he lived so close by that he considered himself a good risk.

We spent the day in Silver Creek country, and the timing couldn't have been more right; the mourning doves were ganging up for the annual migration, lingering in the abnormally warm weather to fatten on the abundance of the little wild sunflower seed. No stranger to dove shooting, Ernest forthrightly said he'd never seen anything to match their concentration. Driving slowly down a ruler-straight seven-mile stretch of State 23 along the east high hills bordering the basin, that he called Monotony Road, one drink long, we were lucky to catch the birds on the move to water following the morning feed; and like me, Ernest was flabbergasted that hunting pressure on our nation's number one game bird was nonexistent. He wished that he'd known it and come earlier. "Tuck it between our ears, Marty. Keep your fingers crossed for another fall." The basin supported a healthy balance of Hungarian partridge—a grand little upland bird—plenty of the big lumbering sage chickens, the largest of our native grouse. Both were good for the cause.

Ducks! They were the headliners. I chose a little used road on the slope of the south bordering hills, stopped on its high point where in a sweeping view some forty-odd square miles of a shotgun heaven spread out before us. Confidently, I labelled it such, added "if there is such a thing, and if not, I think this will do until one comes along." Ernest nodded, got out his binoculars and put them to work. It was a near-windless day, not a duck in the air, but his ears told him the story, pointed his glasses for him. In a quarter of an hour up there, his "This is it" said it all.

Then the true exploration began, for we were directly above the joining of all feeder streams, looking down across a lush mile-square meadow, the main stream flowing through small ponds, their mirror surfaces dimpled by feeding lunkers—rainbow trout up to five and six pounds; mallard ducks dabbling along the tule-fringed banks in singles, twos, and threes. In his uninhibited elation Ernest asked which way would we go from there. The creek system was an open book to him so I said we'd look it over as such—from the beginning.

"Put your glasses on the big mile-square marsh about a mile due west, then look for a small slough of open water in its southeast corner . . . that's where we go next."

He had missed it since the flat angle of vision made the marsh appear as a long deep-green finger that might have fringed a stream. I considered it our first ace-in-the-hole. Ernest took a long look, lowered his binocs, and never will I forget his look. That shallow slough was about three acres in size and its surface was black, and noisy, even at the distance.

"Jesus! Must be a thousand of 'em . . . big ducks, mallards, every one . . . this, Marty must see, close up."

At risk it could be driven fairly close to, a thread of an old wagon road ankle-deep in alkaline dust, cut by shallow puddles of underground seepage. There is no mud known to man more slick than alkaline, but wheel ruts in the puddles were solid if the Buick's belly would clear. I hesitated. Ernest said, "I brought it to use." At the last of them, a long one, it looked too tricky; Ernest spotted a willow stick, said:

"I'll walk the ridges and probe it . . . back off for a start . . . I wave, you come."

It worked, except that he waved a bit too soon, then just stood there; I had no choice but to floorboard it and keep it there. The Buick roared on like a Cape Horner before a gale; the most I saw ahead was a leather vest sticking straight out behind, a big man in it, feet and legs a blur. He made it, barely, heaving like a blown horse when I pulled up on the dry.

"Quite a bit of speed you get out of that rusty knee, doctor."

"Funny what you forget when you damn well have to . . . and we didn't spook a duck—yet."

On a rise where the dim trail turned west, bordering the big marsh, I unlawfully spooked them off with a rifle I brought along in case of an epidemic of coyotes, sent the bullet over their heads. While we drank a beer, "new" ducks dribbled back to the slough. But what he saw in the setup was its isolation and the difficulty of footing it across a quarter-mile flat of the greasy mud—sharply calked soles were a must.

"Wanta try it?"

Damn right, he wanted to try it. With Marty between us, a mutual assistance thing, we made it. There hadn't been a hunter's blind on a strip of dry ground along the open water in years, though at some time an old hunter had contrived to raise it somehow.

"Probably with a team when it was frozen over," Ernest said. "Boy, it's a beauty deal, best I've ever seen, but if a four-legged critter ever went down on the flat . . . like a deer down on ice."

He asked if I'd ever used a machete. Would I cut off my own foot?

"Nothin' to it." He grinned. "Know where I can get the real thing, I'll send for a couple . . . no law against cutting sagebrush to make a couple of blinds with, is there . . . if we don't break our goddamn necks dragging it out here?"

Slithering our way back, Marty said:

"Gentlemen, I could write about this, and it would damn well be unprintable . . . title: 'Runny Nose Flat.'"

But down on a particular stretch of the main stream was the clincher: about a three-hour float trip—the cream of the wildfowlers' dish—jump-shooting from a boat. The beginning of it was at a highway bridge just thirty-two miles from Ketchum. We had squeezed in the time to run it a few times that summer, time it, figure it carefully —for our own use, naturally. Sure, we'd share it with ol' Ernie, and not noise it around, and there was only one man in the country who hunted it in a boat—a little one-man kayak. The entire run was within a privately-owned ranch where we had an "in" and our sneak boats were the canoes.

"The best," Ernest said, savoring the short bit of the stream visible from the bridge, that looked placid and harmless. "If you know what you're doing . . . so open and handy."

It was indeed a delight as a pleasure trip; the stream so meandering you met yourself and the only direction you were certain of was downstream. Silver Creek's secret as a trout stream was also its danger—the long streaming moss in its near-constant temperature that was the food of the tiny fresh-water shrimp the fish fed on. A fisherman tangled up in it called it Circe's hair. Ernest called me a hold-out, which I was because how did we know whether he'd relish such tricky craft on tricky water. Hell, he got lots of his boating education in a canoe on the Des Plaines River that ran through his home town of Oak Park, Illinois—and some other education, too!

On a two-leg country road around the ranch property there were two access points to the creek with a car—a little ranch bridge—a portage-around which we called Picture Bridge—and a road bridge. We had our lunch on a high point in the road between the two, where a short mile south the road joined the highway again at a tiny town and the ranch headquarters mingled as one; a loading point with stock pens and chutes on the Ketchum branch of the railroad paralleling the highway. The sort of behind-the-scenes connection in all of this was that the contracting builder of the Union Pacific's branch lines founded the ranch back in the eighties when it was common to acquire property as part of the deal. His grandson, just out of college, had come to the ranch the previous summer to start learning the business under its manager. A very grand, solid guy named Bud Purdy.

Our personal connection had come from a first-year fishing guide at Sun Valley who had a little store and gas station in the tiny village; Ellis Chapin, called Chape, dabbled in photography very well, took us on our only duck shoot in '37 with guide Pop Mark. Chape was now my cameraman. He sold his business to another mutual friend, Chuck Atkinson, an Ohio boy come West to marry an Idaho girl and raise two cute little towhead boys who played in one of the canoes we kept at Chuck's store.

Chomping on a sweet Bermuda onion like it was an apple, Ernest asked where the boat run ended.

"Just a half mile on down the highway, a little this side of where you hit the pavement after that bitch of a road from the Craters of the Moon. Then it was just a spit and a holler to that tall grain elevator beside the tracks at Peekaboo."

"What . . . where?"

"On your road map you saw it as Picabo, the town at the ranch, but you're in Rome now."

"P-I-C-A-B-O . . . Piece . . . S . . . ! . . . Peekaboo . . . and sure as hell it doesn't fit from here . . . Marty, there's a title for you to build something on . . . fool hell outa them with that one."

A half hour with Chuck and Floss Atkinson—where Ernest wangled a bet on the coming World Series with Chuck was a "good sign-in"—we ran across Bud at the ranch store, and so went another half hour at the population-50 metropolis of Silver Creek.

On another way home I stopped at the foot of Timmerman Hill where a portly old German lived alone in the back of a little beer bar, a single gas pump as another source of his meager living. No one seemed to know him by any other name than Dutch Charlie, but his place was a magnet to many with certain tastes. But you had to give with at least a hint when it came to edibles—when I gave it, old Dutch had two new customers beating me to his door. His magic was a recipe for pickling trout, precooked, I guess, and brined in something. At two-bits apiece, with Charlie's good tap beer . . . 'nuf said. Ernest had a half dozen of them wrapped in newspaper under his arm when we left.

"For Hemingpickle's Harry's bar . . . I feel half pickled already. A premature

Lovable Ab Womak (*center*) putting together the saddle destined to be buried with its owner.

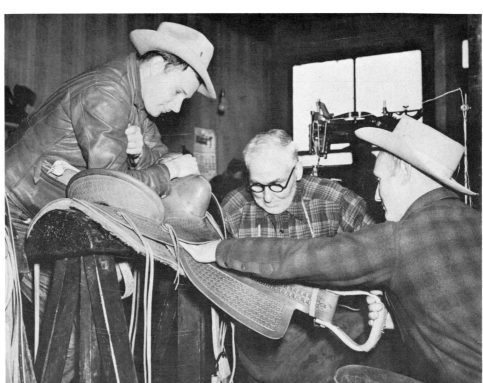

thanks for a fine day, Chief . . . you can pass checking us in with the sheriff, the game warden and the local padre . . . we'll get to them another day . . . or they'll get to us."

One more stop in Hailey to pick up some leather shell bags that Ernest had left for restitching with saddlemaker Ab Womak. Ab and his cluttered old shop, where Ma Womak did the shoe repairing, were collectively a Wood River institution. I bought my horse from Ab; he was to take his time, all winter, at building me a saddle on a tree I had him order that morning. But, you could wonder just who would ride the saddle, me or Ab's new customer. He knew a roper from a bulldogger tree when he saw one. He liked these earthy people, the smell of honest leather, the sweat smell of horse from old gear left for fixin' and the lingo that quickly dispensed with "Mr." He apologized to Ab for the musty odor of his leather goods, and Ab said, "Oh, that's all right, Mr. Hemenway, it smells worse'n that when the boys git it about ankle-deep in here from yarnin'."

"Often I'm accused of making my living at dishing out the ankle-deep, Mr. Womak, so I feel at home."

"That's the stuff, young feller."

The young feller couldn't wait to get Marty outside to tell her the compliment was better than a stiff shot of booze—which we had at another valley institution next door to Ab's.

I had told Ernest that of all the bars in our country, I figured he would rate Al Lewis' little Snug as the Harry's bar. He did, the instant he set foot on its floor so clean you felt you could eat off it. The Snug was more a man's saloon, no bar stools, but tall "goboons" nudging your knee behind the rail of the mahogany; never crowded, always quietly pleasant and your gal was welcome in Al's place where an apology for no places to sit was out of place as a poker game standing up. One of the old school boys, Al was proud of the little museum that he'd been years in accumulating—stemming from the old mining days. In one glass case of old photographs was a picture of Ezra Pound—the familiar one of the poet sitting cross-legged with arms clasped over his knees. Pound was born in Hailey—in 1885—"by accident" as natives said. A few old-timers remembered him as an infant; the father came west in connection with the mining, then quit the country to return to his native Pennsylvania. Ernest wasn't sure of Hailey as his birthplace, but it rung a bell when checking his road map. He said little about it, beyond a pointed remark that he considered Ezra Pound an invaluable friend, forever in debt to him. "It's-another-small-world thing," he said.

Tillie was waiting for us on the Inn porch. Come for a drink at Glamour House, and a chore I was asked to do: rustle up a couple of glass jars, if possible. I found them in the kitchen pantry—about two-quart size. Riding over on Ernest's lap, Tillie asked what for.

"Old Papa's got a recipe . . . gonna pickle a couple of rabbit's-foot charms, shot some jacks by the marsh today . . . make 'em safe for democracy, grace the pocket."

"I don't believe you," Tillie said. "You wouldn't touch the mangy infested things." (Tularemia was rampant in rabbits in those days.)

"I'll dig up another recipe then, and while we work on it we'll have a go at Dutch Charlie's recipe . . . his standing order from you if he goes by there, Pappy says . . . and did I say we saw enough ducks today to have wintered the rabble at Valley Forge?"

"That I do believe," she said. "Did you see any snipe?"

"A few, and signs everywhere . . . my favorite target, snipe, trickiest that flies . . . and I know why you ask . . . that little story Pappy told us . . . I'll put it in a piece some time."

Since he never did, among many others, a sketch of it:

I was about ten years old when my father took me on my first try at Wilson snipe in the Missouri River flats. My little gun threw too-tight shot patterns and I touched nary a feather; so off to one side I saw a few killdeer, the funny little bobbing up-and-down shore birds of similar size. They looked easy, so for practice I nailed several and left them. The pater caught up with me, gave me holy hell, made me take them home and clean them as if for the table, but for the family cat, instead.

"My father had a name for killdeer, Ernie, 'teeter-ass snipe'."

"And you came close to losing some hide off yours for that great deed . . . tough teacher, your Pop, you don't waste what you shoot."

His recipe was a joke on Tillie—with a purpose. In the lunch box he had about three hatfuls of oozy-ripe little damson plums that we picked from stunted trees on an old derelict farm where we often had lunch when dove hunting. Ernest spotted them—a favorite fruit of his, from his youth in the Michigan summers—and the twinkle in his eye had tipped me off. Now up in Glamour House he put her to work with himself—pinching the plums to break their skins when dropped into the jars. He drowned them in Grade-A brandy, using the better part of an unopened bottle— "Let 'em cook for a week, then. . . ."

"Pretty expensive recipe, you big clown." Marty laughed.

"Yeah, but plum jubilee beats cherry all to hell, too!"

3

Saturday morning we got Ernest and Taylor Williams together—a half-planned, half-accidental thing which Ernest went along with, more than glad that he did. He and I were tightening up his shotgun stock for some clay target shooting in the afternoon, working on the counter just inside the door of our shop when Gene and Taylor came. Seeing me fooling with a gun was nothing new and he paid no attention to the big man bent over on my off side. Instead, Tillie was his target in a small production on his promise to bring a dinner of the cutthroat trout she'd never enjoyed but had heard so much about. His answer was the voice back of me:

"I heard that, Mr. Williams," then he saw the face as it came up over my shoulder. Mr. Williams didn't bat an eye, tipped his hat at talking angle, put out his hand, said there was an old rumor going that he might show up some time—he *was* Mr. Hemingway, wasn't he? A single word describes their come-together: click! It was quite a little while before the tomfoolery took over, so we three waited—off on "our" planet—until it came, Ernest the trigger. He hinted quite strongly that his gunnery might win him the necktie that the colonel wore—hand-embroidered with trout fly patterns. The hell his gunnery might, the colonel said—that tie was a lady friend's gift and he wasn't getting it for money, marbles, or chalk!

It was Ernest's exuberance over Silver Creek and the prospects of jump-shooting it in canoes that opened the next circus. Neither Gene nor Taylor ever shied from relating their experiences as white-water men on Wood River at runoff time, and up to then Ernest knew nothing about that. But he had noticed the slight hop in Taylor's gait, and the stiffness in the fingers of his left hand. He remarked on them as he came down the walk. He got it all, on the spot, but the colonel's eyes could flash fire with their laughter when he'd speak of the "sour old maid nurse who should've been one to a veterinary" and "that old social doctor who worked like hell all day looking for five o'clock on his watch." Had Ernest ever been attacked by wood ticks in Montana?

"Sure, lots, Taylor; they just fall off me in a hurry . . . with the blind staggers."

The colonel just might help that situation—it was still mint julep weather. Yeah, there was a rumor going about that, too!

With a tidy investment in five figures, and rounded out that summer, Sun Valley's shooting layout was quite impressive. But did it have a handtrap or two in its inventory, Ernest wanted to know. No, it did not, but the district Western-Winchester man had been around so much on equipment installation that we counted him a member of the family. A twangy-voiced, sleepy-eyed character, Bill Marsh came full on with a gun in his hands and split your ribs with his humor. He dug around in his car trunk for his handtrap sample and made the layout a present of it. It was Mr. Marsh who called the fun that afternoon "a riot of 12-gauge mayhem." He knew how to use that little three-dollar gadget, had more tricks up the sleeve of his great arm than an all-star pitcher. Excepting a murderous shooting game called the quail walk, Ernest had little interest in breaking targets thrown by mechanical means—the proof of what he said in our first talk, the all-out shotgun man, underlined and in capital letters when his targets wore feathers and were edible.

Afterward, perhaps because it was late Saturday afternoon with all the guides checked in, there was a casual gathering in the Ram. I mention it mainly because the greatest of all namers I've ever known got one for himself that he liked. Kindly Pop Mark, a wit to keep up with, sort of teamed up with a big shuffling guide about my age, with a sense of humor far ahead of his physical gait. Pop called Art Wood "Big A." When we shot the quail walk Pop and Art played the piano—the row of release buttons for the traps. Pop had Ernest in a laughing dither on one walk-up, said, "Sure dealt you a heap of misery that time, Big E." Big E looked a bit startled, then exploded in laughter. I've often wondered what men other than Pop or Big A could have gotten by with it. Besides those two and Taylor, there were two others— genial Jack Redden and Clayton "Stew" Stewart, a lad of twenty-one—who spoke of themselves as a bunch of stinkin' fishin' guides. Following the tall yarning Ernest spoke of them as a fine tribe, of which he was the only unpaid member.

On Sunday, September 24, Tillie and I got acquainted with another side of Ernest Hemingway—one that we could guess, even at that early stage in the game.

A one and only in existence, according to the angler, and about the end of the book for freshwater fishing anywhere.

On that first Saturday night on the town, when it was going good on the roulette wheel at the Alpine, he proposed a picnic for Sunday—on Silver Creek. Hadn't he said he was the biggest of all suckers for picnics? So Sunday morning, Ernest left his car for the gals to follow us around noon with a picnic basket, meet us at Peekaboo. I took down a station wagon to bring the canoe back for a bottom painting. Ernest had not picked up a license of any kind, but Gene and I both had our rods along. Gene netted a couple of nice rainbow from a good stretch of water near the portage at Picture Bridge, about midway in the float trip. Lauding Gene's skill, Ernest again said that it would not do for him to get involved, though he did take my light rod and got himself a fair fish—"daudle fishing"—in tennis shoes from the bank. Reading his thoughts, we spoke them for him. Sure, it would be great to take a little canoe run, plenty of time. I went for the boat and we put in at the last bridge—about a forty-minute float through an immense marsh of head-high rushes that we called the Chutes. Once in it you ran it all, no other choice, down to the pullout alongside the highway below Peekaboo.

On the stern paddle, where you get the true feel, Ernest saw at once that the creek wrote the rule book, you followed it, or else. A warm day, it was an oven in the Chutes, where the shooting would be sporting, but drop your birds in the stream. Nothing could retrieve a duck dropped in the impenetrable jungle walling the creek itself. So, fishing was the lost subject, until in a deep pool a big rainbow as long as my arm rolled up alongside, took a look at us, impudently flicked his tail and moved on ahead.

"A friendly cuss," Ernest said.

"I doubt it, Ernie," Gene said. "He just came up to see what it is in his creek that's bigger than he is."

"I suppose you're right, Gene . . . a rainbow is a tuna is a whale."

A short silence, then: "And if either of you accuse me of a steal, accuse me of one that makes sense."

It made sense to get the hell on with the paddling—the mosquitoes and no-see-um gnats were eating us up. Chuck Atkinson met us with our station wagon, and over a beer with him at his store, plans for the afternoon were changed. We intended to take the lower route out of the basin and go south for a look at some pheasant country around Richfield, then on down near Shoshone where Gene had an errand. It was a rare day if you saw a pheasant around Silver Creek; too much snow in the winters. But they were on Ernest's mind, for we had seen a couple of them, drifters up from where they wintered, as were the ducks we'd seen. So, following our picnic under a big lone cottonwood tree from which you could toss a pebble into the stream at Picture Bridge, we took the canoe to the upper bridge on the highway, for the full run. Outweighing me by a good forty pounds, Gene insisted that he and Nin run his errand, they'd come by on their way back, about matching our time.

Well, a load we were indeed, for a light sixteen-foot craft: Ernest's two hundred-weight, Marty outweighing Tillie's hundred by too much, my scant 150 in the stern, where I insisted on paddling so the eager "gunner" could take the front view. In truth, we had a hell of a time balancing for a fairly level ride, Marty between my knees, and we very nearly rolled over getting underway. Damn fools, I thought to myself, and so did Ernest, from the look he threw me over his shoulder. He spoke truth when he said a canoe was a good part of his boating education. He was as good as any man I'd ever paddled with, and I could match him in all but the power in those huge shoulders, long arms, muscles rippling under a red plaid shirt—all but off him in the warmth of the day.

Once underway we got along fine, and it would take a chapter to do justice to the delightful trip—isolation in a big flat pastureland where you felt you were off in another world, a thousand miles from nowhere. A healthy population of ducks nested and summered there in the little sloughs and marshes along the low banks, and they put on the show that Ernest was looking for. He made a cute response to an enraptured remark by Tillie. It was her first look at the basin. She loved the water anywhere (though she couldn't swim a lick), but had never experienced anything pertaining to hunting with me. On a sharp bend screened by a finger of tules we sneaked up on a few mallard drakes and susies that rocketed straight up in startled flight, washed Ernest's face in a spray of power-stroking wings, then against an azure sky dappled with fluffy clouds they hung on their props like planes in the split second of levelling-out—a sight that veterans seldom see. Tillie gasped in delight, said, "Oh! Calendar ducks, just like what's-his-name would paint them for Brown & Bigelow."

Ernest turned his head, grinning his own appreciation, searched a moment for words.

"Yes, Tillie, weren't—they—beauties! Say . . . if you'll split that title with me I might do a piece on the calendar ducks . . . 'Ducks in the Afternoon.'"

In the upper half of the trip there were a number of obstacles: a low bridge or two, an abandoned irrigation flume, old moss-laden fence strands, and a shallow gravel-bottom cattle crossing a bit rough on our thin-soled feet. So we lightened the boat by getting out, slid it along with the girls in it, our footing equally precarious on the slanting approach. I slipped on it, and went to my knees a split second before Ernest did the same. He cursed outright, I called it "slick as hell, this four-letter stuff of cows that once was grass."

He let loose of the boat, stood upright, laughing like crazy, his eyes on the knees of his pants.

"Goddamnit, will you keep still 'til we get across this son of a bitch. . . . It'll be just our luck, Chief, to drop a duck on this s—— every time we run it." (I offer three guesses as to his prediction.)

Around four o'clock we eased out on the low grassy bank at pullout. Gene had left cold beer in the carryall, we split a couple and were about to load the boat to wait at Peekaboo. From there was a stretch of about four hundred yards, straight as a ruler, man-made to avoid the highway some fifty yards distant. No carrying of the boat, the car was parked a dozen feet from the bank—a fishermen's approach. At the end of the stretch was a sharp bend to the left, the stream disappearing in the walls of tules. From the road only, I knew of the old decrepit place beyond the bend, and Chuck or Bud Purdy had said that an odd old geezer lived there, raised turkeys and trapped muskrats in the big marsh for a living. A bridge in his yard crossed the stream, they said; it might be a better place for a pullout. No, it was not a part of the big ranch, not much of anything as a property. The current was oil-smooth, but deceptively fast in the straightened channel. Should we chance it? See for ourselves? Ernest asked. I said no, rather flatly, for on either prow side of the canoe the name Sun Valley was a flag in bright yellow letters—an odd old geezer might resent such intrusion from the big plush place up north. True in a place or two, in our first-rate relations with natives about the country at large. But, Ernest kept eyeing the water, and of course I went along—sure, we could talk our way out at the bridge.

Using our blades only for steering we went down at an alarming rate, over bottle-green water denoting depth. Near the bend there was a noticeable pull in the current; we heard the sound of falling water. We didn't glide around the curve, we shot around it, hugging the inside left. But for a low bank clear of tules, with little sage-brushes to grab, we'd have gone right over a two-foot-high fall—a rock ledge across the full width of the stream. Twenty feet beyond it was the bridge, so low a duck couldn't pass under it. A trap? You could call it nothing else—made to order for the old geezer!

On a patch of open ground about the size of a cabin porch he stood like a bellig-erent statue—the counterpart of an old river rat I used to see on the Missouri. His hands were tucked abib in old overalls, hip waders rolled to his knees, a burlap sack at his feet, and some traps. An old Army campaign hat shadowed his face, its brim snapped low, its crown pinched tightly fore-and-aft like those worn in Spanish-American War times. In the big yard beyond, on the bridge itself, a solid sea of turkeys fattening for market. At our eye-level it was a sea of red heads and necks —all talking at once. The statue remained glaringly silent at Ernest's friendly at-tempt at amenities. All four of us were hanging on for dear life, the prow actually hanging over the little fall. Ernest raised himself, got one foot on the bank, jackknifed with his stern skyward, then the statue came to life—audibly.

"Wh-wh-wh-wh-whatcha th-th-think yer g-g-g-gonna do?"

That explained a thing or two, but Ernest tried like a gentleman, got nowhere: them turkeys didn't know strangers, disturbed their eatin'—all said in the length of two pages. I tried: It was a long pull back up that fast water. S-s-s-sure it was, but we came down it, we could go back up it. By then the air was charged, lightning silence before the thunder, then wham-o!

Ernest's behind hit his seat hard enough to break it, his paddle blade on the bank shot the prow broadside like from a catapult. Of the three canoes, the one we kept at Chuck's had no keel. Lateral resistance of one in that water would have rolled us over in the wink of an eye—why we preferred it for the creek. Even so, I'll never understand how we got turned around. There was a wild man forward, a Paul Bunyan on a rampage, my paddle biting more air than water to help control. My voice was useless against:

"Thanks for your g-g-g-goddamn c-c-c-courtesy! Stutter man, son of a bitch! Son of a bitch, stutter man! . . . and furthermore you can take the goddamn turkeys . . . no, by God, we should do it. . . ."

As we struggled against the tide I stole a split-second look at the man before the bend cut off the view. He had not moved a muscle. But the fury up front was blowing itself out—we couldn't get enough air in our lungs, for clouds of gnats liked the sweat of our labors. Marty's sharp reprimand, shaky-voiced, brought the slow-up to a halt—our anchor, handfuls of tall rushes. Tremulously, Tillie said, "Anybody wanta buy a turkey?"

"Jesus! Wasn't that an awful show I put on back there? I should drown in the sweat of shame for mocking the man. But dammit, he could have let us out. I'm sorry, Pappy, you called the turn, on the nose."

More than just a bit miffed at him, madder than a wet turkey at that overalled Horatio at the bridge, mad as two at myself, I said, "Shall we laugh and forget it, charge it to you-know-what?"

"Yes," Marty said. "If someone will tell me where he got that hat."

"Probably the old son of a bitch voted for the big T in Roosevelt." Ernest grinned sheepishly. "I couldn't tell whether he was forty or a hundred and forty . . . did he look at anybody else but me?"

No, not that we could see.

"Then, by God, I'm the spook, I guess."

We struggled on—like climbing the Matterhorn—Gene watching us from where we went astray: "Wait'll he gets the gen on the turkey man, and Chuck and Bud, we'll get it with both barrels . . . if ever I suggest a move on something I'm a stranger to, just give me the hard tap in one way or another."

We were not through with Stutter Man, nor was he with us, by a long shot. Nor was Ernest hesitant or shy in clearing the air for us while we loaded the boat. In elaboration to the point of excess, he said if Silver Creek's potentials were made to order for his working program, he was not a damn bit in doubt about the country's other offerings. Of course, too, it was a hell of a note that a man had to work with it dangling in front of him, and guessed he could stand the wait for pheasants on October 15 and ducks on the twenty-second.

The work program started Tuesday morning, put off a day to go with us on a day-long trip to firm up plans with the packer who'd take Taylor and me after elk. He lived in the best of the Idaho antelope country, which Ernest wanted very much to see. The fleet pronghorn buck (the right name for the antelope) was a favorite with him, and when he said he had hopes for the following fall, some one of us said, "Fine, if we're not in the war up to our chins by then." He said:

"We won't be, I'm betting on it, long odds . . . but it's coming."

We left early Monday morning and our loop route through the very heart of the state's highest mountain country was one of rough, dusty, teeth-rattling roads—in the main. The worst of it was the old mining road at Sun Valley's back door, northeast over Trail Creek Summit, a hair-raiser, to put it mildly, and the very thing that appealed to Ernest when we started clawing our way up the canyon wall. In a word: little used, unspoiled. He liked the immensity, the far-reaching look of the gaunt Lost River Mountains country, the range itself the state's roof; the one he had seen from the monotony of the Arco desert, reminding him of parts of Spain. Then when we wound down from a high Lost River pass into the upper reaches of the Pahsimeroi River Valley, he asked that we stop, give it a thorough casing from the distance of a high vantage point.

The Pahsimeroi is still off the beaten path, and in those days you heard of it in a way that suggested the mythical to an active imagination. It is old Indian country, the western hunting range of the Shoshonis, Sacajawea's people. Its musical name is legendary, sprung from the oddity of a small stand of pines along the river where the nomadic Shoshoni set up their lodges for the fall hunt. In the aridity of the vast high valley the trees did not belong there, so the red man revered the region as sacred. Ernest agreed that it had an indescribably different look about it, and that it was also a bit of Spain in our hemisphere, the likes of which he hadn't seen before.

The special "permit-by-drawing" hunt opened the next morning, September 26, so, undisturbed, little bands of antelope were everywhere, some close, some far; then down valley in the scattered ranch hayfields the "Pahsimeroi beef" helped themselves with the cattle.

Literally draped in ringnecks taken in Rancher Tom Gooding's *(left)* fields. Ernest said: "Idaho bird shooting is the best in the world." It must have been—he did aplenty of it here, right up to. . . . Gene Van Guilder, at his left, and I. (October 15, 1939.)

"I'm hooked, men," Ernest said. "Glad you got good connections in this country . . . we old Shoshonis will see it again."

In the little one-street dusty town of Challis on the Salmon River we met Bill Hamilton—a rawhide, pine-knot character epitomizing sprawling, five-thousand square-mile Custer County. One of a vanishing breed of men of whom Ernest said in the car when we recognized Bill's oxbow legs moving him along like a sore-toed rooster:

"From here he looks the guy you'd go anywhere with in the mountains and he'd make it good for you whether you connect or not."

Gene or Taylor yelled at Bill who threw us a toothless grin, yelled back, "Tie it n'git down, bin waitin' fer you birds long enough."

"I guess that's Hamiltonian, gents, for 'park the buggy, old cowboys don't like to drink alone,' and I say he's not about to."

Ernest wore his old round-toed cowboy boots, otherwise dressed as I had first seen him, with the addition of his big, battered old Stetson worn *Afrikaner* style—floppy brim, high pinched crown, tipped well back off his forehead. Bill kept eyeing it and shortly asked Ernest what part of the West he hailed from.

"Montana . . . when I'm lucky," he said. "I mean that's the part of the West I use mostly, Bill."

Bill had the name pegged all right, but walking down to a little bar, he suddenly looked up at this big Westerner who hadn't satisfied his curiosity.

"Ernie, you write Westerns?"

No words to describe Ernest's face, or ours, when he jerked his head around, grabbing at his falling hat.

In a small cafe where very long talk was made, and short work of some delicious grass-fattened steaks, Ernie got his other little gem of the day. The single waitress was a buxom, jolly gal who obviously knew how to fork a horse as well as hay, and butcher out what fell to her rifle, too. The writer of Westerns was right at home, so in joking about how rough the going was where he just might go with Bill, he told her it could be too much for him—he hadn't had much experience.

"Oh, don't worry, Mister," she said matter-of-factly. "You're big enough to get yourself an elk with a stick."

He fumbled a bit in his retort to that one, and when she turned away:

"Best compliment I've had since I was invited to the White House."

We took the Salmon River route home, the gravelled Highway 93 hugging the river through the scenic heartland of the state for a hundred miles—to cross it as a tiny creek at the foot of Galena Summit, an hour from Ketchum. It would be hard to find a more satisfying hundred miles than following the storied River of No Return to its trickling source. Looking back on it from a high switchback on the snaky old Summit road, Ernest said softly:

"You'd have to come from a test tube and think like a machine to not engrave all of this in your head so that you never lose it."

The following dawn the work on the novel continued as scheduled, so we learned at a lingering lunch, and that it went better in mountain cool than it had in months of heat in a hotel in Havana. He said he was on the rough of Chapter 13, and had worked the name Sun Valley into it. We lifted brows, how could he do it, time-wise? He grinned.

"The freedom of fiction."

Teaching Marty the art of shotgunning was his other immediate task. Frankly admitting that she could take it or leave it, much preferred to ride, she responded to his wishes with a firm will—when the handicap of her malfunctioning little gun was removed. A .410-gauge pump gun, it had a bug in it, would not repeat, so Taylor loaned her a perfect fit from his department's rack—a fine 20-gauge Winchester double barrel. She surprised herself with it, her professor, too, and the colonel said, "That's the stuff, you're a big girl now," and half under his breath, ". . . that damn popgun anyhow," of the .410. He was on the right track, Ernest said he'd buy her a Model 21 when he was back in the dough again, adding, ". . . and what'll you give me for the popgun, Colonel . . . and furthermore?"

The colonel cackled that it wasn't his!

As September drew to its close, Gene put out his first release to the press—on Ernest fishing. Busy himself, Taylor chose Pop Mark, who was never a Silver Creek fan. He selected Big Wood River below Magic Reservoir, splendid water for nice rainbow trout. There was a bug in that deal, too. In a grove of cottonwoods a short way up-

Bride-to-be Marty Gellhorn with her first loot taken with a gun.

stream from the action that was immediate, a very dead critter made the air thick enough to cut with a knife. The stench was almost unbearable, but the place was right, including a background for my very hastily made pictures on a broad gravel bar. Ahead of that I got one action shot of Ernest fighting the fish, and while on the posed shots, Gene stood by with a red bandana handkerchief tied over his face, just his eyes twinkling above it. Ernest burst out a big guffaw, said:

"For Christ's sake, Jesse James, fetch the bottle of Scotch."

Jesse had it in his hip pocket, tipped it up under his mask for a swig, and passed it around. We did the rest of our fishing at Timmerman Dutch Charlie's place on our way home.

The date was September 28, the one and only time that Ernest seriously fished for trout in Idaho. He told me later that the "come hell or high cow" episode about closed the book on his freshwater fishing, and that the action picture was the only one of its kind in existence.

To even the score, Ernest went along with Marty's fondness for riding. He rode quite well himself, though his sitting a horse might be described as rather "leaden" or deadweight. Gentle with his mount as if it were a kitten, he didn't rate equine intelligence very high, a remark he'd make with a hearty laugh: he figured the horse was damn well aware of it. Perhaps so, for every mount that Bob Miles picked for him, a different one each ride, the combination was not so good. Ernest was one of those people who made a horse nervous, break out in sweat. Bob's ranch foreman and boss of all things horse, Spike Spackman, accused him rather flatly of running his horse excessively, not the case at all. But it was done good-naturedly and then Spike's horse sense solved the problem.

In some 125 head there was one that could do the job: a grey chunky horse named Antelope who let nothing bother him. He was a risk horse, something of a clown, and had been used by movie units from Hollywood, Sun Valley country then quite in demand for locale. Ernest became buddies with Antelope, rode him up the big mountain with Gene and me—a five-hour ride with no trouble at all. And in the interim he learned something about Antelope's high rating. In the preceding spring of '38 the opening scenes of the fine motion picture *Stanley and Livingstone,* were shot out of Sun Valley, in the Boulder Mountains ten miles north, with Spencer Tracy and Walter Brennan. One of them rode Antelope in the scenes showing the great reporter in the West covering the Indian fighting, sent for by his publisher to embark on the search in Africa for Dr. Livingstone. Riding along happily one afternoon, Ernest said, "By God, ol' Ernie's gittin' up in the world, riding Spencer Tracy's horse." Antelope's flicking ear said thanks, then a little farther on:

"But, Antelope, actors are phony, writers are phony, and I think we can class you as a phony, too . . . any minute you just might unwind and pitch ol' Dr. Hemingstone in the sagebrush, flat on his ass."

Dr. Hemingstone never suffered such indignity, nor would he allow me to include him in an informal picture of the riding tribe—six of us. But something came out of the riding, and he spotted the area before we rode into it with him for the first time. North of town on the west of Big Wood River, Adams Gulch is very pretty country, dominated by a high, rocky, timbered butte of the same name. Ernest said that it would be ideal if his current work should some time be produced as a movie. We rode in the big gulch several times, high up in looking it over thoroughly; then, since Bob Miles was responsible for Hollywood's interest, Ernest suggested that come spring we photograph Adams Gulch in light lingering snow—have the pictures on hand in case. His was a shy suggestion, and the movie locations thing was a lucrative business, too, for the resort. We assured him we'd do it.

Right up to the last minute almost, Ernest counted on going with us after elk. He bought his general license, an elk and a deer tag, had a saddle scabbard made for his Springfield, bought mountain boots that he didn't have in his gear. We sighted-in our rifles on a rainy Sunday afternoon, October 1, our takeoff slated for early Tuesday, the third. Like me, his concern was for Taylor on whom it could be an ordeal; opening of elk seasons are famous for sudden early storms. I assured him that Taylor was well aware of his limitations due to his setback and that I could handle his pride in holding up his end if the going got rough. On Monday afternoon, a bright clear one following the threatening day, he came by the shop, asked me to come to Glamour House for a thorough rundown on the situation as I saw it. That had an odd ring, for we had gone over it plenty; there had to be another motive.

A procrastinator of the first water, Taylor had ordered himself a heavier-calibre rifle for the big deer that, oddly enough, he had not hunted in his years in the West. In error, or as a substitute, the model 70 Winchester came with an open-notch sight mounted well forward on the barrel. His own model 70 in identical calibre to my light rifle for antelope and deer was equipped with the receiver-mounted aperture sight close to his eye; of the old school, he had not yet taken to 'scopes. The air turned blue around him, he would take it anyway and be handicapped, then Ernest took advantage. I know there were sincerity and disappointment in his back out: he was in correspondence, and a phone call or two, with his editor at Scribner's, Maxwell Perkins. Walking to the Lodge he told me that he intended sending his Springfield .30-06 with Taylor, instead, if he had to take him down and sit on him for agreement. He called him over in a while, made a big to-do of driving home the fact that bullets are like medicine—if a little is good, more is better: a 130-grain pill was not enough medicine for a big dangerous critter, his 180-grains would leave no doubt about a cure. In those days it was "status" to a hunter owning a custom-built Springfield by such masters as Griffin & Howe, and the colonel was reluctant to take it. He stood as much chance as a snowball in hell: the patinaed, mellow-with-use gun—one that Ernest really cared for, personally, above others—was thrust upon him, and that was that. It had served its owner well, and it was good Indian-sign—even old witch doctor Hemingstein backed up the medicine man in that. He went into his bedroom, returned with a small leather pouch bag about the size of two clenched fists—a primitive thing that had been around a long time. Pawing around in it, his fingers turning up things that our curious eyes scarcely believed, he fished out a good-luck piece for me, and watched while I buttoned it safely in my shirt pocket.

"You have to shoot pictures, too, Pappy. Sorry I don't have anything in that line."

His grin was straight, and I said, "Hell, who of us doesn't draw on the squatting around a fire in a loincloth instincts buried deep within us?"

"Hmph! Anybody who says he doesn't...."

The colonel took off in a high lope, said he'd be back in an hour; I said to Ernest, "Three guesses, and your first is the right one."

Yeah, he guessed he'd call the tribe for the shindig; and the old Kentuckian outdid himself, if such were possible, with the mint juleps that he had glasses being frosted for. No one ever figured just how he managed so late in the growing season to produce those heavenly mint sprigs when by all the rules they should have been

Ernest hard at work—when he wished he were butchering elk far to the north.
(October, 1939.)

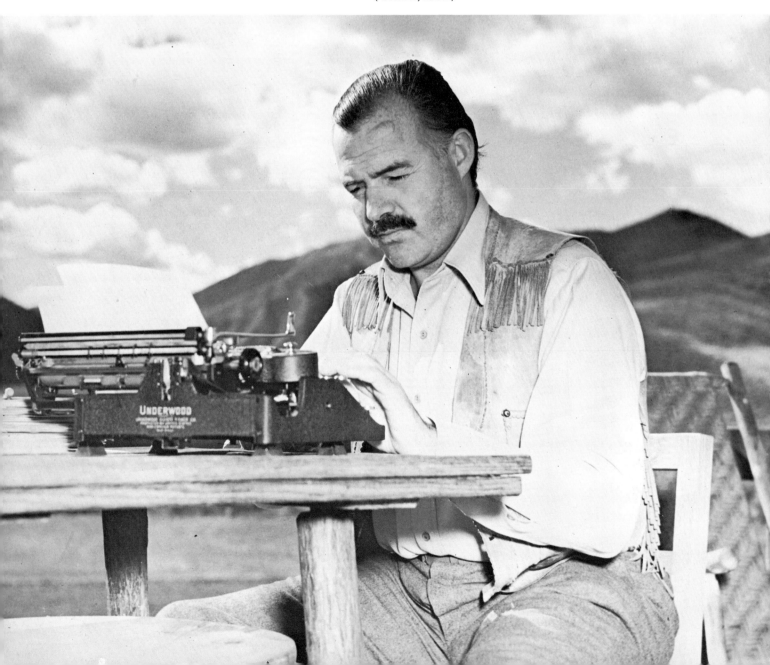

strong. They'd be even better, he'd say, if his mint was grown on the shallow grave of an old confederate soldier. Was he damn sure he hadn't lifted one complete and transplanted it in Idaho? "Christ! This is good, how long before a man can't get up and walk out by himself?"

I said that the colonel had finesse, and restraint: you had one, plus a small dividend, and you knew you had been on a journey!

With plum jubilee for dinner dessert, we wondered if we'd make an early rising—three o'clock—for the long drive into Montana, then back across the high pass into Idaho to our road's-end camp. We made it with a further send-off: still leery of our success in the dry, overly warm weather, Ernest got out of bed, threw a trench coat over his pajamas and robe and came over to the Inn square where we'd parked our loaded carryall; not only to send his regrets to Bill Hamilton, but to admonish us again not to leave the "delicacies" when we butchered-out our big wapitis we were sure to get, one way or another. I can say with feeling that as our lights stabbed a hole in the stygian black on the summit road out of the valley, we felt the old Indian's presence. Maybe he upped good fortune in another form, too—Bill Hamilton could blow an elk bugle made of a hollow stick to make your nape hairs stand on end—the rut was still on and there was much music in the Selway.

On Sunday afternoon about four—six days absence in all—I backed our car to the

This reporter sharing an apple with mountain hunter Bill Hamilton, who got his literary identities a bit mixed up. My first elk hunt, one on which Ernest Hemingway had so badly hoped to go. But he was hard at work on his "Big One."

Inn kitchen dock to unload a thousand pounds of meat in quarters with the hide on, in perfect condition for curing; two above-average antlered heads skinned out and caped for taxidermy, two growths of whiskers and strong smells about us. We'd left the Selway in the wee hours; the colonel slept most of the way home. But now as I saw to unloading, he warmed up reporting in to the Old Man, and was on high C when he phoned Glamour House. The doctor was in, Harry's open for business, but we'd have to leave our whiskers on to prove that we'd been out in the hills, let alone back so soon. (We'd knocked four days off our estimate.) But we'd clean up otherwise, then be over. A hell of a good idea. The doctor laughed—he'd been elking a time or two. If we didn't clean up, any stray dogs around the place might swamp us!

The colonel's pleasure was the first order of business: He fished from his pocket the single deformed bullet we'd dug from his nice big bull—dropped as if pole-axed when hit high in the neck at three hundred yards with the strange rifle and iron sights —remarkable shooting under the stress of labored breathing and hard stalking. We verified the yardage with the rangefinder on my camera, in totalling distances between obstacles in our step-off measure. Ernest's exuberance was that of having made the shot himself.

"I told you, I told you, Colonel, that you could shoot that rifle, didn't I now?"

I gave him back his good-luck charm—the bullet that had killed his first Wyoming elk—its copper jacket now green with age, but a bit pocket polished on the high spots —and I had a single bullet, too, from my first elk. He ran me down, almost, on a dim trail that I couldn't get out of, spooked to high heaven at Taylor's shot, so mine was in self-defense.

"And did you make like pup not broke to house?"

"What do you think, Doctor . . . he looked the size of a locomotive."

He bled with us in our tale of having to walk out of the country, some eighteen miles, leading our packed saddle horses because of the sudden, vicious wet snowstorm that gummed up the works by stranding half our pack string supplying another camp. We walked out to save our meat from the thaw warm-up that followed immediately. Ours was a trip worthy of writing up in a story that Gene took full notes on to do for an outdoor magazine, but there's a highlight or two from that evening of our return.

Did we bring all the "goodies" as promised? Yes, Bill said to tell ol' Ernie that he took care of them himself, from hearts to nuts, and the rest was up to us—get the hell for home once we got out to base camp through that knee-deep snow.

"Well, great, guess I'll have to check over the livers good when we go over to eat . . . might want to trade mine in on a new one."

Should he put that in the story, Gene asked.

"Sure, I know an outfit or two who'll pay extra for that item."

The complexion of things changed when the colonel fixed the doctor with a steely eye behind a levelled finger, and told him that the magic, voodoo, whatever the hell he called it, that he dispensed in the guise of good-luck wishes was damned suspicious now—every possible eventuality talked of had come to pass. He got his laugh for all the good, and the feeling for the bad. The old boy was purple-faced with exhaustion from that walkout that as the kid of the trio I broke trail. He scared the wits out of Bill and me—that remarkable piece of human rawhide, who waited a long time that night before sipping a small hot toddy.

The other was an item to get the ear of any old mountain hunter. When packing in the meat to our hunting camp Bill and I had a thrill: a magnificent big bull in his prime, his nose full of the scents from the loads our weary horses carried, wanting to fight, blowing, stamping his feet, at some fifty yards against a mist-shrouded canyon, a neutral void as a background of a picture the mind's eye sees but once in a lifetime of hunting. Bill threw a stick at him and yelled an insult, and the regal old boy slowly turned and ambled out of sight. I said to Bill, "Didn't he remind you of the trademark on Hartford Insurance Company calendars and ads?"

"I think he was an even better one," Bill said. "Not doctored up by a paintin' feller who prob'ly never seen one where he belongs."

"Aren't you glad you had yours on the horses?" Ernie said. "He's the kind that's good to leave for seed . . . let's hope nobody gets him."

Nothing to do when we went to dinner but to inspect the loot in the cooler boxes; the Old Man with us, and big Ray Daly, a cook and the genius who did marvelous things in his smokehouse—"with tough old bull meat" which in the case of prime elk is often not true. Then out in the service hall, where our group stopped to listen to Ernest extol the virtues of a smoked elk sandwich in a future duck blind, a lady guest who knew all us staffers very well gave us the treatment, greeting the assembly:

"Why, Mr. Hemingway, this must be an occasion for something."

"Yes, lady, it's an occasion, all right, our friends are back from a successful trip, and we are happy about it."

Well, from our collars up, Mr. Williams and I were badgers, not men, and the old basking biddy said:

"Why, I have missed you two since we came the other day, have you been prospecting?"

"No, Mrs. (Whoope-te-do), we've been hunting elk."

"Why, of course, it *is* the season, how stupid of me. Did you catch one?"

The Old Man had ducked like a scalded cat through the Ram door and Mr. Milquetoast was edging away. A long arm went about Taylor's and my shoulders and the hissing voice close to our ears said:

"Yes, they caught two, would you like to see them? . . . They come in five pieces each, with the hair on."

Swish! Skirts through the closest exit.

At the table: "Did you *catch* one? Obscenity! Why that old counterfeit would think your Hartford elk was a goddamn kangaroo."

By then, having worked quietly at his mail and phone, Gene's euphoria for his November affair was at high level; high attendance was assured; he had fish salted away, smoked sturgeon from the Snake River—a slab of it already being worked on? —and he hoped that we of Sun Valley could round out the bill-of-fare when the bird shooting opened. It was warming to witness Ernest's pleasure of Gene's own, and you liked the sincerity of him saying, "Sure, I'll make a speech of no more than six words—if you write it, Gene." By an odd quirk of reporting by a fellow staffer, Taylor and I sneaked out at daylight two mornings after our return and brought in two fat young deer, taken a half-hour's ride away. We tried to get Ernest to go, but he said, "You guys get 'em, thanks ever so much . . . I'm on a good stretch in the running and I can't let loose of it."

The joke of the speech he'd make brings us to how Ernest and Gary Cooper met, by telephone. Coop had promised back in the spring that he'd do all possible to make it that fall—against a probable schedule of filming. It materialized, but in later communication on another matter, Coop said that he might make it for a few days of hunting, around the time of the potlatch affair. Coop meant it, thought a lot of Gene for whom he'd done a couple of nice things—which Coop did not do like taking a drink of water. Ernest was in camp when Gene got the last word from him, so with all of us in a gay mood Gene proposed that he write Coop a letter advising him of Ernest's presence, write the letter "in quad" as he dubbed it, suggesting that Ernest sign it with Gene, Taylor, and myself. He said, sure he would, didn't Mr. Cooper owe him a drink or two—he'd contributed to his career in a small way, hadn't he? In the morning Gene thought differently of it and I said if he said he would, he'd sign that letter gladly. He did: "It looks like a good booking up here, try and get a piece of it with us. E. H."

Exactly a week later, when we were at dinner in the Ram, Coop called. He was doubly sure that he couldn't make it, but there was a vague chance. When we all three had a few words with him, Gene waved the instrument to Ernest who came without a second's hestitation, with a shy grin and a bright crack. But he was taken with the nice voice, its easygoing, shy buildup to a stranger.

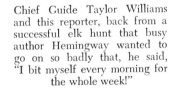

Chief Guide Taylor Williams and this reporter, back from a successful elk hunt that busy author Hemingway wanted to go on so badly that, he said, "I bit myself every morning for the whole week!"

"Sure unwinds with the talk when he gets going," he said.

Looking at his watch, the colonel quipped, "About four bucks worth of his money, Coop writes letters like a bald man uses a comb."

Fate's docket had it that they would not meet in the flesh in the lovely fall of '39.

4

The little tribe grew to size before and while Taylor and I were away: two socialite New Yorkers out for six weeks in residence, the legal requirement for an Idaho divorce. Eleanor Young Bacon, called "Cookie," was the daughter of financier Robert R. Young, head of the once speculator-ridden Alleghany Corporation—the man of great dreams of railroading who said: "A hog can ride across the nation without changing trains, but *you* can't." Cookie, a cute, cherubic-faced brunette, was the Glamour Girl of '36; small, charming, and great fun to be around. The other, a lovely full-blown blonde, was Mimi Richardson Smith—a photographer's dream girl. When we returned, Pop Mark had the girls—"Pop's chicks" in tribal language—well on their way as fair shots, and raring to go for the bird shooting. Mere kids, barely of age, it was hard to tell who watched over them most, Pop or Cookie's mother, a sweet, charming woman, the sister of painter Georgia O'Keeffe.

The oustandingly "good Indian" to arrive in our absence was poet-sportsman Christopher LaFarge. A homely, bespectacled sliver of a man possessing wit like crisp dry bark, Chris was a great wing shot, a student of nature to match Taylor Williams whom he fell for on sight like a ton of bricks. Of the two, watching and listening to them hitting it off, Ernest said, "There's going to be a team, if ever we've seen the makings." He'd been out with Chris, when Gene took them by way of Silver Creek to the lower country, to savor the pheasant prospects; so he knew him well and already there was a thing going about competition in snipe shooting which was a great thing with Mr. LaFarge. Built like one, and teetering like one when he shot skeet, he earned for himself the handle of Teeter the Chris, which he loved. A Rhode Islander, Chris and his lovely wife, Louisa, made Sun Valley their home for all but the summers of the prewar years.

On sheep rancher Tom Gooding's wintering place near Shoshone, and literally draped in pheasants taken from his fields, we got the pictures and a potent statement from Ernest for Gene's second press release. A debatable statement made in great enthusiasm, the caption of one picture said: "Hemingway called Idaho's bird shoot-

Left to right: Cookie Young; her father and mother; and Mimi Richardson Smith at a Trail Creek Cabin party in 1939. Sadly, Cookie was killed in the summer of 1941 in a private plane crash at Newport, R. I.

ing the best in the world." Actually, we held up the release a few days until he hunted the country a little more: Hungarian partridge, and quail in certain fringe areas adjacent to the rich farming areas. But the aggregate was so good that he kidded about shooting over his head—also a debatable statement. As he said of Taylor Williams, he "shoots like a machine." And shooting with this companionable man afield, he made you shoot over *your* head, little doubt about it.

5

Old waterfowlers never get too excited when the season opens and you're comfortable in a tee shirt; take a few local ducks, they say, to satisfy the appetite and wait for weather to bring down the northerners. So it was with us that fall: more parties shooting than were counted on—and the locals were quickly scattered. Ernest was more than happy with a couple of runs on Silver Creek, once with Gene and once with me. Then, coming up from pheasant shooting one night, with a few ducks in the loot, he handed Gene a press agent's gem: He'd write an article on Idaho's great shotgunning; he knew he could plant it for winter publication with his good friend, Arnold Gingrich, in *Esquire*; make it long enough to run as a series of two or three. Great, Gene said, but for heaven's sake, not at the expense of his regular work. Hell no, he said, he could tuck it in—"Ammo money"—and he meant it, entirely his own idea.

The idea grew with Gene, a natural that brought the Snake River into the picture: there was something of a novelty, when conditions were right, in Hagerman Valley. Taylor knew it like the palm of his hand, so Gene called him to describe it to Ernest. Sure, he said at once, it was entirely possible to shoot both ducks and pheasants on river islands and along the east bank that was a veritable jungle of cover where the long mile of waterfalls plunged into the river—itself a long finger lake of quiet water at the valley's upper end.

"But," he said, "it can work hell out of you, too, and you can do the same many places in the lower country."

He knew what he was talking about, and the valley with its "Thousand Springs" aquatic display is a lovely scenic attraction—right alongside the highway. From it came the suggestion to take a day of the October 28-29 weekend to look it over. "Sure, make a picnic of it, take the gals along, see something we haven't seen before."

But it didn't work out that way, and Gene was unduly worried of a shortage of ducks for his potlatch. The result: we took a canoe, our wives for the outing, and, for an extra gun and license, Gene asked a willing young man on the staff to go along. He hunted birds regularly with Pop Mark and his girls, paddled a canoe well, and he talked a hunter's language. We left Friday afternoon, intending to return Saturday night. Saturday was scarcely worth the effort, but the potential was there, and we decided to stay over for at least a try at it Sunday morning. We were set well enough in a little tourist cabin layout; Gene called Ernest, who said he still liked what he heard—we'd set it for the next weekend, hoping for some good old-fashioned duck weather in the meantime.

Sunday was worth it, with considerable effort, and by about one o'clock we called it quits, with but a few birds short of our limits.

While we paddled the half mile up the west shore, ducks started to stir, raised by a distant pleasure boat. I paddled stern, Gene forward—his turn to shoot if something passed close enough to a little tule-fringed bay we ducked into. Our companion, whom I'll call Dee, was the midship passenger, having finished a fair morning in a makeshift blind on one of the islands. Something did come along shortly, drifting down on the water, dabbling busily along the low tules. Gene thought the little ducks were teal—the best of eatin' ducks, bar none—the backlight glaring the water fooled him. When in easy range they skirted the low tules concealing us. Buffle-heads, little diving ducks, and I said, "Let 'em go, Gene." My voice didn't raise them, and I thought he would let them go. Then, tightly bunched, they took off, straightaway, and Gene fired both barrels, in normal succession. Six birds down, but two were winged only, and under they went.

"Now we have some chasing to do, mark 'em. . . ."

I was cut off by a violent roll of the boat, a sharp thud on its bottom, a single shot —out of the river a cripple surfaced where I thought he would—a silence, an ominous silence! Look, look! Something went wrong, boy! I looked, and I saw, clearly, in an instant. Poor Gene had triggered it himself, a series of tragic errors.

To flush the ducks, and shoot, he stood fully upright in the narrow prow, without the slightest movement of the boat being felt. In easing himself down, he turned to grasp the gunwale with his right hand, his gun held high in his left. He was frozen in the half-turned, half-crouched position when my horrified eyes saw the hole just under his right shoulder blade. The smoking muzzles of Dee's double barrel 12-gauge were directly in line, its buttstock resting on the canoe's ribs, held by its grip. Then I knew that the shots downing the ducks were singles from both guns. Recoil upset Gene's precarious balance, the lurching boat upset the rest.

It's an old, unspoken—too often taken-for-granted—rule governing the shooting from a boat. Unless from a solidly anchored and specialized craft for the job, it's a one-man show—period. Weapons other than his are put aside—empty. Who knew that rule so well—one pounded into him so thoroughly that it was instinctive—so much so that he made no warning when we ducked into that little bay! Questions you ask of yourself, but now there's no time to answer.

No mortal power could save Gene, and the best that I could do was make him as comfortable as possible from his fall into the boat while Dee tore for help—a group of men in a farmyard some distance downstream. The wait of fifteen minutes was eternity; and well as I knew him, loved him as a friend, I've never ceased to wonder at the courage and honesty in the remarkable man who was Gene Van Guilder. He had a number of things to say, and we managed them all, some to be nearly as hard to pass on, and try to carry out, as watching him die. It came quietly—in the shade of the little farmyard about two o'clock.

Now the old pro had to put aside the hurt and go to work. The closest town was twenty miles upriver to the south; there was no difficulty with the coroner, the reporting to the sheriff—both friends of Gene. I had Nin's confidence, so went ahead with all arrangements, mindful of the hundred-mile distance from home. Tillie handled the messages by calling them to Sun Valley, fortunately getting the head secretary —perhaps the one outstandingly efficient gal on the staff. The Old Man was absent and at my suggestion she called him about the potlatch dinner. Cancel it, was his immediate decision; without its architect it wouldn't be any good. In the interim, Ernest was alerted and the first thing he asked me: "Can I handle the newspapers for you?" Indeed, he could, I had everything at tongue's tip, then warned him that the flash news would be on the radio shortly, there could be a deluge of phone calls. Put it out of mind, he said, he was in the hotel office with Flo Reilly, had called Taylor, who was standing by—he had correctly guessed that all our gear and birds were left in our haste at the river place, and time was the need now—get home. The stuff would be sent for the first thing in the morning.

All of this a roundabout way of saying that in harsh criticism of myself back there on the river, I hardly knew how to begin. He was like talking to my father, a mountainous man when you were in trouble.

With others there for the follow-through, he was waiting for us on the Inn porch at eight o'clock, between phone calls, and he'd scarcely been off it in the two hours since I'd talked to him. The messages to company officials still had to be dictated and sent immediately, so he helped us in wording them crisply informative. The one to Steve Hannagan personally was separate. By then, the tension was commencing to unwind and he came to our room for a short while, when our first bite since breakfast helped to stem it. He said good night, after asking if I would have breakfast with him and we'd talk good—if he wasn't being presumptuous. Up to then I wouldn't have bet very much on him sticking around—for the obvious reason, and another.

Shortly before, we had learned that Marty had been angling for a European war assignment with *Collier's*, had landed it, and was waiting for word to leave. Ernest sensed what was on my mind and promptly said he was not going anywhere. He was both sympathetic, and very severe, about the rule-breaking, the bad gun-handling.

"So, how can we call it anything else but impulsive action? No, you and Gene were a fine team, and didn't go about telling each other what to do, and I admire your stand, but I won't buy it. If you insist, I'll take the stand with you . . . I'm involved, too."

Very curious ever since his arrival, I thought it was a good time to ask if he knew the story behind his coming over from Montana. Why, he supposed it was dreamed up in Miami Beach. So I told him of the '37 trip to Montana, the overnight stop in Cooke City. It was all news to him, and he was genuinely surprised.

"But it figures, I might have known . . . modesty like that in a man is something to be envied. Sure, I know that service-station man, I must get to Bob Miles about it."

A phone call from Gary Cooper broke it up; when I finished, Ernest talked with him at length; they made a tentative date for the next fall. Then, walking down to the shop with me, he said:

"Now, you have lots to do and I'll stay out from under your feet, but I'm going to check in with you, my way . . . you won't mind, will you?"

No, I wouldn't mind at all; my first task was to write a letter to Steve Hannagan, and I figured it would take the rest of the day. A noble thing to do, Ernest said, a must, so I said I might check in with him for approval of what I wrote. He said, "Sure, kid, we're going on as best we can."

He checked it the following morning, approved it, and said he had struggled with something very difficult to write, too—since dawn and part of the night before. I knew what it was; Nin had told me that she had asked Ernest to write a tribute to Gene, and read it at his funeral. He was glad to do it, but humbly said, "Gee, I wish that I could redo it for someone else to read . . . I'm no good in crowds, I don't talk well, kids, you know that."

He had it with him, typed on onionskin paper, rolled as a narrow scroll, and asked us to read it, see if we thought it "too flowery." We were glad that he turned to look at pictures, but as we went along, its sheer perfection and fitness overwhelmed our tears. Tillie handed it back to him, said:

"Papa, it's beautiful."

She had called him Papa for some time—his encouragement, of course—and now he said he'd try his best to read it good, and that he was glad that Nin had asked us to wear our everyday clothes to the funeral, in keeping with Gene's love for all things Western—"I never bring much in the way of clothes when I come West . . . who dresses up in towns like Cooke City, especially after the tourist mob clears the country?"

He spoke truth; had an old tweed jacket and one pair of flannel pants in the way of dress-up.

6

We buried Gene in the shabby little Ketchum cemetery on the clear, warm afternoon of November 1. In firm, steady voice, of the man he'd known but a short six weeks, Ernest Hemingway read his tribute:

You all know Gene. Almost every one here is better equipped to speak about him and has more right to speak of him than I have. I have written down these thoughts about him because, if you trusted yourself simply to speak about Gene, there might be a time when you would be unable to go on.

You all know that he was a man of great talent. He had great talent for his work, for writing and for painting. But he had something much more than that. He had a great talent for living and for communicating his love and enjoyment of life to others.

If it was a fine bright day and you were out in the hills with Gene, he made it into a better day. If it was a dark gloomy day and you saw Gene, he made it a lot less gloomy. There weren't any bad days when Gene was around. He gave something of himself to all those who knew him or worked with him. And what he gave us all was very precious because it was compounded of the rarest elements. It was made up of true goodness, of kindliness, of fairness and generosity, of good humor, of tolerance and of the love of life. What he gave us he gave for good.

We have that from him always. When I heard that Gene had died I could not believe it. I cannot believe it now. Yes, technically he is dead. As we all must be. But the thing he gave to those who knew him was not a thing that ever perishes and the spirit of Gene Van Guilder is not a thing that will perish either.

Gene loved this country. He had a true feeling and understanding of it. He saw it with the eyes of a painter, the mind of a trained writer, and the heart of a boy who had been brought up in the West, and the better he saw it and understood it, the more he loved it. He loved the hills in the spring when the snows go off and the first flowers come. He loved the warm sun of summer and the high mountain meadows, the trails through the timber and the sudden clear blue of the lakes. He loved the hills in the winter when the snow comes. Best of all he loved the fall. He told me that the other night riding home in the car from pheasant hunting, the fall with the tawny and grey, the leaves yellow on the cottonwoods, leaves floating on the trout streams and above the hills the high blue windless skies. He loved to shoot, he loved to ride and he loved to fish.

Now those are all finished. But the hills remain. Gene has gotten through with that thing we all have to do. His dying in his youth was a great injustice. There are no words to describe how unjust is the death of a young man. But he has finished something that we all must do.

And now he has come home to the hills. He has come back now to rest

well in the country that he loved through all the seasons. He will be here
in the winter and in the spring and in the summer, and in the fall. In all
the seasons there will ever be. He has come back to the hills that he loved
and now he will be a part of them forever.

When the casket was lowered to ground level, kindly Ab Womak put on it the
hand-stamped saddle he'd made for Gene, hooked his silver-mounted bridle and
spurs on its horn. The old man's eyes were misty and his toil-worn hands trembled
as he covered these things with the saddle's blanket, then bewilderingly turned, as if
lost. He had put down his hat while at his task, forgot it, but the big young feller in
the old hunting jacket two sizes too small for him picked it up and handed it to Ab.
And so, we were seven as the shovel was passed from hand to hand.

In our time together I had covered a lot of ground with Gene Van Guilder, knew
that he had a host of friends. It seems that we were close to an hour talking with
them—of the good things that were. As said, the little burial ground was not much
in those days, typical of so many detached communities. But somehow the neglect

In center, Spike Spackman, boss of all things horse, a former Paramount stunt man from
'way back.

Gene Van Guilder trying out a recent inheritance, a shotgun which he did not own until that summer, on Sun Valley's trapshooting range with a crack shot, if ever I saw one.

of the living seemed not to matter in the serenity of the big land itself—"In all the seasons there will ever be."

We had walked the mile over from the Lodge so we walked back, up the gentle slope of the cutoff road past the cone of little Penny Mountain. Near the crest of the low pass we stopped, automatically, I suppose, to look back where the big mountain's shadow line halved the valley in the bright light of day and the grey of evening, the silence toned by the murmur of the distant river.

"You know, men, we let Gene down a little today . . . as long as something had to be sent with him, we should have put in his ax, his rod, and his frying pan."

"And six-gun to knock off a fool hen for change," the colonel said. "But he won't hold it against us until we get there."

"No, the opposite . . . now do we each turn around to the other for a swift kick?"

Sounds a little rough—yes—but true; a practical expression of feeling, understanding, for those left in the game—backed by a mountain of waiting generosity. No one turned around; we walked on to meet an old friend of Gene who'd come over from Boise—a man I'd met that summer. Taken with him, Ernest asked him to come to his place and we'd talk.

7

In those few words there on the hill was more than meets the eye in reading. The roots of a ridiculous situation were already down and growing fast—so ridiculous that we wondered why Ernest didn't reverse himself, pack up, and get on his way elsewhere. In fact he wavered a bit, in view of Marty's departure—tentatively about November 10. Without mention of it, he foresaw it clearly; that there would be a scapegoat, the target of snap judgment and thinking that didn't know a gun from a broomstick, or how it is when men hunt together. Suddenly, it came to me by telephone, later in a face-to-face blast: the whole Snake River business was a lot of nonsense, more play than work—giving me the attitude that says: to hell with it, rack your guns until some reason returns. I couldn't step off the property for a few days, writing a detailed report in conjunction with a thorough investigation by the Claims Department agent—a legal mind who understood a few other things when he got the facts. But in the interim, the local fuss made things a little shaky. Then, in my estimation, the stature of Ernest as a man went up tenfold. In short, he acted as a friend—with other reasons behind his method, simplicity itself.

At Ernest's "good medicine" party, given for the recently widowed Nin Van Guilder, right foreground. At her right is Chief Guide Taylor Williams. Mrs. Frederick W. Spiegel is at the novelist's left.

Gene had inherited a shotgun that summer, one that had belonged to Nin's father in New England. Probably twenty years old, it was sound as new, but a little neglected, exterior-wise; a top-grade Lefever double barrel 12-gauge, a woodcock and squirrel gun—short, lightweight, very handy. Gene shot his first clay targets with it on the trapline with Ernest when Marty was learning to break her first ones. When he got it, I patterned it for him to determine its exact shot-patterns by the usual paper-target method. The artist in Gene liked its slim lines, the tiny old-fashioned "sliver" fore-end, the "wart" on its stock that in the old school made it a pistol-grip stock. He shot it very well, considering, and certainly, shooting afield with Ernest, his appetite for shotgunning was whetted no end.

On the river that fatal day he dropped it into the water; it was overlooked, and retrieved by the kind old gentleman at the cabins who took care of everything for us. He took steps to prevent rust, then I cleaned it thoroughly, took it at once to Nin. Appreciatively, she simply said, "I'd like it, if you'll keep it." Ernest saw it in my rack, and something in his expression tumbled me to his thoughts. He said, "You'll use it, won't you, kid?" and I said, "Sometime, I guess." He looked a bit troubled, asked if I'd been told to stay in my own field. Not exactly, I said, but about as close to it as hints could come. In a few minutes he had me wondering if I were man or sheep, talking through his own disturbance, repeated his remark about his own involvement in the whole thing. He said abruptly, "It needs some work, the barrels reblued . . . fix it up, give me the tab . . . no, no, I mean it, I want to do it." I said, "You mean . . . do it now." He said, "Yes, if you will . . . and as to what people who don't understand wish to think about it, well, f—— 'em!"

Some of the tautness was banished and I smiled; he grinned, as if to say, "Now we all three understand, don't we?"

A Hailey gunsmith did the metalwork, our shop carpenter—a cabinetmaker—fitted and shaped a modern fore-end to match that on my other double, and refinished the stock with a straight grip—three days' time, all told. I showed it to Ernest when he was lunching and working on Glamour House sun deck. He grinned, said, "Good God, what gun is that?" It was a blur in his hands when he tried it on. "The perfect jump gun for the creek, kid, just as fast as your little twenty, and it simplifies your ammo thing . . . wanta go down in the morning?" I was finished with all that other, so I said it was up to him.

This time there was no flip of a coin to see who took the "throne" at the put-in. I punched a few holes in the sky until I got the hang of the gun, but had my limit well ahead of the halfway portage. Wanta try it, I asked. Sure. Lighter than his Browning, he overshot with it on a rise or two, but we ran most of the Chutes with a full house. Loading the boat, Ernest said, "Now you can retire the little twenty, she has served you well."

"Yes," I said. "I'll retire it to my two little nephews back in Nebraska."

"That's the way it should be," he said. "Their grandpa will like that, they can learn on the Platte where he did."

8

Ernest "crammed" his pupil Marty into all the hunting that he could before she left, but the only evidence of his displeasure that we heard was a remark of Taylor's that he often repeated:

"What old Indian likes to lose his squaw with a hard winter coming on?"

He used it enough that one day on a ride, my outspoken wife risked having her ears pinned back when she told Marty she was really foolish to leave Ernest now. She said, "Tillie, I suppose you're right—but it's in my blood and I *have* to do it." On the eighth of November he went all out with a nice duck dinner party at Trail Creek cabin for her. As hinted, Mr. Rogers' forte was good catering, and he could really get into a kitchen crew's hair on a special occasion. If you liked your bird blood rare, or burned to a crisp, that was the way you got it—whether you were a staffer, VIP, or the King of Siam. As Ernest had said to me, "We're going on as best we can," and that included everybody. His grass-roots medicine—"you heal nothing by running from it"—hastened the process; and we happen to know that it wouldn't have been so were it not for him.

Marty's *Collier's* assignment turned out to be the winter hot spot in the spreading world conflagration—the Russo-Finnish War. Ernest laughingly expressed one final beef about her leave-taking: "If I could just get her out every day of this short week of pheasant season that's left, it might cure that itching in her feet." She left on the afternoon train out of Shoshone, so there was quite a busy and long lunch in the Ram, then the two came to our room for a little token of good luck for Marty. She said:

"Keep your eye on this big clown now, Tillie, see that he's shaved and cleaned up when you go out on the town, and to the little parties—I'm depending on *you*."

"By God, I'll mind Tillie, be a good boy . . . got a period of discipline ahead, or until the management throws me out of the joint, or snow forces a southward migration."

"Shall we leave now, so you two can say good-bye?" Tillie smiled.

Oh, hell, that was all done—"Long dry spell coming, just call me Camel Hemingway."

9

He toiled like one in a day or two, the hardest I ever saw him work. He insisted that he help us build the pair of blinds at the slough in the big marsh, took a full day off. He invited himself along when I went to personally settle with the kindly couple in Hagerman Valley. He wanted to see the place where, "We lost to it, Pappy, the worst of all bad luck . . . but that's the way of the Plan . . . we can't tamper with it." Then we returned by a roundabout way that he hadn't seen, to meet Taylor with the material for frames on which to tie sage that we cut with the vicious machetes that he sent to Cuba for.

"Pretty handy, these things; show you how to cut onion slices that you can see through."

"What the hell for?" I said. "The way you gobble them."

Through local recommendations it was this man—Austrian Count Felix Schaffgotsch—who advised Averell Harriman that Ketchum was the ideal locale in which to build Sun Valley. Felix was lost in World War II.

"Oh, it's fun to inhale 'em once in a while, and I guess we need to inhale something to get across the flat with all this stuff, huh?"

An onlooker on the puddled "foot race" road might have taken us for a pair of drunks while we slipped, fell down, cursed to high heaven, dragging roped bundles of sage too scratchy to carry; but it might have been better than the plastering in mud from head to foot.

"By God, Tillie won't have to stand over us with a broom tonight, gents, a hog would turn up his nose at us now."

Indeed, a hog would have, and the colonel had wanted to know several times why in hell he had to get in on it when he could have spared a man for the job.

"Because, goddamn it, it's good for me, Colonel, that's why, and it's in the share-alike thing . . . more than ever I wish that I was in the dough enough to get an option on this property if you can't get the company to buy it."

He meant that, had said so when I showed it to him that first time. Taylor was pushing the Old Man on it, who was with him, but biding his time for the right moment. Anyway, Taylor's artistry and our labors finished the blinds in time to fool a few flights of ducks before sundown. The weather was still the bluebird kind, but, ". . . we're organizoots now, for when she comes."

There were three days of pheasant season left, and I've called '39 a golden fall— a freak in the weather records—and that "she comes" weather passed us by until opening of the winter season—barely in time then. Its mildness proved out, however, as a definite advantage, and the program fell into a distinct routine at once— emphasis on that discipline thing. Chief Guide Williams made his second trip into the Middle Fork of the Salmon River Primitive Area— his special clients: Mr. Young, Cookie's father; a friend of his, and Chris LaFarge—the first deer hunt for any of them. Ernest, Tillie, and I closed the pheasant season in an agricultural fringe area a dozen miles east of Shoshone, near the tiny village of Dietrich on the main line of the railroad. Little hunted and semi-isolated, it was fantastic shooting, and I chose it because of the rising population-cycle of jackrabbit pests. We discovered the particular small area or two within it when varmint shooting in the spring with Coop. Curiosity, more than anything else, made Ernest want to see it, and when we stopped at the farm of a kindly old German named Frees, who told us the pests were eating them out of business, we went into a square mile of undeveloped sage land where the pests went before us as an "undulating sea of rabbits"—quote not mine. There were always several hundred rounds of ammo in Ernest's car, and we eliminated close to that many pests for the old man who kindly allowed us to shoot his cornfields—high crop that rabbits couldn't rob. A lasting friend was made that afternoon, and Mr. Frees guessed that our method was pretty expensive.

"And so is the sport of clay targets, Mr. Frees, but they don't eat your crops."

The old man said the cycle peak was a year or two ahead; we were welcome to his place any time—if he was able to hang on!

Leaving his place, Ernest said, "Christ! that's as much fun as doing what the rabbits do to. . . . Sure keeps your gun barrels hot, don't it?"

Thus, it was more circumstances than anything else that paired Ernest and me as a hunting team; I had plenty of work to do, pinch-hitting at Gene's job of advance publicity on the coming winter season (the big mountain development a very hot thing, the first of its kind in the world), but I did it easily in half-day stints, so had the free time to, as Ernest happily put it: "Split the paddling for ducks in the afternoons." (The new Hannagan man, by the way, arrived with the place opening for winter, early in Christmas week.)

The duck season would close on December 5, but Ernest set no definite time for departure; had an old friend, Toby Bruce, coming up from Key West around that time, said he might work a little longer if he wasn't in the way, and play a little—"roulette, blackjack, craps . . . might get lucky and pay expenses on the long drive home."

We spent so many afternoons on the creek that our favorite canoe was a "floating establishment," honored with the name Stutter Bug—and we became so good a team that Ernest said we didn't ride it down the creek, "We pull her on like an old pair of pants and wear her down—she's a habit, after behaving so good at Stutter's place." Custom-fitted, too. When I took it up for painting, I got the good carpenter to make a new prow seat and brace, set them rearward about ten inches to make room for Ernest's size thirteen waders (he liked foot comfort, plenty of socks in his boots), a broader flotation base under him for the fast movements in snap shooting—and make for a level ride, with any lightweight paddler. A board, hooked onto the seat, made a normal position "throne" when he paddled. There was a wisecrack when he first tried it on for fit: ". . . and room to hang a roll of necessity and a hook for the *Police Gazette* when business is slow."

The migration that fall was a dribbling one, steady and since Snug Bar Al Lewis ran the creek mornings only—about twice a week—business was never slow, the duck variety sufficient, so that we passed up all but the best table ducks: mallards, pin-tails, and greenwing teal. It was an agreed time deal with Al, who joined us in the wonderful blind shooting on weekend mornings. Memorable times, those, with two marvelous dogs handling the retrieving—Labradors Hickory and Bullet from the rep-utable Harriman kennels at Arden-on-the-Hudson. Field-trial champions, the dogs had more duck-smart between their silky black ears than most men—real gentlemen, too—always addressed and spoken of as Mr. Blind shooting was Chris LaFarge's fa-vorite (much driven grouse shooting in Scotland responsible), the colonel's too, and a regular weekend joiner made us a party of six. He was the old friend of Gene Van Guilder's who came to say hello to me at the cemetery, and went to Glamour House for the long talk afterward.

An aviation man, a former Midwesterner who'd learned to fly as a mere boy in Wichita, Pete Hill's and my path had crossed briefly once before—at a big Midwest air show; so our eyes popped in dim recognition when years later we met on a dusty mountain meadow airstrip, when Idaho pioneered in planting fish by airdrop in re-mote mountain lakes. Pete had known Gene since their late school days around Twin Falls. Not only was Pete a born flyer, the stuff of the out of doors was built in, the sort of good Indian who fit—by mutual adoption, on sight.

We'd split into threesomes in the blinds—by the coin-flip method—then the com-petitive camaraderie was something to behold. That morning shooting was short, but, oh, how fast and exciting! Repeating shotguns were not allowed, only double-barrels, when the betting was on—two-bits a duck over ties. Then we'd scatter over the basin, hunting afoot for the elusive, zigzagging Wilson snipe—his wager value, ten cents, but upped to two-bits when the going was rough; then we'd rendezvous for the tally and payoff—sometimes as much as a half dollar involved in the total monetary switch. So, in the ebb and flow of sniping, the quintessence of the sport was attained, with LaFarge and Williams, Incorporated, generally on top. Keenly competitive, of course, fast-shooting Ernest gladly paid through the nose to that pair —the delectable little birds all went into the tribal pot, anyway, for the evenings that about equalled the fun of "catching" them.

In mid-November, Nin Van Guilder went back to Chicago, for a much needed change, with Mrs. Freddie Spiegel. Clara, a Sun Valleyite from the first winter on, a confirmed one in summer, called in reponse to Tillie's telegram and caught the night train at the time of our great loss. Nin desperately needed her true friends, Clara was one of them, and to us others. Though they had never met, Clara left the day be-fore Marty and Ernest arrived in September. Ernest said to her: "You know, Clara, when I do see Freddie again, I'd better have some dice-rolling dough in my pocket . . . or the interest, at least . . . I don't believe we went to bed on the boat going over, back in '18." Which, I guess, happened to be true—from the loser's mouth, later.

Next to go were the now-free gals, Cookie and Mimi. True to his promise, the old inexperienced, non-native guide (their tease name for him) was cleanly shaven, hair combed, his best clean blue jeans on and the old tight jacket; saw them off with a long white box of flowers to brighten their Pullman compartment. Couldn't they open them there, and before all well-wishers, pin a boutonniere on him? No, old guides would be disgraced in that company, and too, he was allergic to those particular flowers—lovely as they were. And truly, we hated to see those gay kids go—mutual, too. When their bus pulled away, the old guide about went into convulsions of laughter, and I said:

"Better be at your phone along about their train-stop time in Pocatello."

"Of course they'll call," he said. "And I'll bet that I get a drink on them the next time I'm in the big town . . . haw, haw, haw . . . you deserve to be along, kid!"

The call came all right, late that afternoon—from the station platform phone—Cookie talking. First thing she said: "Listen, you wise old ——, know what the porter said?" "Shoot," the wise old —— said, about to explode again.

"He said, 'Whadju nice lil' ladies do to git dat fo' a bouquet?'"

The bouquet was a great horned owl that we spotted the day before in a cotton-wood grove along Wood River—preying on ducks in a place we occasionally hunted. My varmint rifle was in the car, and I nailed him with a long shot, the fast bullet passing through with no visible damage. They're a big feathery bird, say thirty inches long, and suddenly the devilish gleam showed in Ernest's eyes. We took the owl home, held the baleful yellow eyes open with little strips of adhesive tape, put him out on the terrace and the cold night air set him up good—after a careful smoothing out:

"By an old ex-undertaker . . . and this kid didn't ass around all those summers in the north country for nothing . . . this'll give the kids something to talk about. . . ."

In the young days of grand old Sun Valley, the work was heavy, the nights long but never dull! Long-time Sun Valleyites will remember these fine Austrian boys with much nostalgia. The young man at the far left is not an Austrian but he learned enough of the language—words which could not be included in this book.

On the phone, Cookie said they both nearly yanked the emergency stop cord, as huge lifelike eyes stared at them, big talons open, poised and ready. We'd learn that they did have something to talk about in the big town.

10

Play and hard work! Reverse the order and you have it—the work, at all times, was uppermost. Not rigidly a five-day program, Saturday morning was occasionally used in the grind—Sundays never, church afield: "I'll have to settle with the Padre, and maybe some morning before I leave I'll make it for the seventh inning!" High noon, however, was mainly knock-off time—a quick lunch and then go, or lunch on the run. More than once, Ernest frankly said that all the relaxation was great, but that an afternoon of lazing it down the creek was the best of all—and why not? Not that he shunned heavy physical exertion, as we know; it was the peaceful quiet, iso-lation—and certainly it relaxed his mind from his work—he'd never mention it there—then the tingle of a sneak-up, the quick action from a rise, and a good shot by his companion was as good as one by him. He loved a good dog and Mr. Hickory, Tay-lor assigned to him to use as he was needed. He was "crew" with us, always. One afternoon we left him behind—too much load because Papa kept urging Tillie to come along on one full trip, if only for the ride.

"We just want to show off, Tillie, how good we are," he joked. "And you might be good luck and we'll get some teal."

Teals were regulars, but he put on a spectacular freak on a rise; a mallard drake and susie that rose under his nose, sharply to the right—a swing that a right-hand shooter can't make sitting down. He switched the gun to left-hand, the buttstock in the crook of his arm, and cut loose. He got the drake cold and winged the duck—instinctive shooting, I guess, like an unconscious finger-pointing. Watching unbe-lievingly, I made a paddling blooper, ran him straight into overhanging willows that he fell over backward into the boat to avoid; Tillie got her hair tangled in them and we all but went over in water a dozen feet deep, and fast. No mind, we had a time getting out of the mess, two times running down the cripple.

"You see, Papa, you brought the wrong dog today."

"Sure, Tillie, but see what we got for showing off, too . . . my boots full of water and mud . . . now I know how a squealer feels when they plant him in a tub of ce-ment."

Fresh in our minds, and still laughing about it that fine day, was a recent episode worth telling. Down in the Chutes Ernest had made a nice shot on a high-overhead mallard drake, tumbling him straight down like a cartwheeling bomb. I tried my best to veer the canoe to one side or the other, he as confused as to which way to dodge. Had the bird hit him in the head . . . ? It hit him low on the back, took with it a light cashmere sweater rolled loosely around his waist, bounced three feet off the bilge. Laughable, yes, but spooky as all get-out at the moment—and a good yarn for the evening table. Enter now LaFarge and Williams.

Then into each of us about fifty cents in the snipe race, we were endlessly needled about it—by the worthies who liked their snipe cooked blood-rare, a contrast to our tastes. We liked ours at least heated thoroughly! So, in the bag that day was a pair of coots—mud hens that in Hemingwayan were dirt hens. When he shot them, Ernest laughed delightedly, "Damn 'em, we'll do 'em a little dirt with these." He took them to cook Daly and told him to barely warm them—for his dinner guests. Ray's smile was a suspiciously odd one, I thought, but Ernest was skinning the birds and didn't catch it. The raw serving to our tormentors was something of a sensation, but imagine Ernest's explosion of hilarity when his serving was a mallard done perfectly to his taste, but wearing a sweater! The leg of an old wool sock, a row of little buttons sewed down the front.

"Well whaddaya know . . . roast whole duck by Abercrombie Williams and Fitch LaFarge and Company . . . and me without a tie!"

11

We recall our greatest sensation that fall as the privilege of reading twenty-four chapters of *For Whom the Bell Tolls* in partially self-edited form directly off the typewriter. Up to his offer, Ernest seldom mentioned the big work—we kept hands off, strictly—but we learned a couple of its characters' names this way: On one of the Adams Gulch rides, Ernest called it "El Sordo country." Then long later he came to lunch in an ebullient mood and Tillie said:

"Papa, you're in fine fettle, it must have gone good this morning."

He laughed, said, "Yes, Tillie, it did. Now you take Pablo, for instance, I haven't known what the old son of a bitch is gonna do from one day to the next, but finally I got him figured out . . . it isn't going to be good, and I wouldn't want him doing it to me, I can tell you that. . . . Would you guys like to read it?"

A picture that I made at the author's request for the dust cover of *For Whom the Bell Tolls*, December, 1939.

"Would we?" Taylor said. "When do we start, Mr. Author?"

Mr. Author grinned, replied, "Well, you should tell me to go to hell, but I guess a few stanzas of it when you're ready just might lead to that."

Our installment reading was done at night, propped up in bed, the twenty-fourth chapter finished in early December. But as we went along it was obvious that the hero's reference to his father's suicide was based on facts in the author's life—of which we still knew so very little. Then one evening when we were just in from hunting, Tillie came to Glamour House to join us in a drink, and brought a sheaf of the manuscript that we'd finished. We were in a discussion on fine points of certain shotgunning techniques, as we boys were taught by our fathers, and in some mild disagreement, too—both of us right in our own approaches—so it was a good-natured argument with some laughs going. Papa (I was falling in line with the name) often said that his father was a great wing shot but not as thorough and patient as a teacher as mine, and that we were lucky in our environs, affording our father so much more time with us than his had. Then, a repeat of his oft-spoken: "And you were lucky in competition with your older brother, and it would have been awfully good for me, too, if I'd had one to kick the hell out of me now and then, if I needed it or not, just to keep me in line. . . . My competition was a surrounding of sisters, and a brother just a kid when I was grown up and on my own."

Tillie chided him, asked if he was feeling sorry for himself. No, not at all, taking it very good-naturedly, then sensing the question in our minds, he told us of his father's suicide—in detail—of illness not too serious at his age; of a minor financial problem, magnified in his mind, and already solved had he taken the trouble to open his morning mail. But, he said that the basis of his father's dilemmas was domination, ". . . by my mother, she had to rule everything, have it all her own way, and she was a bitch!"

Horrified, Tillie gasped, regained her breath, burst out:

"Why, Ernest Hemingway, how dare you! How can you say that about your own mother?"

"Daughter, I can, and I do, because it's true . . . and I say it at the risk of losing your respect."

He went on: "True, it was a cowardly thing for my father to do, but then, if you don't live behind the eyes you can't expect to see all of the view. I know that part of his view, and I suppose he was mixing it up some . . . and you do such a thing only when you are tortured beyond endurance, like in war, from an incurable disease, or when you hasten a drowning because you can't swim all of the sea."

To appease her further, he put his arm around Tillie, said, "I'm sorry I burst out with it that way, should've kept it to myself, Tillie, but look . . . you know me now. Can you imagine me trying to learn, forced to be a musician? . . . I learned to play the first six notes of 'My Country, 'Tis of Thee'. . . . Hmph! . . . And there went my liberty. See, I'd have done better at poetry."

"Papa, you devil, how can I give you hell?" Tillie said, and switched the subject to the great reading we were enjoying. From then on, if he was casually asked by the colonel or us, "How'd it go this morning, Papa?" he'd grin, say, "Oh, our book went great this morning, but yesterday. . . ."

12

Our book's progress slowed a bit in late November—a few days of warm, rainy weather—northern birds were down in numbers, the shooting "something to write about." A verbatim quote, that, of an incident one morning so funny that I'm still wondering why Papa Hemingway didn't work it into something. He and I threw a sack of decoys in the boat and Taylor worked afoot down one of the drainage canals within the loop of the creek, and met us at a little slough. We set the decoys, concealed ourselves and the boat in low willows, waited but a short while for some business. In a short windy squall the rain turned to thick, blinding, wet snow, visibility maybe a hundred yards. Then, out of nowhere came the rushing sound of old canvas being ripped apart, and any old slough rat will recognize that only one species of duck makes such a racket when they buzz your stool for a look: lesser scaup, commonly called little bluebills—short-winged acrobats with other habits exclusively their own. Absolutely fearless when they want to get down out of a storm. We almost had our hats taken, they came so low on the first pass; circled into the murk, and we got set. In action so fast that it's blurred in memory, we had time for but a glimpse of perhaps a hundred black specks boring straight at us, the van let loose and tumbled like bricks into our blocks, the followers coming so fast there wasn't room on the tiny open water; they zoomed up and we cut loose—three double guns, six shots. We shut our eyes and ducked our heads. Papa got one square in the belly; one hit my boot and half drowned me in icy water; one hung but an inch or two above the colonel's hat, in willow branches, and fell into his lap. Those six shots produced a baker's dozen and the dogs didn't know which way to start first. A half hundred bewildered bluebills bobbed among our decoys, not twenty yards out, and took off when a voice out of the gloom said:

"Sounds to me like a bunch of kids with more firecrackers than they know what to do with."

Chuck Atkinson, out hunting the canals with his dog, his coat bulging.

"You missed a good show, Chuck."

"The hell I did, a grandstand seat . . . how's your belly feel?"

"You'd have to come from a test tube and think like a machine not to engrave all of this in your head so that you would never lose it." The main Salmon ("River of No Return") flowing past the principal Sawtooth Range and the little hamlets of Lower and Upper Stanley.

"Okay . . . I guess . . . I haven't called foul yet, but he was awfully close."

Ours was a first experience of its kind, something we'd read and heard about only —the kind of which you say: one's enough, but I wish they'd do it again, soon. Up on the big marsh, the morning and evening shooting was also something to write about; we closed shop there, disposed of our blinds to avoid self-invitation by others snooping around the basin the following summer. Toby Bruce arrived December 1, Papa folded up his work, said that it was time to loaf and play before packing up for the departure. On Sunday, December 3, we had our second encounter with Stutter Man, in a surprise discovery in late afternoon. Papa and I did the lower half of the canoe run, not doing very well in a stiff wind, the day bright and sharp; Toby and Taylor waiting for us at pullout with the car. Up in the Chutes a ways we saw for the first time several flights of ducks, really carrying the mail, winging in over the long rocky ridge fingering down from the higher hills, its foot jutting out into the marsh. An odd behavior, but we figured it quickly; coming in from the open water of reservoirs some miles east, the ducks cut the corner instead of going around with the creek's meandering flow—to rest on its sheltered waters for the night. Papa was up front and he turned with the impish gleam in his eye: just beyond that ridge was Stutter Man's old place, perhaps a hundred fifty yards to his backyard, a hundred feet lower in elevation.

I said, "Papa, you ornery bastard, what are we waiting for?"

"For two bastards to get up there," he said. "That's pass shooting, boy . . . deluxe stuff, and if we're not real careful we might rain down a little shot on his bridge . . . no turkeys there now, that's for true."

The colonel said he'd noticed that freak behavior, but kept it to himself, knowing damn well what we'd do. "Get up there," he said. "Take me across in your boat and I'll work the dog down on the flat, but I'll tell you this—you're going to have to shoot like you haven't shot before, this fall." He was so right—we missed four out of five until we realized just how great was their speed. The old place below was forlorn and deserted-looking, some wash hanging on a line; then suddenly old Stutter appeared from an old log outbuilding, flailing his arms like a windmill, yelling something we could not hear for the wind, and running pell-mell for the house.

"Jesus, kid, we'd better stay behind these rocks . . . the old muskrat may be going for a musket, and if he shoots like he talks we may come out short in the deal."

He came out on the porch with something in his hands, but we stayed low, downed one limit of ducks, watched them tumble slantingly for several hundred feet, bouncing off the flat like rubber balls. We let it quiet down then, and Papa stood up, yelled down his thanks for Stutter's courtesy—and that was the finish of the '39 fall shooting. It was hell getting up and down the rocky steepness of that ridge, but calling it a shooting banquet, under *those* conditions, is putting it mildly! Act Two for Stutter Man.

One might wonder if we ate enough game to grow antlers and feathers—almost, at that—but suffice it to say there are always "customers" for excess game of any kind (the staff disposed of much when the potlatch was cancelled), and from our indulgence came a byword, or by-phrase, if you will. One late day we stopped at the Snug and left a few ducks for Ma and Ab Womak, had a drink with Al, and speaking of the fall as a whole, Papa said,

"Well, Al, it's like Pappy's ol' pappy used to say when plenty to eat from the family guns had graced the table for some time . . . 'we're eatin' high on the wild, kids,' and I say that's better than high on the hog any day."

"I'll buy one to that," Al said.

13

Still keeping ahead of my work as the fall flew toward its close, my major chore was getting out the winter opening issue of the resort newspaper, the *Valley Sun*, and putting it into the mail via the extensive guest lists. It was a biggest issue, full of pictures, some photo-art work, all on the opening of the big ski hill. My stumbling block was writing the main article on it; I was the only one to do it, so you know who offered to give me a hand, when he came in one day and heard me cursing the stuff that came off my typewriter. A long piece, when I finally finished it for the printer, it certainly did not sound like me! I said, only suiting the situation: "Ernie, the damn thing should carry your by-line, mine following in very small type."

Thumbing through the finished product, he complimented the whole, then in a moment he looked up, grinned a bit sardonically, said:

"Nice of you, Pappy, me taking on a ski mountain, hmph! . . . but I was glad to help you, as you've helped make it so good for me . . . you know how I stand on that, in spite of that other, the slight to us both . . . inexcusable, and unforgivable."

What had happened embarrasses me yet, to some extent. In that personal letter to Steve Hannagan I included that I would stand by to do the best I could until he got a new man; that I would have full publicity cooperation as assured me by Mr. Hemingway—in fact, I quoted his: "we're going on as best we can." Steve's reply was prompt enough, and he thanked me, but said briefly that his office would advise me of any needs and he did not mention Hemingway's name. How Ernest found it out was simple: I met him in the post office one morning, and looking for a reply that would please us both, I opened the familiar Hannagan envelope, read the letter in his presence, and, in spontaneity, blurted out: "Well, for Christ's sake!" I had done the damage and aware of my embarrassment, Ernest was rather hesitant in reading it. In his inimitable way, he laughed harshly—yes, that's the word for it—said:

"Well, by God, I guess this is what we call being ignored, huh, kid? Maybe thinks you're responsible . . . no matter how nicely you wrote."

That was the angle that he'd foreseen, and I had not, of the *total* ridiculous situation. By then it was fully driven home that certain of humanity resent a little man's good relations with a big one—seem to think that such is reserved for the high and the mighty.

But the foregoing explains why there is no mention of press releases on Ernest Hemingway following the good one at pheasant season opening. There were none allowed, though when I spoke of being asked by headquarters to make a bird shooting addition to our big game hunting film—a thing I wanted to do from the first fall on—I got started on the footage and finished it the following fall. Ernest figured considerably in it, fully cooperative at all times. I used a lightweight 16mm camera, hooked to an old adapted gun stock—from my shoulder. The few still pictures I made were personal for-the-record ones.

On December 8, two rainy days ahead of the departure, a group of us gathered in the Harry Morgan Room, drinking up the bar "dregs" and shooting the breeze—a man's party for "the work's all done this fall," as someone said. Pete Hill had flown over to say so long; Toby tended bar; Big A Wood and Pop Mark tried to out-yarn Big E; Al Lewis came up, brought a nicely tanned coyote pelt that someone had given him, no room for it in the Snug; but "Ol' Ernie the Coyote" could make good use of it—"And if you don't like Coyote, just call me Packrat, men." The dregs got in their licks, all right, but not so much that I couldn't frame an image on a camera ground glass. Ernest said he'd been out of the big production so long that he didn't have an up-to-date picture for the dust jacket of the forthcoming *For Whom the Bell Tolls*—a book, by the way, not yet titled, but F.W.T.B.T. was in the running. I got a camera and made "sunshine" pouring through the open bedroom door with extension flash; made three quick shots and had prints out before dinner that night. I didn't care too much for the best one, Ernest liked it, said he at least resembled a working writer rather than a half-drunk gent whooping it up with the boys. The picture made it, so, maybe the dregs were all gone!

On Sunday, December 10, we enjoyed a leisurely lunch with Lew Hill at his Alpine in Ketchum. Outside, a soft drizzling rain fell steadily; the Buick's "best back seat passenger there is" a chop box rigged up for the trip, an ice compartment in it, and packed to the lid with high-on-the-wild to "feed us to Texas, and maybe to New Orleans." Its top insulation was the prime coyote pelt, held down by a couple of cased shotguns. But there was a concerned vein in our good-byes, too.

"Be sure and let me know if Nin will have a job this winter, and if you have snow for the opening . . . wouldn't it be awful with that big mountain all ready to go, and bare as my head in this rain?"

Diminutive Toby Bruce took her out of town about two o'clock, an arm waving semaphore-like out either side, a broad dark face grinning back on the right.

"Well," the colonel croaked to Tillie and me, "what do we do now?"

On December 24 I sent a cable to Havana: affirmative on Nin Van Guilder's security for the winter; the same on the snow, "down for the winter" in snow country talk. I had been to the cemetery, on skis, to place a few pine boughs on its dry, fluffy whiteness. On Christmas morning came the cabled reply:

"ARNOLD VAN GUILDER WILLIAMS AND EVERYBODY ELSE—SUN VALLEY IDAHO
MUCH LOVE AND MERRY CHRISTMAS FROM IRON MAN BRUCE AND DOCTOR HEM-
INGSTEIN STOP THERE ISNT ENOUGH DOUGH IN CUBA TO SEND MESSAGES TO
EVERYONE AM FOND OF THERE. HEMINGSTEIN"

A photograph made October 16, 1940, on Silver Creek's Picture Bridge, our original camera platform for fishing movies and one that brought national news-clipping records. Shown are a trio of atavistic primitives; they were the ones I knew best.

Ten-cent birds, Wilson's snipe, until the rough going upped them to two bits, any money, so long as it was good for the "red" to grace them at the table.

Membership cards in a select society

Christopher La Farge with a record-spread Wilson's snipe—"trickiest live target that flies."

3.

The '40 Fall ---
'''No Work and Big Dough...'''

1

Preparations for the '40 fall began early. As a result of his great enthusiasm and curiosity for the saltwater fishing he'd never done, Taylor was invited by Papa to come to the Florida Keys, then over to Cuba to fish the Gulf Stream with him. The colonel took leave of absence, left on a cloud in early April, returned in mid-June. On his way he stopped in his old home town of Fort Thomas, Kentucky, to visit his aging mother, and his only brother Phil, in the sporting-goods business across the river in Cincinnati. Phil's good friend, Dave Roberts, sportswriter for the *Cincinnati Enquirer*, got acquainted with Taylor; a column in Dave's paper appeared soon, a lifelong friendship was established—and the start was made on a "second profession" for Taylor Williams. In a word, he became a more-than-casual, self-appointed press agent for his good friend Ernest Hemingway. When he returned he was the color of copper—"damn near all over"—ten years the younger in manner and talk, and in his pocket was the money for a general hunting license and the small fee to accompany the application for the special antelope hunt permit.

"Papa's going great guns," he said. "Working like a beaver, and he hopes to make it for dove season the first of September. I told him that we'd get him fixed for that permit if we had to blackmail somebody."

I had heard something to that effect in our meager correspondence. In May I sent over a hundred contact-size 4x5 photographs of the "El Sordo" country, some gorges for "the bridge" and other locale within easy driving distance. Bob Miles and I worked off and on a month at the job. If F.W.T.B.T. was to be made into a movie —an idiot would know that it would—damned if it wouldn't be made where part of it was written! The author responded with enthusiasm in his letter. In August Taylor sent the application to Boise for the permit drawing, and as to the result: What do you think? The result of that was a telephone call from Papa.

"Damned if I don't believe your *governor* was blackmailed."

Right on the heels of his call came Toby Bruce escorting the boys by train.

Their Papa's phoned instructions were simple: "Get them licensed, warm 'em up on a few clay targets, and have us a dove feed on hand when we get there . . . I doubt that we'll make it on time, and if so, I've got work to do first."

He and Marty drove out in a new Buick convertible (how he got it so soon he wouldn't say, just grin), and arrived September 6. The work that he had a rush on was the check-out of the final galley proofs of the book. He brought them to our shop for packaging up on September 10, came through the door sideways in his elation at completing eighteen months of toil. The package was airmailed to Scribner's that morning.

"And damn," he said. "We were sorry to miss the fun . . . how many shells per dove, boys?"

"Awww, Papa, you're not supposed to ask us that!"

Seventeen-year-old Jack, called Bumby, was (and is) the real freshwater fisherman

The Master, and invited Taylor Williams, on the fishing machine *Pilar* in Cojímar, Cuba,
the locale for *The Old Man and the Sea,* in the spring of 1940.

My first 1940 fall task, ". . . make me a picture of my gang while Toby's here and we're not involved in essentials—yet." Toby Bruce, Key West, in jacket.

of the Hemingways—a dry-fly specialist to command the respect of our experts, with only a little of his know-how talk. The blond, blue-eyed, and handsome counterpart of the old block in so many ways. Twelve-year Patrick and nine-year Gregory— "Mouse" and "Gigi" in that order—were the little shotgunners on their way up. Their reply to their father about their shooting speaks well enough of the strong ties; or maybe this is better: There were enough doves on ice for several feasts and the kids had held up their end. One of the first things their father asked the little boys: "Who does this nice lady remind you of?"

"Our mother," they said, and, blushing, Tillie hardly knew how to answer that one. The second child and eldest daughter of a large family of brothers and sisters whom she mothered from a child herself . . . well, I guess that in itself tells a few things. The youngsters were "allowed" to call her Tillie; the "Pappy" business had them shaking their heads until they got the habit—much to their Papa's amusement.

A great favorite picture, because of little Gigi's fascination with a myriad of his new friends.

Needless to say, there was a small celebration in Glamour House when the galleys were away, and I was asked if on the morrow I could take a few pictures "of my gang before we all get involved in things and Toby's here?"

I said, sure, and he hadn't unpacked all his clothes yet, so asked me what he should dig out to wear. I just looked at him and grinned.

"Sure." He laughed. "I'll get out my bulldogger's outfit."

My first casual glance at him that morning in '39 brought to mind a big top-name rodeo performer whom I knew well from the Sun Valley shows. I told him so in our first talk, but said, "Who in hell ever saw a rodeo hand bareheaded, sleeves rolled up, and wearing a leather vest?"

"Nobody." He laughed. "You'd call him a damn phony."

So out came the identical outfit and the following morning I made the few shots over around the lagoon in the Inn village square; and, his publisher was asking for something special in conjunction with their promotion of the book. Right then there was not a damn thing for him to do that, in the public image, "looked like Hemingway," as I frankly put it to him. His fishing gear was packed away, and, in discussing it, here was the sort of situation that flustered Papa—yes, embarrassed him, and me. I said, "Oh, hell, Papa, you and Toby just lean there on your car and I'll make an informal shot or two of you talking or looking at something . . . pick out an object. . . ."

"We'll look at the bell in the Opera House belfry." He laughed. "And be thinking it's that time . . . about to toll five o'clock. How's that?"

"All right, be tasting the drink," I said. "So you won't look so damned stiff, you know."

More by accident than anything else, I guess, he wiped the laugh off his face, and always at ease with his old friend Toby, he put one foot up on the log bordering the drive, a hand on his hip, the other arm leaning on the car. The finder showed it perfect for a second and I tripped the shutter. With a tongue-in-cheek attitude I said, "That'll do." He laughed, said, "That's the way we like it, short and snappy." I did the lab work myself, printed that casual shot "full" and in a tall "panel" of Papa alone, cropping-out Toby, who understood what I was after. Then the laughs.

"Damned if I don't look like I'm tasting a drink, Pappy . . . but I like it. It's a fine

Gigi Hemingway "hard-rolling" Sun Valley's Canada honkers and bread-heavy mallards, whetting his appetite for things to come—soon.

Of these two apple-cheeked characters—Tillie and himself—Ernest quipped: "On you, daughter, cute . . . on me like a horse. . . ."

One of the best shots of Ernest Hemingway—in my opinion—in those days, his peak years, I'd say, as a literary factory. (September, 1940.)

picture . . . know why? . . . My hands, they don't look like *hams*. You can't call me the old bulldogger with them . . . hell, maybe I should've finished out as a 'cello player, after all."

So, my brief glimpse in the finder paid off: when Scribner's got the print they borrowed my "hands picture" negative, and I was told they printed it in a life-size panel in their book promotion. Indulge me at this writing to say that whenever Papa Hemingway comes to mind, that is my "image" of him, 'way back when; forty-one years of age, full of "*p* and *v*"—to quote him—savoring a monumental literary success. My images of him are many, but that is the first and foremost; there's a laugh in it too. Foremost in his mind when my shutter clicked was the itch to get his rifle sighted in, sweating out the twenty-sixth of September when he hoped to get a buck antelope lined up in his sights. Instead he doffed his bulldogger clothes for shorts and a tennis racquet! ("Have t'watch my talk today, the Padre's playin' with us.")

In his gun rack was a new Model 21 Winchester double barrel in 20-gauge, factory fitted with an extra set of barrels for long-range work. His promised gift to Marty on her birthday. So the sweat-out interim was enough tennis to "go along" and stay in good with the amiable, social Father Daugherty—a good hand with a racquet himself—and lots of times at the shooting grounds. No finer double guns were ever built than the 21s and hers was a good incentive for Marty; and her successful efforts with it occasioned a memorable incident.

We made up a trap squad one day and locked the trap for straight-away targets —the "sleepers" that so often fool the experts because they look easy. As said, Ernest did not care for traps, so he was the puller on the old pump handle cock-and-release; Marty, Tillie, Taylor, Stew Stewart, and myself on the line, moving through the full five positions, as usual. No one noticed a strange elderly couple watching from their car until we finished a round and the old man came out to ask if we intended another round—he hadn't shot trap in years, and would it be an imposition to shoot with us? Stew loaned him his gun and went to take over the pull stand; Ernest said no, he was enjoying the exercise. He delivered our targets perfectly on call, the old gent set a nice pace as lead-off man, and shot like a house afire. In short, we had fun with the nice stranger and shot a second round. When finished he thanked us all like the perfect gentleman he was, and tipped the puller boy a silver dollar. Again, there are no words to describe his chameleon-like expressions as the old man walked away.

Marty said, "Well, sonny, now that the trap season is about over, what'll you do then?"

"Well, let's see . . . three squads an hour is about average . . . three bucks, not bad wages . . . I'll put in my application for next summer now."

"I thought you were going to kiss the old man, Big E," Pop Mark cracked.

"I think I would have, Pop, if one of you had suddenly goosed me . . . first tip in my whole life. Pretty proud of this dollar."

On the hunt a good average pronghorn buck fell to the trusty Springfield—high on the west slopes of the Pahsimeroi. I didn't put in for the hunt (tied up with a special group of railroad guests), but at the time I had in mock-up the resort's first hunting brochure that Advertising had turned over to me for copywriting and illustrations. Chape got a couple of good close-ups of Papa and his antelope. He had told me that I could use any pictures that I thought suitable for such purpose. I showed Papa the one I preferred, and since paid-space advertising legally requires them, I had no choice but to ask him, of all people, to sign a model's release! I hear his laughter yet, but he said, "Hell, yes, Pappy, make it a blanket release until further notice, might set me up with the John Powers Agency if times get rough."

"I'll do that, Papa, thanks very much . . . now since we're not allowed funds for model fees, we always make some sort of gesture, you know, and don't you rate pretty high?"

"You're damn right." He laughed. "Since I feel pretty cocky, no work to do and back in the big dough again."

The part that was tickling me was that he was kidding and I was not. The guides wore fine Pendleton woolen shirts—a special deal with the manufacturers through Jack Lane's Inn store—and they had given me several shirts in return for promotional pictures; I had shirts to burn. I went to Jack, traded one of them for a large size,

Stalking the buck with Taylor Williams. ". . . gits around pretty good, with a rusty knee, don't he?" Of the vast and different Pahsimeroi Valley, he said: "Country so much like Spain that you taste, smell, and feel it. Hell, you're there!"

First Idaho big game for
Papa—1940.

The first "must" discharged in the '40 fall—September 26—for which Papa
won a shirt, as model fee, and from me, one big resounding laugh about it.

from a very limited choice of pattern colors. I just rolled it in a paper so that anyone
would take it for a bottle. Now, Johnnie Walker Black Label was the favorite
Scotch, but the package didn't indicate a square bottle, and Papa was pleasantly surprised when I simply put it on the long table behind the couch in the H. M. Room.

"Your compensation, *sir!*" I said. "Will Black and White do?"

"I'm being overpaid, *sir!*" He chuckled and picked it up, tumbled when he felt it
carefully, then the paper flew.

"Pappy, you bastard, you weren't joking . . . in inch-square black-and-white
checks . . . well whaddaya know? Now the Chief Guide will have to recognize me
. . . I'll get to take out the beginners!"

The real joke behind it all was that back in the winter there was a rumor going
around that Ernest Hemingway actually guided hunting parties—for pay—his first
fall in Idaho. Cookie and Mimi had come back for a vacation, and admitted that
they joked about it—which, of course, was misinterpreted and distorted, as usual. In
one of my few letters I had mentioned it, much to his amusement, and sure—it provided a small degree of flattery, that he mentioned in his reply. He liked that fine
shirt, wore it immediately and for a very long time.

On September 28 the Coopers arrived in midafternoon, were put up in the closed
Lodge as usual. Coop came straight to my place with some hand-loaded big-game
ammunition. He really had some awfully cute ways about him, made quite a cover-up to-do, talking our usual. I was leaving in a few days on another elk hunt in
the Selway, taking a guest along. So, after so much palaver he eased into it, shyly:

"Now where you hidin' this fella Hemingway who I feel I know?"

Tillie had Papa on the phone, they talked a moment, and Coop said:

"Thanks, Tillie gal, Podnuh, see ya later, ah'll bet."

First in-person meeting of Gary Cooper and Ernest Hemingway, September, 1940

Though we knew the two would dovetail, we were intensely curious to witness this in-person meeting; but we had to be satisfied with a fitting description by Taylor: like two strange schoolboys sizing each other up, a line scratched in the dirt between them until "they got 'er done" in a hurry. They seemed as old buddies when we arrived there. The following day they got the measure they both looked for: we had a couple of hours over on the quail walk with the guns, and a round or two of skeet with Rocky, she who could shoot the pants off all of us at her specialty. Afterward came the incident that I'll never forget, and I remember it with warmth, and something else.

We pulled up in Coop's car in the square, for Papa to pick up his papers at the drugstore newsstand, and he'd said, "Will you run over the hill with us, you know?" For a second I didn't know, then caught on from his manner: he wanted to show Coop what Nin had had done for Gene's grave. She had remarried back in June—an assistant manager of one of the hotels—a quiet, nice chap named Winston McCrea. As soon as the ground was suitable in late spring, a local mason did a fine job of surrounding the two-plot space with a low stone wall, or fence, about a foot high— solid, permanent as the mountains. The headstone is a large natural granite boulder, its bronze tablet carrying Gene's name and the pertinent dates: 1905-1939. Beneath them is the last sentence of the eulogy that Ernest wrote and read:

"HE HAS COME BACK TO THE HILLS THAT HE LOVED AND NOW HE WILL BE A PART OF THEM FOREVER."

Behind the stone she had planted two small lilac shrubs—altogether a very fitting whole, set well back from the looping cemetery access road, pretty much by itself. Papa had been out with Nin to see it, was impressed with its simplicity and expressed himself fully. Really, I was a bit surprised—I can't say why—that he spoke of it to Coop right off. Our visit was brief and simple.

Coop with an Idaho bob kitty, a foot-of-the-bed rug for little daughter Maria—her second one.

Little three-year-old Maria Cooper is fascinated by her first snow. She is with her papa
atop 9,200-foot Baldy Mountain—Sun Valley's perfect ski mountain.

"A hell of a guy," Papa said softly; Coop spoke in a soft affirmative, and that was all.

On October 3, our guest, whom we were nursing along as a fall regular, and I took off on our elk trip; I went on "company time" but otherwise on my own, and not for a trophy, but for good meat. I got it, with Bill Hamilton again at the helm, and we were back in five days. Again Ernest hoped to go, but was in correspondence and had phone calls about the book's publication. Of course, the meat was for the "pot" and I had to fight him in his insistence that he split my mild expense with me. I said in truth that I helped promote the thing for the fun of it, so he reluctantly backed off. In return for the good bourbon whiskey that he sent with me, Bill again made special effort to see that the "delicacies" came back with me in perfect shape.

No joke about those, they were the special treat, while the quarters were curing. I've often mused that were it not for other things going on, Papa would have promoted their consumption around a campfire, like on safari.

The Coopers stay was not a long one, about three weeks, but as Coop always said,

"We got in the good licks, didn't we?" Rancher Tom Gooding again hosted us on opening day of pheasants; something of a small army moved into his ample fields and those of his neighbors. Old Mr. Frees's area absorbed us nicely off and on, and the "general" put his army to use there in annihilating hundreds of the rabbit pests in the adjacent sage areas where they holed up during the day. The old man was right about the population rise; there were a couple of drives on his place that fall, and would have been more but for other factors. The duck season opened earlier that year, so some of that had to be tucked in with Coop. We had one good day in the blinds and one memorable one on the creek during his stay.

He shied a bit at the canoe trip, and it's a cinch that neither Taylor nor I could have got him into one, but you know who did. We made a leisurely fun day of it, took down another boat, and on the snaky upper stretch of the run with lots of shore growth for concealment, Taylor and I on the paddles, we drifted quietly side by side, the gunners taking turns on the rises. It was more fun watching the two big kids at their fun, both of them more than willing to spell us, but not arguing about it. We had both dogs along, did a little business in our "bluebill" slough, and loafed over lunch on Picture Bridge—breaking it with a sortie or two on foot for snipe. They were the first that Coop ever shot "at" and let me say for the record that the old easygoing cowboy's vocabulary could match a Seventh Cavalry trooper's any day—when the going was rough. I remember of no day in many years in his company when he had more fun.

Up to then, the only press release on Ernest was the antelope hunt. This, more than anything else, not to "push" the publicity on him (we'd get that anyway in the press notices on the book, and another deal); don't make a big thing of it was the dictum. Pictures had been made only on a couple of Trail Creek parties, more or less for fun. I had a camera along that day, used it casually around the bridge—no objections at all, the opposite, in fact—then, waiting for the later flight movement we just sat around talking on the log rail of the bridge. I had my boots off, having shipped a little water, and suddenly Papa picked up several snipe, kidding Coop about them. Of course he was inviting me to take a picture of the three of them, the dogs included. I popped one, it looked awfully good as a casual, so I made another and "directed" that one. That did it, so we horsed around at making a number, just for kicks. But didn't we all know better? We were home early and I brought proof prints to the dinner table late that night. They were all personal hits, but that one with Papa holding the snipe in his hand, Coop in the middle, Taylor kneeling with his gun for a staff, was "my" picture, and I knew what to do with it. Sure, you bet, was my answer. The Hannagan man, a genial, laughing Irishman, kicked it off in a release. Probably long forgotten now, it was syndicated, the clipping returns came in by the sackful, a record for a long time.

All of which is to say that's how it was with Papa Hemingway—easy, casual, no fuss about it—and rewarding. And let us not forget to place most of the credit with the environs; a warm, golden, shirt-sleeves day, the soft murmur of water, contented

Gregory and Patrick Hemingway on their first duck hunt, Silver Creek, Idaho, 1940.

canine companions—a party of *basically* atavistic primitives. They were the ones I knew best.

On October 22 the airmail brought a box of the first edition of *For Whom the Bell Tolls*—about a dozen—all of which were pegged for certain people about the premises and elsewhere. By then that "no work to do" business was a laugh—an elated one. Mr. Author needed a full-time F.W.T.B.T. secretary, a private switchboard to handle the phone calls, and the daily mails swamped a favorite bellboy. As expected, Hollywood was hot on the scent for film rights—one notable producer-director had already visited Sun Valley and there had been talks, but no deal. Then from Hollywood came the man who got it—the head of the story department of the Myron Selznick Agency. He was Don Friede, of whom Papa said he felt was the one before he came—a long-standing obligation. Friede was once an editor for an early publisher, as we got it, and helpful in the struggling days. Don was a quiet, all-business sort, was in camp two days and spent practically all of it poring over the book. We wondered how he absorbed it so fast—the trained mind, of course. Tillie and I were having a late lunch with Marty and Papa when Don joined us, still on the last chapter while he half-ate his meal. It was time for us to take a powder, but Papa said quickly, "Don't go if you don't have to, there are no secrets about our book." We may have wished that we had; those figures talked gave us apoplexy. Afterward there was a phone call to Papa's lawyer, the deal was settled, and Don took the bus for the afternoon train.

Prior to that was an amusing incident relevant to the record price that the story brought. It was a drizzly day spent in Glamour House on reviews, columns, and God knew what all—some drinking too, but not excessively, tempered with lunch sent over from the Inn. This in a period of about six hours, then suddenly Papa jumped up from a heap of papers and periodicals, said, "Let's go shoot some targets." A damn good idea—fresh air was a must. Not a soul on the grounds but Stew Stewart

A pair to tie to—one with pose know-how; one who cared less'n nothin' for sartorial finesse

locking up the skeet layout. Okay, we'd shoot the unwanted skeet because?... How he did it, I don't know, but Papa broke twenty-four out of twenty-five. In the midst came a phone call from Hollywood, there was some cursing, going to take it in the shack, then on the porch he said to Stew and me:

"Goddamn, that was big dough I was talking to, shouldn't have been so short with 'em, I guess... but Christ! I wish they wouldn't call during our working hours."

It was one of several calls from Twentieth Century Fox, but Paramount got the story.

2

Early in November the long-coming divorce from Pauline materialized. Little comment here, other than Papa often saying that they were friends with an under-

Two kids watching their dogs retrieve mallards.

standing, and they always would be. I remember but a single change of pace at the time: a sober, non-talkative ride home from a pheasant hunt. There were just we two in his car, so I know that it was real.

Also early that month came the good break, and the other reason why our mild publicity was soft-pedaled. Papa's friend from the Spanish Civil War days, photographer Robert Capa, came out on a story for *Life* magazine, an arrangement no doubt with the Hemingway finger behind it. Intended as a story documenting the book and its eventual filming, it also covered the goings-on at Sun Valley. It came out in the January 6, 1941, issue, after the November Hemingway-Gellhorn wedding, so Capa's picture story was shot with that in mind, too.

The little Hungarian, short, dark, beetle-browed and moody, eternally dangling cigarette squinting his eyes, well, Capa was different; what he did in his field had size to it. He shot his 35mm cameras like miniature rapid-fire guns, and put some meaty human-interest stuff on film. We took him down the creek in the canoe, scared hell out of him a time or two, but you didn't scare him long—he had nerve, plenty. One segment of his piece concerned our habitual hunting on a poorly-run thousand-acre farm in the fringe area west of Shoshone—fantastically good pheasant cover on most of it. The little farmer's name we could not pronounce—about a foot long on his mailbox; he was Balkanese—so Papa simply called him John Myers. John had thirteen children in stairsteps up from a nursing infant; a house so small that you wondered how they were stacked for sleeping; they ate in relays, but with freedom in other necessities due to a collection of decrepit old buildings fit for firewood, and little else. So concerned with the business of eking out a living on the run-down place, the Hemingway name meant not a damn thing to them. Needless to say, we seldom took a bird home from John's farm, for a butchered elephant carcass could have been ditched about the clutter of buildings. John shot with us, and when our party had enough guns, one of his youngsters would mount a horse and follow to carry the

Not exactly an essential Hemingway game

Nor for a pseudo Montana cowboy. ". . . the critter's bound t'go under the fence, instead of over it!"

birds. I've seen the feathered load outweigh the boy more than once. One cold fruitful day we came in, Mrs. Myers cooked a noon meal, and Capa had a time of it getting his angles in the cramped house. We headed out again and finished up in mid-afternoon, then before leaving we went to work in the yard on a gallon jug of claret—the snakes were bad.

For a few days Papa had been trying to figure a graceful way to get John's pickup truck back in the running. It was sick with clutch and transmission trouble, there was daily milk to get to town, for which John had to depend upon a neighbor. Papa asked me if I thought it was worth fixing up, and I said, yes, and it was. Suddenly we "had to go" behind the barn: how much cash did I have in my pocket? Between us there was enough, plus a touch on the colonel's pocket, to be sure. When we left, Papa slipped the half-full jug on the truck's seat, told John to have it towed into town by his neighbor and get it fixed—we'd see him in a few days. The jug was corked with familiar green paper. The fall party was about to break up so we did not see John again for a year. A straight statement to Capa who'd caught on:

"Report that in your story and I'll wring your neck."

He smiled with it and Capa kept his word, but. . . .

There was one incident in which he didn't, ignored the explicit word that he got on it.

When we went behind the barn that day, Papa took his gun along, for there was a weed patch down a short slope that often produced pheasants. My weapon was my gun-stocked movie camera, and I hadn't turned a wheel with it. We finished the monetary thing and Papa said it just might be our luck to walk out there and do some business for both of us. I fell in behind him, and damned if a cock pheasant didn't roar out, a sharp-angle shot that he missed with his under barrel, and winged the cock with his upper. The bird recovered from his bouncing fall, but gave Papa time to slip in reloads before he took off like a quarter horse. He ground-sluiced him for the count and I was able to get into position to grind off film on that much of it. My

The Cooper getting-acquainted party at Sun Valley's Trail Creek Cabin. *From left*: the Coopers; Mrs. Winston McCrea (widow of Gene Van Guilder, now remarried); Satirist Dorothy Parker, a most gentle lady belying her career; Taylor Williams; E. H.; Winston McCrea, by the wall; in the foreground, Miss Parker's husband, script writer Alan Campbell; Tillie Arnold and Martha Gellhorn at the right. (October, 1940.)

Record of Cooper's getting-acquainted party. Photo credit to the giver, by remote control flash.

The 6.5 mm. Mannlicher Schoenauer rifle that done in poor Francis Macomber

old print of the film shows Papa walking into the camera, the wings flopping; he drops the bird, picks it up and comes on (pretty good actor, too).

The cock was a magnificent specimen, in his prime, and I made a couple of koda-chromes for myself with my Leica. Papa said: "This is about the heaviest pheasant I've ever hefted . . . boy, isn't he a beauty!"

Here was the "lead" picture for the Idaho part of Capa's story; I said so, and Papa agreed, yelled out in the voice you heard a mile, and Capa came on the double. Whenever I look at its full-page spread in my file copy of *Life*, I think to myself: this is as fine, and typical of Papa Hemingway in that era, as any picture I know. Then I smile to myself, too. The caption reads:

"Photographer Capa reports that Dead-shot Hemingway, in ten days of hunting, never missed a bird." The caption angered him plenty.

His beef was that in view of *Life's* great circulation, countless gunners would laugh up their sleeves, knowing full well that the best wing shots do well in averaging 60 percent, in rare cases perhaps 70 percent. Fine shot that he was, Papa's average was in the top bracket, his misses in proportion. In this, he was scrupulously honest, and had told Capa of such averages. In a letter to Taylor and me he said that when he saw Capa again he'd have a boot poised for him—sidewise, so it would lift him!

Another incident in Capa's visit was a classic, the occasion a pre-wedding, going-away party at Trail Creek cabin. Marty's mother was out from St. Louis, a gracious lady whom Papa called a rare jewel. As he put it, his party was for her, Capa, "and everybody who's made everything so good for us this short fall." All males put on their party-going rigs and wore ties! Chape and I took a camera between us and used it sparingly, for fun. The cabin bar in those days was very small and boxed-in, entered via the kitchen. The drinking was mild all around, and of course Papa perched himself on a stool and remained there until the dinner gong. With his jacket pockets full of flashbulbs (the big ones that were all we had then) Capa fired away at his favorite human subject, then finally got up on a stool behind the bar for some bizarre angles, I guess. Every shot that he fired showed Papa with a drink in his hand or on the way up—and at it. Papa told him three times to get the hell down off that stool—"What're you tryin' to do, portray me as a rummy?"

Capa let up on him for a bit, but stayed up there, then started sneaking a few shots when his subject's eyes were turned. He had a spring-loaded ejector in his flashgun and accidentally kicked out a spent bulb—smoking hot— and it would have burst on the bar right in front of Papa. He caught it in both hands and flipped it right back, catching Capa square between the eyes! The whole maneuver so fast you could hardly follow it. Capa said not a word, got down with the sullen look of injured, insulted pride, while Papa's "Now, goddamnit, am I a friend or just a son of a bitch of a target to you?" injured him further. He came out into the room, laid his camera down carefully, then the torrent broke.

He tore off his loosened tie, flung his jacket in a corner, and lit into Papa like he was ready to kill him. There were probably thirty of us present, and I doubt if there was a closed mouth among us. His tirade was half-English, half something else, and for a bit we wondered if he was about to get tossed outside in the creek just off the

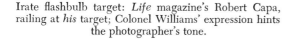
Irate flashbulb target: *Life* magazine's Robert Capa, railing at *his* target; Colonel Williams' expression hints the photographer's tone.

Paddler, Beartracks Williams; cameraman, Robert Capa; grinner, because they're flyin' good, Papa H.; gun platform, Stutter Bug. (November, 1940.)

ın Silver Creek's sloughs a greenwing teal and a fat mallard have fallen to the O/U Browning. Paddler, Taylor Williams.

front porch. Papa told the barkeep to fix his madman friend a drink and put a little castor oil in it at the instant my flashbulb went off, catching the scene. I just couldn't resist it, I guess. Anyway, the flash broke the tension, Papa commenced to laugh, and slowly Capa turned on the sheepish grin, wound the film in his camera back into its cartridge, and gave it to Papa who put it in his pocket—still laughing. At the table, Capa went noble. He picked up his empty camera and a fat candle in a wrought-iron holder and made a picture of the about-to-be-weds. The date was November 14.

The boys had departed by train—to catch up on their schooling—and for reasons of their own, the wedding was not to be in Sun Valley, "just somewhere down the line on our way home." Finally, Papa hit upon Cheyenne as the place, said they

Basque friend Frank Unamono, with Gigi and favorite bellhop Marv Foster, appointed guides when Papa worked. As Gigi says today, "Darned if we can remember when we went to school those days." But we guess he did, Dr. Hemingway.

would tie the knot simply—"give the string to a Justice of the Peace . . . we like peace and justice, don't we?"

While the packing was in progress, Marty said, "By all the dusty old standards, wouldn't it be nice if we had a wedding picture . . . wonder who'd make one for us, just a casual something?"

They were casual, all right, but good—profile shots using only natural light on the sun deck—one with Ernest (Marty's only address for him) pointing at an imaginary something toward the afternoon sun. We ran off prints in a hurry, and agreed on that one as the best.

"I'll bet that I can plant this as a full page in *Harper's Bazaar*," Marty said. "The more I look at it the better I like it."

"Now if Pappy and I had our way we'd plant it in *Field and Stream* . . . more in keeping with the life we live out here . . . but say, I look like I'm pointing to the dark future."

Once again the bulk of the gear, books, were stored with us; the Hemingway confidence said there would be another fall free of war involvement. I, the pessimist, did not go along with him, but in standing his ground he'd merely grin, say, "You'll see, kid . . . of course, I could be wrong." Tillie and I were flattered, and touched, by both Marty and Ernest urging us to go with them—to Cheyenne, to Omaha, Denver, anywhere along the line as we saw fit—or, "Hell, come to Key West with us, and on over to the new place in Cuba." He meant it, would stand getting us back by air or train (we with railroad pass privileges); and their next destination was New York; he wanted to work out something on that. We don't fully recall why we didn't take him up and have always regretted it. Pete and Dorothy Hill had flown over to say so long, and offered to fly down to the Wyoming capital, or wherever, and bring us back. There was one teasing thing ahead at the time: a special late-season deer hunt in the Middle Fork Primitive Area, but I would've passed that up. The departure was November 19.

On November 21, a Cheyenne justice of the peace did the honors, and on the twenty-second Tillie and I got a telegram from there:

"WE HOPE THAT WE CAN LIVE UP TO OUR WEDDING PICTURES AND ALSO TO BE AS GOOD A PAIR AS YOU TWO."

Typical Idaho "lower country"—pheasant heaven—in October, 1940. *From left:* Chief Guide Taylor Williams; Robert Capa, on camera for *Life* magazine; Neil Regan, Hannagan press agent for Sun Valley; Hemingway loading the first bird of the day on a horse ridden by farmer John Myers' boy.

When she read it, my seldom-swearing Tillie did say:
"Damn it, why didn't we go with them, at least that far?"
On December 9 came this telegram from New York:

"PICTURE US TWO ERNEST POINTING DARK FUTURE WITH RIGHT HAND TAKEN BY
HARPER'S FULL PAGE SPREAD EXCLUSIVE WITH BYLINE YOURS STOP PLEASE
DON'T GIVE TO ANYONE ELSE HAVE ARRANGED WITH LIFE NOT TO USE STOP
EVERYTHING FINE HERE CLOSELY RESEMBLING LIFE IN RUNAWAY ELEVATOR
STOP AM OFF TO BURMA ROAD SOONS POSSIBLE STOP ALL THIS AND HEAVEN
TOO LOVE TO THE GANG. MARTY."

No surprise at all in the Burma Road announcement; that had been a sharp burr under the Hemingway blanket most of the fall. Marty angled hard to get the *Collier's* assignment to cover the China-Burma Road theater that was the headline news on that side of the world. Someone else got it, then was decided against, and Marty landed it.

Silver Creek ducks never seemed to mind a big safari Stetson

"Well, all right, but by God, she can't go alone . . . it's too rough a trip, especially for a woman, and I won't allow it, and I'll wangle some sort of deal as an escort."

(He did, with the newly organized *PM* magazine headed by Ralph Ingersoll.)

While with us it was an out-in-the-open bitch about the whole thing, and Marty was assailed from all sides. Again, Tillie's arguments against it were friendly interest and were accepted as such. Marty simply told her that she wanted that assignment "more than anything in the world."

The informative telegram was followed shortly by a note from Papa; it did indeed confirm the runaway elevator theme, and said he was carrying around a six-figure

One of three handsome Middle Fork muleys, taken in the fall of 1940, when Papa wanted to go with us, but said, "Gotta date with a gal and J.P. down Cheyenne way."

The big one, same trip, slowed with a leg shot; Taylor Williams and Mike Finch, guide, finished him off. Long-term Sun Valley-ites will remember the three heads adorning the Lodge lounge mantel until a few years ago.

Measuring the antler spread on two Idaho muleys—heads that won the 1940 National James L. Clark competition. Hemingway urged the two local hunters to enter their animals.

check in his pocket and guessed he'd better deposit it before the digits were worn off. Near Christmas we wracked our heads to figure some cute tokens as gifts and good luck for the coming Asiatic trip. We had gone on the deer hunt—Taylor, Chape, and I—a successful one netting us three record-book heads that adorned the big Lodge lounge fireplace for many years. With our gifts we sent pictures to Papa who expressed his delight with our success—as pleased as if he'd been along: "We're going to have to go into the hills together some time."

There were some nice gifts for us, Tillie's a thing that she wore for a long time, and the affectionate note with them was signed thus:

"With much love, always. Gellstein and Hemhouse."

4.

The '41 Fall ---
'"That Unshakable Hangover . . ."'

1

The foregoing quoted excerpt was spoken to us that fall, but the insight behind it was gained much earlier—in the Far East, the China-Burma theater. There were complications in their preparations during the winter, and it was early spring before they got underway. Delayed a few days in San Francisco, Papa called us from there one night. In contrast to his beefing back in the fall, he was quite airy about it, but in the conversation he said that they'd had so many innoculations, so much needle-jabbing into their anatomies—Marty was still dragging with aftereffects—that he guessed they were both eligible for the Purple Heart.

"I hear San Francisco is lousy with needle artists and I'm gonna find me a good one and have mine tattooed on my ass!"

It was good, however, to hear him so cheerful; they would let us know when they set foot on home soil again—and by God, it had better be damn well ahead of fall! They flew the Pacific and we got word from Havana in July that they'd made it. Taylor had fished the Florida Keys that spring and had seen Papa briefly when they left for Asia; so he had the fall gen and acted upon it.

In August he sent Papa's application in for another antelope permit, and damned if the big "H" wasn't lucky again! Taylor drew one, I missed—and was disappointed because there was a free time spot around the date. The three boys again arrived—by train—ahead of the dove season; Toby Bruce took factory delivery of a Lincoln Continental convertible and drove it out to Idaho for Papa, arriving September 6. It was a beautiful car—one of the all-time classics of design, remember—a dreamily comfortable thing to drive; to be sure, it was a prestige car, but it sure as hell was not for Idaho "safari" use! It was September 14 when its owner and his equally still-tired bride arrived. Toby met their train in Shoshone.

The "deal" with Sun Valley was finished in '40, and Papa decided to try the Inn —their quarters on the second floor of the wing jutting out into the Village Square. Plainly utilitarian, they were far handier to all services, but a minute or two to everything. The trip to the Asian scenes of the war was a harrowing thing, an experience, a circus—and revealing! Since I vowed only personal experiences herein, I'll say that it was great listening to, spread over the fall, and that Marty's honesty confessed that she'd never have made it without Ernest. She said she was never so glad to see anything in her life as the sight of the Golden Gate Bridge on their return flight.

This time Papa flatly declared that he'd swept his docket clean of work, only answering the most important mail. "We'd better make this a good fall, if we can," he said. "I see an interruption, not too far off." The invigorating mountain air banished the weariness quickly; there was an active season ahead, as the booking showed, and the fun started at once—with the elegant sage green Lincoln, its top folded down, and bulging with seven of us.

The general had to inspect the Silver Creek theater right off—went to church with the little boys first—and took the wheel himself for the jaunt. Everything went fine until the country road around the creek run. At a midway place called the Point-of-Rocks there was a persistent mudhole—a seeping spring—that the general knew like the palm of his hand. But somehow he missed the right wheel ruts and promptly bogged her down, square in the middle of it. We pushed and heaved to no avail. Toby tried to drive it out, I tried. We didn't know what automobile history now concedes: the original Continentals were notoriously underpowered, and we got the hunch then. We saw a Sabbath-working farmer plowing a field with a team and got him to pull us out.

"Why, this 3-G son of a bitch can't pull itself over a fence post the size of my arm."

Translate 3-G, please, General.

"Just a few thousand bucks worth of gutless green giant, that's what, but ain't she pretty though, mud dripping off her belly like an underslung sow!"

The pretty sow took us on an immediate trip up into the Bitteroot Mountain country of western Montana. Taylor had several elk hunts booked in the Selway and had to arrange with packers to "spread them out" in the area. We only mentioned it, and Papa said it was the perfect time for him to see the country he'd missed twice, keying himself up, admittedly. There were four of us: Papa, Taylor, "Big A" Wood, and myself, and we picked up Bill Hamilton on the way. Winding up the Trail Creek Summit road, which that fall got a first improvement on its lower half in sixty years, a rolling rock knocked a hole in the exhaust pipe. We yelled ourselves hoarse for forty miles to Challis and a mechanic with a welding torch for repairs. "Sure growls like a bear, anyway, thanks to the Ferloin Road over the hill." That was the colonel's name for it, had called it so when we first took a fairly spooked Ernie over it two years before. The name stumped him and he asked the colonel to translate: "Simple, like the old butchers called the poorest cut of meat, ferloin steak —the fer piece from the loin."

"Ah, hah! a perfect name for this son of a bitch, a hell of a fer piece from a boulevard!"

Gigi, at ten years, was as handy with a shotgun as most men.

Indeed it was, as much of it still is, and probably always will be.

While in the Bitteroot country we went on up to Lolo, Montana, and west over the historic Lewis and Clark Trail—then merely a crooked little old wagon road down the Lochsa River in Idaho—to our old base camp. With our sleeping bags we roughed it overnight, the smells of the big wild in our nostrils, of steaks broiled over an open fire, on a wire grill that we bought on the way—not planning on it, but taking advantage while there. In the morning, sniffing the good bacon and coffee boiling, Papa said that of the many places he'd seen, the big down-timber, rough and rolling Selway was as typical an example of a man sensing his rightful place in nature's scheme of things as you'd find. That was as close to that sort of thing as we

The Hemingway "chips"—John (Bumby), seventeen; Patrick (Mouse) twelve; and Gregory (Gigi) nine, at Sun Valley in September, 1940. Once, when admiring this picture, Ernest said, ". . . when I retire, we'll put the Bum in the movies, the Gigi in the prize ring, and the Mouse will *manage* all four of us—and good."

ever got together—but it's a glimpse of the man Ernest Hemingway, stripped down to the essentials, that left an indelible impression on me.

I said little on that pleasant trip about him elking with us that fall, but knowing that I was itching to twist his arm until I near broke it, his remark to the effect was: "We'll see what the toll on the antelope hunt is, Pappy . . . damn, I wish that you had drawn a permit too, I feel like a cheater . . . don't we, Colonel?"

A little incident when we got back almost tipped him into going with me and another guest—farther south in the Selway, closer to home. He called it a good-luck omen, and maybe it was—says the perspective of time to me now. A cook in the Inn kitchen had a little 6.5 caliber Mannlicher-Schoenauer carbine—identical to his except for double-set hair triggers. Too short-range for our Western hunting, the rifle was, and is, a classic in design, workmanship, and general appeal. I had tried to buy the gun just as a pride-of-possession thing (though they'll kill anything that walks under proper conditions), but the cook wouldn't sell. Then, quitting the Valley for somewhere else, he put it up for raffle—tickets a dollar each. One of the Ram waiters told us about it at dinner, said there were a half dozen or so tickets left. Fairly well taken in the juice of the grape we dug in our pockets and came up with about that much between us. Sure, hell yes, close the raffle now! Within minutes the cook "shook 'em up" and a waitress reached into his tall cap and pulled out ticket number 27.

"Now, we're partners in something of material value, Chief . . . what in hell will we do with it?"

"Set it in the rack and admire it," I said. "Something to brag about, our luck, to our jealous friends, huh?"

And so we did—because the rack had to be full. ". . . so that we look well armed in season, prepared for any emergency."

The antelope hunt turned out as quite an event, worthy of Papa Hemingway writing it up "for dough" years later in a popular man's magazine. The prelude part of the trip seems more important now, as Hemingway history. I present it as it appeared to me—the deed of a good Samaritan, and more.

Impressed with Taylor's and my success with our light .257 rifles, Papa itched to try the caliber on an antelope. We did our best to focus the 'scope on my converted Springfield—the action he naturally preferred—but his eye would not take it, so he switched to Taylor's Winchester and its iron sights; Taylor used my gun. I went along as cameraman, hoping also to augment good movie footage that I'd made in the summer with telephoto lenses. Ours was a sizable party; two other guest hunters guided by Jack Redden; Papa took the boys, Bumby to fish the Pahsimeroi River, the youngsters for the ride. We set up camp in an old bunkhouse-cookshack combination on Ray Hamilton's ranch well up in the valley; Sun Valley sent a cook with us, the best in grub. Bill Hamilton had ridden the slopes on the valley's west side, reported ample average heads, one buck of record-book size, another a true freak. The pronghorns' headgear is unique in the animal world—distinctly American—and this

Calf-riding Gigi Hemingway on Ray Hamilton's Pahsimeroi Valley ranch, performing for an amused railbirding audience.

fellow had horns that curved sharply forward, out over his brow, in profile resembling an eyeshade, instead of the majestic upward flaring straightness. Papa said he'd go after him—no good for seed—and one of the hunters suggested they flip a coin for him. Taylor put his foot down, told all his guests to go for the best—he'd take the freak if we could find him on the morrow.

It was settled over a fine steak supper in the smoky lantern-lit bunkhouse, with Ray's ranch hand joining us, and heavily hitting the jug of a good red wine, his back to the heat of the old wood-burning cookstove. We knew him only as Wild Bill—a big, jovial, strapping man, Papa's counterpart in build—in his mid-twenties, and rarin' for fun, which he knew where to find. At the head of the forty-mile-long valley there was a feverish mining activity at a place called Patterson—a mushroom camp, wild and woolly, in pursuit of the vital metal, tungsten—so much in demand as war material in the Lend-Lease program with Great Britain. Wild Bill was bent on going to Patterson, and Ray warned us to stay away from the place at night—off-shift miners had little to do but drink and fight. But, fascination of something different was the lure, so Papa, Jack Redden, and myself ignored the warning and about nine o'clock we went with Wild William—he feeling little pain, we in very good shape. I drove my own car (thank God) and Ray warned Papa not to wear his big hat, and to pull his pant legs over his boots, not tucked into them. That, he did, but wore the hat. Ray's reasoning was sound: he said that a drunken miner might take big Ernie for one, too, and tell him that he was a better one—what then? Papa said:

"I'll agree with him, Ray, and get the hell out of his way, if it's out in the street even, with lots of room."

Street, hell! It was a dusty lane of dozed-off sagebrush, dimly lighted with naked electric lamps hanging over the void, bordered by eateries and saloons—all mere thrown-together shacks. The bedlam emitting from them was deafening, the air the kind that you could grab in handfuls. We parked in a dark vacant lot beside one of the saloons that Wild Bill recommended in fuzzy-voiced enthusiasm. Crowded to capacity, its mob was friendly, yelling out "Hi, Bill," on all sides; the whiskey was good, the price high—the barkeeps poured with their eyes shut. More was spilled by jostling than was drunk of the single round we had, edging away from the raw wet planks of the wall-to-wall bar. Bill's choice of the place was quickly obvious: a huge man—as big as any I ever saw—mean-looking pig eyes slitting hate at Bill who, in his state, tried to return it, doing a fair job. Weaving like his boots were nailed to the floor, he'd have tackled the giant had Papa not edged his way between them. He hissed to us:

"We'd better get the hell outa here, there's a few guys taking this in, maybe friends of the big one, and there'll be hell to pay if either of these two make a move."

But the big man had his plan—fairly drunk, too—and edged away, then headed for the door, Bill trying to follow him, Papa holding him back with a body block. We waited some time, things looked normal, and I headed out, said I'd start my car. Good. Nothing in sight, so I turned my lights on dim, left the doors open, and went back onto the flimsy plank porch to see our bunch talking outside with some "good guys," obviously. I nodded that the coast seemed clear, and the dusty street was empty in all directions. Suddenly a young man about my size appeared, carrying a battered tin suitcase, heading straight our way—a drifter, no doubt, looking for a bunk tonight, a job tomorrow. Before any of us could stop him, Wild Bill lurched down the steps, hauled back a long right and walloped the slender man on the side of his head, sitting his behind in a cloud of dust. Weaving over him, Wild Bill said he was not the son of a bitch he was looking for, mumbled an apology, and just started to help the man up when the one he was looking for lurched out from the shadows of my car, cocked and ready. His right hit Bill high on the head, and Bill got in a lick and went to his knees, the big man staggering back against my car. He recovered quickly and moved in, a long leg and a huge hobnailed boot primed for the business. In a swift leap off the porch Papa was between them, his right hauled back and in a blur landed on the side of the man's face, whacking like a lath on a barn door. His towering target folded down like an accordion, his lolling head barely missing my bumper. Shaking in our boots, Jack and I left the porch in jumps, a mob boiling out the door behind us. Papa pulled the innocent to his feet, who asked who and why. His reply was: "Don't wait to ask the cooled one. Get going, and thanks for having that suitcase for him to kick outa the way first."

He and Jack heaved the half-out Bill into the car, and we were off in a cloud of frantic low-gear dust, nobody saying a word, but hanging on as I drove out of a mess like I'd never driven before. Safely out, with no lights trailing us, Papa leaned forward in the dash lamp glow to seek the answer to my question: "How's the hand, Papa, it sounded bad to me, that crack . . . you're supposed to shoot with it tomorrow."

He grinned up at me, a still-spooked look in his eye.

"Okay, I guess, stings a bit, but I saved it with my grips."

I thought that his right came from his jacket pocket, which he now reached into and came up with a half dozen of our hot hand-loaded .257 cartridges, saying, "How's our boy Bill, Jack?"

Bill mumbled something to Jack's, "All right, I think, a skinned knuckle or two, some blood."

"Sure, he connected with the big guy's collarbone . . . in the morning his right will look like a green cantaloupe—with fingers. Jesus, I'm lucky the biggest man in a long time was boozed up, and I never saw such boots in my whole life."

He was right about that, and a man's head might have been pulped that night if fast-thinking Papa Hemingway hadn't moved like a streak of human lightning. We got Bill into bed, sneaked quietly in ourselves, and in the morning it was covered up by Papa joking that someone bet Bill he couldn't put his fist through a ply-panelled door—hit the frame, instead. "Come on, kid, I'll saddle your horse for you." Like a similar statement: nobody was kidding nobody.

At ten o'clock, with Papa and the boys far off on a ridge holding the freak buck's attention, the colonel stalked afoot to a low ridge and nailed him clean with a single shot at a long three hundred yards. When Papa rode down, he said, "Great shooting

The results of this antelope hunt, September 26, 1941, are given in the text. Note the "fancy hat" on Taylor Williams' buck (*second from left*). Brothers Ray and Bill Hamilton (*third and fourth in the back row*) hosted the hunters. The high-horned buck in the center is of record-book class.

Second head of big game (two antelope only) taken in Idaho by Ernest Hemingway,
September 26, 1941—this one in a spectacular long shot. Note the mark of the bullet's
entrance in the buck's shoulder. Youngest son Gigi admires with his father.

with a strange rifle once more, Colonel . . . it's a fine little cartridge, good for antelope, good for fisticuffs—minus the Queensbury rules."

There was nothing wrong with the big-bodied buck that we could determine in
dressing him out—as the colonel said, nature just saw fit to equip him with a fancy hat
—and he was alone when shot, an outcast to the apparently finicky antelope ladies.
Good Samaritan number two, Mr. Williams.

We fanned out on our horses then, searched hard for the big buck Bill had reported; passed up some ordinary heads and ate our lunch on the high backbone of
the Pahsimeroi Mountains as they dipped off to the Salmon far below to the north,
shining brightly in the warm September sun. Our glasses eventually picked up a

small band headed by a good average buck and the long stalk down commenced, the boys following slowly, well behind—instinctive little hunters needing but little instruction. We worked it well, got into position behind a low and rocky ridge that afforded concealment. A nod from Papa said for me to belly up, take a look, and use my judgment on trying for some telephoto footage. It was there, all right, the band about two hundred yards off, grazing along quietly, slightly below me on a long flat. Then I almost loused up the whole deal by forgetting that my long lens barrel was a brightly polished raw metal. It surely flashed a sun reflection and the band took off in a buff-colored streak, due broadside to me, down toward a long fingering ridge that, if reached, it was good-bye, Mr. Buck. I frantically waved for Papa to come on the double; he did, cursing a blue streak, ran on by me twenty yards, skidded to a stop, raised his rifle, and in a barely perceptible pause in lineup, let off his single shot. The buck, as usual in the midst of the does and fawns, just disappeared as the rest went over the ridge. I silently cursed myself, but breathed a sigh of relief as Papa stood there, not believing it himself.

"How far would you say, Pappy?"

"Pretty close to three hundred," I said. "And for a minute I thought there would be no shot to ask about . . . sorry, Papa. . . ."

"What spooked 'em, kid? . . . It was a perfect setup."

I spoke of my theory, and he said, "Sure, that had to be it, I didn't hear your cam-

A formidable-looking character who tangled with a miner bigger than himself—and won.

era running. . . . Well, good! . . . I've made fair shots in my time but this ranks them all . . . what a hell of a cartridge, a hell of a rifle."

"The understatement of your life," I said. "You still haven't got your wind back."

The buck was in perfect shape, hadn't run far enough to heat him up for meat-tainting; was hit at shoulder point at an even two hundred seventy-five yards, carefully stepped off on the easy terrain and double-checked with my range finder. Accuracy-stickler Papa was in charge of that, modestly shy about it, but happy as a kid in genuine awareness of the luck element coupled with the know-how of the born hunter.

The man who was my partner on the elk hunt got the big head—a fine trophy animal—and all permits were filled. Needless to say, there was no Patterson proposal for the night following that successful day, and his antelope was the last big game that Papa Hemingway collected on his home continent.

Ten years later he wrote it for *True* magazine, published in its July, 1951, issue, a piece entitled "The Shot." In its leading paragraphs he said of his good friend Taylor Williams: ". . . who can kill you dead with a borrowed rifle at three hundred yards!" It was a typical Papa to not mention it to the colonel who had fished the Gulf Stream with him but a short while before the story appeared; instead he sent us copies of the magazine. I sat right down and wrote him for both of us, kidding him that he left out the reason that he made that remarkable shot with a slightly sore hand. His reply made no mention of that, but it said:

"I wish, Pappy, that it were so we could come out to Idaho this fall and spend the dough that I got for the piece with you guys."

2

Again luck smiled on me in the Selway. I returned with a fine meat animal on October 9, drove in shortly after the Gary Coopers. There was a fresh liver feed that night, when Papa had us all in stitches with a rundown of high points in their Oriental trip; and as a storyteller Marty could match him any day. We got the serious side of it, too, when the Hemingway crystal ball flatly said that our entry into the world conflict would come in the Pacific.

"We'll probably get it for a Christmas present," said he. "Or maybe wake up New Year's morning with an unshakable hangover."

Actually, of course, there loomed the ominous fact of our relations with Japan

Rocky and Coop at Little Redfish Lake in the Sawtooth Mountains—a picture that Papa Hemingway liked very much, and of which he had a fine print.

having gone from bad to worse, when that summer President Roosevelt had frozen Japanese assets, which effectually cut off her oil supply. That is what would eventually embroil us, Papa Hemingway predicted. So, to repeat him, we made it as good a fall as we could—and it was—a great one, in which the general had some notable additions to his little army of gunners.

Following the Coopers from Hollywood came Director Howard Hawks and his willowy attractive wife, called Slim; Producer Leland Hayward and his actress wife, Margaret Sullivan, who liked to be called Maggie; the handsome actor Robert Taylor and Barbara Stanwyck—then Mr. and Mrs. and both riding high on their careers. From Washington, D.C., and the White House, came busy Lend-Lease administrator Averell Harriman and his younger daughter, Kathleen; and the John Boettigers—President Roosevelt's daughter, Anna, and her husband. It was more for true than joke that Papa, before this group arrived, kidded about going "on a binge with Mrs. Benge." Mrs. B. had a little shop in Ketchum, in which she designed and turned out leather jackets, coats, and vests of real class and of the finest chamois, antelope, and kid skins—any colors—and a specialty of hers was pullover hunting shirts. There was no bigger sucker for fine leather stuff than Papa Hemingway, so he went all out, had several things made, including a white capeskin hunting shirt—"going Hollywood" to quote him—"don't you think I'm as handsome as Plainsman Hickok Cooper in this fancy shirt?" Well, he was pretty handsome, at that, at least his coloring was a striking contrast in the neat white party rig. Anyone would know there would be plenty of parties with that group in camp.

It was Mr. Harriman's first fall visit to his big baby out West, his time was short, and he didn't intend to hunt—something we never associated with him. He came to

Marty Hemingway; Winston McCrea; Coop and Rocky; E. H.

the shop one morning when I was there alone, honing down a welded ejector rod that had snapped in Papa's Browning. I saw lots of him when he came, but seldom did he visit the shop, so I had a hunch that he was wondering why the Hemingway quarters were in the Inn that fall. The two had never met. I went on honing while he asked about the hunting, and directly I was asked where in the Inn Mr. Hemingway lived. I pointed out his windows in the wing not sixty feet from us, where Papa sat typing at a little table—the broken gun kept us in that morning and I was trying to get it ready for an afternoon shoot. In his pleasantly blunt way, Mr. Averell grinned, said, "See that you do, looks to me like you might." I knew that he didn't expect me to get them together, and he seemed in no hurry, so I went into a brief dissertation on the Labrador dogs he'd given the Valley, said that I was sure he'd hear praise of them to make mine dull. He thanked me and went on his way. Late that afternoon I saw him in the lobby; he took the trouble to say how right I was about the dogs, and the praise he got on the great Idaho hunting. I said I had a hunch he might be going afield. He grinned, said:

"We might, at that."

We hadn't gone out that day, and sure enough Papa told me that he and Taylor were to take the big boss and Kathleen on the canoe run down Silver Creek, separately in relay, that Mr. Harriman had sent for guns. I said, "You're quite the promoter, Papa." No, he said, he had just told the truth of how it was—great stuff, and it was good duck weather right then, a little rainy, and they'd hold good on the creek. They did, on a wet cold day, the only hunt they made, a good one. Now the punch line, a Papa tale, but it rang true.

He admitted, when he was on the throne, that he overreached himself and his gun, made some good shots, and missed a few, deservingly; then, in his well-meant blunt way, Mr. Harriman told him that he was lightly disappointed in him—didn't quite come up to his reputation as an unbeatable shot.

I laughed outright when he told me about it—so familiar, I said—and asked his retort.

"I kept my mouth shut, for once, but I wanted to say, 'Well, Averell, just how damn long did you play the game to rate as a seven-goal man at polo?'"

"Well, why didn't you, Papa?"

"Because what I know about polo you can stuff in a .410 shotgun shell and have room left for what I know about a balloon."

Anyway, Mr. Harriman apparently accomplished in his behind-the-scenes way what management had been urging on Papa for some time—move over to Glamour House, which both he and Marty missed so much. The Inn was all right at first, but when the weather concentrated the horde of tame ducks on the big lagoon so close to their quarters, their morning clamoring was not so good when Papa worked early at his correspondence. Too, it was the independent "avoidance of obligations" streak in his nature that made him reluctant (the Hollywood bunch housed at the Lodge had nothing to do with it). Later, he confessed that this one did: One rainy midmorning he walked down to our shop with Tillie, and out from a mob of begging ducks a mallard susie stopped squarely in the path, looked up at him, said: "Quack?" He stooped over, his pointing finger almost touching the old glutton's bill, which she might have taken for a morsel.

"You, you bitch, I'd know your voice anywhere." He laughed heartily.

Tillie poured it onto him then and there, in effect: "They seem to go out of their way to heckle you, Papa. Now get moved over there. You can accept a favor, what's so wrong about that?"

A typical Trail Creek party, at which a turned-up collar or two in the bunch was par for the course. ". . . you don't catch cold in cool fresh air."

Same party, the table shot from this angle in order to show the two record-size mule deer heads flanking the fireplace, the ones Ernest urged the hunters to enter in national competition.

Well, he might, he said, but did nothing about it, then shortly an amusing complex occasion made up his mind—or so it appeared.

Of the frequent Trail Creek Cabin parties, one is outstandingly memorable, a sizable one that the gals had the full hand in. It followed an inclement-weather day of "all male" hunting, and of course we were late getting home—Dutch Charlie's place or the Snug Bar—which didn't set so good, especially with one independently-natured lady, all of them dressed and waiting. We hurried in trying to soften things, Marty and Papa to ride up with Tillie and me. They knocked on our door, Papa in his shirt-sleeves, carrying a leather jacket and his white capeskin hunting shirt on his arm. Which should he wear? His moral support decreed the white one:

"All right, I will, but why in hell did I sucker myself into this damn thing, anyway? . . . have to be careful and not get jostled with a glass of red in hand . . . that would fix things good, huh?"

Quite to his pleased surprise his white hunter garb was a hit all around, and the large evening got in gear quickly, the male contingency around the bar beside the roaring hot fire. At the time it appeared that Howard Hawks was a cinch to direct the filming of *For Whom the Bell Tolls* for Paramount, and the principal roles were decided upon, though there was *no* insistence by Papa on Coop and Ingrid Bergman as Robert Jordan and Maria. Yes, his preference was an influence, no question of it, but he did not tamper "in the face of such a hell of a deal I got on it." So that was the subject, then it gradually evolved into a favorite topic—boxing—due to a recent event involving Papa and we locals (too lengthy for space here). We were all feeling the glow and soon a few were taking mild swings at the Hemingway midriff—muscles that he could tighten up like a rock; nor was he hesitant, when in the right mood, to challenge your hitting power. He laughingly challenged the wilful good sport, Howard Hawks, who strongly hauled back and delivered a haymaker. Both winced at the impact, but nothing happened, nothing gave, nothing broke, including the much-vaunted Hawks' "broken wrist." Nuts! Charge it to the myth department, news-gathering, magnification of minor incidents resulting in the buildup of the false image. Shortly we'll know how "broken" the wrist really was.

The gals broke up our kid stuff with their "soup's on, fellas," and with the fine meal the "Noble Experiments" were drained and repeatedly refilled with top red wine (the Noble Experiments were the imported wine lifters under which your glass was raised to open a valve for the gravity draw). But the wine-loving Papa had his white garment in mind and stayed with his Scotch highballs, instead, a rarity, indeed. In fine, talkative gear, he harbored a hangover from the boys catching hell for being late from hunting, so he eased it a bit by asking the leader if her husband was as good in bed as he was to look at across the table! The frown he got, then the smile, then the bright laughter, could well be interpreted as her, "What do you think?"

That perhaps, was Papa's own door-opening to get drunk, and that he did—not staggeringly so—shall I say, grandly, nobly drunk. The first, and one of about three times in all the years that we saw him so. The parties of those days generally wound up with a Virginia Reel or two—the Cabin's terpsichorean specialty—and Papa did his dancing in a chair. Finally he figured he should take quiet leave and selected Tillie to drive him home. In a drizzling rain, she stopped in the driveway tunneled through the Inn at the Square. As he left the car he said:

"Tillie, I'm not going up the straight stairs, I'm going down the hall and up that bastardly circular staircase . . . if I make it all right, I'll stay in this place, but if I come to grief I'll be goddamned if I'll ever, ever see them again."

"Papa, I'll help you." So up they went, and Tillie had a time of it, on the inside narrow end of the tapering treads, no hand rail, and two hundred pounds of man draped around her neck. The barked shin, however, was not hers.

About nine the next morning he bounced in as bright as a dollar, laughed about last night, but said he guessed he'd made up his mind to move to Glamour House —could we do it unobtrusively, get his favorite bellboy to take charge? I said, yes, and "I think you put on something of an act last night, were you as boozed up as. . . ."

"Oh, I was, all right, ask Tillie, and I should be apologizing . . . Glamour House, we'll know you again, soon!"

Spaced in with regular hunting, at intervals of several days, were the big rabbit drives around the Frees farm. I'd say that those were the most satisfying affairs to the general who organized them, lined his army up to twenty guns on a couple or three—out across the big sage fields for safety and efficiency; no one even so much as felt a stray well-spent pellet, though it may appear that it were probable. The mixture of the group: the Hollywood greats; the Washington, D.C., elites; we local

Totaling the take on a best rabbit pest drive—2,200 done in by a couple of dozen guns. Flanking "the General" are son Bumby, John Boettiger, and Producer-Director Howard Hawks. (November, 1941.)

"Recess" during one of the massive rabbit pest drives, November, 1941—Gary Cooper, the "General" of the massacres, the poet-sportsman Christopher La Farge. On the ground, a newsreel cameraman is changing film—hoping to get something from the "carnage."

regulars, plus the resort's tennis pro and pharmacist Bud Hegstrom; a couple of favorite Ram waiters; the Hemingway boys; a poet—and even a newsreel man whose company got wind of the drives and sent him up to see what he could do with such "carnage" for the public movie screens—amused him as much as anything about them. There were five of the drives all told, the newsreel man tried his best on two of them, admitted it was not a tasteful subject and just about impossible for a cutter to do anything with his film. General Hemingway said, "Hell, Bob, concentrate on my fine army, the non-shooting gals helping with the herding. Where will you find an outfit like this, and you're getting it for free!"

Certainly, it was not sporty shooting—a massacre instead—but a service to the farmers, and we just about cleaned out the pests in that area. Then we'd all gather in Mr. Frees' farmyard for the day's tally, and the old man would say:

"*Gott und himmel,* think how much less little rabbits next year!"

On the peak day that netted close to twenty-two hundred, the gang brought plenty of condiments to go with a fine chicken dinner that the Frees women put out (quite a family of them), eaten out in the warm sun in the yard. The amount of ammunition shot up was subject for a joke that the big makers owed us all a Christmas present. One "ranking" soldier of the army echoed Mr. Frees' comment that it was quite expensive annihilation, but the general chuckled in an aside:

"Hell, they can afford it, the country's damn good to them, let 'em do it a favor, the kind that counts." Wasn't too soft-voiced about it, either.

Smack in the middle of it all, there was an accident—one most painful to think about even now. On a duck shoot, John Boettiger was using Taylor's Browning over-under trap gun—the model that does not return automatically to safe when opened, like the field guns to which he was accustomed. Jump-shooting, with the dogs along, the group stopped for a moment; John laid the gun down to one side, but, probably in the excitement of the hunt, didn't break it open, sure that the safety was on. When he picked it up, a weed stub on the ground nudged the single trigger, the under barrel fired and mangled a hind foot of Bullet, the junior of the Harriman Labradors. Poor John was beside himself, said that the damn fool who would do that should be shot himself. The Hemingway temper flared at the moment, and agreed with him. Taylor and one of the guides rushed the dog to Sun Valley, but the doctors could only stump the wound, so the dog was minus a foot.

(Actually—poor solace, this—Mr. Bullet lived out a useful life; was spared field work, and a genius at the stable fashioned a cushioned leather lace-on boot that he got around on very well until quite old; was about as good as ever in the water.)

I was not a witness, but drove Marty and Papa home, he cursing everything in general, himself the most for losing his temper to say what he had. As men do, we went straight to the Ram bar, and the wise Taylor nipped the round there and we headed for his room—the "boar's nest," in hunting season, the proper place. John was all for throwing in the sponge, and when the bottle was considerably lowered

The family and a bag of pheasants. (October, 1941.)

Papa would have none of that; things would go on as before. November was well along then, the weather spotty, and there were a couple more rabbit drives booked. Then the season's highlight, entitled, say, "Leave it to Papa Hemingway."

Wild ducks commonly decoyed to the tame ones, right onto the lagoons, and in spring we often saw wild geese going over in the northward migration, but never in the fall. But south on the big reservoirs they were hunted quite commonly. One morning Taylor and I were on the Inn porch watching Pop Mark feed the ducks, and hoping for the pretty sight of our tame Canada geese flying up from the lake, or from the small lagoon into which you could toss a pebble from Glamour House sun deck, or the small balcony off the Harry Morgan Room. It was snowing, a wet sludge of it on the warm ground, and suddenly we saw a pair of geese flying up the creek, and heard our geese set up their call from the Lodge lagoon. As the wild pair circled between the hotels we saw that the smaller goose of the pair had a leg down, flying erratically, badly hurt; the gander a big one, going good, and leading her down. (Canada geese mate for life, almost without exception, and the goose was not for long, obviously.)

We had talked to Papa but a few minutes before; he was shaving to come for breakfast with us. Taylor looked at me knowingly—heavy goose loads of No. 2 shot were always in a separate pocket of our hunting coats—coyote medicine that had been successfully used two falls before on an old dog about to keel over from starvation. So, we knew what to expect and were not disappointed: the pair circled back beyond the Lodge and disappeared in the murky sky, then in a matter of seconds came two sharp cracks—full-choke 12-gauge cracks. The colonel chuckled:

Anna Roosevelt Boettiger, perched on a fender of the 3G Lincoln Continental; Christopher La Farge; Taylor Williams refreshing himself; Roland Bloomstrand, pheasant-shooting tennis pro at the resort.

"Well, the Good Samaritan got 'er done . . . let's go arrest him for shootin' on private, restricted property."

"Let's," I said. "You do the pinching and I'll go around to gather up the evidence."

The colonel stepped in to the bell desk phone that was already ringing.

"You'll have to take me as I am, men, pajamas, lather face, and all," and laughing so that the colonel held the instrument at arm's length. Here's why:

He heard our old pair calling the strangers, took a fast count of the family, had a time finding his goose loads, the pair coming in almost at eye level. He got the double French doors open to the small balcony and got his shots off from *inside the room!* The pair fell almost directly under him, he saw that he'd got them clean, then a wild-eyed dishevelled Marty burst into the room:

"Good God, Ernest, you *didn't* shoot John Boettiger, did you?"

"No, Miss Mahtha, I shot me a pair of geese, trying to register into this joint, and I'm going to let John in on your nightmare."

(Miss Mahtha was addressed as such by their cook at the Finca in Cuba.) John, and everybody else in the bunch was let in on it, and a leather medal was proposed for the Good Samaritan—to be hung in the Lodge lobby for the hotel being the most plush, expensive goose blind in all the world. Needless to say, it still holds that distinction!

Nor, from the hunters' point of view, was the goose incident the season's only

A pause between drives on a rabbit-pest shoot: Anna Boettiger, Gary Cooper, and Howard Hawks.

John and Anna Boettiger, top-shooting soldiers in the General's army.

highlight. Due to the early departure in '40, and the mild weather at that time, we had not observed the evening movement of ducks into the basin via the shortcut over the rocky ridge off old Stutter Man's backyard; but the old boy and that great shooting were not forgotten, by any means. The canoe run was still almost exclusively used by Papa and me—occasionally by Marty and him—and we ran it often to help keep ducks moving for the others scattered about the basin. Sure enough, we saw them coming over the ridge one windy November afternoon, but did not go up there when we finished at pullout. Nor did I have to be a clairvoyant to know what was going on in the think department up front. We itched to climb up while we watched the ducks, in intermittent small flights, spread in a pattern two or three hundred yards wide, so that several guns could use the ridge at once.

"Now, kid, we can dish up a little good medicine for the old boy, if it's only a lot of noise . . . and we'll introduce some real shooting to the boys, huh?"

The "boys" still in camp were Coop, Howard Hawks, and John Boettiger, and the doctor couldn't wait to get them up there. They'd heard nothing of it, so, in a day or two they wondered what in hell was going on when in midafternoon Taylor had them at pullout and our canoe came down the creek to meet them and they were ferried across one at a time—not so happy about it, either, right at the head of that straight, fast current that we knew so well. When all were safely across, we brought Taylor and Mr. Hickory over, and Papa said, "Now we got a little time to kill, men," and they naturally thought of a small open slough that lay up and in back of the tule jungle of the Chutes part of the creek. It wasn't long until the talk was interrupted by the soft, swift song of mallard wings passing overhead—out of nowhere, from behind them, then fading fast in speed. Goggle-eyed, they looked around at the ridge, saw the next flight seeming to fly right out of the rocks along the crest— the moment the doctor was waiting for.

"That's what we thought when we discovered it." He laughed. "It doesn't make sense, shooting ducks off a mountain ridge. Any takers?"

They couldn't wait to get at it; Taylor stayed on the flat to work the dog, and the fun commenced when we spread out after scrambling up the north face in rubber boots. When he hit the crest a small flight barely missed Coop's hat—winged bullets, literally—and a bit more than startling at first sight! As expected, not a feather was touched for a few passes, then the "lead" was found by the boys and they commenced to connect on about one out of three. Then we all got a surprise. A bullet whacked against a rock and ricocheted off it in a zinging whine, followed by the report of a rifle. Papa and I expected a shotgun pattern thrown up there by old Stutter—in a high arc of fall for scare. It was Coop who said, "Jesus, what was that—sounded for real to me!" Then we had to divulge the joke that was on us, too. We went right on, staying down and back out of sight, and a few more bullets zinged our way, figured as an old obsolete .25-calibre, by the report and snap of one or two that went overhead. Papa laughed, said, "It's one for Ripley's 'Believe It or Not,' huh?" Coop said, "Yeah, and them ain't blanks like in the movies, Podnuh, and I ain't gittin' paid fer it, either!"

Truth is, the angles were such that it's doubtful a single pellet fell in Stutter's yard; the ridge was not even a part of the property he rented; his turkeys were

One for Ripley's "Believe It or Not," ". . . see, flyin' right outa that rocky ridge, gents?"

gone to market; and a final kick in all of it was, we had learned that he was a bachelor and his name was, of all names—Cecil!

"Fits him about like a saddle fits a hog."

So in Hemingwayan the ridge was "Stutter's chancre that we'll turn into a carbuncle for him."

Stutter gave up the bluff with that one try, did a lot of yelling on the almost daily flings we took at it right up into early December. In certain weather conditions it was fair in mornings, too.

3

It was around Thanksgiving time when a headliner in the nation's news was the presence in Washington, D.C., of the Japanese diplomat, Kurusu—the "double-talk" mission, remember—that Papa Hemingway remarked in dead seriousness that he'd bet the 3-G Lincoln on the Christmas present, or that unshakable hangover around the New Year—to be delivered in the Far East, the Philippines his first guess. Remembering World War I times so clearly, I don't believe I would have bet against him—for money, marbles, or a ball of string.

Then, on Sunday, November 30, the Old Man called me to his office, to tell me that once again I would have to pinch-hit in getting out advance publicity and news releases for the resort's winter opening; the Hannagan man was to be replaced, and in timing with that he was a Reservist in one of the Armed Services, and was alerted for something. So my guns were hung up—until? . . .

During that first December week I did take an afternoon to go down on the ridge with Papa Hemingway and Coop—the day before Coop left—and photographed the setup in a series of shots that I put together for them in a long panorama print. We had learned of the possibility of the almost worthless property coming up for sale in the near future, they toying with the idea of buying it—for a private "duck reserve." A little work on it at no great expense was entirely feasible. The big marsh up in the springs area—the real prize—was tied up in an option. Also, during that week, Papa was talking about packing up for Cuba—the Finca Vigia at San Francisco de Paula, just outside Havana, the place that he and Marty had acquired a year or so before.

Early Sunday morning, December 7, he and Taylor went down to shoot the ridge with Bud Purdy and Chuck Atkinson. Behind in things, I was trying to catch up,

On the ready for something to explode out of that field: Howard Hawks, Marty H., and Coop, in his field-going best.

writing captions for a deep stack of news photos on my cluttered desk. A little after eleven o'clock my startled wife called me out to her desk where her little radio was blaring the news of the disaster at Pearl Harbor. About the same time, the hunters on the creek were just pulling out the canoe from ferrying back from a fair morning on the ridge. Chuck describes it as chilling cold in a brisk wind, they in a hurry to get to his store for a warm-up. They, too, could not believe it when Floss Atkinson gave them the word. I guess we who can remember it so vividly can well say, "Well, who in hell could be expected to believe it!"

It was a very concerned and troubled Papa who said later that day:

"Well, I missed it a couple or three weeks, and where we'd get it . . . watch it explode all over that side of the world, now, citizens!"

On Monday, the eighth, no one saw hide nor hair of him until midafternoon. Marty called us when we were at breakfast before eight; she hadn't heard him leave, the Lincoln was gone, and we inquired around throughout the morning; I even went to town and discreetly asked if he'd been seen. No, from all asked. The road from town was watched, the cutoff road past Penny Mountain over to join the highway, too. Nothing. In midafternoon, Tillie and I were at Glamour House with a desperate Marty, holding ourselves back from calling the sheriff, the highway patrolman—do something! Suddenly, Papa walked in, looking sheepish—very much ashamed and apologetic for the worry he was responsible for—but quickly explaining that he hadn't slept well, and just had to get the hell away from everything and everybody to think out a number of things by himself. Sitting where I was, I knew damn well he hadn't come by either of the roads mentioned, but that he could have come down from the Ferloin Road—Trail Creek Summit then closed by snow, but the valley floor and well up the canyon as bare as the carpet. I said nothing then

Coop and Marty cutting a rug at the cabin

—or ever—but he sensed my surmise and said, in his oft-used Indian talk: "I found a quiet lonely place, like old Long-think, and had it out." When he told me of a part of it, I couldn't believe him, thought he was joking, until he reminded me of a few things that an idiot should have thought of.

Within three days the Philippines had been hit—our bomber force at Clark Field knocked out—the British capital ships, *Prince of Wales* and *Repulse,* sent to the bottom of the China Sea; our home radios warning of the coming domestic gasoline rationing—everybody get where they're going, in a hurry. So, the pack-up was fast, bulky gear left with us for safekeeping; the now quite augmented Hemingway library a biggest item; I would find some place for it ahead in the unknown. Then I got the word on Papa's scheme—from himself. The Caribbean Sea and the Gulf Stream were hotbeds of German U-boats and he would rig his thirty-eight-foot Wheeler fishing boat, the *Pilar,* as a search-detector craft, in the guise of a fisherman; arm it with every feasible weapon it could carry—in addition, "for just in case," he said. I said, more or less as a disbelieving jest, that I couldn't conceive him taking aboard his favorite small arms—like the Springfield, the little Mannlicher of Pauline. He grinned, said it was still only an idea worth working on, and that some weapons he would hate to risk—he had boys growing up.

"I said, "Take *our* Mannlicher, Papa, nothing attached to it but the price of a bottle between us." He laughed heartily.

"You're right, Pappy, at that, I will take it . . . hell, who can tell what I'll end up doing, at my age, but I won't sit aside and watch . . . now speaking of guns, I wish that you would change your mind and keep the Duke of Alba shotgun; if you leave here, well, that's up to you."

I refused again, for the very reasons just mentioned. The gun was an ornately beautiful piece, done in quiet good taste; one that he'd picked up in the Spanish Civil War, had a story about how. He brought it out in '40, said to me:

"I warn you, Pappy, it's a lightweight and will kick hell out of you with heavy duck loads, and it doesn't fit me well at all . . . so if you can handle it, and I know you can, she's yours."

I was gape-mouth surprised as I looked at its lovely engraving, a stock and fore-end of the world's finest walnut—black-streaked Circassian—the tightly-choked thirty-inch barrels, a pigeon gun, and for stuff like pass shooting at range. It fit me like a glove when mounted so I knew that it fit him. Cover-up, of course, and I was moved almost beyond words that he wanted *me* to have that "bloody museum piece" as he joked of Chris LaFarge's matched English Purdeys.

"Papa," I soon said. "This gun should not come to me, it came of personal experiences of yours, like my father's fine old double is in my brother's rack, and one of his rifles in mine, I. . . ."

Don't let anyone tell you that Papa Hemingway was not capable of visible emotions in its presence on another. He said softly:

"Well, you're right, Pappy, but the kids aren't nearly ready for it, and . . . oh, well, I'd better take it home with me, then if we join up again after this mess is over, and we will, we'll talk about it."

Whether his Duke of Alba name for the gun was just a story, or not, it was obviously custom-built for someone of note—and cash! I was gun student enough to know that. I put a lot of ammunition through it those falls; Papa made a few spectacular shots with it, and a few misses too—one that I recorded the results of in my bird-shooting film. I'd have given my passport to hell for that gun.

The younger boys had gone home by train around the first of December and out of high school then, Bumby, at the time of Pearl Harbor, was away on a short trip—about a job with a contracting firm with big defense jobs going on Wake and Midway Islands in the Pacific. At military service age of eighteen, Pearl Harbor changed all that.

Ours was not a tearful good-bye—too much pressure to get going—simple, to the point:

"Keep in touch, now, as best we can, let us know what will happen here with Sun Valley as soon as you know," and he joked me in wishing that instead of an aging forty-two and a half, he was a young thirty-five and a half.

"I'm warm to the touch, Papa," I said. "And you know what that is in time of war . . . maybe I can take pictures of ship building, or something like that."

When he kissed Tillie good-bye, she felt something round and thin pressed into her hand. With the Lincoln's exhaust fading away, she opened her hand and saw the old 1890's silver dollar, and then tearfully remembered hearing:

"Just so we'll never be broke, daughter."

5.

1942 to 1945 . . .

1

Business as usual at Sun Valley that winter, but an imbecile knew that as the belt tightening increased the railroad would eventually close it. The company's president made that clear when he was appointed by President Roosevelt to head the synthetic rubber-for-war industry into high gear. W. M. Jeffers was a public-conscious operator, announced to management that it could hold out as long as there was personnel to run it. Thus, I made a fast trip down to Hollywood in May of '42, with a canful of 16mm color film taken as background selling material for a proposed Twentieth Century Fox movie starring the pinup star of the era—Betty Grable. I got the job done with the director of *Springtime in the Rockies* but I would have bet a modest sum that neither that picture nor *For Whom the Bell Tolls* would see a foot of film shot near Sun Valley. Director Sam Wood had "Bell" in his pocket by then, and while down there I spent a few hours with the Coopers at their home. Coop agreed with me that the California Sierra country was so much closer, but he also agreed that it would be fine and in keeping with the author's wishes that it be filmed where a third of it was written. In my pocket I had a letter from the Hemingways—a mere note—to show them; they had a similar one to show me. Both said that it was not very good fishing in the Gulf Stream, but there was hope that it would get better. Taylor Williams was there at the time; how he made it in view of restricted travel only he would know, so I hoped to get some word of the "fishing" from him when he returned in June. He didn't make it in time, for early in the month the military found the old carcass good for something.

The last word we had from Cuba was a short letter that Tillie had when she came to see me in Arizona in November, 1942. There was, naturally, no word other than that everything was fine and that the immediate future was "unforeseeable."

By early summer of '43, disappointed in not getting overseas, I was set in a desk job, but smack in my line so that I at least knew what went with what. Sun Valley closed in December of '42, Tillie returned to Iowa, and joined me in Texas later.

By that time we had word that the United States Navy had leased Sun Valley as a rehabilitation center. The Old Man was great in keeping in touch with his boys, let us know that Taylor Williams was on the skeleton crew the company kept on for basic maintenance—such as it was.

The next clue only that we got was when I came in from the base one night and picked up the June 26, 1944, issue of *Life* magazine on the way. We gasped when we opened it to see the full-page Robert Capa picture of Papa Hemingway in a London hospital bed, wearing a tremendous beard, his head swathed in a turban-like bandage fastened by safety pins. The caption said he was the correspondent Hemingway, and had managed to provide copy for the rest of the correspondents by becoming an indirect casualty of the second front. Read on: On his way to his quarters from a sober party a few nights before the invasion, his car crashed into an unlighted water tank in the middle of a blacked-out London street. Hemingway, the driver and a passenger and the water tank spilled all over the road; the brawny novelist landed in the hospital where surgeons put fifty-two stitches in his pate!

"Good God!" Tillie said to me. "Enough to sew back the whole top of his head . . . poor old Papa, and it says that from the mess he's got water on the knee, and they say he's forty-six . . . he won't be forty-five until next month."

The caption said that he had already landed with invasion forces on the Normandy beachheads and was flying missions with the R.A.F. and that Marty was also covering the war as a correspondent.

That fifty-two stitches business bothered us no end, but I had to smile when I remembered: "but I won't sit aside and watch. . . ." I had joked him about being the old firehorse answering the bell when last with him; he had tapped his knee, said with a laugh:

"You saw me run once with it, maybe I can again if I'm out front and scared."
We don't remember just when it was that we stood in line for tickets to see *For Whom the Bell Tolls*, but we do remember whispering to each other that they opened the film exactly as Papa had predicted:

"They'll have to do it Hollywood style, you'll see, the scriptwriters will blow the train right off, instead of it opening quietly in the forest as I wrote it . . . and ended it."

2

When the shooting was all over, we stopped in the Midwest for a visit with our families, picked up a small trailer of stuff we had stored there, and headed west—half in the notion of going on to the coast. I had word of my old friend, Vince Hunter's doings, and could well have rejoined him in the motion picture bureau he was giving full time to as part of the railroad's Public Relations Department. We hung on indecision all the way to western Wyoming.

It was a brilliantly clear day in late September and the horizons ahead were clothed in white, and there was a month of fishing left up in Idaho where a grand old friend just might have a plate of freshly caught brook trout on ice in the little house that he lived in on the Sun Valley property, at the foot of Dollar Mountain, but a spit and a jump from Trail Creek. We turned northwest!

Late the next day we drove into Ketchum, found it looking the same except for the sea of Navy blue—operating personnel at the Sun Valley setup, most of them living in town, and the "patients" with nothing to do but wish they were home—so we knew it was useless to even ask for lodging. We phoned for a hotel room in Hailey, then from Lew Hill at the Alpine we learned that Taylor was over in Stanley Basin, would be back tomorrow, and then Lew told us a sad story. The colonel's eldest son, Taylor III, was killed in the last major European offensive—the Ardennes. His father was in the dark about it for some time, eventually learned that as a prisoner of war, Tay was machine-gunned to death with a host of others in a mass prison break. Tay's widow and their little girl, born in her father's absence, were up from California, seeking a little mutual solace with Grandpa Williams. Hearing it in advance was bad enough, but it would ease things somewhat when we saw him.

I knew Tay quite well, from the summer he'd worked at Sun Valley, and when he and his younger brother, Bob, were called to their father's bedside in '38. This was a second tragedy in widower Taylor's life; there was a daughter Betty between the boys, and though separated so much from his children, well, we knew their strong ties. We still entertained an idea of looking around a few days and then driving down to California, or doing some corresponding in that direction. When we met Taylor the following afternoon, I think we practically abandoned the idea.

The boss was away, had his secretary with him, so she obliged us with her town quarters until their return in a couple of weeks. The young widow, Bert, by shortened name, and a talented girl well employed in California, left in a few days after

"... this boy was a better 'buck' than me any day!"

our arrival and Taylor suddenly loomed to us as a lost soul—in truth, he was. His exterior generally hid the inner man, so for a week or more the three of us went fishing every day, ate fish until we grew fins, prowled about the country, and, best of all, went to see an old native who'd given us a price on some building property in town, back in 1940. I hadn't the foggiest notion but that the price would now be exorbitant, in view of the usually expected postwar boom that was freely talked about, even then. The seller kept his promise and we tied it up with a short-term option. When the Old Man returned and told me that I could go to work at trying to gather the scattered files and other things of our operation while the Navy was commencing in its slow, ponderous way to move out, we finished the property deal and told the colonel that we'd put down a root of our own, at last.

"Come on," he said. "We'll go to my shanty and water it!"

Within days we learned of a career Navy man retiring and we knew his landlady in town, got the house on the spot—a four-room, primitive affair, equipped as in 1910, but livable and a home after the former hotel life and the transient period. By then we had quite a bit of the gen on Papa Hemingway, then in Cuba, his marriage broken up. That pained us, remembering the great times with Marty, whom we still speak of as a "hell of a gal," the kind you never forget. However, we felt that we understood how it was, and perhaps even how it might have been, from our knowledge of both of them, from the beginning. Only a hint, please: Too much alike. Though it was only a joking remark at the time, we thought it ironical when we heard of the breakup:

". . . I look like I'm pointing to the dark future."

Taylor was in touch with Toby Bruce all along, and with Papa before we arrived. There was no divorce as yet, but we were told there was a very attractive lady who had firm claim to Papa's heart. Oddly, all of this had escaped us until back in Idaho. We didn't write, and by the time we were settled and had found all stored stuff (hidden so well we almost forgot where) Papa answered my cable in a long letter to Arnold, Williams, Ltd., Ketchum, Idaho. A most important word in it was that there were Idaho plans for the fall of '46.

I barely got started at the near-impossible ahead of me when both Taylor and I were called by the boss for quite a surprise: Coop and Rocky wanted to come up for a little hunting, six in their party; a short stay, Coop said, about ten days—was it possible? The boss arranged by phone with Mr. Harriman for them to stay in his private cottage on the grounds—out of the Navy's control. The others in the party were Rocky's uncle, Elliott Gibbons, and his wife Irene, costume designer of note for MGM, whom we knew slightly; and late of the U.S.A.A.F., Major Clark Gable, and a lady friend. Taylor said:

"Hell, Mr. Rogers, Coop don't need a guide, what are we supposed to do?"

The Old Man laughed, said, "Well, you're his friends, aren't you, and he's a friend of ours so knock off what you're doing and be set for them . . . Gable's a guy we'd like to have as a regular." He told me to use my judgment in how I would handle subtle publicity—in view of the place not reopening for perhaps another year. Simple, I said, just use a Ketchum dateline—Coop *had* to get back whether Sun Valley was open, or not. The party arrived in a few days.

The pheasant shooting—no pressure during the war—was, to put it mildly, out of this world. Clark Gable was indeed a fellow we'd do well to have on our list—a fine, easygoing, ready-to-bird-dog in the field, share anything, sort of guy. A born clown, too. They had a local lady for a cook, Taylor and I had a small deer hanging in the old woodshed back of our little house, and our sizable kitchen with its old wood-burning cookstove and exposed hot-water tank must have been quite a contrast to that bunch—but you'd never get it with the good stuff on Tillie's table. Clark fell in a ditch full of icy water one day, soaked to his waist, and came up cussing and laughing—just like in the movies—but for real in environs where you do things for real. Here was a guy who'd hitch right off with a guy we wished was around to join us; we talked a lot about that fellow whom Coop had in mind when he got Clark to come up and taste the country himself. He handled a shotgun like he handled a movie role, was a good rifle shot, proved it by a long shot on a coyote that was feint-stalked by Coop, on foot, and it worked. We were convinced of him coming back when the party left.

Our next visitor was Bumby Hemingway, out of the Service after a harrowing time as a prisoner of war, a wound—behind him an impressionable tour with the O.S.S. He was out to pick up his old car left in Sun Valley care, and to check on the curriculum at the University of Montana—a long day's drive—at Missoula. Bumby

Center: Gloria Batis, Basque epicurean without peer, and owner/operator of the Rio
Club in Ketchum—a Hemingway favorite at all times.

stayed with us, we talked ourselves hoarse, and so got the gen pretty much firsthand
on so many things, including an indirect introduction to former correspondent Mary
Welsh, whom Papa met in London when she was on the staff of *Time* magazine.
Shortly after Bumby left for Cuba in early December we got word of the Hemingway-Gellhorn divorce. A Christmas greeting from Papa said that there would be
a wedding before long—but no set date.

In mid-February of '46 the boss left on a business trip and put a sizable order
in my lap. The Coopers wanted to come up for some skiing, Clark Gable to come
with them, and Dr. and Mrs. Peter Lindstrom—"Mrs." being Ingrid Bergman. At
the time every facility, hotel, and what-have-you in Sun Valley was a shambles of
the Navy move-out coupled with repair crews trying to put the place back in shape;
no materials to do it with, the Harriman cottage being renovated, and I was to do
what I could for them in Ketchum accommodations. Such was much like finding a
pheasant with teeth and I was busy making ski action pictures with a few returned

March, 1946. Bumby Hemingway; film stars Ingrid Bergman, Gary Cooper, and Clark Gable. The picture responsible for a long-standing false impression (*see text*).

employees—climbing on skins because the captain in charge would not permit use of the ski lifts. I told Rocky the problems when she called, but they insisted on coming, so I went to work, managed to find lodging with an old friend and owner of a complex on the main drag called Brandt's cabins, lined up a cook, and told the Hollywoodites to come ahead, and play it by ear. What they found awaiting them wasn't much, but they were delighted, and had to use skins to climb Dollar Mountain for a few days until the old captain was "charmed" into allowing use of the lift on Ruud Mountain—the jumping and slalom hill—provided we ran it ourselves. That was easy enough and everybody was happy.

Then in early March Bumby Hemingway came down from school in Missoula, stayed with us, and we rustled about and got him fitted out for some skiing. I made pictures and put out a news release, handling it like on the fall hunting. One picture was a lineup with Bumby, Ingrid Bergman, Coop, and Clark Gable. It produced news-clipping returns by the sackfuls and a lasting public impression. For years we were asked about Ernest Hemingway being a consistent skiing pal of the people in that picture—and the "dark future" picture that appeared in *Harper's Bazaar* in January, 1941, facing a winter spread, was also a public convincer that he was a ski fan. It lasted until the latter years, when I said to Papa:

"Goddamn it, dig out that old pair of boots of Bumby's, put them on to come and stand on my skis and lean on a pair of poles; I'll make a negative and we'll hang a print of it in every hotel room in the place."

He howled, said: "Sure, and I'll write the caption for it, maybe that will straighten them out for all time, huh?"

I'm sure that it would have—for in truth Papa never so much as had on a pair of ski boots in Idaho, and when he was in a small audience to my Friedl Pfeifer *Ski Skill* film back in 1939 he enjoyed the picture very much, but tapped his knee and said that skiing was not for him any more, the legs were no good for it at an ancient forty years of age! In that little group in our room was the great Hannes Schneider himself—the father of modern skiing, then established as the Arlberg School. Friedl was a protégé of the grand old man and he and Ernie had a great time talking of Alpine skiing—Ernie's *sprachen Deutsche* always leaving something to be desired.

During Bumby's March stay with us, Mary Welsh became Mrs. Ernest Hemingway, there were telegrams exchanged, and some laughs at a news picture of the couple, of which Bumby said that he'd never seen his father so nicely gussied up as he was in his dark, pin-striped double-breasted wedding suit. We hadn't either, and no one enjoyed our comments about it more than Papa. We let him know who was with us one night—by telegram—when the Coopers and Clark were at our little house for dinner. His reply was a joint one to all of us, and I wish that I had it now, or had made a copy of it. Clark said that here was a guy *he* wanted to know very much and intended a fall hunting date.

In April my parents came to live with us, Mother in fine health, my old dad thin and wan, but bright as a parrot, with a lift in spirits that at last he was in the West. A realist, my father, no secrets about anything. In early July the last of the Navy personnel departed and Sun Valley was still a mess, everyone hoping that it would be in condition for the December reopening. A pessimist would have said it couldn't be done.

By late July I was receiving boxes of gear shipped from Key West while I still searched for suitable living quarters in town. In his letters and a phone call, Papa stressed economy, said he'd had an expensive time of it getting organizoots again at the Finca, and felt there was no better place to start off the new era with his family all together than the Idaho hunting and the simple life. He said "Miss Mary" was a fair cook, so find something with a good kitchen in it, and as much privacy as possible; use my own judgment, get it for three months starting on September 1—"We're going to make it for the dove shooting, at last!"

With the Navy gone, it was still crowded in town because of returning Sun Valley people, many who would live there, but not yet. Just across Trail Creek, outside of town, was the best setup I knew of: MacDonald's log cabins in a long row set back from the highway. Mac was redoing his modest comfortable owner's quarters for long-term rental purposes, so I was lucky in timing, got it tied up in mid-August when Bumby Hemingway and the younger boys arrived to "make out" with Taylor in his little bailiwick—with sleeping bags—and get with the fishing. What a time those two weeks were!

Patrick and Gregory—now borderline age—seemed to us as having grown past their "Mouse" and "Gigi" names, and the three of them climbed into Bumby's old car, then hiked up into the White Cloud Peaks lake country and brought back a stock of fish for the family icebox. A good thing they did—the absence gave the colonel time, with Tillie's help, to air out his "boar's nest" and start over again! A good thing, too, that our kitchen was a big one, with a big table and plenty of chairs —such as they were. As August drew to a close, Mac handed me the keys and the boys got moved into their quarters down the row from headquarters-to-be, and all stored and new gear was put in place for the arrival. Then the phone call from their father—in Casper, Wyoming—and I'll never forget it.

It was the dusk of evening; I was at home alone, resting on the porch from mowing the grass. In greeting me again like there hadn't been one in years, the tone of his voice told me there was something wrong—seriously wrong.

"Pappy, we're delayed over here in Casper, and in trouble . . . Mary's in the hospital following emergency surgery . . . almost lost her and she's not out of the woods yet, but we think that she'll make it. . . ."

He did not tell me what it was, and I didn't ask; said he couldn't know how long the delay would be, and to speak to the boys about it in a way to not spoil their fun if I could. How was I fixed for money in case they ran out? I said in effect: don't worry about that for an instant. He would call or write every day, gave me his number and the time to call if I felt it necessary. On August 31 he called me about nine in the evening, with the dope this time; and with a background for basis, I had a hunch of what it was.

"Pappy," he said, very straight and level, "there was an addition to our family on the way, early on the way, lost it in bad luck . . . and now there can never be any more . . . so I guess you know what I mean. . . ."

I could have cried, recalling the time when my mother's life hung in the balance with exactly the same thing, and our anguished father—parents who desired, and fervently wished to give their eager young boys a little sister. My second of silence was like an eternity itself, but I managed something, for Papa Hemingway knew, so further talk on it was not for the moment. He switched the subject by telling me that I could again beat him over the back for missing a dove season, for he was sure of a couple of weeks there—so how were we fixed for shotgun ammo? I had answered that one as "fine" in previous contacts, so he said:

"Sure, the colonel's foresight back at close-up time, so shoot good, everybody, and kiss Tillie for me."

"Do it yourself, Papa, if over the phone will do for now," I said, and put her on —the best medicine I knew for the moment. When I finished with him, his voice had the familiar tone again, then, typically:

"Say, kid, suppose it was me . . . maybe I'm getting old?"

"You?" I said. "That'll be the day. . . ."

"That's what I like to hear." He laughed. "Thanks ever so much."

Forgive the mileage that I'm adding to a well-worn subject: the lifelong Ernest Hemingway desire for a daughter of his own; one that we'd heard expressed many times, even then; so I can't help classing the time as a low point for him; and instinct born of the things we'd heard of Mary whom we felt we already knew—said that she shared it with him.

By September 11 she was able to travel, and on the twelfth I got a telegram from Cody, Wyoming, on the favored old route west:

"PLANNING TO ARRIVE FRIDAY EVENING LOVE TO ALL PAPA."

6.

The '46 Fall...

1

How often we've laughed with Mary in recalling her introduction to the complex upper Wood River community, part of it old as the hills and known everywhere as Sun Valley, Idaho. The faithful old Lincoln got them here a bit after five o'clock, they checked in at the cabins, okayed them, then by what Papa called our private connection road (actually the original wagon road into Ketchum, from near the kitchen door of Mac's, across the creek on a rickety log rail bridge and past our little house), he followed me and drove right up to our front porch. Like she was a doll, he picked Mary up in his arms and took her into our kitchen where a well-cushioned, old-fashioned rocking chair awaited her—on the far side of the room opposite the old cookstove that I had fired up good to heat the oven for a heaping platter of mourning doves for the welcoming meal. Mary's obvious embarrassment at meeting strangers this way was so short-lived as to be almost nonexistent. Papa as good as knew my parents, addressed them as Mom and Bill, and he felt as much at home as the boys. An immediate remark that he had made was an apology for their arrival falling on Friday the thirteenth! But he looked at the platter of birds, the heaping dishpan of the little fruit that the boys and I had picked on "damson plum lane" while dove hunting, and he said:

"But, by the looks of things it might be good luck now, Mom's going to make jams and jellies . . . the best there is with good wild red meat."

I fixed him with a whimsical look. His eyes twinkled.

"Come on, let old Papa in on it."

"Double the thirteenth," I said. "On the twenty-sixth I've got a date with a Pah-simeroi antelope . . . then we'll divide him by two. No arguments, you hear?"

There were no arguments, instead a tribute, well put, in an adaptation of his own, to my parents:

"I'll bet, that as we always have, we'll eat a little higher than high on the hog."

"Give me a week," Mary said, "and I'll be on my feet to cook it."

In the foreground, Dr. John and Mary Ellen Moritz. Doc never minded "Sawbones" as a handle. He's patched more ski bones than Carter's made pills—including one on a matchless hunting dog!

One look at her, hearing the firm will in her voice, anyone could believe it. Since Mary was from the great state to the north of our native Iowa, one that we knew so well from its great fishing, I called her the "tough Minnesota Indian"—but the first I ever saw with a boyish blonde haircut and bright blue eyes.

The best of medical care and know-how was available to speed Mary's rapid recovery. Back in 1939, by his own resourcefulness, a prince of a man from Nebraska sold company brass on the need of a hospital at Sun Valley; they gave him a third-floor wing in the Lodge, and he put it into operation in December of that year. Dr. John Moritz, back from war duty with the Navy, was a respected friend of Papa Hemingway and everybody else in our community. So, it wasn't long until the simple life was settled in for the fall. In some ways it was destined to not be so simple.

On the twenty-sixth I got my antelope buck—a fat young meat animal—in two shots of the absolute worst and the luckiest best of any shooting I've ever done. I slid off my horse and missed him clean at a long hundred yards, on a ridge that he calmly walked off of before I could bolt another cartridge into the chamber. Pretty smelly with a four-power 'scope! In a near duplicate of the '41 performance I've described earlier, I ran but went prone because of the distance to make my steady-rest shot, panting like a lizard. My bullet literally cut his throat at 326 carefully paced steps. With me was a young Sun Valley staffer just back from the war named Jimmy Saviers—who became a postwar fishing guide with his older brother, George, also just out of the Navy and then in medical school. Jimmy was my confirmation that night when we got home and I told Papa Hemingway of my crazy shooting. I got his typical response.

"Well, I put the good sign on, didn't I? . . . and that was great shooting, kid, for true . . . but the colonel and me got you beat yet . . . we both made ours with borrowed rifles!"

"Rub it in, Papa, you so-and-so," I said as we hung up the split-down-the-back

The Hemingway "fall pantry" in the airy old barn at MacDonald's Cabins in Ketchum.
Note the "butcher goods" hanging in the background, remains of a buck antelope and a
smaller deer—"soup stock."

buck in a big rickety airy old barn in back of Mac's cabins, which, he said, we were welcome to use for hanging game for aging, and ducks and upland birds heads up for the curing that tenderizes and enhances the flavor—the European method and old-school in our own country when primitive facilities demanded. The nights were frosty sharp by then, the old barn held the temperature well during the warm days—a perfect setup but thirty feet from the kitchen door. In the first days of deer season I slipped out one morning and got a small spike buck while Taylor took Patrick Hemingway up into an old area of his and the boy got a handsome well-antlered buck in perfect meat condition. He used his father's old Springfield that he practically slept with for days beforehand; and, indeed, Papa was proud that on his first try at big game, Patrick was the meat-getter; and that his good friend with the know-how showed him just where to place his bullet for a one-shot kill.

So, as said, economy was stressed, and both establishments were off to good starts at living off the country. Austerity was a necessity with us, too, for we were pouring every cent we had into the building of a home—a trying task, shortage of materials, in the nation's reversion to a peacetime economy. I was lucky to get a mere shell up by then, with a roof over it, base-sealed only for winter when my much-in-demand workers had to quit me. Papa went up with me one day to look it over—perched on the hillside of an undeveloped part of town that was yet only a village townsite in community ratings—one of the finest locations, the house arranged for an "enormous view" out over town toward the big mountain to the southwest. That was great, in his view through the big window opening, but his warming repeat of an earlier remark is a significant one, in my view.

Deeply respectful of our strong filial ties, he said:

"Doing what you are for your folks is not covered by a couple of well-worn ones like loyalty and duty . . . you're going about it as a privilege, and that is something that is to be envied . . . it's so rare in families. . . ."

"That's a great compliment, Papa," I said. "But then, too, we're the sort that like a table of our own to put our feet under, remember?"

"Yeah, I know, but what I said still holds good in my book . . . you'll always feel good about it, I can tell you that."

During the dove season, and later in the month, a situation developed that permanently altered relations already tainted. The railroad's colorful President Jeffers had retired early in the year and now there was one of an entirely different sort at the throttle. A small, officious man, he was a Jekyll and Hyde type who could make things quite rough when in the latter garb. He fancied himself a hunter, which he was not, nor was he physically up to it, most of the times that we saw him. With none of his guides back yet, Taylor took the new president and his companion down and introduced them to the dove country, all that he was asked to do. Then in a couple of days the game warden called on him with bona-fide reports from ranchers in Silver Creek basin that the railroad's president, of all people, was seen riding the fenders of his car, shooting doves on the go—a flagrant disregard for the law which could throw the book at him for such. The warden was a friend of Taylor and to Sun Valley, the relations record a flawless one, much of it to the colonel's credit. It was up to him to handle it quietly, and he did, but firmly—there would be no more of that. The big boss took it, but naturally resented it, coming from a mere employee, a company subsidiary employee, at that. As said, the colonel was brusque as a rule, but he was a gent this time, no harm done, supposedly. Then, later, the president stopped by for a go at the sage hen shooting and Taylor guided his party. That time they locked horns, but good, so the man's intent was quite obvious. Caught in the middle, Mr. Rogers had a time of it; he was loyal to Taylor, always, and absorbed their attitude at the time when Averell Harriman and Mr. Jeffers heartily agreed upon the colonel as Chief Guide. He stood as solidly as he could in defense of Taylor who otherwise would have been sent packing, on the spot. As it was, he was demoted to "one of the guides" and the title of Chief Guide became a thing of the past. In truth, the boss had his own neck out a bit for not reducing him to some menial job.

This was borne out when in October the president stopped off on business and suddenly decided that he wanted to shoot some ducks on the way back to his private car in Shoshone. The boss called me in late forenoon when Papa Hemingway had stopped by the shop and we planned to take in the evening shooting at the big marsh—our first postwar duck shoot. For some reason I never knew, the president was always very nice to Tillie and me; we knew him well when he served under Mr. Jeffers, who definitely was a friend. So I didn't mind taking him hunting for an hour, but had to get help for his party of three. Stew Stewart was back as the new Sun Valley postmaster, so I went straight to him, Papa walking to his car with me. Who should we bump into but the president being shown the overhauling progress by Mr. Rogers. The men were introduced, chatted a moment, and the president told me he hadn't even brought a gun, could I fix him up with one, and some boots? Sure, and we went our ways, to meet at three o'clock. Then barely heard by us, Mr. Rogers was asked:

"Well, is that great white hunter still around?"

Well! That went over about like a lead balloon, bristling with needles—for how else could it be taken? Little—unprintable, of course—was said about it at that moment. Stew said he'd be glad to help me, and I took along a former sports desk employee under Bob Miles, who returned to Hollywood after the war—this chap becoming Director of Outdoor Activities in Bob's place, more or less as the result of helping me see to it that ducks went to the cook of the private car that night. I half carried my "client" halfway across runny-nose flat, he quit there and I planted his party in some nearby willows. His was the only gun and he didn't fire a shot with it, though we sent numbers of ducks his way.

All told, it was no less than a ridiculous, uncalled-for state of affairs; embarrassing to all, damaging to the colonel's pride and prestige. Papa Hemingway openly said that really it shouldn't be any of his business, but even so, by God, it was, be-

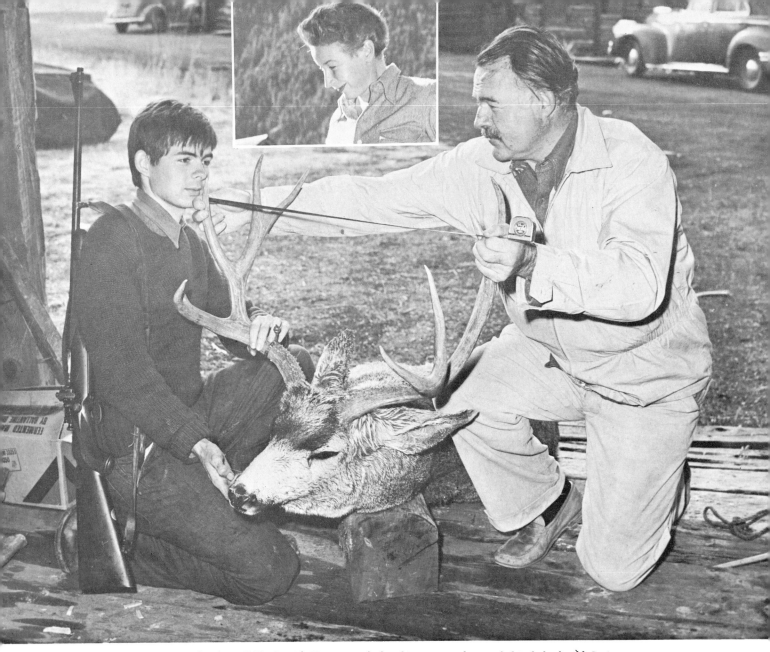

October, 1946. Patrick Hemingway's first big game, taken with his father's old Springfield. *Insert:* "Miss Mary"—the Hemingway bride of the previous March. '46 was not a "picture" fall.

cause Taylor was his friend and it was unfair to a damn good man. Up went a wall that remained, permanently, and what in hell could any of us do about it? Nothing. For instance: when Patrick got his fine deer I made a good picture of him and his father measuring the antlers in the door of the old barn at the cabins. Naturally it was a first-of-its-kind and I asked Papa's approval to put out a news release. He said:

"Sure, kid, but use a Ketchum dateline on your caption . . . this is where I live when in Idaho."

I did so, on a straight informative caption for half a dozen of the prints and sent them to the Hannagan New York office—no objection to that. The clippings returns were average, the dateline was Sun Valley and the bulk of the caption headings read: "For Whom The Bucks Fall." Neither did that go over so good, but there was a later thing to take the sting off tampering with the great title. Several old Sun Valleyite friends of mine sent me congratulatory notes on my clever caption writing!

2

The next upset of the fall was not long in coming. Down in Hollywood, producer Mark Hellinger took the great Hemingway short story—"The Killers"—and with vivid imagination in scripting, rounded it out as a first-rate full-length movie—the one that put Burt Lancaster in the big time, a boost for Ava Gardner, too. Mark himself brought a print of it up to Ketchum for a little "premiere" for the author. At the time our movie "Opera House" was in a state of overhaul, one projector only was operable, the rear-screen speakers removed for replacement. Mark had to return the print quickly so I got our electrician and we rigged up a makeshift—a public-address horn hung on the projection wall behind our small audience of perhaps a dozen of us. The sound was not so bad, but the effect was awful, aided by projection interruptions for reel change—for the man who notoriously did not like Hollywood versions of his work. This one he lauded, asked for a re-run of one particular reel. Too, he liked Mark Hellinger—a nice, charming man as I remember him, seeing him but little. Papa joked that he liked the picture so much that he was tempted to redo "The Killers" in full-length form himself. But it was not a joke that he and Mark had a long-term deal on the fire for other Hemingway stories, and judging from that one, it's a logical assumption that they would have been different in quality—story faithfulness, that is—than an eventual production or two, like, say, *The Snows of Zanuck*, or another scornful one perhaps less known, "The Short Happy Life of Francis Macomber."

Their deal was wrapped up after the showing, then Mark was around for several days, staying at a new combination motel-restaurant gambling-casino place at the outskirts of town called the Thunderbird. It's rather ironical that a notable member of the prewar shooting tribe had a sizable interest in the TB where Mark went on at least part of his gay and expensive spree—which is not to say that it was the only joint in town where the operators ignored the age-old principal that says you must not kill a goose that lays golden eggs. Whichever, and whoever, Mark Hellinger was fleeced, and set himself up for it, but good. Papa Hemingway tried his best to avert it—I know, for I was an observer on occasions when he would not touch a drop with Mark. All men run their course in such, and finally Mark returned to California. In ten days we got the news of his sudden death from a heart attack!

For a day or so, Papa said little about it, an interim when your own dials read: Let him do it. He did, a flood of it, coming up from the creek one night in a cold rain. He flatly said that he feared something like this, could not understand why Mark had to go off the deep end. But, in his "glory hole" (his pocket, a desk drawer, or maybe a cardboard box, for safekeeping) was Mark's check to him—a sizable one of five figures that anyone would have deposited before the ink was dry. But not he; so maybe he had his reason in that case. Whatever, he returned the check to Mark's widow. In return for his decency and fair play, we happen to know he never received an acknowledgment.

What we heard about the whole thing, in sum, was this: That had the deal with Hellinger been carried out as planned, over the long pull it meant "so much dough that I'm almost afraid to think about it." On the sideliners, like ourselves, worried about another angle of the long pull, and I, like the colonel, came right out with it in blunt terms. Papa was thinking the same thing.

"It's a bad thing, taking a guy like that. But damn it, after a war there are always changes, elements that move in and give places like this a black eye. Let's hope it doesn't spread like a disease and spoil it."

Thus, the total setbacks naturally created a considerable air of gloom. Mary could do little more toward hunting than occasionally go along for the ride. But the shooting was great, the little bright spots along the way heightened the morale—take it in stride, so to speak. We recall one night of taking it so—surprisingly. It was a short walk from the cabins to the Thunderbird; Papa knew that excellent food was served there—naturally, a come-on—so he asked Tillie and me for dinner with Mary and him. We had a fine meal, plenty of good wine, a little time on the rou-

Duck hunting along Big Wood River in November, 1946: Rocky and Gary Cooper, Gloria McLean, and Taylor Williams. Gloria is now Mrs. Jimmy Stewart, of Hollywood.

lette wheel, and Papa tried his hand with the dice, the latter a deliberate move on his part. Nothing happened. It was a pitch-black night outside, and I guess old Mother Earth was passing through a comet's tail, or some sort of cosmic fallout: the sky was a mass of flaming meteors. Remember the superstition that when you see a falling star, speak a wish for good fortune and it's visited upon you? The idea grew on our walk to the highway and the turn-in to the cabins. A fiery streak would slice the sky to the horizon, followed by Papa's finger and loud voice:

"Money, money, money, money, money!"—which quickly became a quartet, or a foursome of idiots. We were hoarse when we went inside for a nightcap, of all things. With it, Papa turned his pockets wrong side out.

"All that horse . . . out there didn't net us one damn thing, did it?"

The Coopers came up late that fall, made their own arrangements for the Harriman cottage at Sun Valley. Clark Gable sent his regrets with them—a picture schedule his reason—and we never saw him again. Pheasant season was finished by then, so it was ducks only with the Coopers and their friends—Ned and Gloria McLean (Gloria later became Mrs. Jimmy Stewart, of Hollywood). Their November stay was a short one, and Coop and Rocky had hopes of returning for the holidays.

So the hunting tribe was a small one, its pace slowed down as the fall advanced to December because of miserable weather that not even a duck enjoyed.

The postwar reopening was also Sun Valley's tenth anniversary, for which quite an event was being prepared—on Saturday, December 21—the bookings showing a very busy season throughout. The younger boys left for home in midmonth, and Bumby Hemingway lined himself up for a Lodge front desk job for the winter. Then because their quarters were available until January 1, Papa suddenly decided it would be great to spend a Christmas in Idaho, see the country all in white,

". . . see the country all in white, for a change from the semi-tropics. . . ."

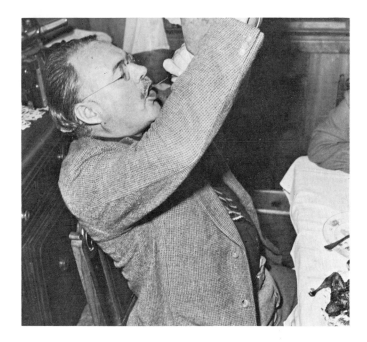

November, 1946. "Inhaling the red" from a bota in the dinery of a wonderful Basque cook—who knew how to cook Idaho birds, too.

for a change from the semitropics. His decision came as a surprise to us, for actually the euphoria wasn't very high during that draggy time. It did not drag for us, it was pell-mell preparation time, and almost by demand, we moved back to our former quarters at Sun Valley, and arranged an easy setup in town for my parents. For half the month we hardly saw Mary and Papa.

The Coopers made it for the resort's opening event, along with a small contingency of other Hollywood winter faithfuls, and a host of old-timers. The elite of the parties was held in the Lodge dining room, a big anniversary cake to be cut and served by the railroad's president. The Hemingways' invitation to attend was personally delivered by Mr. Rogers who was openly embarrassed by it. So was Papa, who hedged on it, and I was asked to see what I could do.

Who, me? How could I when I got an owlish grin and: "White hunter friends don't go much for pastry." So the lead picture of the event that was well publicized was an elegantly shy Gary Cooper, by himself, the recipient of the first cut of the cake.

A lanky Montanan proves he can inhale it with a cigarette in his mouth—and a bib over his shirt!

Or maybe it was ladies' night, instead. Elliott Gibbons, Irene's husband, at left.

Looks as if "ladies night" is about over. *Center,* Rocky Cooper's mother.

So, busy as bird dogs, we nonetheless got away for an hour or so on Christmas morning to go down to the cabins for a bit of cheer, and to exchange the simplest mere tokens of gifts, just in keeping with the spirit of Christmas. Coop and Rocky went along, and the "Chamber of Commerce" was embarrassed because that all-in-white business had not materialized; the lower slopes were passably skiable but on the valley floor snow had to be hauled for Santa's dog team to pull into the Inn village square for the Christmas Eve program. Christmas Day, though, held the threat of storm, warm overcast, a few flakes drifting tantalizingly outside, the mountain horizons lost in the pall. We had a fine time, nonetheless, lots of laughs over the trinket-exchanges, and with a little good cheer from his glass, Coop just had to kid ski-bug Rocky, so he came forth with a dischordant stanza or two that started off with "I'm dreaming of a white Christmas, just like one we wish we had. . . ." Loving to kid Coop, always, it was the moment that Papa had been waiting for—and let me say that Mr. Cooper, in right occasions, was quite a master at it himself, as the following little tale should confirm—one he did not know had been passed on within the year past.

When Clark Gable fell in the irrigation ditch he was blue with the cold as I drove the old station wagon we had that day for all it was worth to town and the J. C. Penney store. He sailed in, joked the few goggle-eyed salesgirls who were accustomed to the familiar Coop, but not this clowning character who said he'd wet his pants and was some very wet money good for some long johns and pants—just any kind of pants, so they were good and warm? It was, but the small town store's one dressing room was occupied; so what, the car would do for a place to change as we headed north for home. But a mile-long U.P. freight train beat us to the main-drag crossing, so as it snailed along we waited on the cross-street; Clark shiveringly pulled off his soaked boots—and everything else from the waist down. The heater in the beat-up prewar fleet car acted up, put forth about a match flame of warmth, so Mr. Gable was in quite a hurry—in the back with Taylor, Coop up front with me. I felt Mr. Cooper's elbow in my ribs and followed his winking eye with mine to see

But a good-night always ended with a modest nightcap and some serious talk—most
likely about the war just over.

a neat young woman—obviously a schoolmarm—tripping fast our way, and thoroughly familiar with whom she now knew she would finally get an autograph. Coop obligingly wound his window down as she said, "You can't get away now, Mr. Cooper," never taking her eyes from him. At that precise moment, a pair of scratchy, heavy iron-grey long johns were at half-mast up those hairy Gable calves, and Mr. Cooper said:

"Sure, lady, but first there's a fella in back, kinda busy, but he drops everything t'scribble an autograph . . . here, I'll open the door, the window's stuck. . . ."

And he did, and Mr. Gable dropped everything to grab the door, Mr. Williams leaning back out of his way, and his other hand was pretty busy, too! For about three seconds it was quite a show; the young gal gasped, gulped, stared, turned three shades of red:

"Oh! . . . it's, it's. . . . *Clark Gable!*" Her hand flew to her open mouth and she thereupon took hasty leave, most likely hearing but the first half of: "Yeah, my dear, it is, and come back when I get my pants on and watch me cut the throat of a long-legged son of a bitch from Montana. . . . Say, cowboy . . . she's a pretty cute kid at that!"

A favorite picture from the postwar era —a Hemingway party at Trail Creek Cabin. By window, Karl Geppert, original maître d' of the Continental, Sun Valley's Challenger Inn.

We laughed for twenty miles, then pulling a long grade near the lava beds our tired engine threatened loudly to throw a rod. While I hitched a ride to Bellevue to call for a tow-in, Coop spotted a coyote that Clark nailed for a fine pelt.

The tale we had told Papa, who liked what he heard about Clark Gable. So at the precise moment of quiet he said that Christmas morning:

"Say, Mr. Cooper . . . I hear ya bin shillin' fer The King."

"Huh?" Coop said, bluest of blue eyes widening in surprise.

"Hear ya bin shillin' fer The King . . . come clean, got a witness."

Tall man caught up with it, grinned bashfully.

"Yeah, and when I shill, I shill good."

"The champion shiller . . . did you ever get cornered with your pants off in town, and shoot a fine coyote, all in less than an hour?"

"Well, they don't call ol' Podner The King fer nothin' ya know."

The departure for Cuba was the day after Christmas, with a stopover in Salt Lake City to visit old friend Charlie Sweeney who'd been up for a visit in the fall. Had there not been considerable gear stored in our lockable attic in our shell of a house, it would have been an easy matter to think we might not see Mary and Papa the coming fall. Several times he'd said he'd have to get into production on something pretty quick; he was, "runnin' out a credit a little too fast." But Mary was in fine shape then, had been for a long time, and when we saw them off that morning they both said:

"It will be great if we can make it by September 1."

Nor were any instructions left about keeping a finger on a repeat setup at Mac's cabins.

The crack of this picture: "If George Brown ever sees this shot, he'll beat me down to
size—for free!" (Hemingway, 230 pounds.)

7.

'47 --- the Good Postwar Fall . . .

1

During the '47 winter, Taylor Williams bubbled with enthusiasm for his spring trip to fish the Florida Keys. The correspondence flowed between him and Cuba, for Papa Hemingway had made quite a to-do about him coming over for a good go with him in the Gulf Stream—on the *Pilar*. Taylor always made most of his fly rods and now he was knee-deep in heavy saltwater rods—beautifully done, too. In late winter I photographed them, made letter-size prints, then typed a long letter for him, advising his host that on April 1 he'd be on his way, with his shotgun, too, for the fantastic Cuban dove shooting. Papa's replies to him made you ask yourself which was the bigger kid of the two, and wish that it were so you could be included in the deal.

His reply was back to that one when fate, as if she had been soft with him, dealt the colonel another blow. He was at our door one morning before we were dressed, so stunned that he couldn't speak, handing us the telegram advising of the sudden death of his daughter, Betty, in Arizona. I don't recall ever seeing a more shaken man. His family was wiped out but for a single grandchild and his one surviving son, Bob, a seafaring man living in Portland, Oregon; a loyal son, indeed, but remote from his father because of his work. Self-reliant from the core out as a rule, Taylor was no good now: I got his emergency rail passes for him, almost packed his bag, to get him on his way. At the bus he asked if I would write Papa and tell him he might be a bit delayed, if he could make it at all—he was not sure of all circumstances and what might evolve.

I cabled a brief message, followed it up with a special-delivery letter. I got a phone call from Papa immediately; his word: do everything humanly possible, calling upon him if need be, to see the colonel on his way south. He said: "He needs it, Pappy, he's had enough grief. Find out what you can and let me know." I promised that, but, the loss hit Taylor more ways than one, and upon his return he was on the fence about going. We talked about it at length, and in the interim I got off a brief cable. A second phone call then, to the colonel, so on April 1, he was on his way. With little demand for fishing guides before late June he returned in time, with the old spring in his step. Had some orders for me, too, which I discharged at once.

It was September 20 when Papa and the boys arrived in a new Buick Roadmaster convertible, the delivery of which held him up a bit (he said he had to retire the old Continental as an "errand" car to and from Havana). Mary was to arrive in a few days by air—for there was some difficulty, or suspicion, on the part of the Cuban government, about excessive arms at the Finca. Papa snorted about it, and a ruse of some sort was figured in getting the favored guns out of the country and Mary brought them with her. Naturally, there was the beat-up old pump gun and the faithful Browning double among the load, but he had a sad story to tell me. He had forgotten to bring the Duke of Alba shotgun the previous fall, for he had not changed his mind about passing it on to me. On a dove shoot he'd loaned it to a guest, and the man's carrier boy stumbled with it, plugging both muzzles with mud —the lad not knowing what could happen. On the next drive of birds the friend cut loose with it—no barrels left! Papa was sick about it, would have sent it to the Spanish makers for new barrels, but his reasons for not doing so are obvious—he wasn't exactly a hero in Spain, following the civil war and the "book." In his own way he gave us both hell, and I joined him as to my refusal in the first place. But the kick was, he brought along the little 6.5 Mannlicher we'd won on the raffle in '41.

"She's done me all the good it can, which was little, so you don't owe me a half bottle . . . we don't know what it accounted for when the cook had it, but it has a shark to its credit now—a big fish-eating shark."

(Though the little rifle has accounted for very little for me, it has an honored place in my rack today.)

First postwar party, given mainly for visiting old friend/correspondent Quentin Reynolds. Reynolds was no stranger to Sun Valley—he had spent his honeymoon here early in 1942.

For two good reasons of his own, Papa and Mary stayed up at Glamour House until October 15, then returned to the MacDonald cabins that I had reserved for them—austerity again stressed. But, the old taut, ebullient Papa was with us again, in sharp contrast to the fall before, and how good it was to see. He was much too heavy, just around 230 pounds, is all—"Aw, look, see how solid, how hard I am, hit it good"—and fighting a touch of pressure, too. He heeded his own and Dr. Moritz' advice: not to even think about going into the higher country for big game. I had neither the time nor money to go for elk, so I hunted mornings for a deer while Taylor guided Mary for a first try at big game with a rifle. She was not the take-it-or-leave-it type, she married a man who lived to hunt in stride. . . . All right, she wanted to be the hunter. The surrounding country at the time was swarming with deer hunters, more of them returned veterans, and what war does not spawn an army of "budding" hunters now familiar with a few things they wouldn't ordinarily have known? Local hunting was like in war!

Then the colonel was called off the local effort in taking actor Ralph Bellamy down on the Salmon River for deer, Papa and I got our heads together and, in touch with Bud Purdy, who earlier had suggested an outlying summer ranch of his not far from the Craters of the Moon country—open, high-rolling wintering area for deer. I had not hunted it, or even knew it from talk, only from logic and instincts. Bud was right about it, but neither he nor we could know how much Mary Hemingway's first head of big game would demand of us before his hang-up as meat in the old barn at Mac's place.

At four o'clock in the morning of Friday, October 17, Mary got breakfast while Papa whipped up lunch sandwiches for us, in his pajamas and robe. We had fifty miles to drive up into the foothills of country we could not hunt by horse because of its openness. Well before sunrise we climbed steadily on shank's mare, Mary's sea-level wind much improved since her arrival at the approximate six-thousand-foot level. Miles later we topped out on a high bare knob of a miniature mountain with no choice but to sit there for a bite of lunch and some needed rest, and to glass a vast sweep of country with my binoculars. Not one to discourage easily, I was then, after our full hour up there, as plainly visible as the Eiffel Tower to mule deer optics—and where in hell could they be? Nowhere, in my view, and often since we've mused at recalling Mary saying, "Pappy, we simply *have* to get me a 'beastie' you know, and I agree it looks hopeless. . . ."

Mary's rifle was Taylor's .257-calibre Winchester Model 70 bolt action—the borrowed rifle of the '41 antelope hunt and later "The Shot" magazine piece. A super-accurate rifle, tuned for such by the colonel's painstaking metal and woodwork, its stock was a man's length, but I thought of Miss Mary's fine shoulders for a small gal, arms of a length that did things, and had seen her handle the rifle at the sighting in. Find the right setup and she'd turn the trick. Pick up the glasses and try for it! It paid off in a little while.

Far down in a wide, exposed canyon, something moved in a small stand of aspens

—about two miles—and it turned out as a fat doe, barren of that year's fawn by her color. She moved out from the midday siesta, looked about, then straight into my glasses. Don't move a muscle, Mary, we'll have to sweat her out, hope that she'll start to browse on that gentle slope above the creek. She did, and there was a glint of movement in the aspen gold—sun glint on a head of polished antlers! The rut was well past and this fellow should be in fine shape—if he'll only move out for a good look at him. We had it made—if we could get off that knob an inch at a time, as cats do in stalking a bird, and over to a dry, twisting gully of countless spring runoffs draining the whole face of our big hill down into that little creek. We accomplished it somehow—time and patience—and started down on as tough a stalk as a hunter could find, and I certainly did not feel like one on that exposed hill. In an hour or so we made it, peeked over a drop-off, screened by brush, to appraise a fine buck at some two hundred yards below us—a forty-five-degree down-angle shot that is toughest of all with a rifled weapon. The buck stood broadside, sniffing the air suspiciously, his attention down the canyon, the does in the aspens. I wanted one of them for meat.

Then both our spirits sank to zero when down the canyon a rifle shot rang out—not too far off, and it sounded to me like the familiar old "thutty-thutty" caliber. A critical moment—the buck jumped a few yards, held it, his radar in full operation; not a second to lose. Mary lined up on him, as best I could tell her, and, yes, she said: "Back me up." I did, but needn't have: her shot stopped him cold, then he moved with the shock and I put him down with the advantage of my 'scope over her aperture sights. We scrambled, fell, down the steepness, then a doe broke out for a clean shot and I got her.

Who the hell wanted it that way? Sorry, Mary, but your bullet was first. She good-naturedly argues with me yet—to my equally good-natured dismay. Never mind, at four in the afternoon her handsomely antlered buck and the fat doe were field-dressed when a man and his wife came footing it up the creek and the woman said that she had taken a shot at an owl in a tree. She carried a battered .30-30 Winchester carbine; I could have beaten her with it!

We flagged the carcasses in a place easy to pack out in the morning by horses that Bud Purdy would have in driving cattle back to his home place at Picabo. But our trek was back up the draw to our car in another canyon. I felt considerable compensation in the fact that there was a tough little blue-eyed Indian in my footsteps up the long climb. We stopped at Picabo, had a lift from Chuck and Floss Atkinson's bottle, and a little talk on the phone to Ketchum. He said:

"Aw, gee, great! . . . Fresh liver for breakfast, pheasants at noon!"

True, so I took off at daylight to get the deer, then go on down to join the hunt on the old Frees farm. Bud met me with horses that he wasn't too sure of about packing; one took the doe just fine, docile as a kitten; the other took the buck all right—until we got out in sunlight where the shadow of those antlers walking along beside him seemed not to his liking. His load was well balanced, and secure, but his jitters were those of a short-haired dog on an anthill. When he uncorked, the action was literally an explosion: he headed for the creek bed, rolled the buck under him when he tried to rub it off on a tree, fell on him, crushed the rib cage flat and split the skull block—halving that fine head of antlers, of which a sharp point gouged a nasty cut on his foreleg. That took the starch out of him. We relieved him, gave him first aid, and packed the buck on Bud's saddle horse—but I was sick about the antlers. It was a head worthy of mounting, and a first for Mary—'nuf said.

I got to the farm but a little ahead of noon, and gave that poor old horse all kinds of hell when I reported the bad luck. The general lifted the tarp, saw the well-cooled perfect meat, and he said:

"Tough luck, sure, but who's got the recipe for cooking horns?"

But black is sometimes white, too: so far as we know today, those antlers, re-aligned perfectly on a panel, still hang in a bedroom of the Finca in Mr. Castro's Cuba.

2

For good reason, old habit and precedence were broken that year in opening the bird season. Rancher Tom Gooding's old wintering place in a heavily farmed area was in other hands then, so he and Papa scouted out the fringe country, and Mr. Frees reported plenty of pheasants on his place—bring the army and come down, the place is yours, said he. By then the hunting pressure was greatly increased in the lower country—about ten guns afield to one in the old days, but the grand old farmer was a loyal one, and never forgot favors. We had much of that area to ourselves. It was as good an opening as any we ever had. Papa took down a car trunk full of fixin's to go with a good old fried chicken dinner that followed the first go-around for birds. His little army was somewhat different that fall, too.

The best hunting pal anyone could ask for, Chris LaFarge, was missed so much by all of us; his lovely wife died during the war, so, as in Hemingwayan, ". . . we lost old Chris." We had two pairs of Coopers—Rocky and Gary, and Major Dick Cooper, ex-officer of the British Army, and his wife from East Africa. Dick was the friend who advised Papa on the original African safari with Charles Thompson of Key West back in the thirties. Out from the *Cincinnati Enquirer*, to write it up in his column and shoot like a champion, was Taylor's friend, Dave Roberts, who was a tribesman from then on—and when Dave wrote it, it was for true. Our regular pheasant pal, Ketchum druggist Bud Hegstrom; old standby Tom Gooding; the colonel, back from success in the Middle Fork; the Winston McCreas from Sun Valley; Clara Spiegel from Chicago, and ourselves and five Hemingway guns made us a small swarm to whom its general did a little showing off—by accident.

It was a gorgeous warm day, so our fine dinner was an in-line helping in the kitchen to any place you found in the yard—the tongue or seat of an old horse-drawn implement, the well curb, or the bumper of a car; high-tailed cats from the barns and chickens competing for your scraps; and against a deep azure sky punctuated with wind-screen poplar gold a hundred feet tall, noisy ravens flapped over

"A feather for your hat, Madame, compliments of Dr. Heminghopper." A great hunting day in the fall of 1947.

for a look as if asking: What in hell's going on at the old Frees place today? Fly over once more, loud mouth, and you'll find out. One did, Wham!

"A feather for your hat, Madame, compliments, Dr. Heminghopper."

Ours was a long fool-around, for the buildup back into the cover for a final afternoon drive, but even so, on such occasions of leisure you never caught Papa Hemingway very far from an arm's length of his gun. There was always the empty hayrack in the farmyard for the daily hauling of feed, and that is generally where you'd find the old Model 12 pump with its breach block open, a shell poised on the elevator of the action for a quick shuck-in. The cover, even close about the buildings, was good and the buildup of birds was evident when a cock pheasant cackle was heard down the long row of poplars, and one of the party picked up his gun and took a swing in that direction—an eager beaver. He got results, but not for himself. Still nibbling at something on his plate, Papa leaned against the hayrack, the butt of the old gun but a foot or two from his shoulder; then the single shot down the tree row—all heads up! Exactly as the raven had done, here came the cock pheasant roaring over the open yard, the trees his screen from the eager beaver. The plate was quickly swapped for his gun: Click, Wham! Without moving from his tracks, the hilariously laughing hayracker reached down and picked up his fine specimen of pheasant!

Hunter robber! City hunter! Arrest him for shootin' game from the man's yard!

"This beauty I think I'll have mounted . . . give him to me for Christmas. Make me a picture with him, Pappy, in case I eat him, instead."

Not long afterward, near the end of pheasant season, we enjoyed a distinction of some note: our second throw-off from property. We were four: Papa, Taylor, Bud Hegstrom, and I—on a chill raw day of drizzling rain. The owner of the farm, a friend and old neighbor of Taylor, had given us permission to hunt it, but his tenant saw fit for no logical reason whatever to kick us off. He was an ex-service man, indirectly and loudly boasted about it, when he said, yes, he'd heard all about certain people who had reputations as tough guys—he could be a little tough himself. Nobody was tough with him until he lit the fire, then fanned it persistently, abusively. All he wanted, naturally, was for the big tough guy to take a crack at him, on his property, but it didn't work, though for a short interim it was frightening. I'd seen that temper once before, but not quite like this—and, certainly, it was justifiable this time. We'd made a big circle of the farm and had not fired a shot, or seen a pheasant. Then revenge came served in a neat package.

Our car was parked about a half mile out by the main road, at the corner of the farm, where just inside its fence were a few cottonwood trees on a little knoll. It was then raining quite hard and a "gang" of cock pheasants had moved under the trees in a tight huddle that we didn't suspect until we surprised them, too—roaring out from almost under our feet. Our four guns got six of them, and every bird fell inside the fence! About a half mile down the side road, the hard-boiled ex-G.I. was just approaching the farm buildings, stopped to look when our barrage let loose;

but from the distance and angle, he'd have a time proving a thing. Then our tough guy took over. Within minutes Bud stopped his car right at the front gate of the farm, a loud-talking Papa dangling six cock pheasants in his hands, banging them against the door, calling the toughie everything that his vast repertoire of obscenities had at tongue tip, plus a few not yet invented. Not before or since have I heard a man take a going-over like that one. He stood in the yard not fifty feet from his gate, frothing at the mouth, a pitchfork over his shoulder. Bud Hegstrom possessed something of a hot-fused temper himself, plus a terrific sense of humor, too. Howling in glee, he cut in with his torment:

"Look at him, wouldja, fingering that pitchfork handle, like whipping out the 'Flight of the Bumblebee' on a flute!"

The echo to that one comes under the unprintable, also.

And the '47 fall produced an absolute first, though I've reported a narrow squeak or two in past years. Old Silver Creek finally won a round on its terms. Old Stutter Man's place in two postwar years was forlorn and deserted, and we felt the twinge of conscience more than a time or two when we'd heard that in the war years someone had missed seeing him around, then discovered him dead in his bed. Then two old bachelor brothers took over the place, rather odd characters, but friendly enough, who had no objection at all to our shooting the ridge for ducks. We saw to it that they had ducks for their table. Then one miserable cold day, Papa and Bumby floated the usual run in a keeled mate to our little *Stutter Bug* canoe that was lost in some way as a Navy casualty of war. At pullout they were short a few birds and decided to explore the winding stretch of the creek below Stutter bridge, about a long half mile of it to the lower highway bridge where the creek flows out of the basin. None of us knew it, of course, only from the highway and the down view from the ridge. To fly fisherman Bumby it looked good for another year; there were ducks, too. Also, it proved deceptive in current and speed. They got within a hundred yards of the highway where, on a sharp bend, the canoe was incapable of bending, and over she went, dumping the works in some ten feet of water. Papa was in hip boots, Bumby in chest-high waders, but no problem due to the narrowness of the stream, on whose amalgam bottom of just about everything to raise hob with guns, lay the Browning over-under and the old Winchester pump —the veteran with the proverbial nine lives of a cat.

On vacation then, using every hour I could, working on our house, I knew nothing of the mishap until the following night around seven. Just putting on my coat to go and eat, then return to finish a small job, I heard a rap on a big end window of the living room. A glance at Papa's face peering in from the dark plainly said: We're in a bit of trouble. I let him in and he told me all about it, cursing himself and things in general—with a laugh in it, too. He said that when he felt his butt hit that water for a complete immersion, he swore that it was the hand of old Stutter's spook he saw pulling the canoe out from under them. It struck my funny bone so

"...make me a picture, Pappy, in case I eat him instead."

that I sat down on a sawhorse and let the laughter rip so hard that I thought my company might stalk out on me. The opposite:

"Yeah, and to think of the times we've run 'er, then pull a stunt like we did. . . ."

"That spring-fed water gets awful cold after some miles on the surface, doesn't it, Papa?"

"Jesus! Make an Eskimo drop his teeth." He laughed and pulled a flask from his pocket, looked around at the mess I had to get ready for our winter occupancy —or bust, figuratively speaking.

"Think you'll make it before you open up at the Valley, or maybe by Christmas, kid?"

"I'd better, Papa. I ran the loafers I've been paying off the job today. Once they get inside where it's warm, you know. . . ."

"Sure, when they let you have it below the belt . . . then you'll get it done, I know you will, here's to it."

Well as he shot his old standbys, and understood their functioning, Papa was simply out of the running on things mechanical. (For example, like he was with cars: one son once joked that he was just about the world's worst driver. I argued that I'd settle him in third place, the colonel had firm claim on numbers one and two!) Now he apologized for coming to me for help in disassembling his guns completely for the cleanup, and since I'd partaken in so little of the duck shooting but had shared the loot, I said, wasn't that too bad? Tillie was already at his place. Dinner was in hatch. So, to keep it safe and not blow the place with fumes of high-test gasoline for washing gun parts, we took to the airy barn with cracks in its walls you could pitch a cat through, and poured a little high-test into ourselves as we worked —for what is colder on bare hands than highly evaporative fuel in near-zero weather? By midnight or thereabouts the guns worked smoothly again, and the hunters were back in business. I had a loyal helper every minute, who said, "Hell with

A good bar—the Club Rio—in rarity, too good!

"... all kissed and made up ... everything's okay now."

that" when I'd suggested he go to bed. It was a split duck season and there was little left of the first half.

Not long afterwards we got a pleasant surprise: Papa announced that their quarters were available into the winter and they would stay over until—perhaps all of January. Mary expressed an urge to try her legs on skis, and had already done a little shopping in that direction. So what in hell are you going to take up, Papa?

"Snow shovelling." He chuckled, patting his impressive paunch. "I might hire out to the city, keep the walks open to the joints in the block ... the Rio Club, I'll do for free." (The Rio was the Stockmen's Saloon of the old days—run by Basques, still, and a favorite, always.)

For the holidays, and well into January, there were gentleman guests up from Cuba: scholarly young Roberto Herraras, and seagoing merchant ship captain Juan "Sinsky" Dunabeitia. Roberto's English was passable anywhere, Sinsky's a language of its own—but who ever heard of Spanish-English language barriers in a

Juan "Sinsky" Dunabeitia (Spanish merchant ship captain); soprano Donna Gidley (my sister-in-law); baritone (pretty good, too) Papa H.; and a Ketchum "club man" whose identity escapes me. I think he was responsible in some way for "Blackdog."

house of Hemingways? Another way of saying: never a dull moment in that interim.

The winter opening that year was December 21, with a healthy booking for the entire season, so in the usual pre-Christmas confusion I tucked in time to get moved into our house—barely livable, but passably comfortable. I finished late the after-

Christmas night in Sun Valley, 1947

noon of the twenty-fourth, and a very pleased Papa Hemingway, sympathetic of my round-the-clock efforts at the last minute, was one of its christeners. He showed up at dusk with a couple of bottles of a choice wine for our Yule table. It was bitterly cold, little snow down so far, and the rascal had walked the few blocks up from the center of town. "Needed the exercise, but I'm damned if it's worth it this night," he said, going directly to our fireplace—and a good laugh. The mason had finished it but a day before and had told me that we could have a bit of cheer from it—just so we didn't try to heat the whole damned house. So my father had the matchstick blaze going that was the laughable disappointment to a fellow expecting to warm his blue-with-cold bare hands. Dad said it was a hell of a welcome when a man calls to say Merry Christmas!

"It sure as hell is, Bill." Papa chuckled. "But good things start small and our Pappy said you'd all be here by now, or else. He's made it and I think he needs a drink —don't we?"

He had that in his pocket, too, and chatted with Mom and Bill while I changed into warm clothes to help the boys cover the Christmas Eve program at the Valley. Music-loving Mary liked to join the big choral group that formed around the Opera House, so when I drove down to get her, Papa rode with me, and he said:

"That bunch will freeze half stiff up there tonight . . . Donna's good soprano will sound like somebody's breaking dishes."

Donna was Tillie's young war-widow sister, a lively, effervescent bundle whom Papa would miss a meal to kid—held her own fairly well, and in the couple of years she worked for us, she conducted the group, and very nicely, too. But Papa was so right for that frigid occasion. Normally, the programs were lovely, moving things that Mr. Rogers went all out for: torchlight Ski School parade boarding down Dollar Mountain; the varied vocal numbers; Santa Claus around the huge Village Square Christmas tree for a jillion kids. But a twenty-five-below-zero temperature stiffens the bearings of all things; it even froze up the bark in Santa's sled-dog team. The boss put out good money to import a fine young violin soloist who, in that temperature refused to deliver, for he said if he hit a high note on his valuable instrument, the thing would explode in his face. The Old Man went purple with rage but the lad stood fast. Donna was an hour thawing out under our shower and Mary said she could pinch herself Christmas morning and just feel it.

But we got a "deep" white Christmas—late. It warmed up during that day and by nightfall a real dandy commenced laying it down—visibility, two town blocks for a couple of days. When it cleared, Mary Hemingway took her first ski lesson on the kindergarten slope of Dollar Mountain, and late in the day I went down on an errand and caught a fellow who needed exercise, getting it with an "idiot stick" clearing the snow from the path out to the game pantry. There hung a number of wild-fowl meals still (all legally covered, license-wise) and what he estimated as the equivalent of fifty bucks in red meat over the butcher's counter and a month's supply of soup bones! Believe me, he didn't joke—Miss Mary wasted nothing in that line.

3

The usual New Year crowd poured in, Hollywood never so well represented—a list of noteworthy names to fill this page. Old Sun Valley was really jumping that gay winter. The year 1947 went out in a wild whoopee with the elite event at Trail Creek Cabin—now expanded with a big dining room addition that both rounded it out as the ideal party place and spoiled the cozy charm of its younger days. That party, Papa Hemingway readily consented they take in, admitting more curiosity on his part than anything else—its attendance three parts movie crowd, one part Ski School. Without doubt, most of his interest was focused on Ingrid Bergman. His table was a corner one in the big room, and if either of them left it for hours on end I don't remember it. Coop was a frequent stopper, joining the intent conversation, the laughs, sipping at the inexhaustible champagne. Before the meal was over, Papa's jacket came off; he wore a soft wool shirt of neat pattern weave, but left his tie snugged up where it belonged—"Goddamn it . . . hot in this noisy place!"—and remained in his shirt-sleeves until the party faded out in the wee hours. Much has been reported of the author joking of Robert Jordan making love in the sleeping bag, with his shirt on, and that is when and where it was done. So far as I know that is the only time the three were together—the author and costars of the movie version of F.W.T.B.T.

But that was about the sum of the social side of the simple life; Papa made no bones about avoiding involvement: "too rich for my blood, right now." His friends stayed until well into January, the usual stormy month of getting the season's snow down—a good fall of it that year. One snowy day early in the month he came stomping into the shop and one look at him prompted my question. He said, yes, in many ways he was enjoying his first winter visit, but time did seem to hang a bit heavy occasionally. Quite sure that I read him true, I tucked it away for the time being. Coop skied quite a lot in those days, as much to hold up his part of "being in the swim" as anything; he could take it or leave it—by a varmint rifle shot, any day! After so much of it the old hip injury which gave him that little hitch in his git along would commence to bother him, then he'd be among the missing in the ski lift or chow line at the Roundhouse on the big mountain. Often in past winters in the stormy times no good for my work I took an occasional day to prowl about the lower country with him in quest of a few jackrabbits, a bobcat in the lava beds. I was en-

New Year's party, 1947-48, at Trail Creek Cabin. ". . . how do you make good love
with your shirt on?" E. H., Director Henry Hathaway, "Robert Jordan" Cooper, "Maria"
Ingrid Bergman.

couraged by management to do so if my program permitted, keep the guy happy,
and I enjoyed every second of them. So, sure enough, it wasn't long until Coop came
to the shop one cold morning to tell me he got a fine "bobkitty" the day before; it
was a good pelt that he'd have made into a little bedside rug for little daughter
Maria—to match one she already had from an Idaho kitty; he wondered if someone
could take a picture of him with it. Someone did, then and there, and he asked me
when I might sneak a day or two with him. I read him true, also: Sure, I could, any
time, and had he seen, or called Papa Hemingway who might like to do a little
prowling too? Yeah, he'd seen him, but maybe he was working, had his guests to
consider, hadn't asked him. By the same token, Papa wouldn't interfere with Coop's
skiing, and didn't know that he'd about had his fill of it for that year. I said to
Coop: "Try him, and see."

He did, when Tillie just picked up her phone and called Papa, said Coop wanted
to talk to him; and I thought to myself: funny, these two, their first time together

January, 1948. A memorable occasion was hatched from this picture—requested by Coop,
possibly with the hint in it. In any event, this was the sort of "skiing" that Mr. Cooper
liked best.

in the community, in circumstances different than in their accustomed falls, when
everything is automatically a cut-and-dried proposition.

So, for the balance of the Coopers' stay, there were several good prowls; the lower country seldom had more than a hint of snow; Timmerman the dividing line
where it dwindled to nothing as you went on south to the big river. On his off days
from his relief checker's job on the ski lifts, Taylor joined us. On his insistence we
used Papa's Buick, for a good reason: being a convertible, it was easy to shoot from
with all the windows down. Against the law? Well, out in the open, miles from nowhere, and "on the prod fer a pesky er vicious varmint" in Coop language? So, like

in the movies, Papa rode shotgun, I did most of the driving, and I'm sure I needn't say that ours was largely a foursome of kids at the cowboys-and-Indians stuff. Which is exactly how it was on one of the prowls—as much by accident as plan.

Both Papa and Coop had often expressed their curiosity of the historic Oregon Trail where, beyond upper Hagerman Valley, it skirts the Snake River bluffs, then cuts across a vast desert plateau to storied Three Island Crossing many miles farther downstream. Nothing much to see, it nonetheless awakens something in the imagination of romantics. For some botanical reason the sagebrush along the ridges of the numerous and deeply eroded ruts of empire grew tall as a man on a horse, and by sight alone you could follow the trail for miles. It was Taylor who said that jackrabbits liked those ruts—shelter from the incessant wind—and coyotes were always around. Cruise parallel to it, and there could be some action, if we should bump into one out in the open where little flora grew other than dry grass and dust with scattered stunted clumps of sage. In miles we saw nothing, then doubled back, topped a low rise close to where we'd started. There was Mr. Coyote trotting toward us at an angle, heading for the tall sage rows; changed his angle and would have made it, but the big Buick was a powerhouse and cut him off. Like a furry streak he took off across the open country toward a slope of normal sage a good mile away. Papa yelled,

"Take after the bastard, step on it!"

I hesitated, but heard the action of his gun slam a shell home, a rifle bolt locking behind us, seconding his motion. I tromped on it with a heavy foot and the smooth land ahead was ten times as rough as it looked; yelling in my ears, scarcely heard above the blast of cold wind; fists banging doors—"Jesus, did we take off over that one!"—and I hoped that the springs and tires would hold. By a miracle they did, but I was hard put in catching that coyote and dared not get too close—he'd turn on a dime and the chase would be over. The old pump gun barked a couple of times to keep the pursued in the notion and the protection of the sage was coming up too fast. I saw an open spot ahead, slammed on the brakes in a skidding stop and a cloud of dust and Coop lowered the boom on him in a dead straight-away shot.

"Pretty fancy shootin', that, Mr. Cooper!"

"Did a little yerself, podner . . . saw him take on about seven knots per when you nicked him with a few . . . and pretty fair herdin' this hoss, did we say Tallyho, there goes?"

"I guess, and I'm almost afraid to open the hoss's door," I said. "It might fall off the hinges."

"Aw, we didn't hurt 'er none." Papa grinned. "It was worth tearin' up a Deusenberg for, huh, Coop?"

I say that the little episode and the other pleasant days of gadding about were well worth it—just for a fellow who otherwise might have come down with a quite common winter disease known as "shack happy." Even so, it was knocking at his door when well along in January Miss Mary sprained an ankle, putting her out of the ski business. The packing up for home commenced at once, and this time a little Idaho native who'd tail-wagged his way firmly into the affections of the Hemingway hearts would ride in style in the well-loaded Buick, to make his home for the rest of his life at Finca Vigia, San Francisco de Paula, Cuba.

We remember the young canine best from a bitterly frigid night when Papa hatched up a little dinner party for Roberto and Sinsky just before they left. Too, he thought it would be nice to bring in a cook, in relief to Mary, who'd had plenty of it. There was an attraction in big Joe Hannahan: an ex-pugilist and trainer, a good one, obviously, no signs of it on his good-looking face that was a map of Ireland. Fine tenor voice, too—sang with Mary in the choral group. Tillie and I and her singing sister were there, and a nice young bartender from one of the joints in town. All well and good, but where in hell was the cook? He lived up at Sun Valley where he worked a day shift, and he liked the Club Rio bar quite well, too, the first one you hit coming down from the Valley. I was about ready to drive there and work my way back through town in a search for him when we got a hint: it sounded a bit like "It's a long way to Tipperary." It had been a slow one for Joe—a very obvious argument along the way with a snowbank! His nose was an icicle radish and a flip of your finger would snap off either of his ears. Seven jumps ahead of the whole business all along, Mary calmly put on her apron and went to work while we thawed

Miss Mary "pinch-hitting" for big Joe Hannahan, a first-rate chef himself— most of the time!

Comb-harpist Hemingway rendering a classic—not for canine ears!

Joe out enough so that he could contribute a little verbal help to his specialty—which proved that he wasn't fully embalmed. The dinner was the usual success, then the party swung into quite a songfest; Roberto rendered his weird Moorish chants in a high falsetto voice, and our host made a little music on a comb with a piece of wax paper folded around it. The accompaniment to those two was the mournful, ear-shaking cries of the friendly young dog who'd run for a handy pair of knees on anybody to put his head between and shut out those God-awful sounds!

Not keeping track of canine waifs so common around Ketchum, I can't recall how the mutual love affair originated, but it was quite obvious that the friendly fellow was but a two-varieties dog: Springer spaniel out-and-out, in all but color—a silky coal black, with a tiny white patch for a collar button. Hence: Blackdog. As Taylor often joked of the Finca as the farm of cats, Blackdog possessed a thing or two in his makeup, for there's little question but that he carried top rating in the affections department. He was on his way to his new home at the end of January, 1948.

"Blackdog," a canine orphan from Ketchum who lived out his long life in Cuba

8.

The Fall of '48 ---
End of Idaho Chapter 2 . . .

1

When Taylor Williams returned from his spring trek to the Keys and Cuba there was a shadow of a doubt that Papa Hemingway would consider it worth while to come West that fall. It is embraced as an era in the waterfowl history of our continent as an unhealthy one. Spring hatches were down and it was known that we'd have another split shooting season that would not be attractive, time-wise. In contrast, however, to the over-all situation, the local one was good for ducks. So when the dates were published we mailed them to Cuba immediately and were a bit surprised in the immediate response: Coming anyway—line up the MacDonald cabin setup again. The waterfowl dates: October 29 to November 14—December 23 to January 8. Tucked between was the upland bird season of exactly three weeks ending November 21. So what does an all-outer do in shotgun country in a full "dry" month of the fall?

The arrival was a late one—mid-October—and we had the pantry well stocked for an appetizer and some main fare. By then it was something of a round-heeled joke about the continuous missing the dove season, but it was now a well-established institution—you weren't in the swim if you didn't "shoot them little things" which made little things out of quite a few who talked awful good gunning, and knocked you down to get to the table ahead of you. But it was the colonel who took the kidding of his life for how he bagged the big meat. The small crew, who in summer "manicured" ski trails on the big mountain, reported to him a big lone mule deer buck that holed up during the day in a small stand of pines in the "Bowl Area." Well, he'd be damned if that wasn't a square deal, so he—of all people, who scorned all but the old-school ways—hopped on the ski lift with the crew and had the big buck down squarely in the middle of Easter Bowl, on a 50 percent grade, by eight o'clock in the morning. Big as a small elk and in perfect condition, it took four of us to pole-pack him down to where we could drive a Jeep. That was a short week before the Hemingway arrival.

"I wonder if it will do me any good to ask if there's any of the liver left?"

The inevitable snort: "Who knows better than you that deer liver spoils in twenty-four hours unless you eat it."

Mr. Williams drooled for a solid year for that treat—he and a lot of others—and leave his method to him: It took me several days to collect a little one-spiker that I could pack in on my back alone. There was liver left, but it had to be joked about.

The younger boys missed that fall, and Bumby got in but a few days of pheasant shooting—awaiting his call for another tour of duty with the Army. On a picture, Coop was conspicuous in his absence. The first half of the duck season was excellent, and we had Silver Creek practically to ourselves, Mary and Papa making good use of the canoe trip. The Frees farm area was also pretty much ours but generally the lower country was under heavy hunting pressure; weekends were something to avoid, and though the bird population was good as ever, the wily pheasant was just a mite wiser. Nonetheless, we ate as good as ever, too. Then the dry December rolled around and there was an on-the-fence interim about staying on for Christmas, our attempts at persuasion not at all subtle. We lost, and we knew that ahead was a period of absenteeism; we had known for a long time that it was inevitable.

We got it all at once, sitting around the table one evening—a very gay one, reminiscing more than usual. When it was announced that he hoped they'd not have to miss more than two falls, Papa asked about our attic room. It was all his, we told him, and asked how his supply of pencils was.

"Oh, if times get rougher I'll send up for a hatful, or if I dig around I might still have some from that hatful you guys loaded me with."

(We had—in '39, when he settled down to work—wished him good luck when several of us showed up at Glamour House, each with a pocketful of company "issue" pencils. He dumped them all in the old Afrikaner Stetson, picked up a cased fly rod, said that if we'd have it painted white he'd work the streets on Saturday nights and get off relief.)

There was little doubt of his intent; he said he had the outline of a big work in his head and it might take him two years to do it, so a small truckload of gear was stored with us: rifles, fishing rods never used but once, sleeping bags, a tent, boxes of odds and ends, and two small trunks of clothing—plus a very nice roomy bookcase that Sun Valley's carpenter shop made for him when they were in Glamour House the short time the previous fall. He left about a hundred books with it, and I joked him that if he left the stuff more than a couple of years I'd charge him rent.

"Let's see, now, what is your favorite brand?" He laughed. "But we'll do our best, kid, and maybe when the colonel is down in the spring we'll know more then."

The departure was on December 15.

2

During the winter Mary wrote that they would soon head for Europe, and she gave us the Paris address of the Guaranty Trust Company for mail forwarding. From an earlier hint only, we bet on northern Italy, which it proved to be: old haunts country, Cortina D'Ampezzo the hub, mostly. Later we got it by public news that Papa had a serious infection from a bit of shotgun wadding blown into his eye by wind while hunting on the marshes near Venice. Their intent of a few week's trip stretched to nine months, in which *Across the River and Into the Trees* was largely written. Neglect on our part is reason for correspondence being almost nil.

That year went out on a sad note for us: my father died a few hours into New Year's Day of 1950. He didn't make the "five years at the most" that our old family doctor predicted for him when I brought my parents West. Taylor offered to write the Hemingways while we made our fast trip back to Iowa at our busiest time of year; but I said no, Papa obviously was hard at work (back in Cuba then, as I recall) and why bother him then—for I knew he would sit down and put his respectful feelings in writing. Taylor Williams was the best personal messenger I ever knew, so he took the word on his spring trip. Papa knew that I was well prepared for the inevitable, saw the stamp on my father when he talked with him the last time. His warming words came back with Taylor.

And what about that fall, we asked him. No, not that one, he said, maybe the next. The new novel was serialized in *Cosmopolitan* magazine, but we were damned if we'd read Papa in installments this time. We read John O'Hara's review on the book in the *New York Times*, issue of September 10. But when we got our hardcover copy inscribed by the author later in the fall, his inscription didn't hold a warm personal candle to those in the six volumes of the special "Sunrise Edition" by Scribner's back in '39. Oh, it was personal enough, but that "touch" wasn't there. Two falls in absentia. How many more? I, for one, with good reason, felt there would be plenty. I was certain of it-when in the summer of '51 he sent us "The Shot" story and wished it were so he could come out to spend the dough with us that fall.

Remember his remark that I reported at the time of Mark Hellinger's tragedy: ". . . let's hope it doesn't spread like a disease and spoil it." Another one, much farther back: he "spooks easy." Well, Papa Hemingway was, basically, just about as spooky as they come—perhaps because of the uncanny accuracy of the crystal ball between his ears. Our little community did split its own pants seams in a fizzling-out postwar bust; certain of the newer element boys got a bit greedy running their games of chance; there were justifiable complaints that got to out-of-state competitive ears, and plenty of in-state ears, too, that had been awaiting the chance to pounce. So, the law cracked down on the always illegal gambling—hard, and suddenly—and out went a way of life that fit the country, as we knew it in the older days. It was the change that caused Papa Hemingway to flatly say that he doubted he'd ever return to Idaho. I repeat, too—he never forgot, or forgave, what had happened to Mark Hellinger, speaking mainly of the fleecing he got. Which is not to say that he was an addict of gambling—about as close to that as I am of a halo overhead. It was a carry-over of the Old West to him, an expression of individual freedom, and if hurt, it was your own damn fault. The slot machines hung on until near the mid-fifties, then the competition got rid of them, too, via legislation. Their licensing provided a tidy revenue for a little town like Ketchum to operate; that was

". . . and out went a way of life that fit the country—the West—and if hurt, it was your own damn fault!"

cut more than in half, and it's been church-mouse poor ever since. In spite of a steady growth, urban and surburban. I know what I'm saying about running the town, not on a shoestring, just the empty eyelet for one, for a blind citizenry elected me Chairman of the Village Board for a four-year term in '55. I'm still spoken to by everyone, but, it was no picnic. The pay was—thanks for the try. It's our home.

But we know that we claimed a piece of Papa's heart along the way, and by "we" I mean the "package"—the people, the country, the still good hunting, yes, and again, that simple life. I have no better expression of his feeling on it all than the following.

When Taylor Williams returned in June of '52, we saw him hop off the bus almost before it stopped rolling, and come down the path to our shop in a half dogtrot. Oh, oh, is it glad tidings this time? From his jacket pocket he pulled our copy of *The Old Man and the Sea*. We had read it in *Life*, in spite of our avowal, and we were almost afraid to open it to see what the "write something in it" was.

> For Pappy and Tilly
> with much love
> PAPA
>
> We miss you awfully bad
> ; the worst Time is the fall of the year.
> Please kiss Miss Tilly for me
> PAPA:
> ERNEST HEMINGWAY—Finca Vigia—1952

And of course I kissed Tillie for an always very honest Papa in that department— she who said of the inscription:

"Look at the punctuation, and the second 'Papa' printed so small . . . like he wants to hide for not being back . . . and I wonder why the formal signing of his full name; he's never done that before."

Papa didn't write often—Mary was chief correspondent—but he always got his pen on Christmas greetings, one in particular: a half-tone reproduction of a photo of *Pilar* heading out into the Gulf Stream, her master on the flying bridge—

> I love Tilly
> Pappy is my good friend
> We miss you very much
> Please kiss Tilly for me

—pretty much a standard pattern, but in the note with that one I caught a reprimand with our standing invitation to come with Taylor—change our vacations to spring, if possible—and for me to bring my hopped-up Graflex camera and telephoto lenses; Papa felt that with my action-shooting experience I'd do a good turn on leaps of big game fish. In the absentee interim the resort developed quite a spring convention program, so we never got to enjoy such a trip. I think that Papa shared my confidence that I wouldn't freeze on-camera at my first sight of a marlin

A picture brought to the writer by Taylor Williams. It was taken in Cuba sometime in the early fifties, perhaps in Cojímar, where the boat *Pilar* was kept, in the locale of *The Old Man and the Sea.*

or sail in a grand leap, for once he sent back a tale with Taylor of a visiting cameraman whom I knew well. A cracking good one, too, but a specialist more in personalities who used the wrong equipment. A specific shot in his assignment was a grand leaping shot, with the master in his close foreground, on the rod. As he described it to Taylor: "I got on a good fish, and Gregorio kept the boat lined up at exactly the right angle, and then I horsed that beauty up and out of the water so many times that my arms about played out on me, then it all went dead . . . know what the guy said? . . . 'Mr. Hemingway, if he'da jumped one more time I'da got him.' A hell of a nice guy, too, but the son of a. . . . Colonel, I think. . . ."

"'Bout time for a mint julep, Mr. Hemingway?"

Had I missed on that many tries for a picture, I think my question would have been, "Papa, sir . . . how long is the swim back to Cojímar?" and asking it as I went over the rail in a not so grand leap of my own!

3

In late spring of '53, while Taylor was in Cuba, I got a letter from him, and Papa, to ship things to the stateside outfitter, Abercrombie & Fitch in New York, for the second African safari that Papa and Mary had planned after a summer trip to Spain. Taylor requested that I ship his Model 70 Winchester .270-caliber for Mary —stock to be fitted to her by Griffin & Howe—and his heavy Colt target revolver. From Papa's glory hole in our attic went the old Springfield .30-06, a couple of plinking rifles; heavy clothing that in my judgment was right—for Idaho falls are about on par with those of East Africa—altitude and weather-wise. In Papa's letter was a warming long paragraph wishing that it were so I could go along and, in quote: "Your good eyes, and my good nose, and your long lenses and that movie box that you shoot like a gun . . . hell, we might go into business." I laughed because of his crack about his nose, which was, indeed, a good one, and not because I thought I was being salved. I had fun putting little notes in pockets of the old latigo leather vest and the folded flat-as-a-pancake old Stetson hat.

The visit to Spain that summer was the first since 1939, and a thank-you note from Nairobi in late August said that his welcome was surprising, and pleasing. The next news, of course, was of the African plane crashes in January of '54. Like Hemingway history says, the obituaries were all ready for release—and some out— when the truth of it all finally came. It scared hell out of us and an aviation expert was on hand who feared it more. Pete and Dorothy Hill had come over from Idaho Falls to see us, and Cessna airplanes were part of his business. When he heard that it was a 180 type with spring-steel legs on its fixed landing gear, well, in brushy terrain their craft would be flipped over with a broken back. Hell, it was curtains with that in mind. Busy, or no busy, I went with old pilot Hill into the Ram to heist one for our old pals now gone over a hill—the big one. Heist one, heist two—we held a wake, that's what we did, and ended up at the old corner table, staring red-eyed at that empty chair with its back to the wall next to the outside window where you could "watch for the bad ones comin' and case the whole joint— especially for writers and correspondents who drink more than a share of the Noble Experiment at the eights-and-aces table when it's runnin' good." A couple of tolerant wives and a worried Mr. Williams broke up the wake before it got fully out of hand—or me fired!

The story of our doings eventually reached the ears of him who enjoyed it most—
from Mr. Williams, of course.

"Well, being treated to a wake by two old drinkin' pals is a signal honor, by God
. . . and except for weddings and a funeral now and then, neither of them's been inside of a church in twenty years!"

That was our very limited—and nonsensical—side of a near tragedy, but in this not-
too-limited view, there is little room for doubt that those two crashes were a turning
point from which there was little—if only temporary—remedy, or correction.

Next on the docket: much of the latter part of the year of '55 was spent on "that
bloody picture"—in scornful Hemingwayan—a three-way deal between Papa, Spencer Tracy, and Leland Hayward, as writer, star, and producer, in an attempt to produce *The Old Man and the Sea* as a film classic to match the written one. From its
beginning in the Cuban locale, a series of bad breaks haunted them—like a couple
of hurricanes, for instance. Then further efforts for the huge fish the story called for
were made off the Peruvian Pacific coast in early '56. Big fish were caught, fourteen
feet and over, as I recall hearing, but none big enough to satisfy the so-called ge-
niuses who finally resorted to special effects. Speaking his disgust of the whole
business to Taylor early that summer, Papa sort of masked it with a flashback. He
said certain things might have gone better if they'd had old Antelope—his and
Spencer Tracy's horse—on the crew.

"Fishing for a big one from horse would've made as much sense as some of the
stuff we had to put up with, I can tell you that."

Certainly it was a not-too-well physical Papa who went through the mess—the
business he abhorred anyway; but it is quite obvious that he was looking for something, and was willing to try.

The result of one of our winter prowls, the exact date I
cannot recall and did not record, but in the late fifties, I'm
quite sure. The point is: If
the countless times "we did it
again"—from 'way back, until,
. . . each occasion with "good
ol' Coop" was comparable to
a sculptor chiseling deeply in
timeless granite. On this occasion, due to deep snow, it
took a Tucker Sno-Cat to follow the keen noses of the
hounds—bobcat hounds.

On February 6 of '57 Taylor Williams' seventieth birthday was celebrated in a gay party at our house. Though he did not show it, or act it, the old boy had failed quite a lot in the past couple of years; was quite deaf, and the "family" problem was getting him to wear his hearing aid—"squawk box"—in normal conversation. Fully eligible for retirement, self-pride would not permit it. He had a small house in Ketchum, one that Clara Spiegel moved off her property when she built her part-time residence kitty-corner across the street intersection from us. A very talented man with his hands, he took his time at rebuilding and modernizing it, held his regular winter job on the lifts, but at other times he was more or less "carried along." The guide service was long since a thing of the past at Sun Valley, so he fought a little boredom, too. He lived for the annual treks to Florida and Cuba, took leave-of-absence to go, and as Dr. Moritz said to me one spring when Taylor boarded the bus: "Best medicine in the world for the old boy." He looked after him very well, as did Dr. George Saviers, who had joined his staff when he completed his internship some years before. Having guided with Taylor in the postwar summers, George's interest in him was more than professional. And the little local family watched after him, too; our latchstring was as familiar to him as the buttons on his shirt, and "Miss Till" was his "daughter" whom he always thought as much of as if she were his own. Thought a lot of my mother, too, who was in splendid health in those years.

Then, twenty-two days after she'd had so much fun at his birthday party, she slipped quickly away to join my father. Ours was a very empty house for a long period of readjustment.

Though he'd done no mountain hunting for some years, a bit slowed in the field, Taylor missed little of the latter. Then in the '57 dove season he scared the wits out of us. Opening day was a very hot one; he insisted on jumping his birds in a rough fallowed field of wild sunflowers, and the old boy was doing well; but it was plain that the going was too much for him. We tried to talk him into sitting in the shade of an old deserted barn, smack in the flight line to another field and shoot with our old friend Jim Kennedy who had a pair of folding stools. Nope, that would violate his pride. Suddenly he was missing the easiest shots, cursing himself, stumbling along like a blind horse. The old blood pressure had him. Shooting near him, Tillie rushed over and led him back to the shade and set him down. He readily admitted it, and that finished his days afield.

In March of '58 he suffered a mild stroke, about three weeks before his intended departure for Cuba. The good doctors pulled him through, but Dr. John told him to forget it for that year, and privately to me that he doubted he'd ever go again. So, while hospitalized, he asked me to write to Mary and Papa Hemingway. I did, for his signature, then got off a short one of my own, told them I'd report later. When he was out of the hospital and taking it very easy I sent them a favorable report. Then I took a short trip to investigate the possibility of rejoining my old colleague, confidant, and good friend, Vince Hunter, whose motion-picture operation was on the verge of an expanded program of promotional railroad films. The door was left open to me, but I wrote it off for several reasons. Reluctantly I returned to settle back into the old rut that a once wonderful place to work had been in for a long time.

There was a turning point in lovable old Sun Valley's history: the record snowfall winter of 1952. A dangerous area was needlessly opened to skiing against better judgment and a January avalanche killed three guests and a ski instructor—the last body not recovered until June. It shook hell out of things. Pat Rogers, *Mr.* Sun Valley for fourteen years, asked to be relieved of his post to return to the Utah Parks operation. To his surprise, his request was readily granted. As one sage observer remarked: "Now all the color will go out of the place—expensive color, true—but now what?" A good question. To justify this reluctant but necessary report I'll span the years to the early sixties when the company finally shed itself of the deserving place, and the president publicly stated that running a resort was always quite remote from running a railroad.

Its pace-setting winters generally held their own, but as a year-round thing it steadily declined as a fantastic money loser in spite of all efforts and individual initiative. As to ourselves, we had to serve an impossible faction, a hangover of the long defunct publicity setup that was a yearly contract proposition in its heyday. In short, you can't pull it in through one door and give it all away through another. If the faction knew what it was doing in one phase, that would have been acceptable; in another phase, it did know, and there was nothing we could do about it. So, back to the rut.

I was home but a day or so when, on May 8, the special-delivery letter from Cuba came. Written by Miss Mary, it opened with their grave concern for "our colonel" and a few relative things on our end, then the balance of it was indeed a revelation. A paragraph dripped of nostalgia, poetic prose, stuff like: ". . . out there, all cluttered with look of the reeds and grasses along Silver Creek as seen from a canoe, the quakers trembling gold among the pines, the smell of the sage and the wideness of the sky and the brown velvet hills around Picaboo. . . ." Then:

They were both fine, Papa thinner than he'd been for a long time—down to 207 and in good health the past year, for the first time since those crashes in Africa. He was working like a beaver, or an IBM machine, had all winter, and very well, too, but no plans for publishing anything so far, and no plans for any travels, either, but . . . "We must have a reunion with you guys sooner or later."

Well, now! said this old pessimist to himself—sounds a little more like it should have been for years. I could not show the letter to the colonel but told him that bit. I could have heard his retort in my sleep: "Well, what've I bin tellin' you, goddamn it!" And the faithful Miss Till echoed him—emphatically. My retort was something like:

"Yeah, I know, but remember how Papa often said of an old bull elk using a country so long, then he goes over a mountain to another one that he thinks might be better?"

"Sure," the colonel came back strong. "But he said the old bear went over the mountain too, to see what he could see, and that's about all there was to it. . . ."

And that was about all there was to that—until later in the summer. Then came Miss Mary's long letter dated August 13.

"It's long after midnight and I have to get up early tomorrow morning, but I can't wait to tell you that just today, Papa decided that we better, pretty soon, get out of this climate for a while and head for Ketchum. We've had it too hot for too long and I feel sure the change will do him good.

"We haven't figured out routes or means of transportation, etc., yet; but are sure of two things. We'd appreciate it so much if you could let us know when this year's beast and the bird seasons start—doves, Huns, pheasant, ducks—or whatever you may know about now. If no season opens until, say, the first of Oct., we won't plan to arrive much before that.

"Second thing, Papa is deeply involved in a book and he will want a place that is peaceful, quiet—no interrupters, etc., where he can work mornings—shooting in the afternoons or say 3-4 days a week, having fun the other days. There will be just the two of us but, to be comfortable, and give him a decent working space, we ought to have a cabin with two bedrooms—and of course, *a view,* and a *fireplace,* and a *kitchen decently equipped.* I'm going to be the cook, and will hope to find somebody to make beds, clean and wash dishes, if possible. (But that's not so bloody important now.) The important thing is a snug, sweet place for Papa to work and for us to live for, let's say, a couple to four months (quite impossible to be specific about it). I'd like to shoot a deer and eat him; we once went to Italy for two days and stayed nine months; if the weather is lousy consistently, we may pull out.

"Bumby, who left Monday for his new office in San Francisco, says Chuck and Floss Atkinson have a fancy new motel, which may be the answer for us—or maybe the old ones on the road to Hailey where we used to stay. (I may have to tote groceries from town on foot, who knows?) Or some completely new place, with space and plenty of daylight, and lamps that can be adjusted for reading at night. A Glamour House with a kitchen, in short.

"Dear Fellas, as usual we are imposing on you, asking for this sort of gen. I do hope it's not too much imposition—even now at 1:55 A.M., I'll dream of you and Ketchum all night—no reply was ever waited more fervently."

Scribbled in pencil across the whole letter heading was Papa's short view, angle, whatever:

"DEAR PAPPY AND TILLY: Just read this!" Then he went on to say that his idea was to stay a month and then see if *no publicity* and not bothered, and if any shooting they could stay on; he repeated: skip ideas of publicity, then would not have interrupters that "make it impossible here now!" Certainly would be wonderful to see you guys again. Love to Taylor—would figure to hire or buy car if they came, and:

"Tilly, we have a date for the World Series, if you'll go." (By car radio in the old days.)

Tillie and I were elated, saw no problems except that no one bothers to rent out his house for only a month; a season was the rule. Four blocks down the hill from us, a block past Sun Valley road at the upper edge of town, was the ideal "Glamour House with the kitchen" that Mary hoped for. I put in a call to its owners in the lower country, and since I could not tell them who I wanted to rent the house for, they would see me when they came up for their usual weekend. On the Sun Valley road was the motel that Chuck and Floss Atkinson, as partners in a small group, managed, and also there was a fine market in the same block—all told a very neat combination in the community; the market was located in the fancy structure that was built as the plush old supper club and gambling casino back in '38, and called the Christiania (its name synonymous with the glamorous history of Sun Valley). We knew that their Christiania Motor Lodge was not adequate for their living quarters, but a minute's walk away was Mary's tote-distance for groceries, and Tillie laughed, "Shoot, even Papa might tote a few from there, because they carry a lot of groceries that we know he likes."

The lady on the spade, Ann Southern, breaking ground for the Christiania Motor Lodge in Ketchum. On her right, Floss Atkinson, and on her left, Peggy Kneeland, a partner, and Chuck Atkinson.

So I got off a long letter in our ebullient hurry; and since I knew that Papa would expect it, I outlined a lot of things local—too much, I would learn—of changes I knew he wasn't aware of that also would not affect them in the least—especially in the off-season when now even Sun Valley closed completely in the falls, and, miracles of miracles, some of the bars in town. Mary's letter indicated they did not know of them, so I reported the addition of that wonderfully sporting game bird now doing very well in our country—the exotic chukar partridge. Not remembering the spook of the old days about rabbits, I mentioned that in the past couple of years we'd been taking the delectable little western cottontails, that we liked better than pheasants—legitimate game animals of the state with a fixed season on them. Hell, I was raised on cottontail rabbits, so why wouldn't I mention them?

Mary's reply was fast, dated August 24, and in the same envelope a hand-written one from Papa, dated August 26. I read it four times, and it took the wind out of my sails; because of a thing or two of the changes, I'd made my remark as a joke, more or less to be smart, I suppose. Mary's letter was a short agreeable one, told me not to overdo it, the house hunting—get something comfortable for a while, then she would house-hunt if they decided to stay. Obviously she'd written it, addressed the envelope, and handed it to Papa for his comments to me in the usual way. He thought it over, then wrote a page, starting it off:

"DEAR TILLY AND DEAR PAPPY: Remember it's been ten years since we were there. . . ." Then he said that if I thought it was so changed that they wouldn't like it any more don't be afraid to say so for fear that they might think that they weren't wanted or weren't welcome. Just write frankly! For instance, the fishing in the Gulf Stream was completely changed and almost nonexistent; if anyone wanted to come down for the old fishing they would have to tell them how bad it was. It was simply gone. If Taylor had come down that spring he wouldn't have had any fun. Yesterday there was not a boat out and the town was so changed that an old-timer wouldn't know it any more. He'd tell anyone truly not to come there. Felt maybe we weren't warning them off because we didn't want to seem inhospitable. They would understand *completely*, and he would truly appreciate it. Write back as soon as I got this. Best love, PAPA.

Well, for heaven's sake, where is the old confident Papa whom we knew so well? Yes, our personal messenger had been a good one until, as said, the past few years. Tillie called my attention to the sealing flap on the envelope:

"Those cottontail rabbits were what spooked me! PAPA."

I dropped everything to get off my second letter. When I figured it had reached them, I phoned Toby Bruce in Key West. Note that there was not a mention of a fermentive political situation going on in Cuba then—in the eastern provinces of the island, and I had given too little thought to it. Knowing Toby was a best fixer, and that we talked a common language in this case, it figured he'd get through by phone easier than I, especially if there were calls in the offing. In a word, I asked him to bear down, say, in effect: Get the hell out here to Idaho, it'll be good, you'll see. And I guess he did, for he called me in an hour, said the spooks were pretty much banished, and for me to go ahead with arrangements as I saw best. I'd say I most dropped the phone in relief: I came within a few silly words of lousing up the whole deal. Yes, it had been a long ten years. All right, pitch in, like you always had.

I got the house without a bit of trouble, at a modest rate; Marge and Clark Heiss I had known since I came to Idaho—Marge a daughter in the Brass family who owned the old ranch that the Union Pacific bought to build Sun Valley on. They took my word that our mysterious friends were sound and reliable, would care for their vacation home as if it were their own. The only hitch was, they had to have it by Christmas—their daughters would have college mates in tow for the holiday. I took it for granted a three-month deal—to December 15—would be acceptable, and wrote for an immediate reply. It was a prompt yes—they hoped to arrive by mid-September. Mary had already joked that they would miss another dove season!

That was a disappointment, due to an unavoidable delay on their end. The only item shipped to me—highly insured by the sender, Toby Bruce—was a small luggage piece containing the manuscript currently in work. The express agent caught nothing from the shipper's name, so not one local soul knew what was in the wind. Mary and Toby's wife, Betty, flew up to Chicago, where the men met them in the station wagon they had driven up from Florida. In a couple of nights we were just breaking the news to Taylor, yelling our heads off, his squawk box parked in his hat, when our phone rang: Cody, Wyoming, calling—a Mr. Bruce. Their caravan was moving west a day ahead of my guess. By the time Papa got on the phone, the colonel's sixth sense had tipped him to something, brought him out from his easy chair —far from the phone—wiring himself for sound. I said, "Hold it, Papa, I'm being stabbed." The squawk box got a workout!

And how good it was to hear that voice again! I actually sensed, and heard a snatch, of slight hesitancy as the phone was handed to him. Then it vanished like smoke rings in the breeze of exhilaration.

"The Bruce and me got womans with us this time, fixing the drinks while we run the boat."

Remembering nineteen years before, when the two had run it the other way, laughingly wishing they had womans for a hell of a long grind to Florida.

"And I guess you're doing the navigating, General."

"You're damn right, I could do it in my sleep. . . ."

"Then we'll look for you, say, between five and six tomorrow night."

And you could bet your bottom dollar that in that instance you could set your watch by the team who had been at it for such a very long time.

Then we got our tongue-lashing, and in a way deserved it from the colonel. Goddamn it, he hadn't been told, and thought we'd been acting a little secretive for the past several days. I sweetened his drink and showed him those written instructions that meant exactly what they said if you knew the man who sent them: no publicity, and no interrupters—for a welcome change. The old fox caught on in a hurry, knew exactly who would rudely, callously, in ignorance of the subject, have had it in the papers—to hell with the man's privacy, his work, his wishes so very simple to carry out. The colonel was well aware that the old fox on his way damn well knew it, too —the fellow who forgot nothing or nobody. And where were they to live? The Heiss house, Colonel, of course—where else? Perfect, he said, because he knew it so well.

Built of heavy logs squared smooth on the inside, its huge main room spoke nice planning at first sight. It was living room, dining area, and kitchen all in one— so arranged for the feeling of separation; the kitchen fenced off by a very long eating counter, the end divider backed up with a spinet piano—its back to that of the refrigerator! "Keep the music cool," as 'twas later said. The opposite wall had tenfoot long bookshelves butted by a big native stone fireplace that could heat the big room by itself in all but the coldest weather. Flanking it was the tightly closing door leading to the roomy, well-windowed double garage with wood storage space to the ceiling on its inner wall. Therein was the combination—no better deal could be found for the fellow who liked hanging his game in a cool, well-ventilated place! A gentle ramp at the room's inner end led down to the three-bedroom wing which looked out on a grassy slope down toward Trail Creek bordering the property. A friend once said of the place that it was the best "camp-and-home" setup he could imagine.

The view that Mary expressed her wish for was not a breathtaking one, but one sunny bedroom I imagined as the literature plant. Its furnishings were simple and a bit aged, including a sizable chest of drawers waist-high on the average man. On my power saw I sized two plywood panels, hinged them together on one long side, edged one to lock over the chest top, the free one for tilting to the proper angle at which Papa liked (and for his comfort) to work standing up. From news pictures I'd seen and what Taylor had told me I raised the chest height by squaring heavy stubby blocks for under the legs—the whole taking about a half hour in my basement shop. I took the rig and set it up the afternoon of arrival, when Marge Heiss saw that everything was shipshape and ready for living. There was wood in the garage so I laid logs on the grate and thought of a sentence in the first letter: "If the weather is consistently lousy, we may pull out." I closed the door behind me, stepped out on a day as warm and bright as early September, went back up a bit early to get my wife and the colonel who, when I saw him last was about to blow a fuse. The date was October 5.

In a couple of days we'd have the last convention that year, but it was stonequiet at the time. Taylor was waiting, gussied up for the occasion: necktie, niftiest plaid wool shirt, jacket, the works, and the only way he could extinguish that fuse was to dampen it a bit. All right, we'd have a short one with him, then we'd git to gittin', for Tillie had kitchen things to do.

9.

'58 --- the Heiss House Fall . . .

1

A few minutes before six o'clock the colonel yelled to us in the kitchen: "Here they come, here they come!" His face had been glued to the window for the past half hour. We rushed in to see a long black Buick station wagon with a white top rolling up the hill, the white-bearded figure pointing to a house that looked familiar to him, and then he saw the figures leaving the window for the front door. The beard parted in a big grin and Bruce swung her around the corner and drew up in a roping-horse stop, doors flying open, arms reaching.

"Aw, gee, we're so ashamed . . . it's been too bloody long!"

An only word to describe the immediate reunion out in the street is: smotherings! And I guess we used more than our side of the street, too. And you knew that when coherence prevailed the bright ones would spring from the bottomless well.

"Why, like you said, it's pretty much like it was . . . if my nose is right it even smells the same."

"Coming through town did you see anyone you knew, Papa?"

"Sure . . . saw ol' Pappy Hanes frisking across the street the same as ever . . . saw Jack Lane locking up his place, and some familiar guys on the porch at the Rio . . . say, Your Honor the Mayor . . . you got any stuff goin' that you can cut ol' Papa in on?"

"Not that will grease your palm in this burg, Papa, and say yourself, you came straight as an Indian goes . . . to our tepee, didn't think. . . ."

"Of course I could find it, helped you build it—with my mouth, didn't I?"

"And again the horse's nose is red and peeling." Tillie laughed.

"It ought to be, Miss Till, I've been pushing with it against that windshield for an awful long way."

Tillie couldn't help remarking of the elegant car, being "old habit" Buick.

"Sure, Till, it's a beauty, and courtesy from the makers for the trip . . . quite a *hearse*, wouldn't you say?"

Papa showed tiredness from travel, but it vanished in no time; and though the beard was as familiar as could be to us via the news media, he was something of a stranger, momentarily. While chatter reigned, it was good to see him and the colonel off in a corner, swapping their own gen in their own ways. When he first walked into the house his attention was called to my cat that he'd heard so much about. He was a big fella for his kind—a Siamese—as pretty as the breed produces, and independent as a hog on ice. His command post was the railing of the stair landing on the two-story inner wall of our living room. Over it hung the big white rug I had tanned from the goat that I shot on my first hunting trip in Idaho back in '37. Chinner loved that thick white coat, a place to lie flat, approve or disapprove the situation beneath him with those deep blue eyes. Obviously, he'd never seen a Santa Claus before, looking up at him, soft voice trying to coax him down so they could be friends. I told Papa to sit down in my favorite chair while he and Taylor talked, and see what happened. I didn't know myself. Kitty was ignored, but in a few minutes he started slowly down the stairs, stopped on the bottom step to stare at the bearded face. Still he was ignored—or was he, in cat sense—and then down the last step, he sat down, looking up over Santa's knee: Stranger, I'm coming up to investigate. In a few minutes he did, light as a feather, crept up on Papa's chest for a long sniff at that big silver foliage. The pair promptly proceeded to smooth each other's whiskers.

"You see, Mr. Chinner, I'm an old goat myself . . . thanks ever so much for your vote of confidence so soon."

Music was going on the hi-fi and suddenly Chinner was cradled in Papa's arms, waltzed about the room and on out through the kitchen, into our big east-wing dining room. It was new to him, a greatly enlarged breakfast room, and when you heard an "Oofs!" like in bear language you knew that Papa was impressed. He liked the big picture windows, the "man" look, the little bar built into one birch panelled wall, the pair of favorite shotguns hanging above it, the long table I'd made of a wide walnut door. He scolded Miss Tillie for ignoring his phoned "We'll go out to dinner when we get in tomorrow night," and added, "but now we'll hope that we'll be invited often to this beauty house we know was such a struggle when you started it." Tillie was frying chicken, for which she apologized for having broken a custom: "The wildest we happen to have, Papa."

"But they had feathers, once." He grinned.

When he'd put one piece away at the table he asked her what she'd fried it in; vegetable shortening, she answered. Good, he guessed he'd have some more, then— he was being a good boy about his weight and diet. In the hour before we ate, he nursed along a Scotch and soda with a dash of lime, in a normal-size old-fashioned glass.

The Heiss house was a hit at first step into the front door, and a bit of a surprise in that the Bruces could be their house guests—the cozy loft bedrooms above the big room. The windows in the "work" bedroom rattled with the laughter at the elevated chest of drawers, especially at the box of shotgun shells that propped the hinged top at close to proper tilt. Papa nudged a shirt button up to it, checking the "height for write" and said it was right, and my reward was:

"By God . . . Pappy knows what to do . . . Mister Pappy, sir! I'm stiff with gratitude, or I'd bow."

"Mister Papa . . . if I'da tried it just one more time. . . ."

"Sure, Mr. Pappy, but you forgot to varnish these fancy legs . . . no, truly, it's a fine place to work."

He vaguely remembered seeing the house when my letter described its location, but remodelled since, it was strange to him. When he opened that door beside the fireplace he thought it led out of doors. His grin opened from ear to ear to Mary:

"Come here, Kitner, look at this, will you? . . . you just back the buggy in after a good day, and hang 'em up!"

It was noticed at once that the house lacked a TV set, for we'd advised that when Chuck Atkinson moved to Ketchum he "wired" the town for reception by permission of the Forest Service for antennas atop 9,200-foot Baldy Mountain, the signals amplified in the line down, then cables buried in streets and alleys for piping into homes. His idea was the most forward stride for the town in years—for otherwise it was isolated. He stocked sets in the market and youngest son Stan was service man.

"Gotta have one, Miss Till . . . for our World Series date."

With five games played, the Milwaukee Braves were one up on the Yankees, and Tuesday was traveling day back to Milwaukee to decide the Series in one game, or two. So we said goodnight with a date for tomorrow—do a bit of prowling. Basic things for breakfast were in the refrigerator, the travelers were tired, and you knew that everything was going to be all right.

Betty Bruce was a confirmed rock hound, so the colonel knew exactly where to take them while Mary and Papa and I went down to check in with Bud Purdy and poke into nearby hill country where chukar partridge were reported. As I recall it, the talk most of the way down was of the current situation in Cuba—and I got it thoroughly, as they knew it, salted with the analytical, future-wise. It was cause for me to blurt out something like:

"Why don't you two pack up your choicest things and get the hell out of there, close up the Finca until the thing runs its course, one way or another."

I hit the right key, all right, but the response was:

"Easier said than done, Mr. Pappy . . . still have to have it looked after, people have been loyal to us, with us a long time . . . can't just turn them out, you know. . . ."

So the little touch of an idea I had was put to sleep, and the subject was tacitly switched to the business at hand. When they passed it the night before, it was noticed that the old Stutter Man place was deserted, the house a windowless shell, outbuildings crumbling and half fallen in. The gate from the highway was wired up but stile steps for fishermen's access straddled the fence, so we walked in to the

First loot of the '58 fall, the exotic and very sporting chukar partridge. A gourmet's delight, second to none of the upland birds.

creek, hearing duck talk on the slough farther back in the marsh. A deaf mute would know that something was on Papa's mind but nothing but duck was talked and: "It's a good place here, the old bridge and all, for hunting, picnic lunches . . . know we won't be kicked off, anyway . . . hah!"

Dark, youthful, seemingly ageless Bud Purdy ran a successful operation on the old ranch, and there were changes in the basin, inevitable ones; but the gen was good, as always, and on our way back we drove up into the hills on a ranch road to show Mary her first chukars—the season on them not far off. Papa knew them from Europe but never in his own country. He was visibly drooling, for the bird is not only among the most difficult and sporty to hunt, he's a gourmet's delight of rich light meat on your table. Our rancher friends, John and Barbara Powell, said their gate would be open and he'd keep us posted. The Powells weren't of the old days, and Papa said when we drove out:

"Well, ten years really weren't so long, after all, but it's a shame that the old big marsh and runny nose flat is drained and growing potatoes."

Chuck was working on the cable into the house, so in a cracker barrel huddle around a set in the market we saw the tying game in the World Series on the eighth. (We had not tied into his service at our place, as yet.) For the Yankee victory on the ninth, assistant manager of the Inn at Sun Valley, Forrest "Mac" MacMullen, was our host, with a "bachelor's pride" lunch in actress Ann Sothern's house, which he looked after for her. Mac, like Don Anderson who headed the sports desk's activities, had fished with Taylor in the Keys a time or two, and one spring went over to Cuba for a few days. They both lived in the Canada chalet at the Valley where the colonel's popular domicile was the "Bobcat Bar"—which you had no trouble finding by the skin of the real thing tacked on his door. They "mothered" him too, in return for so much of their know-how of the out of doors that rubbed off on them. Both Idahoans, some of Mac's raising was in Montana, both joining the staff in the postwar days. Something about Mac's curly sandy hair, his ready wit, sharp-nosed features, his neatness, earned him the Hemingway title of "Duke." His little baseball party was a well-timed affair, too, attended by all Yankee fans, not a bit good for old Dr. Bookmaker.

"Just wait 'til Chuck's boy Stan gets our TV hooked up and we play the fights on Friday nights . . . just bring your cabbage and a mild thirst and. . . ."

"Yeah, do that," pipes the colonel, wired for a change. "And the doctor will teach you just how the old cow ate the cabbage, too . . . if you ask me, you'd better stay clear of the joint on Friday nights, unless you feel high in the green."

Our last convention left on October 10 and Sun Valley locked its doors for the fall. Tillie and I took our three-weeks' vacations starting with the bird seasons and fixed it for some extra time on our own. The Bruces drove the Buick back to Florida after a week with us, Clara Spiegel left for Chicago, and Papa accepted her offer of her dependable old Chevy station wagon to use for a hunting car. It was roomy, and perfect for the job. The duck season opened a bit ahead of birds, and on our first try at them on Bud's place we got cheated in one choice spot.

Along the bordering hills of the ranch ran an old winding drainage canal several miles long—great for jumping them afoot, its raised outer bank offering concealment in most places, a single lane road atop. We drove over to the canal on a bright Sunday afternoon, and up along it a short way, more or less looking over the situation; Papa driving slowly, reorienting himself, Duke and I the lookouts approaching the bends. On a very wide sweeping one rimming a big bowl in the hills it was a cinch where we could put up a healthy rise of mallards. We called a halt, Papa remembered it now, and quiet as mice we loaded guns, got but a few yards from the car on the perfect stalk. Of a sudden, about two shotgun ranges in distance a swarm of mallards exploded into flight. We straightened up from our crouches at the same instant a stealthy coyote got up off his belly on the low opposite bank of the canal. He just stood there, grinning at us—you swore—and trotted off into the low sage, an ear showing now and then, a bushy tail. Mary's rifle was in the car.

"Git the Mannlicher, teach the son of a bitch a lesson . . . even if it is his private domain."

We uncased it in a flash and Mary sent him over the top of that high hill, and he might be going yet by the looks of the bushy appendage propelling him along when we saw him last. Big joke, getting skunked by a smart gentleman on a first go-around, and of course the bark of the short-barrelled little 6.5 spooked some more farther along, but no matter. We got ducks to hang in the new pantry. Canoes for floating the creek were a thing long since vanished, but "Coyote Bend" would produce again, and other old canals were unchanged, too.

Following the lean postwar waterfowl era, Federal law finally reopened the snipe season. They were not plentiful any more, but in certain short grass meadows in upper Silver Creek you could count on a little shooting in the warm open weather. When Papa, Taylor, and I went to make a precheck of the lower country we got into plenty of them in a couple of places. The colonel, not shooting, climbed a post in a fence corner and marked them down for us, as sharp hawk-eyed as ever. As Papa laughed after many long years away from them:

"Well, kid, we had to shoot like hell and depend an awful lot on blind luck to get this many . . . don't tell anyone it was more luck than anything else, do we?"

He was so right, and for once in my life I outshot him for a very good reason: I had a fairly new dressed-up Model 12 pump gun in medium-range choke; its patterns twice the spread of the only shotgun that Papa brought with him. He was both over and under-gunned, and I had asked him about the two old favorites I knew so well. Oh, they had faded away along the line, just like old soldiers do, he'd said. When I first saw the double-barrel 12-gauge I recognized it from a letter that he wrote to Taylor in the early fifties in which there was a latrine description of its tight-pattern throwing, long-range characteristics; in fact I remembered those hilarious lines so well that I burst out a big laugh and said, "Hell, I could run my hands over it while blindfolded and identify it." He laughed, too. "Sure, and the front end of her is just as tight as the hog's other end was when I wrote you guys about her."

He bought the gun, well used, in Venice when working on *Across the River and Into the Trees.* It was a plain piece, but handsome in its clean slim lines, made in London, the reputable old firm of W. C. Scott & Sons, for an Italian marketing firm name Angelini & Bernardon. Its only adornment was a small silver name shield on the stock's underside that had never felt an engraver's tool for a former owner. It was the gun that threw the wad from which a wind-blown piece lodged in his eye. In gunners' talk it was a "pigeon gun" and how he shot it! For some reason or other he reached into his literary character file and called it the "Adams gun" and said he liked it as well as any he had ever owned. Admitting that he needed a "bit more open," I offered him my modified choke, and a trap gun opened up a bit for 16-yard targets only—both Model 12's. He tried the field gun and it fit him perfectly, but appreciatively he said, "No, Pappy, I see love in your eye for it, and don't put the field stock on your trap gun for me, I can get along with the Adams all right." Then the fun.

A bellboy owned a Model 12 pump that I knew very well, a 12-gauge with a short stubby barrel to which was fitted a variable choke device. When the short-lived "Flex-Choke" device was being readied for market, the gun was brought out to Sun Valley when the great shotgunner, Rudy Etchen, ran the shooting layout as a lessee. He tested the gadget thoroughly, fired untold rounds through it, found it flawless, and I photographed the tests and did the photo-art work for the advertising brochures and program—hence my familiarity with it. It was an ingenious thing in concept: you wound it up, so to speak, and the gas from each three shots fired tightened the choke successively—from improved cylinder bore, modified, then to full choke. Or it could be locked on any one by turning a flush collar on the bulky affair. The Model 12 is a pretty gun—one of the all-timers—but that gun, on the whole, was just plain damned ugly. Perhaps that's why the guy gave it to Rudy who sold it to the bellhop—who now wanted to sell it cheap. When I told Papa about it, he gave me the one-sided grin: "Oh, you mean one of them whore's dream arrangements, huh? . . . haw, haw, haw! . . . a club . . . well, we'll take a look at the W.D. gun, and if she cuts the mustard we'll deal with the kid."

I got it, and we wore out our arms throwing clay pigeons with a handtrap. As he said, "Takes one sucker to prove another . . . but by God, she shoots like a dream, whether for legit or prostitute." It actually fascinated him, and it was a handy piece, for its short length made for fast swinging and lineup. We'd accidentally knocked the midrib sighting bead off it, so took it to a fine gunsmith we eventually got in town; and the price of the gun was so low, "the damn thing could have a germ in it we can't see." Bill Jones fitted a new bead and assured the buyer he got his money's worth.

"Thanks ever so much, Bill, we'll take your word, but I think with its looks the kid shoulda thrown in a bow and a set of arrows, don't you?"

I'm not the only one around who can vouch for some phenomenal performances that came from the combination—shots that I wouldn't have the nerve to describe.

2

Though the area was still good, the old Frees farm setup was no more when the old couple retired in Shoshone, so we opened the pheasant shooting with Tom Gooding and a friend of his in Hagerman Valley. It was a fair day, though we worked for every feather, and the noon trigger sounded like the barrage at El Alamein. It's a memorable day otherwise, too. Six of us drove down: Mary and Papa, Taylor and Duke, Till and I, and just a bit late getting started on the hundred-mile run, so I had to step on it when the going was good. On a stretch north of Shoshone at seventy per a black cat tore across the road toward home, and Papa swore that our front tire nicked kitty's tail. He let out a long breath, crossed himself, said we'd do okay with that half-good omen.

Swearing he'd take it easy the colonel was along, for how could it have been otherwise? Got his birds, too, loafing near the car while we sent 'em to him from working the cover. We had a little respite at Tom's friend's place in the afternoon lull, then finished out not quite full up after all able hands bird-dogged a field with little for the effort. Then, casing our guns at the car, my somewhat disappointed little wife opened the theme—unwittingly—for the long drive home. She looked at that fine-looking field, shook her head:

"Gee, how I'd love to see a big old (male pheasant) get up."

The three-second silence was broken by a roar, then the chorus. Her face turned at least two shades, a long arm about her.

"Why, Miss Till . . . ," but he couldn't go on, and if so, no one could have heard him.

Duke drove home, and we took State 46 north from Gooding over the high pass that drops down into the big Camas Prairie wheat country—a continuation of the Timmerman dividing line. It was chilly, for when the sun deserts you in the lower country and you are climbing steadily, you know you're not in the banana belt—especially when you rode in a car with Papa Hemingway, his window always well down, and you wished you were penguin-dressed and Eskimo-blooded. He'd pull that old stocking cap down over his outside ear and to hell with sissies: they would-n't catch cold that way, nor be asphyxiated with a leaky exhaust pipe, and the damn heater fries your feet in heavy socks and boots! Tillie was snuggled down between him and Duke, whose cap was barely visible behind his collar; Mary between the colonel and me. The little bar in the glove compartment took care of Till and Mr. Polar Bear, who was quite sure that we had some booze buried somewhere, but asked anyway. Yeah, we had some—hundred-proof vodka that Miss Mary had poured into a plastic facsimile of the pint whiskey bottle size.

Climbing up to the pass it was steadily getting so eggs would freeze in that car; one of us would mumble a complaint and the window would go up an inch! Duke's head made like a scared turtle's, his voice wondering how the boys were win-tering over on the Popo Agie! Would the colonel back there like a nip of Scotch—he who hated vodka, nohow? You're damned right he would, mumbled a gratuity and retired into his burrow. You could pitch a cat out that window when we hit the top of the hill and a blast of icy air from the distant Soldier Mountains was like we drove into a sharp box. The colonel came up.

"Goddamn it, Mullen, if you'll pull up and let me out, I'll run on ahead and have a fire goin' when you fellas get in!"

Mary had fumbled around in the gear and pulled forth a jug. She took a belt of it, made an awful face and passed it to me. I made two and nearly gagged, but damned if the heat of it wasn't heaven. I held the bottle up in the glow of the dash lamp, saw that it looked normal and wondered why the whole thing hadn't dis-solved in its contents! I looked at Mary, she looked at me: four bucks-plus per fifth over the counter. She reached for it:

"God, Pappy, we may as well be numb as the way we are . . . and what are we, anyway!"

The window went up another inch and the contents of the jug steadily dimin-ished to about six drops as Duke pulled in at the Heiss house. It was sort of quiet in the back and Mr. P. B. wanted to know what in hell had been going on. We got out and Mary held forth the jug to him.

"Taste it, Papa," she said a bit thickly. "It's great."

Eyeing it suspiciously, he raised it up to the light—a spoonful couldn't poison him, surely; he tipped it up, a grimace like you never saw before, a roaring guffaw.

"Jesus Christ, men . . . these goddamn rummies drank a bottle of this!"

The jug disappeared in a mighty heave out toward the creek.

"Damn good thing there's a kettle of soup on the stove!"

About the end of October we got just a touch of rough weather, our first of the fall, when there was a mishap. In climbing over a high tight-wire fence, Papa sprained an ankle, some of the damage in the heel ligaments, too. It was enough to lay him up several days, as anyone could tell when his boot came off with diffi-culty. No, a doctor wasn't needed, said he, but we called Sun Valley's hospital over slight protest anyway, and Dr. George Saviers stopped on his way home with the necessities. The two were strangers, but felt as if they knew each other; had barely missed a meeting back in '46 when George fished and made out with the boys and the colonel before taking off for medical school. Remembering Jimmy so well, he knew he was being treated by a Saviers from the brothers' great similarity. Theirs was another "click" on sight. A not too disgruntled Papa said he'd spend the time working, goddamn it, and he did, hobbled about on an old cane.

At the time there was thought of going to east Idaho to hunt geese with Pete Hill in the upper Snake River area, man's hunting, strictly. The accident loused it up, as well as the weather; Pete was to fly over for us. It all worked out for the best, the timing perfect for a pleasant event, which could well have been a highlight of the season for Papa himself. Certainly it was for us. He got a letter in his mail forwarded from Cuba, when we picked it up coming from hunting on his first day out after the accident. It came from his Polish translator in Warsaw, Poland, a man he did not know, not even his name. He was due in the U.S.—his first visit—auspices of the Ford Foundation and the Institute of International Education. His hopes were that perhaps he might have the opportunity of meeting Mr. Hemingway, if only to get acquainted, say, in New York. There was no business attached. His schedule included a stop or two in Florida also. The letter was late when Papa got it; the man was in Los Angeles for several days. He got him on the phone at once, learned that he would be in San Francisco on November 10 with some free time— he was committed for the following Monday. I heard no part of it until Papa had hung up the phone, his coat, said suddenly, "This man I'd like to know, he's no interrupter. . . ."

Knowing that I was one of two emissaries for the Hailey-Ketchum-Sun Valley community who helped to bring feeder-line air travel into Hailey, he asked me to get full gen on connections, provide the man with as much of his free time in Idaho as was humanly possible. He smiled and simply handed me the phone, said: "He says that he likes to hunt but has had no opportunity for any since the war . . . that's one damn long time, you know."

That was a bona fide order and not easy; the local service meeting the coast flight into Salt Lake City required an overnight stop there, cutting into the next day. How could that be avoided, he wanted to know.

"Only one way, Papa," I said. "Johnson Flying Service in Hailey, and Larry himself is the only pilot, busy flying hunters in and out of the backcountry every day. . . ."

"Call him, if you will, you speak so well of him. See what he can do . . . if not, maybe Pete in Idaho Falls. . . ."

Larry said to give him a day's notice and he'd fix it. Papa called Los Angeles then and there—a most interesting little talk. It was November 8. He told the man that his flight to Salt Lake would be arranged and when there he'd have something fixed, not to worry about it. It was, you might say, talk between old friends. The man got perhaps the key question put to him with a small chuckle:

"Mr. Zielinski . . . as a good Pole, will you arrive drunk or sober? . . . all right, then we'll take care of it here."

When it was over, he said:

"Thanks ever so much, Mr. Pappy . . . have you ever hunted with a Pole before?"

"Not one spelled with a capital *P*, Papa . . . does he really talk like a huntin' man to you?"

"Yes, he does, and like a real gent, too . . . he's not at all set for any of this, but I guess we can fix him up."

And so did he on the flight selected. Larry took off for Salt Lake on November 11, to have the man in Hailey around six that evening. The gentleman from Poland had a surprise and a thrill coming. It started when he got off his plane in Salt Lake, the public-address system paging him. He was met by a small, laconic man in coveralls and an old leather jacket, and led to a single-engine—a big engine, he noticed —airplane of which he thought: the upper wing looks as if it's trying to catch up with the lower one. Larry used his powerful bush pilots airplane, a stagger-wing Beech, strange to a European. Then when approaching Hailey long after dark he saw no runway lights, only thin little twin beams pointing diagonally down the landing direction on a grassy turf—two pair on each side—car headlights of Larry's friends. The man was shook up a bit, but felt better when he scarcely felt the wheels touch down, the portable lighting system falling in behind to the dimly lit ramp by the single hangar. Then he got but a glimpse of a big figure dressed in old clothes, a stocking cap with a walnut-size topknot, approaching as a silhouette in the shadow of the overhung upper wing. Local hand to give him help with his luggage, of course. The man opened his door, said:

Discussing the Rape of Warsaw with a citizen of Poland at Heiss House in Ketchum in November, 1958.

"Mr. Zielinski? I'm Hemingway, so glad you could come."

Mr. Zielinski said later that he about fell out. We'd come in late from hunting, took care of our chores at home, the gals made dinner preparations and then we hurried back, barely in time. No question but that all four of us must have looked like hinterland, and primitive America to the good Pole—who did arrive sober on the so-called Champagne Flight to Salt Lake.

A charming man, younger and about my size, there was something about him that you liked at first sight. We stopped at the Snug Bar, naturally, for a round, where he was asked:

"Bronislav, isn't it . . . but how are you called?"

"Bron," Bron said, in beautiful English, so faintly accented as to be negligible. "And I can't believe any of it . . . I came to America and here I find myself in a place called Idaho . . . oh, what do I say?"

"Hi, Bron," Papa said, and Bron paused a second, blinked, said, "Hi . . . Papa." Papa raised his glass to him.

This from the man who wholesomely told me later that he was the man he wanted to know more than anyone on earth. I believed him, and still do.

With his motel but a block from his host's house, Bron was otherwise one of the family; my clothes that would do for hunting fit him; with plenty of socks for padding, he got by fine with Papa's old high Spanish boots. Given his choice he picked my old Lefever double gun because it was European to him in appearance, feel, and lightweight. You knew when he mounted it so perfectly that he could hardly wait to feel its jar on his shoulder, and you felt good in the way there are no words to describe. The day after his arrival the picnic lunch was at the old turkey place, with a

A "latter years" hunting picnic on old
Stutter Man's place.

Left to right: Dr. George Saviers, Sun Valley; Bron Zielinski, Warsaw, Poland; Papa Hemingway; rancher John Powell, Gannett, Idaho.

few ducks taken on the way. I can hear his laughter now, while he got Papa's vivid account of our experiences with old Stutter Man—the works from the near-dumping of the canoe to bullets singing over our heads. For some reason he found it hard to believe that his host had known Idaho so long and that a part of his big work that he translated was written here—until he remembered suddenly that Sun Valley was mentioned in an early chapter.

While there we poked around the marsh, Duke and Bron in a turn around the outer side, Papa and I pussyfooting it up the inner side to the slough. No ammo burned, but walking back, Papa suddenly stopped when we came around the ridge point in sight of the old house, confirmed my previously correct hunch. The old place could still be bought for a song, and he'd been thinking about it; could put up something in place of the house—small, good place to work and stay overnight when the shooting was good. What did I think of the idea? "I still have the pictures you made of it a long time ago, for Coop and me."

I said, "Fine, Papa, it's the only place in the whole basin available in these times . . . you've always wanted something up here . . . this one is good for little but your original idea, and now. . . ."

"Sure," he chuckled. "We could have a bulldozer knock down these old buildings and we'd have the goddamnedest bonfire you ever saw . . . but truly, the trees are still in good shape and we could do it pretty cheap, I think."

I took the bit, right or wrong, because the news mounting in Cuba seemed to call

Bron Zielinski and Papa Hemingway on their first hunting trip together. Papa is taking a ribbing on his spook of cottontails.

for it, along with my own idea in the back of my head, said something like this:

"Papa, I still think you should get out down there. If you come to it, count on me for help if you like; I'll get leave of absence that I'm entitled to, anything to help . . . sorry for being presumptuous, but I don't like it and neither do you."

In rarity, he put his hand on my shoulder, and if I ever saw hint of a mist in Papa's eyes it was then, and I felt like one plain damn slob! But he smiled, said slowly:

"With Bruce at that end, in Key West, I don't know anyone I'd rather have along than you, kid. It's an idea anyway, we'll see, talk about it some more. . . ."

He did, back at the old bridge, to everyone, while putting out the little blaze we roasted hot dogs on; the subject was dropped while we loaded up for back to the

Powell ranch where we got into some very good shooting on chukars. George Saviers was waiting for us with John and Bobby, we worked it slick, we younger "goats" on the hill work, the gals and Bron and the old master on the flats. A favorite photo I made is one of Papa and Bron, the latter with a brace of partridge and a pair of the little cottontail rabbits he'd shot—Papa grandly taking a kidding of them being great stuff—but not for his table. He opened that one himself, remembering what he'd written.

Pheasants the following day, for which we chose the old Frees farm district, and as we crossed the railroad tracks in Dietrich, Bron remarked on the familiar name identifying its little post office resembling a chicken coop. For it he got a full account of our history with the district, including the rabbit slaughters.

"You know, Bron, Pappy and Tillie brought me out here the first time to close the pheasant season and that opened the long thing of the jacks . . . I've threatened a number of times to have Pappy make me a picture in front of that post office and send it to the Kraut and tell her that we got the powers that be to name it after her, and that of a jillion rabbits we did away with, there was not a single meal of hassen-

". . . send her this picture and tell her I got the powers that be to name the place after her."

pfeffer to show for all that ammo . . . you got a camera today, haven't you, Mr. Pappy?"

I had one and the picture was made of him and Mary on our way back and I've often wondered if the glamorous and durable Kraut ever got a print of it. I'm inclined to think so.

Bron was an exceptional man, but not so much that he escaped the norm of being tagged with a name, and he got it for reason other than the "Wolf of Warsaw" indicates. Warning before we ever saw him that we must be careful of our careless "boondocks talk and sloppy slang" Papa himself was the first to forget it when we'd known him but minutes. He understood our language and lingual tomfoolery so well that it became a game, tacitly, trying to trip him up almost from the beginning. He "snapped" them all on the run, hence the name. He howled like one upon bestowment, and I guess we all raised the pitch an octave or so at his farewell party at our house on the stormy night of Friday, November 14, allowing time for his return to San Francisco by train. His host had a taxi alerted to take him to Shoshone—leaving about midnight—to make the miserable-hour connection at 2:00 A.M.

The main fare was roast beef rare on Miss Till's spittin' stick rotisserie that seemed to do the job especially well. Dressed for travel, we got Bron's jacket and tie off him, like we rats in from the sloughs, and while at the bar for the opener, Papa said:

"Wolf . . . she's a pretty nice pad here, don't you think?"

"Sir?" said the wolf.

Bron couldn't say, for he could not see one lying about.

"Ah, hah! Bron, old boy . . . we finally tripped you up, this round we tip to you for the long holdout . . . you know, my friend, most of our slang is not so bad, really, but whoever dreamed up pad . . . hmph! . . . whether it be shack, a tent, a penthouse, or wherever he lays his head, a man's house is his castle . . . the pad namer ought to be, you know, astraddle a log. . . ."

"Yes," Bron agreed. "And the knife forced upon him, too."

When Bron left that night, wet snow falling was so thick we hardly saw the lights in town center but a short five blocks away; but it was a local snow, we'd learned, rain in the lower valley and beyond the "hill." Otherwise there was little doubt that a dangerous road might have been bypassed for an aerial return for Bron. As we were talking it over, I made an attempt on the great few days past, and rather wistfully, Papa cut in.

"Wouldn't it be great, and good for the world, if all of it could be like that . . . if I say so myself, it's been an experience in human relations with Bron here."

He did not lose touch with him, either, nor did we.

3

When I called Pete Hill, cancelling the tentative hunt with him, Papa suggested I ask them over. He hadn't seen them since 1941, the last weekend before Pearl Harbor, which happened to be quite a ripper, I might add. In the postwar years they were out of state, Pete with the Civil Aeronautics Board since shortly after I knew him well. Oddly enough, and to which Papa attached certain significance of his own, they settled in business for themselves in Idaho Falls in August of 1953, the same month the Hemingways left Spain for the African trip. Thus, Mary did not know them. No definite date was set for their visit. Come when convenient for them was the word; when they called us and got no answer they knew we were out hunting, and so we were unaware that they were on their way when we stopped at the locker plant in Hailey to pick up six choice mallards for a roast duck dinner for Bron. The man mistakenly froze the birds, it was almost dark then, and you don't pick and clean "hung" ducks in a matter of minutes. Mary was fit to be tied, fumed all the way up to Ketchum, and who could blame her? Bron's farewell party was set for our house the following night, the menu planned. While Mary stewed, Papa chatted with Bron and Duke, sipping a short one, intermittently humming a little tune. I drove and smiled to myself. Too, it had been a wet miserable day hunting pheasants; we very nearly got skunked. Oh, well, the market would still be open, Mary said. We'd make out with something.

We got home, lit the fire, and the phone rang; Pete was calling to say that they'd just driven into town, brought their Brittany spaniels, hoped they'd help the hunting in such weather. Get the hell out to the house, Papa said. Mary exploded then. As if it were only yesterday when he'd seen them last, Papa said, "Hi, Dort, you've grown an inch, or am I taller?"—to Dorothy who's not much bigger than a pint of soap. The "old coyote" greeted the old pilot with, "Seems to me the last time we flew it the manifold pressure was a little high on all engines . . . am I right, Mr. Pete?" In the chatter of the reunion with these old Papa friends, Mary's mind still whirled about dinner, she who recently had joked that the garage looked like the back room of an old-time poultry market. Like reading their instruments, or feeling it in the seat of their pants, old pilots size up a situation fast or they wouldn't be old pilots. We'd go out to dinner, said he, if it suited everyone, or break it up, what the hell!

"The hell we will," said the old coyote. "This is an occasion, let's see now . . . it's been seventeen years . . . we'll do a production line, organizoots, don't worry, Kitner, nothin' to it, huh, men?"

Sure we knew, because the most abundant of the pantry's stock happened to be chukar partridge, they had not yet been tapped, and Mary had never cooked one. Not wishing to overblow her horn, Tillie in her years in the West had become mighty proficient with upland birds. Mary knew it, laughed, and gave up—the man of the house was having his fun. Skilled hands can peel, draw, and trim small birds and have them ready for the broiler in nothing flat. While the gals fired up other things, that was the production line. Have I not said that Papa drooled for chukars, hadn't had them in years. A disappointed Pete had hoped to bring over a goose or two for the pantry, but the geese had other ideas over his way.

So the meal was a simple one, and a delight, the Wolf of Warsaw, a stranger to them, now understanding why those great little birds were tops on our list. Wolfing for all he was worth, Pete casually said:

"Wonder what all the poor folks are havin' tonight."

"Chukars, goddamn it," Papa howled. "Damn near as good as Lodge Canucks, huh, Pete?"

Lingering long at the table over the old days, histories in between, and all, the subject of Christmas came up by someone asking Bron if he'd be back in Poland for his. It went on from there, and back in the summer we'd been with the Hills and made a date for Christmas at our house. Papa pounced upon it, with a broad grin:

"You wouldn't mind a couple of customers, would you? . . . Miss Mary and me may be sittin' out in the snow somewhere, or in a tent."

Mary chided him, but he wasn't joking: the pot was boiling in Cuba. Fortunately, he was able to keep in touch quite well by phone with headman René down at the Finca. Outwardly you hardly noticed the inner turmoil, but it was there, just the same. And let me say now that it truly was a wonderful fall in the fun department—one to remember. But that little remark at the table was a clue for me, and I simply couldn't help it, like at the slough that day. I decided to try at first opportunity.

That old place down on the creek was fine for the Papa a decade before, but not for the one in '58. Mine down there was go-along talk, and of course he knew it. Actually there was never any further mention of it. The opening came very soon, when Mary was at our house one morning as we readied ourselves for a hunt. She stood looking at the fine building property just across the street, about the choicest in the community—urban or suburban. We had talked of them before, from our point-of-view, lots that Tillie and I had coveted since we'd bought ours from the man who owned them. Papa knew all about that when we were building, and I had said that had we used our heads and waited a while we could have afforded their higher price—four lots in a parcel that the owner would not split in two (topographical reasons, the upper two worthless, except for eagles to build on but assuring privacy). The old man was an eccentric, cagey when approached in property deals, but he liked us and only the year before he'd come to us voluntarily with an offer four times that of his postwar price! We were tempted, even so, but . . . he offered to give us first chance at them should he feel that he had to sell.

So, when I'd loaded our gear in the car I said to Mary, "Come on, that lower slope fools you from here, see it up there for yourself," and she gladly went with me, all over the fine high contours so ideal for the view—many times as "enormous" as ours. When she'd had a good look she agreed to talk to Papa about buying them, almost beating me to the proposal. It was but an evening or so later, unloading from a hunt, that Papa brought up the subject himself, and the silent telegraph he used so effectively was: "Come sit down, we'll talk." We spent the evening, and he unloaded a lot of things, calmly, matter-of-factly, reading "the unreadable future in Cuba as best we can." First, though, he said:

"Mr. Pappy, those lots, though we might not have to put up a tent on them, are a good investment but . . . if I try to buy them don't you think the price will go sky-high?"

"Of course, Papa, but old Frank's word is good as gold, I know that, believe me; my proposal is that I buy them in my name, and I know the right attorney for handling paper work, deed, title, you know, keep it out of the public record for you, as you want it.

He thought it over a bit, "Gee, kid, I'd feel like the robber, you've wanted those a long, long time, but if you truly want to do it for us, frankly now, that's our rule, well, see what you can do and we'll take it from there."

In an aside, let me say that for sufficient reasons of our own, we were not prepared, or quite willing, to burden ourselves further at the time—much as we wanted the lots. Just to make it clear that my offer was no great sacrifice. Papa Hemingway was well aware of much of that, and for the record, he'd not otherwise have listened to any of it. So he was satisfied when I said I'd move quietly at it.

The old man was away at the time, but lived in plain sight of our place where I could watch for his return. Repeating that he was an eccentric, but shrewd as a hawk, he had to be handled just right. I got to him in about a week and told him that it would take me a little time to fix my finances. Could I have an option? Yes, I could, and at his crude dictation I wrote it out, in duplicate, on pages torn from a notebook. We sealed it with my check for a paltry sum that he would hold until I delivered. The option was good until the end of the year. A flimsy way to do business on a sizable transaction? Not in that case. I reported to Papa that I had the thing sewed up and to take his time. He was pleased beyond words, but got around directly in expressing himself:

"I guess we've all got the hunch that we might be staying out here all winter, and we've got to find a house within a month . . . but come spring and we have to pitch a tent up there it's quite a long way to the crick for water . . . I guess maybe ol' Pappy would run a hose across the street for us, Kitner."

Mary, by the way, had building plans in her head, made a sketch on paper and showed it to us one evening. Absorbing his newspapers, Papa made no comment.

4

Of course it was only happenstance, but at the time even the November weather put on a show—a delightful one. Not too unusual, at that, it was almost like a carry-over of Indian summer. We hunted regularly, but at a leisurely pace, as much for the outing and picnic lunches as for anything else. The duck season would penetrate into January, and heaven knew we were not pressed in that department. I think I'm safe in saying that the usual went on in the workroom, but there was little, if any, mention of it as I recall. Duke was idle with the fall closing

"Tailgate Bar" for serving a typical lunch while out hunting pheasants.

and Doc Saviers was our hunting pal whenever he could make it; and I must say that the colonel was not neglected, either. Often along for the ride, he was grand about it, Papa feeling much deeper about his empty gun hands than Taylor did. He'd get a little cantankerous on occasion, critical as a trial lawyer—or like a wise old horse casing the colts.

One lovely bright morning I used to finish splitting oversize firelogs and getting our winter stock in out of the weather, expecting the usual call near noon that we'd head for the creek or the lower country. We got the call, but not for that—it just seemed like a lazy afternoon to have a lazy lunch, talk about the London price of onions. Sure, Miss Mary, we're kinda lazy, too. But we knew something was in the wind, because even that was not quite the norm.

The Bloody Marys were in preparation when we got there, the front door was open and you could sit on its threshold in your shirt-sleeves if so inclined. Shortly, Papa said they had a friend coming, arriving tomorrow by train—did I get all wood worries taken care of? He wanted to show the man a good time, he said, leaning into it a little, as if reminding me that so late in the season, pheasant shooting wasn't exactly like taking candy from a baby—you had to have a few guns, surround 'em and out-smart 'em. A wee bit warm for northern ducks, too.

"Sure, we're in the clear, Papa, sounds like you got a huntin' friend comin', I'd say."

"Oh, he hunts, but not the kind we do, which is about all we do out here . . . but how can you beat it, for us, anyway?"

By train, tomorrow? No Sun Valley busses meeting trains, I thought; but sure, we'll be hunting down that way, pick up the man in Shoshone. No mention of it —then. The friend was working on a television adaptation for *For Whom the Bell Tolls,* he said, and during his stay, he, Papa himself, might find it necessary to do a little work on a day or two so that he couldn't always go afield. Okay, I said, simple enough, glad to do anything.

"Sure," he said. "I won't be tied up much, I hope, and we'll have to fix him up with a gun . . . I think your Lefever double, Gene's old gun, will be simplest for him . . . you mind?"

"It's there in your rack, where Bron left it, cut it out, Papa . . . gee, that's great, doing the book for TV. . . ."

"Well, who knows?" He grinned. "There may be a little life in 'our' book yet, maybe get back in the dough again from it . . . might be we can use a little extra before long, but what the hell, look at this weather, we're in luck and I think it might hold for a while."

Naturally I asked if we knew of the producer, thinking of several whom we regarded as old friends. No, we did not know him, he said, he was A. E. Hotchner, a magazine writer he'd known for some years.

"You know the crazy story of the betting on the horse race in France," Mary said. "When the padre from Cuba was in on it, the priest that Taylor told you so much about . . . well, Hotch is the one who rounded us out as the foursome in dividing up the loot."

Yes, we'd heard the story, from them, and Taylor, a real classic too. We ended up at our house for the evening, fully expecting to go out tomorrow. Papa said, on saying goodnight, "We'll see how it goes in the morning." In midafternoon, just such a gorgeous bright day as yesterday, Mary called. Could we come down to meet Hotch?

We met a slight, dark, friendly man, good talker, the entertaining kind, and right off I said I'd bet he was a Midwesterner.

"I've learned how to recognize one, like myself, Hotch. This fella here had something to do with that a long time ago."

"He would." Hotch laughed. "So I may as well admit it, I'm from St. Louis, but I've lived in too many other places since. I wish that I lived in country like this, from what I've seen so far I think I'd like it better than Connecticut; you know it back there?"

"No, got as far east as Philadelphia during the fracas, only a couple of days, at that."

". . . my priceless trigger finger that I couldn't, ever, do without."

Hotch was sure that he could do all right with the gun, and, thinking the men might wish to talk business, we left shortly.

"Sure, kids," Papa said. "Tomorrow for pheasants, huh?"

We were on our way by midforenoon, and it would be our luck, for a third time in all the years, to be challenged in hunting a place, or being kicked off, in the presence of a visitor. Except that the kicker-offer was a wee bit too late. We chose the Dietrich area where for some time we'd had our eye on a huge cornfield close to a quarter section in size. On the road to the old Frees place it was posted with weathered paper signs so old you doubted the teeth in the "No Trespassing." We hadn't asked to shoot it, thinking that some "dry" day it could be an ace in the hole. Nearing it we happened to meet the game warden cruising the area. Duke knew him, so flagged him down and asked about it. He said, yes, it could be hunted, the farmer was a friend of his, the sort who liked to be asked permission, was all. He didn't think he was home, but stop to see, he suggested, and if not, go ahead and hunt it—he'd be responsible, tell the farmer when he saw him.

"Nice fellow," Papa said. "Don't run into one like that often . . . you can tell he's reliable, too."

Just a good shot of Papa, in the fall of 1958—ebullient, taut, and full of . . .?

We drove to the house on the side road. No signs, and Duke went to the door anyway—no response. So into that big, heavenly juicy field of corn we went, cornfields in Idaho that size so few and far between. We had to work at it, organizoots to beat hell, but we got birds so that our six licenses could each cover a partial bag. So not to be piggish we didn't wear it out, rendezvoused and headed for the car in the road, a short distance from the house. The farmer's teen-age son had come home from school and waited for us—a blustering banty rooster who lit into the apparent leader of our party like we'd pulled the crime of the century. On one side of the picture it was so funny that you felt like exploding in mirth, on the other like snatching that little crew cut bald-headed. The apparent leader was wise to the smooth-tread trick of trying to bluff us to hell out of those lovely big "John birds" with the gaudy dress to match the trademark of Johnnie Walker Scotch Whisky; and he wasn't about to get by with it! Never have I heard such a smooth velvety tongue give a whippersnapper a deflating like that one got—polite, tactful—covered all ratholes, too: identified himself, everyone by name and address, the works. The leader was surrounded by his assemblage by then, and he walked on out, the boy sort of mincing along to one side, trying to figure what to say. Inside, the big leader was about to bust a gut laughing—but plumb disgusted with the youth of our generation. Tillie said:

"Papa, you devil, you missed your calling, you. . . ."

"Should have been a Boy Scout leader, huh, Miss Till? . . . I'll bet that little son of a bitch sneaks 'em all summer with a .22 rifle and swears the tractor ran over 'em."

The area on out past the old Frees farm—fair itself—looked the best, so to do his best for Hotch, Papa voted on it for the next day. The birds were wild, quick to take to the sagebrush, which is how we tried to work them, push them back to regular cover, if possible. We went into it, Papa and I well apart and out ahead of Mary and Hotch, figuring they'd use the pheasant ruse of laying low, then roaring out behind us, into the following guns. A couple did just that, one of them squarely between the two, flaring when he saw his mistake. Both guns went up, Mary a fraction of a second the first to shoot, the feathers flew, she had him clean.

"I got him, I got him!" Hotch cried jubilantly, truly thinking he had, and why not? Extremely close, but the experienced eye sees all the little signs.

"Hotch," Papa laughingly yelled. "I could skin him and draw him before your shotstring went by him . . . and you know if in their company, it's always ladies first."

Like the old saw has it, only damn fools and strangers bet on the weather in the mountains, and it was on its way then. On our first go for ducks on Hotch's visit there was a fresh fall of dry snow, a chill, sharp morning when anything could happen. We chose the old south canal for jump-shooting; I took Mary and Till with me to work from the lower end. Papa, Hotch, and Duke started down from the upper. I used every Indian trick I knew in scouting ahead, needlessly: I saw not a feather, heard no shooting, at their end. I saw that the boys were working our way in a silver fog, miserably cold things of rapid temperature change. Bright sunshine on our end, but we'd get it soon. Empty-handed, we mosied back, for we had the car, to wait; and we said that maybe that old dog coyoty had worked the whole thing and skunked the boys, too. Soon we were enveloped in fog, chilled to the bone from it; I fired up the engine and we were about to climb in to get warm when muffled voices were heard coming our way. They had the happy ring to them. Ghostly figures loomed up. I called out:

"How'dja do, men? We saw nothing, heard no shooting."

But the figures looked sort of pregnant.

"Wagh! . . . we got thirteen, as you can damn well see!"

A baker's dozen is what they had, too—and cold feet. Stutter Man's was the place to build a fire, heat slices of leftover rare roast beef, with our lunch. Hotch had his little 35mm camera, asked that I make a picture of him with Papa. He had black-and-white film, otherwise it was nothing against the grey pall as a background.

"I should at least have a record that I hunted out in Idaho, and look like one."

So I made him a picture and we took off to build a hot fire. It was our last outdoor picnic that year—and not too enjoyable.

Papa and Hotch

A couple of afternoons later, a bright snappy one, Papa was tied up with some work, so he asked me to take Hotch to try again for some ducks. I chose the old faithful canal, just knew we wouldn't miss there. We had no luck on a couple of the upper bends, so we made the big swing to come in on the center of Coyote Bend, Hotch off on my left a short hundred yards. Expectant ears often fool their owner, but I was quite sure I heard ducks, instinct smelled them. We did a good sneak, got fairly near to gun range, when the roar of a hundred pair of mallard wings split the air. They rocketed up, levelled, and passed across Hotch's line well out of range, carrying the mail.

"Now what scared those ducks?" Hotch said, straightening up. "We weren't making a sound."

I suspect that he thought I was laughing at him; I was amused at the irony of it— the thing that you expect yet you don't.

"See that sheep dog trotting up through the sage there, Hotch? Well, he's a coy-ote, and he's laughing at us, taking his time, for he knows if a bullet was due him it would be there by now."

I told him about the hand he'd dealt us once before.

"Cute as hell," he said. "But can he really make a living off that canal?"

"No, Hotch, they live mainly on field mice, rabbits if they're fast enough, but they have a dessert of duck now and then."

His jinx was a good one: all we got was "hunt" the rest of the afternoon—it was just one of those days. When reporting in I said, "Sorry, Papa . . . made a record today, the first complete skunking old Silver's ever dealt us. Guess who?"

He guessed, all right, first try, quite amused. It was to be an evening at our house, Hotch's last night in camp. He headed for his motel to change and I got as far as the door with him when Papa called me back. He had the pencil and note pad in his hand, wrote something on it, tore the sheet off and slid the pad and pencil to me, ask-ing that I sketch him a map of the bend and mark the exact place where the coyote had spooked the ducks. Then how had the old boy left the scene?

"Well, how do *you* think he left it?" I said.

"That's what I thought," he mused. "You've described it perfectly, it would make a fine little piece . . . from the coyote's point of view."

My grin gave me away—I thought he was joking. He was not, so, "Sounds inter-esting, Papa. Wonder how a coyote's thinking on such a trick would read."

"Good, I think what he did to you guys today gave you a royal one. It's the same in man or beast, I'll just spell it with an 'm' instead. Takes two old dogs to know how another one thinks, don't it?"

"I guess so, Papa. Shall I try a howl when I get out in the dark!"

"It's a bit early, kid, but see you in a little while, and we'll *knock* when we come."

When I went past the window outside, he was bent over the pad, writing.

5

For some time we'd had our ears and eyes open for something suitable for the coming move; inquiries on the very few good houses invariably sent the rent soaring when known who wanted them. The company had an arrangement whereby staff of our category could live at Sun Valley—operational convenience. We took our meals there—as part of our salaries, so as an ace in the hole all along, we offered our house. So of course Papa said no, surely something would turn up.

Now there was no doubt about staying into the winter, for Papa began to talk about sending Mary and me into the hills for some meat. Would I go? You bet I would, but hardly thought it was worth the expense for him to have Larry fly us into the Middle Fork where there was an extended season into early December for deer. He brushed that aside. I knew the area well, arrangements were made for a one-day trip, for Larry shuttled daily anyway. On our first take off a murderous snow squall in the high Boulder Mountains twenty miles north turned us back, not a sign of a hole in it to let us through. It cleared later in the day, so we were set to be at the Hailey airport at daylight the next morning—over a mild argument. Tillie had a Twin Falls dental appointment, and damned if she could make the drive herself; word had it that fog (common at that time of year along the Snake River) could very well move in, possibly icing the road. And besides: "I'm not going to sit around on my butt worrying, when everyone is doing something for the cause." Papa won the argument to look after Till, and they did run into the fog—we saw it as soon as we got altitude over Hailey. From Timmerman Hill south it was a blank, clear as a bell for us flying north. Papa said that while Till was in the dentist's chair, he window-shopped and tried to locate old friends, "Big A" Wood and Jack Redden, both out of town, to his keen disappointment.

In the mountains we had a fast-moving, rough, but successful day. We rode down out of the high with our deer to a river canyon airstrip of postage-stamp size, barely making it in time for a daylight takeoff and the lineup to the distant exact dip in the crest of the Boulders, barely visible, even then; when you know that the skill of the bush pilot—men of a breed apart—will take you over in pitch darkness, to hell and gone 'way up there, the wrinkled and jagged hide of old Earth waiting to take a poke at you if he miscalculates an nth degree along the line. Many times I'd heard the throb of that big engine in the black of early evening—Larry's flight line to the back country directly over our house; and a glance at my watch told me that he'd never come out of the Middle Fork as late as we were that night.

An anxious Papa Hemingway was pacing a groove when Larry set her down like a light-footed cat; and he'd come to get us twice, driving slowly, his ear tuned along the way. He saw the signs of butchering on my clothes, the bulging blood-stained flour sack in my hand as we climbed from the plane. A tired pair we were, too, glad that that day was over. He said Till was waiting, with steaks for her broiler, and either of us could have wolfed one raw on the spot.

Within the next few days luck smiled—such as it was—on the house-hunting thing. In the local paper Till saw a house-for-rent ad; we knew the people well, the man a skier-carpenter, season depending. They lived in the house, had another outside of town. She called the lady and was surprised that the house was no-where near finished inside. She put it out of mind, then got to thinking about it and called Mary. When we came in from hunting that night Till was at the Heiss house and from both their manners we knew that our gals had been doing things—like little girls who'd made a drastic goof, or were caught picking a neighbor's flowers. Before we got our coats off Mary set out our brands, said forthrightly:

"Papa, we got us a house, and you guys better sit down with a pacifier while we tell you about it."

He simply looked at her, a sort of relieved smile.

"Kitner . . . if you got us a house, we got a house, great! Is there a place to hang our meat and birds?"

"No, not even an unattached garage and not a lot else, either . . . but the house does have a fine and well-equipped kitchen, everything to do with there, a nice counter that you'll like as well as this one, dining furniture, places to lay our heads at night, and that just about sums it up . . . wouldn't you say, Till?"

"About like it was when we had to move into ours, Papa—raw, unfinished floors; paint where he'd had time for the most essential. . . ."

"We'll make out." Papa cut her off. "Get some zebra and antelope skins sent up right away, have something under our feet to make us feel at home . . . these won-derful Heiss people will let us have the garage for our game. This one we hate to leave, as good a camp as we've ever had up here, but we've known we'd lose it so we're tempered . . . thanks ever so much, Miss Till, now we won't have to kick you out of house and home."

"Thanks for what, Papa, I stumbled onto it, and felt. . . ."

"Good things can come from stumbles, you know, and let's charge it to thought-fulness and luck. We'll go with you tomorrow, take a look."

The man agreed to do a number of things to make the house more livable by mid-December; the rent was fair enough—Papa's only other major question.

Certain things were needed for it, but why spend for a temporary thing? In our sitting room we had a small leather armchair that was kind to Papa's back, with a spare that we put in its place. There was a good laugh over an old floor lamp that barely stood by itself beside a cot in our attic; shade gone, but with the inverted bowl and three-way light making for good reading, if you didn't give a damn for looks. Nobody did, so it went with the chair, and the stored bookcase went too, filling a blank wall in the well-laid-out living room that literally begged for attention, its nice fireplace a focal point. A huge picture window faced the big mountain, much nearer, the house on the opposite side of town center from us, the walk about three and a half blocks. The wall was otherwise a blank, too, so from leftover materials in the backyard, Miss Mary scrounged masonry building blocks for legs and a panel of heavy plywood of the right size for a top. Presto! A coffee table big enough for a quarterback, strong enough to support a horse—but really a place for the ever-present truckload of newspapers and periodicals. The master bedroom was decked out pretty well, but the one selected for a workroom was rather sparsely furnished, a chest of drawers of similar vintage to take the riser blocks and tilting top.

The one feature to catch Papa's eye was a fine adjustable-angle TV set hung from a far corner ceiling of the dining ell of the big main room of the house—viewable from most any corner of it except the sleeping quarters. Another to catch Miss Mary's wondering eye was the height of the counter tops, the breakfast bar separating the kitchen area. The landlady was as tall as a Diamond Horseshoe chorus gal and had her man make the counters a good three inches over normal height. Five-foot-three Miss Mary wondered which end she was short on—the upper or the lower. A small plywood box that she could kick about with her foot from the chopping block to the stove decided the issue for her. By Saturday, December 13, the place was as livable as could be under the circumstances, except the hot-water heating decided not to work, baseboard radiators were as cold as stones. Installed back in the spring, they were new enough to have not yet acquired the habit of operating properly.

Back on the job then, we knocked off at noon, thinking the final moving was done that morning, and that maybe we'd get word to take a late afternoon run down to the creek; there hadn't been one for several days. Coming into town at our corner, we met Papa on foot, turning into the block to the Heiss house. He flagged us down, came to open Tillie's door. The mood was high—a talking mood, the signs read "Then what were we doing—anything special?" "No, I had but one small errand to do up home." He reached for Tillie's arm.

"Make your errand snappy, Mr. Pappy, we got leftovers that we can move easier when they're inside us—and leave your boots at the door . . . the floors are so damned clean for the move-out . . . you know how it is."

The paper bag under his arm had the telltale shape of a large can, tomato juice size. He caught my look, said yes, could I think of anything better than a Bloody Mary at the moment? He was making them his own special way when I got back to the house where they'd have to wait until a call said the heat was fixed in the new place—which already had acquired a name. The people's name was Whitcher—not exactly as common as Jones—and when he first saw it, Papa said:

"It's okay, we'll move to the Whitcher house, and we could wish 'er were finished but that'd take the fun out of being gypsies."

So, Wisher house it was called, as we call it today.

So the afternoon was a lazy one of talking, reminiscing, a pickup lunch, a half bottle of vodka lasting us out—the manuscript, the clothes on their backs, and two "cotsies" (cats), all there was left to move. The kitties were half-grown, pretty grey-and-white things that someone dropped off nearby. "Mr. Peterson" and "Purr-house" kept down the mice in the tiny furnace basement. Brother and sister, Mr. Peterson was the favorite, say a foot-warming cat. Out in the garage there was another, not nearly so friendly, member of the household.

His name was "Owlny" because that's what he was—a small brown owl with a crippled wing—and he'd been brought down with a definite purpose in mind: as a crow decoy for winter shooting down along Big Wood River where they congregated by the hundreds in the cottonwoods. On a November day we went down to hunt ducks on the old south canal on the Purdy place, a bright snappy morning following a fall of about eight inches of fluffy snow. Right beside the highway in a pasture a short mile from Picabo grew a small patch of scrubby willows little higher than your head, and several pheasants, drifters up from the country around Richfield where they wintered quite easy in less snow, had been caught in that one. They clung to the precarious perches of thin willow branches, so we drove on past a bit to try a sneak back to them—a near hopeless thing, we knew. They gave us the slip, all right, but almost from under Tillie's feet the owl, hunting mice in the willows, flew out. Papa took a careful lineup on him, deliberately winged him. Examination on the spot, dodging talons, a snapping beak, showed the wing bones intact, the damage in the muscles instead. Bandana handkerchiefs bound the wing folded normally to his body, same as we once did for a duck that was saved to fly again, and Owlny was put in an empty shell box and taken home to heal up for his assigned future role. His cage was a large carton with holes cut in for ample ventilation, the old cane poked through it as a perch. Owlny's food was the giblets from ducks and birds, a blackbird shot now and then, or a rabbit, for the roughage required in his diet. He resented every damned bit of it, too—better have gloves on if his home needed attention. In residence so short a time when the move was made, Owlny could not yet fly, but the signs said he would one day. To determine that, we tied a string to a foot, gave him a slight boost, but he settled onto my heavily gloved hand, his talons plainly felt through it, and they had to be pried loose to put him back in his box. Papa disdained gloves, always, and his hands were as if they'd been run over with a steel currycomb from feeding Owlny. I hoped that when he was flyable again he'd turn him loose, for actually Bud and his boys on the ranch had wire-mesh cage traps ready for trapping magpies, nuisances around congregated wintering stock. True, a very old trick in the shotgunning book;

tethering an owl in a tree for decoying crows—but "magpie-ing" was much simpler and a service to the ranchers. Naturally, Owlny would be taken care of religiously, the pantry would be visited until exhausted, the market only a block away.

In midafternoon a call was made about the heat: not yet but in time for dinner, they hoped. What the hell, nothing else to do, a bright but very snappy day outside, snowfall in quantity to know it would stay. Good stories and remembrances were going well. The latter came up with the comment that it had been an easy fall on the pocketbook, the rent for the Wisher house the same—and by God it oughta be, no arguments there—and come to think of it, falls in Idaho had never been hard on the purse.

"You've always said, Papa," Till remarked, "that a fellow could have more fun out here at a modest rate than about anyplace you know of."

She broke out in laughter, remembering an old one, and it opened that flawlessly filed store of memories.

"You mean when I first came I was broke, and before the fall was out I borrowed from you, don't you, Till?"

"Yes, and I think you should tell Mary that one."

"You tell it, Miss Till, I'm not sure that I. . . ."

"The heck you don't." She laughed. "But I will because it's the kind we'd have to tease out of you. Come on, Papa, admit it."

He guessed we would, at that, so she told it, about so:

"We went down to the Alpine one Saturday night for dinner, their sizzling steaks at eight-five cents, the come-on for the casino, you know, where we headed next. With a little money between us all, we played the games until after midnight, just seesaw. . . ."

"And Pappy and I both went broke by then," Papa cut in. "And as usual you were the lucky one on the wheel. Go on."

"Yes, I came out seven dollars ahead, after I bought a nightcap at the old Stockmen's Saloon, a habit when we were in town, then Papa came to our room to borrow a book, so we had another nightcap there. At the door he said, 'Daughter, would you mind loaning ol' Papa a couple of bucks?' But he couldn't keep a straight face, so I asked him if he was quite sure that two would be enough, and opened my little pocket purse with the silver dollars. He reached in and took all seven of them. . . ."

"I see," Mary said. "I remember hearing that there were a couple of whorehouses in Hailey in those days . . . was it River Street, or something like that?"

"As I heard it, yes," Till said. "Then he apologized for borrowing it all, but he said he was damned if he'd be but a two-dollar bellows to cool a harlot's lust."

"You got it exactly right, Miss Till . . . showin' off that I'd read the big stuff, wasn't I."

"And when did you get the seven back, Till?" Mary asked.

"In the morning at breakfast, which was rare, but it was Sunday and I went down the creek with these two show-offs, just for the ride. . . ."

"And then I did show off, and we damn near dumped you in the drink again, Miss Till . . . seems we never did things right with you in the canoe . . . well, guess I loused up that observation. . . ."

"Yes, you did, Papa, I went along to be bird dog, don't you remember? . . . Now, tell Mary your good dog story, that one you said was a hot stove tale for duck hunters only."

"Well, we're duck hunters, Pappy was chief witness, and I'll listen this time."

One chilly prewar morning we were at the big marsh, Taylor and the younger boys in the lower blind, Marty, Papa, and I in the upper, with Mr. Bullet, the Labrador, handling the retrieving. Icy wind cut like a knife when we'd rise to shoot, and we had small pressure burners made from old camp stoves for heat—such as it was. Business was good early, then there was the usual lull; the dog's presence in our blind was not so desirable: the air at too frequent intervals was evidence that it must've been "sumpin' he et." We had to take it or in cruelty boot the wet dog out in the wind. Soon a flight of mallards wheeled over for a look and Papa and I nailed

". . . hafta send Bron a print of this just to show him I don't spook from rabbits—dead ones, that is." (He didn't; Bron got one from this reporter when he again visited us exactly seven falls later.)

a pair; the dog tore out and brought the first one to us. I saw the devil in Papa's eyes, but didn't catch on until he raised his head over the blind rim, called out: "Colonel, may get some action now, call the dog to you with this bird. . . . We'll hold off on the next bunch for you guys."

Bullet obediently trotted to their blind, the needler about to burst in glee, and it wasn't but minutes until he did. Taylor's hat showed up, then his screwed-up expression, his shaking fist, then two dark tousled heads that never wore covering in any weather. Their father nearly choked himself yelling down the wind:

"Don't I always say that when you hunt you share alike?"

Shortly we saw the dog's tail wagging from around the sunny side of the blind, then it would disappear, then back outside again—an earthy little pantomime says it best, I guess. We had two thermoses of soup with us and presently Papa shouted out, "Hey, Gigi, you guys want a little warmup, some hot soup?"

"Oh, boy!" came up the wind, but sounding like this:

"Ooooo, buoy!" and the dog beat Gigi to our blind.

"Thanks for the soup, Papa. Bullet's better now."

Just the colonel's eyes were visible above the sage rim as this was all going on. Then in about two minutes:

"Yeah . . . just what we thought . . . Bullet's so much better that he's decayed!"

"Papa, you were a louse," Mary howled.

"Yeah, but who got the double dose, huh?"

Needless to say, when in that sort of groove, it was the old stuck-needle thing as the day wore on with mounting concern for the other house; nothing to be done about it, so back on a track of another kind: two real delicacies in the refrigerator not to be trusted in earlier moving. Hotch had sent a wheel of exotic spread-type cheese; a typical container of near-quart capacity of A-grade caviar, the rule being: "Dole this out sparingly, make it last; if we could stand the tariff, we'd have him send some more." It was well after dark when the call finally came that the moving could be finished. Perhaps an hour passed in our gathering up the finals and closing the door in a little verbal ceremony, a promise in owl talk.

We got things into the house, Till and I not doffing our coats and about to say good-night when it was noticed that the house felt a little cool. It was, and a check proved a dead system in the basement. What I knew about boilers you could engrave on a pinhead; we couldn't locate the owner and finally by phone I found a Sun Valley steamfitter who reminded that it was Saturday night—the last one the locals would have the town to themselves until spring. I was told to push this button, turn that valve, listen for the gurgle and wait a bit. If nothing happened, hit the damn thing with a hammer like we used to do with a balky Model T Ford. I guess we did, for by somewhere around nine we had the place cozy with a roaring fireplace and the cats curled, their backs to warm radiators. So the Wisher house was initiated with a pickup supper, and though it was odd in a way seeing the soft brown

African antelope skins and the bold contrast of zebra hides on a floor in Idaho, well, it was warming to the eye and senses. A beautifully tanned, head-mounted cougar skin—a local gift—hung on the wall above the bookcase.

6

The following Sunday Taylor Williams gave us all a little scare. On the job at the foot of Baldy Mountain's ski lift he was brought to the hospital with a stubborn nasal hemorrhage. On an errand to the Valley I bumped into Doc Saviers who said it was the worst of the occasionals he'd suffered since his stroke in the spring. He let me say hello to him, but thought that he'd keep him quiet another day before letting him go back to work—a physically effortless job. I went back home to finish my Christmas tree trimming, saw Papa trudging up the hill, dodging sledding children, excited dogs stealing their show. He waved his walking stick at me, working by the big front window—his stick an old short ski pole he'd resurrected in the basement. I saw from his broad grin that the mood was high, his hand motion telling me that the tree looked good from the street a hundred feet away.

He parked the stick in the hall and I noticed a stubby piece of corncob stuck over its spike tip; of course it amused me and I said something about it being a one-horse town, but we didn't feed the horse corn on the cob.

"I learned that a long time ago." He laughed. "So the cob came from the lower country . . . spike no good on a walking stick, but it comes off easy for spearing lost dollar bills after a wild Saturday night in town . . . spear a beer can and get a fifty-yard toss every time."

"Got any windows by accident yet?"

"No, but I broke up a hell of a good dogfight with the stick . . . she's a cute little bitch, too·. . . now I know where the rest of the town dogs are."

He'd learned about the colonel, and was putting it off, his expression giving him away—soundly disturbed when he opened up. I told him that I'd seen Taylor but a minute, and that later in the day we could go up, after returning from a late run down to the creek. No, he'd rather not see him down, never had; we'd check by phone. I went on with my trimming, listening to him repeat an apology that he'd made a couple of times to Mary, Duke, Till and me: an incident one day far out in open country, hunting ducks on an irrigation canal—windy, cold, seventy miles from home. The colonel, in the isolation of deafness, couldn't dovetail with us in a worthy effort, gave us hell for not getting out of there and heading up the road for home. In short, he had us biting nails. Softly to us, his voice toned in mixed emotions, Papa said:

"Poor ol' Pop, he's like a grey-muzzled old bird dog . . . not worth a damn any more, but you love him so much that it isn't any good without him."

Now again beating himself in buildup of guilt had his remark been heard, we reminded again how Taylor had made successful effort with his good humor on the road to make up for his impatience.

"Yes, he did," Papa said. "I know that he's awful good about admitting what he

A cold-footed Papa stomps to get his feet warm; "Duke" MacMullen nurses the fire; A. E. Hotchner, visitor from Connecticut, looks on; Miss Mary and Miss Till preside at the grub bench. A landmark of the old days—"Stutter Man's Chancre"—is at the right in the background.

misses and gets cranky . . . but I worry because this thing has been with him a long time."

He wished that he'd retire, but understood why he didn't; why management was so fair in not urging him to retire at overage; nor was living alone in his little house an encouraging prospect, either. Easing off the subject slowly, Papa said, "That's not exactly down his alley, but at this time of year, going into winter, things look bigger. Come spring he'll perk up like a kid, probably."

A good opening and Till took it: "Papa, he's probably a lot more perked up, even now, than we see, his eggnog party is all lined up at the Bobcat, you know he'll beat hell and earth to have that, and here at Christmas. . . ."

"Sure, a bigger kid than all of us put together . . . well, as Mr. Pappy once said of him, 'basically good rubber bounces well' . . . and say, speaking of our Christmas dinner, you said you have the tree for the dining room . . . I want to see it, since Pappy beat me good on that deal."

I had, and we think it as cute a "kid" Hemingway anecdote as any: Time and conditions permitting I always went up-country to cut our tree from the forest, but Papa probably forgot that, for when Tillie won the mild argument to have the Christmas party at our house because of a little more room and other factors, Papa insisted he'd buy a nice tree at the market when he got theirs. It popped out of him at exactly the right time, that last day at the Heiss house, and I said:

"Buy it with what, Papa, when I got my sharp ax and my skis to take me into a canyon where I know there are some dandies. Don't you respect tradition, the hand-down of our forefathers?"

"How about another Bloody Mary, Mr. Washington, the barkeep, Mr. Lincoln, is glad to oblige."

He went on to say that while I was tradition-bent, would it not be nice to have a small tree in the dining room for added cheer, and I said I thought I could arrange it. Good, he was to have charge of the bottled goods department anyway, so he'd pop for a bottle of champagne, in toast to the symbol of Christmas. So with the big trees I found a perfect specimen about two feet tall, so tightly branched a pine squirrel would have been hard put to hide in it. Trimmed with tiny lights it truly was a storybook little thing on a stand that I had to make to bring it up to height in a corner of the room.

"A cone of greenery so perfect," he said, "that it looks good enough to eat . . . but aren't we glad that we can't!"

Unusual in his occasional calls of that kind, he stuck around quite a while, we talked this and that, lightly, laughed at the children, some of them dragging their sleds up the diagonal slope of the lots across the street that were then his—but not in title, and to be paid off in full after the first of the year, for tax reasons of the seller. We did it quietly in our own way (through our old Midwest bank); and Papa joked that at least he was contributing something—he wasn't asked to be Santa Claus for the kids in the town program, only in fun by old Pappy Hanes who needled him every time he saw him all fall. He stayed long enough that I started changing to hunting clothes and Duke arrived, ready for takeoff. He reported that the colonel was doing all right, and that he was cranky as a sore-foot bear. A weight seemed lifted off Papa's shoulders, and we had a fair little hunt before sundown.

7

On Christmas Eve Till and I went to town early on errands and I had to be there for at least the start of the program a bit later, then back up to the Valley for that one. Parking was at a premium, the little town packed, and a glorious display of street-canopied light—quite new decorations for which we could hardly afford to dip into the treasury. We bumped into Papa coming from the liquor store, on foot, his box of goods put down on the sidewalk so he could get back at Pappy Hanes who had him backed to a wall in the usual nonsense. To us he said:

"Gawd! . . . did you ever see so many kids in one small town in your whole life . . . has His Honor appointed a general, a . . . Pied Piper to keep 'em in line for Mr. C. on that hayrack? . . . they'll sink him first round if you haven't."

"You wanta be Pied Piper, Papa?"

"Humph! not bad . . . E. Hemingway, P.P., Ketchum, Idaho. A place in the staid and phony world of titles. Merry Christmas, Miss Till, right here on the street . . . and say, Mr. Pappy, I got an old friend here in the box, you guys got the time?"

We took the time, and him home. The old friend was a bottle of tequila of a particular brand that in the old days we often had a nip of in Leon Bilbao's Tram Club bar—a jug Leon kept especially. The brothers Bilbao, Dan the other, were in Nevada, but they were blocks in the old structure and never forgotten. So they were toasted in our "shot of blowtorch" and Mary was going up with us to sing in the program, then come back to do something similar with a few gals about town. Stay-at-home by choice said:

"If the carol singers come by and throw one for ol' Papa, shall I reward 'em with a shot of this?"

"Not if you want 'em to serve the neighbors and make it last the season out as we used to do."

"Guess you're right." He laughed. "On both counts."

It was mutually agreed that since it was a first practically full Christmas together, we could go a little above the mere token level in our exchange of modest gifts. Tillie hit it on the nose: through a friend who had one, we got a practical envelope-shaped insulated carrier for iced foods for travel, a good-looking multi-purpose piece to go nicely in any luggage company. Orders were to appear at the Wisher house for Santa Claus hour, after he had taken the ten-minute walk down to the Baldy lift to say Merry Christmas to the colonel. The day was a beauty: crisp, bright, the rugged land a diamond-studded fairyland of white.

In a little while, when the gifts were opened, we had to say to Mary and Papa: "You devils, you, you broke the rule."

And we said it after minutes of the tongue-tied warming surprises of all kids on Christmas morning. From a sizable heavy box Till took mountains of wrappings about a beautiful hand-painted Italian salad bowl and plates for eight. What practical gal doesn't take enormous pride in her table; so for her starry-eyed "You should not have done this," she got:

"Why not, Miss Till? When it comes to salads aren't we all part rabbit?"

In the other box was a fine record changer for our hi-fi system, and these schemers had done quite a bit of that. In the past years or so I had replaced all my old components except the player, still going like a smooth-tread tire. I saw a new-on-the-market type I wanted when in California back in the spring. Somehow Mary and Papa pried it out of Till, who'd heard me ask Stan Atkinson if he could get me one when I was ready. Mary got on the phone to Salt Lake City and the thing arrived only that morning—barely in time to wrap it. The tiny card, in Papa's handwriting, read:

"For Mr. Pappy—from an old admirer."

Who, me? you say to yourself, because you don't know what to say aloud; so settle for this one, please. Later, when the Hills had arrived, Papa said to Pete and me:

"Now you guys should have a little time this afternoon to hook it up so we can have moosic . . . whoever heard of Christmas and no moosic . . . but don't hold a wake over the old tired one."

The gag gift of Pete's took the show. The fancily wrapped package was suspicious in its size, deceiving in light weight. Papa shook it, held it to his ear—"Gotta figure how to disarm it or never know what it is"—and slowly got it open.

"Ah, hah! . . . they're loaded with buckshot, too . . . best present of the day, Mr. Pete. If I throw a long high one, nick him in the outfield, I wonder how that will read from the coyote's point of view."

Our women's point of view broke up the morning party before the wake developed there, but well in time we had music without variations in the revolutions. It seems that at least a wheelbarrow of stuff came from the Wisher house, along with the roast turkey; Duke's contribution was the wonderful fat goose roasted at our house.

"Did you get him, Duke, in the traditional manner?"

"You're damn right I did. I knocked on the farmer's door, said, 'I'll take that big underslung boy right there, if you'll run him down.'"

When Papa popped the champagne cork it simply vanished, over our heads, but someone caught a glimpse of the direction; sure, it went into the coarse-grilled cold-air register under the little tree stand. That was supposed to be a bad omen, so we'd fish it out after a while. Later in the evening the colonel said, "What the hell do you think this is?" his finger pointing at the little tree. There was the cork, just an edge showing. Ah! that was a good omen—but don't take it from there now, retrieve it when the tree came down. All of it rolled up into a memorable Christmas.

10.

The '59 Winter ---
a Chapter Finished, One Begun . . .

1

The Sunday before New Year's, Papa said to me:

"Well, kid, another one about gone. . . . We'll see a lot of changes in the new one, some we're not looking for, I bet."

It's a cinch that he looked for the one on New Year's—the Castro take-over in Cuba. The apparently calm exterior acceptance of it we did expect because of the long warning. I think I'd have torn my hair out. Phone calls came from a number of outlets wanting statements of the Hemingway views of the thing as a whole, and we know of only one instance of violation of his hands-off policy—publicly. Till and I walked in on it, when Papa had just hung up the phone—a New York newspaper. The air said we'd better turn right around, forget the business we'd come for. Papa grinned, said no, come sit down—we'd seen him in his own doghouse before for saying things he shouldn't have. He finally gave in to Mary's sensible persuasion that he should pick up the phone and retract his statement. It was accepted without substitute. Papa admitted breaking his self-rule on the Cuban turmoil, but the retraction brought on a burst of bitterness in which he told us of a nocturnal search of the Finca for excessive, or suspicious, arms by the *Guardia Rural* of the Batista government. A watchdog was killed by a searcher's rifle butt (not the Blackdog from Ketchum) and such invasion had prompted Papa to make official protest, of which he may as well have tried to spit out the moon. So the take-over of New Year's Day planted local seeds.

For the first town council meeting of the new year I got our attorney to come up and take care of putting the "ownership" of the lots where they belonged. Papa liked the Twin Falls city attorney, Bob Balleisen, who knew his business, and had done so much for our town problems. Mary fixed us a bite of something to eat in our hurry to get to the meeting, Till had dinner with Mary and Papa. When I went to get her later the three of them were perched about the counter looking at a set of pictures of a fine local house. Back in the spring of '58 I photographed the property inside and out for a selling agent, and then in the fall when property of any kind was first mentioned, I had a set of the prints on file, asked Papa if he'd like to see them. Why did I? Because even a thought of building spooked him; to him it would be a billboard advertising the fact that Ernest Hemingway was about to get out of Cuba and take up legal residence in Idaho. I said at the time, "Why, Papa, people do it all the time, for seasonal or part-time residence, sometimes with the idea of renting it out other times." My offer of the pictures was a casual thing, for I knew there was a six-figure investment in the property, even though it could be bought at considerable sacrifice—about what the average man could retire on, at that time! They were not looked at in my presence, lay on the Heiss house piano for weeks. Now they were out, discussed rather lightly, and I was asked but a few questions of the place that neither had ever seen due to its semi-isolated location. Forget it, I thought to myself, but Papa asked if I needed the prints. No, keep them, I said.

In midmonth the Coopers came up for a short stay, about two weeks, the first Idaho reunion in eleven years. Coop was finished with skiing; we had lost them for a number of years earlier in the fifties when they put up a house in Aspen, Colorado; but the honeymoon didn't last long, and of late they were sort of filtering back to Sun Valley. Coop was due to start a picture in early spring. A first event was a magpie shoot at a private gun club near Bud's place on Silver Creek, followed in about a week with another—the trapping time between. January was its usual stormy self with an above-average fall of snow, so I sneaked off to get in on the fun of both of them, plus a prowling day or two with Coop. For some reason Papa didn't go with us. Coop was not a well man, had been under a surgeon's knife, and in his own quiet, indirect way let it be known that he wasn't riding a cloud over the results. But the little time I had with him was as enjoyable as ever.

A significant entry in the January notes concerns a Sunday night, January 18. The colonel was going along fine and we thought it fitting to have a simple dinner at our house, the Hemingways and the Coopers. Coop was disappointed that we were a bit late in cooking it up as an impromptu thing, a previously made date, so we had it anyway, the five of us. When I went down to drive Mary and Papa up, the snow was coming down in a solid wall of white. At the table we had the drapes open, the backyard floodlights on, the world outside a fairyland, snowflakes the size of nickels dancing to the silent symphony; and you felt like dancing with them, a mental kink in your back, too, when you thought about getting out in the morning! No matter then; the table cleared, we were "playing the game," which meant digging up old times and a couple of big fat picture albums came out from the bookshelves base cabinet, the chatter so thick you had a time getting a word in edgewise. Whenever we could, we'd try to maneuver the talk to a naturally favorite listening that we got in snatches from both Mary and Papa—Africa, a place that this kid had dreamed of from a small boy on—spurred now by my profession. In that respect I never had to twist either arm, they gave forth in volume when at all possible. It is quite probable that due to his great, lasting respect of white hunter Philip Percival whom Papa once labelled "the finest man I ever knew" he so often affectionately called the colonel "Pop" in addressing him in person. And of course the humor would invariably form the finale. Like the big laughs—with respect attached, too— of Papa having been honored with an "African fiancée" by sage old-timers of a village who remembered him from the safari back in the thirties. Invariably we'd ask, "Now how old did you say she was, Papa?" He'd howl, look sideways at you, say:

"Oh, all of twelve, I'd say, wouldn't you, Kitner?"

And Mary would say, "Judging by her size, I would say about that, and cute, too, some mighty handsome people over there; you've got to go with your cameras some time, Pappy."

It was now Papa's habit to take a little lie-down after a good evening meal; Till kept a small car robe on the foot of her bed for him when they came, and when he'd excuse himself the colonel would say, "Well, Chinner's buddy is here tonight, you'll see kitty sneak away from his mat by the fire to join in the siesta; Pappy has to siesta with kitty on the floor, or get his ears pinned back."

"Shhh!" Papa would say. "I'm the best cotsie lawyer in the business, don'tcha know."

The rest of us lingered on at the table and when the records on the hi-fi played out I went in to change them. Sitting cross-legged on the floor facing the book shelves, half blocking the hall to the bedroom, was Papa, the cat stretched out beside him. "Hell, we got chairs in here, Papa." Oh, this was fine, he said, just reach up to where they were handy—he had books out in little piles, on the floor, the cabinet shelf, amusing himself with old inscriptions in his own stuff, like three cute ones in the six-volume "Sunrise Edition" of 1939:

Earliest Book
by Hemingstein
    X
his *mark*   *(In Our Time)*

"Who said this was a dirty book?
Nobody from Glamour House—
(The Harry Morgan Room)"   *(To Have and Have Not)*

"Winner take nothing,
But me Take Tilly
    Hemingstein"   *(Winner Take Nothing)*

plus a big volume that sold for ten dollars back in 1932 when first published:

"Such a Big Book for Hemingstein to have
written day and night for such a long long time.
                       Hemingstein."   *(Death in the Afternoon)*

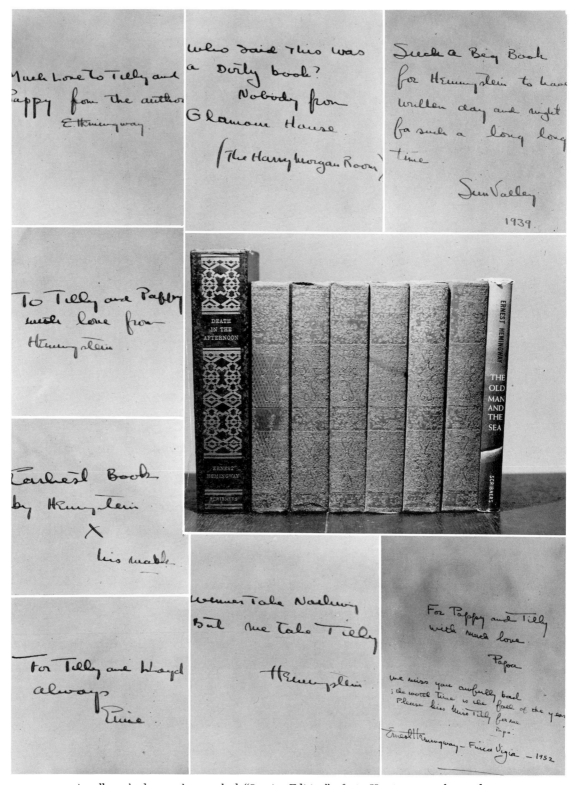

A collector's dream—the matched "Sunrise Edition" of six Hemingway titles, and two
other books, each with the author's warm personal autograph.

The base cabinet was our "file" of memorabilia of a long, colorful period—our time at Sun Valley, my own then totaling twenty-one years: clippings, magazines, negatives and photographs; all in a sort of jumble to fill a couple of wheelbarrows, but in order that we could thumb to in the dark if need be. The doors were open, but Papa wouldn't delve into that; asked me to sit down, he wanted to be sure about dates of a couple of incidents. He had them right, because I could easily show him, and presently he said:

"With all the 'bait' you and Till have kept so intact you ought to do a history of your time here . . . hell, you grew up with Sun Valley, came before it was fully born, helped in a bigger way than you may realize to make it what it is. . . ."

"And to change a lot of things that we don't like today, Papa," I cut in.

"That's a part of it, always in such cases," he said matter-of-factly. "But it's been lots of fun for you, so I meant what I said."

"If I felt that I was good enough to do it, Papa, I'd be inclined to try and vanish somewhere . . . it wouldn't be history of the kind we read in school, you know."

"No, it sure as hell wouldn't." He laughed. "You might feel safe on the moon, say."

"If I ever do try it, Papa." I laughed, for that was my angle of thought. "Shall I include you in?"

"Oh." He grinned. "I guess we could look into the mirror and maybe scratch it a little, but I don't think we'd break it."

We were joined when things were cleaned up in the kitchen, even the colonel overdid himself and didn't ask to be taken home before his dinner was settled. The last music on the hi-fi that night was the only kind that he ever stated a special liking for: Stephen Foster favorites, sung by the old groaner himself, Bing Crosby, whom we both knew slightly from earlier days when his boys spent the summers here. We took the total party home around eleven o'clock, blinded in snow and making it easy with chains on, the new fall up to car door bottoms. While all this was going on, down Hollywood way in California, a needless, senseless thing took place that would change a few things for Till and me.

Early Monday morning I got a business call from our Los Angeles Public Relations office, a routine thing about pictures I had in work for them, then the shocking news and a tip-off. Over a minor domestic spat in his home that didn't amount to a hill of beans, Vince Hunter's first cameraman locked himself in the bathroom, put the muzzle of an automatic pistol in his ear and pulled the trigger. The tip-off was that Vince would call me within the hour and was ready to catch the afternoon train for a talk with me about taking the job. The interim gave me time to think out any number of angles, the background of the situation, and try to understand. I knew the man well as we had worked together on occasion, including a solid winter in the filming of a difficult ski movie for Sun Valley promotion but a few seasons before. He was good in his work. We were not close friends, but there was much in common; thus it did not set well with me to take on a fine job from the wreckage. The other view was that I had opened my door the previous year, the expanding program was delayed, Vince had taken on a raw apprentice to learn the business, and now he found himself ready to go full-out on several major films —a program stretching ahead indefinitely. I told Vince to catch the train.

We spent a full day together. The immediate prospects of the job were even more attractive than I thought, and I had a week to think it over more after Vince left; he would call me at that time. In the interim we thought it best to have made a definite yes or no of our own before talking to anyone. It was, of course, yes, and I called the Wisher house; the man of the house happened to answer, said:

"Sure thing, Mr. Pappy, come on down. Hope it's good, I saw down at the magpie shoot the other day that something was on your mind."

Till and I went down after work and my opener was this:

"Papa, Vince Hunter was up from California, spent a day with us, and. . . ."

"He isn't going to take you away from us, is he?" he cut in on me, not alarmed, but keenly tuned, wanting the works. I outlined it in full, the four of us perched on the counter stools, and I can't remember a better audience in a ten-minute, uninterrupted spiel; the good side of it making the warm response, the from-the-hearts blessings. Indulge me in a brief necessary sketch of it:

Around March 1 I would go to Hollywood for a period of road and studio production work, and return to Idaho coincidentally with the opening of the agricultural season—May, roughly—with two full-length railroad traffic promotional films to make involving irrigation, potatoes (the major industry in Idaho), and relevant activities. My working territory would be immense but, a commonly conceded fact in railroad talk was (and is) the "breadbasket division" for origin of freight revenue was the Idaho division. Thus it was almost certain that as a matter of convenience all around, my working base for at least two years ahead would be our home where I would stop off most weekends, traveling from there to different areas. There was a vague possibility of a change of plans, but this was not likely once I started on the program. I was cautioned, however, to keep a residential move in mind, and be prepared for it. The advantages of the whole far outweighed disadvantages. Right or wrong, the decision was ours—a quote from my audience when the picture was clear, and with us, he was convinced that it was the right one. Papa did say:

"Miss Mary and I could cry with the thought of you two moving from here . . . but we won't think of it in that light; it's the line in your work that you like best and you've gone the distance where you are, don't know how you've stood it lately, from what I know."

He naturally asked how it all came about so suddenly and I told him exactly how it was, had with me the Los Angeles paper carrying the story (the suicide means, the same as his father's had been), and that bothered me, but I had no other choice —news reaches everywhere. He didn't bat an eye, or change expression, but said:

"Happenstance, true, but at an odd time, things changing so fast we can't keep up with them."

Our talk was no more than an hour, and we were especially taken with Papa's: "You've been on one track a long time but you're adaptable, kid. We've seen the evidence, you know."

I wondered about that—I was "coming on 53"—not exactly a pup any more.

Our next tough facing was the colonel, and we did ask advice about waiting until after his birthday party coming up February 6—his seventy-second. We knew that he would bluster like a hen searching out a fence hole, but that his blessings were a cinch in due time. We'd wait, and tell him we'd have cocktail hour and dinner most weekends and that Miss Till would be training someone for her job through the coming summer, and to the resort's fall closing (that was all set). I began at once getting my loose ends picked up, my next-in-line ready to take over.

2

The colonel's birthday party was at Clara Spiegel's, a small group that year, but a perfect gem. His cakes always were gems, too, Sun Valley's head baker knowing him well, outdoing our suggestions with little touches of his own—for that one, tiny, perfectly done bear tracks meandering between tiny pines, a blue sugar trout stream, small bits of something was sage, the trail so for-real that you looked for the little chocolate bruin that made it. Words are beyond me (as always then) for the feeling at Taylor's anniversaries. His "boys," Duke and Don, had duty call after the preliminaries, so for the dinner there were the Hemingways, Doc and Pat Saviers, the hostess and her neighbors across the street—and the neighbor's camera, a pocketful of flashbulbs. Probably the toast to warm the colonel's gay spirits the most was Papa's to their twentieth anniversary as friends. On so many of his facets that evening Taylor was as much like the fifty-two of those long-ago days as we'd seen for some time.

Twelve days later, our old friend was gone.

The fatal blow struck on Tuesday morning, the seventeenth, after we'd had breakfast with him at the staff tables; joking good with a couple of ski instructors, jawing about it being a grey gloomy day outside. It would be chilly in the trees along the river at the foot of the ski lift, the sunshine always welcome there—sharpened a fellow, helped him watch for the chiselers with the phony ski-lift tickets—"the god-

Colonel Williams' last birthday party—his seventy-second—and the twentieth anniversary of a friendship with Papa Hemingway, heavily stressed and toasted by the latter.

damn cheap skates, anyhow!" He waved to me from the path to the Ski School meeting place about nine, as I worked at my desk by the window; his head was pulled into his turned-up collar, and I felt a tinge of something I couldn't call guilt when I thought of how great he'd been at our house the previous Saturday night, putting his good sign on our future. I sat there pondering it a few minutes, then suddenly Tillie yelled at me from out front, to come quick. I was at the door in nothing flat to see an employee and a guest practically carrying Taylor Williams between them as they turned toward our shop.

The poor man was in agony, scarcely able to speak, hands at his chest, sounding like a man half drowned. Somehow I knew that it wasn't what we feared when we set him down at my desk where he couldn't hold up his head. Till had the ambulance there in no time and I waited at the hospital for a word on what to do. I got it in minutes from Doc Saviers: see if I could locate Taylor's son Bob in Portland, Oregon—advise him to catch the first train if he was in port. Fortunately, he was, heading for sea within a day or two. Then I headed for the Hemingways, and George's call beat me there—which helped a little, so you think. By four that afternoon when Papa and I spoke a few words to the colonel, he recognized us in his sedation, squeezed our hands, and wondered what the hell it was that knocked him down in the snow. Doc said he had a clue to what the trouble was.

At ten that night I looked in on him—sound asleep. I saw Papa in the Lodge lobby at eleven; he'd had a very few words with the colonel, he said, but he never told me what they were. He was waiting for a taxi to take him home and talked but a minute outside. For once in my time I saw Papa Hemingway hard put for words, among the few spoken:

"I'm afraid that it isn't any good, Mr. Pappy."

The colonel passed on at 1:00 A.M., and while we were at breakfast Doc Saviers called to ask that I try to contact Bob's train en route. I talked to him by company telephone at an Oregon division stop, got his ready okay for the autopsy Doc asked for. His findings proved his hunch: an atrophied (thinned with age) stomach wall had ruptured upward, penetrating the lung cavity—very rare in medical history, it was said.

"But leave it to Taylor to do it a little different than we ordinary folks," Doc added.

"Yes," Bob said. "It's like Dad, all right."

It reminded me of a typical remark of Taylor back in 1952 when we attended the funeral of a friend, the popular ski instructor killed in the avalanche. The snow was seven feet deep on the valley floor and the looping one-lane access road in the cemetery was opened by Sun Valley's big rotary plow; the grave, like all, were done even in average winters, opened right beside the high-walled swath.

"Finest country in the world to live in," Taylor said to me. "But it's hell to have to be buried in it in winter."

On the phone Bob had told me to go ahead with whatever arrangements I could, and the five-foot level of snow was the first problem: I felt it proper that the colonel's resting place be as near Gene Van Guilder's grave as we could get it—some sixty feet from the road, all by itself for all of those years. I learned while Bob was en route that plenty of available space was there. When I told Papa, he said, "Gee, kid, I was hoping that you would propose that, because it's not for me to suggest."

"Why not, Papa? Bob considers us as much family around his father as himself. . . ."

"Yes, I'm quite sure that he does; I remember him well, and I know he'll approve . . . but it will take a shovel brigade, a small army, to move that much snow out to Gene's; I was out that way not long ago and from the highway I noticed that you can't see even a hump in the snow where the lilac bushes are on his grave."

I guess my one "sin" while in service to the town was in borrowing its equipment to take the place of a shovel gang. We had recently purchased a Michigan loader, a versatile affair for cleaning out intersections following the regular plow; and my good friend and town marshal, Les Jankow, was glad to bring it out when the Valley sent down its rotary to open the long U-shaped loop of the little cemetery's road. The once shabby burial ground was now a credit to the community, due to voluntary citizens' action in cleaning it up; a carpet of fine grass, an irrigating system, and caretaker—paid for by a tax levy. But opening a grave well out from easy access had never been done with a machine. The man handling the sale of the twenty-five-dollar plots buckled on his high overshoes to come along with his map for recording, quite vexed at our insistence on that one spot. Ours was quite the operation on the bright, snappy day, the snow a bit deeper than we thought, due to the sharply rising hill that piled it there on the lee side of the prevailing storm direction. As I was the only skiing man I put on my skis and probed for what seemed eternity because we got slightly off the "key" that was one of two small footstones, right beside the rotary's cut. Papa had insisted on coming along to help in any way that he could, and he was one of the guiding-eye sidewalk superintendents, standing on the high fat tires of the stubby Michigan machine. When my long shovel handle finally hit the low stone wall about Gene's grave my hands and my feet were about to fall off. The snowfield looked like a cribbage board. Then the big rotary came in on an angle to miss the footstones; the operator could run it along a silk-walled tent and not touch a thread; backed out for Les to open a high-banked clearing. It wasn't pretty, by any standards, but the turn-on-a-dime Michigan did the job in no time and high-heeled ladies' pumps could get to the gravesite without much discomfort on the slumbering green grass practically free of snow. I got a welcome nip from a brandy flask, the town got back its gasoline.

Bob's selection of pallbearers included an earliest Idaho neighbor of his father, Mr. Hicks, in charge of Sun Valley motor transportation; old guide Jack Redden; George Saviers; Forrest MacMullen; myself; and Ernest Hemingway—listed last because in his humility, he thought that he intruded over much older friends like retired Pop Mark and much-liked old-time neighbor, Dan Knight. Old guide Art Wood could not make it, and Don Anderson, who had once roomed with Taylor, emotionally asked to be excused.

We buried the colonel on Saturday afternoon, February 21, a bright, almost balmy day in which our jackets were warm enough. As he was so different in life, Taylor's simple service had a touch of difference, too. As long as we knew him, God's great out-of-doors was his church, and the young minister was a newcomer, his subject a stranger to him. Undertaker Ray McGoldrick, of Hailey, called me over to the Opera House a bit ahead of the service, and to my surprise our neighbor a block down the hill in town waited for me—a sheaf of sheet music on her arm. I'd known Frances Campbell since I came to Idaho and hadn't the foggiest notion that

Les Jankow, Ketchum's town marshal

she was an organist. Bob was not there yet, so she asked my opinion on her music. It came so fast for me, I guess, that I said something like:

"Gosh, Franny, I don't know . . . the only music I ever knew Taylor had preference for is Stephen Foster's, and I guess that would hardly . . . or would it?"

I guess that as well as she knew him, too, she had something similar in mind, for she only smiled and turned to go to the Hammond organ. I had to smile to myself, too, in suddenly recalling that back in my professional days we always liked to be able to say of funeral music: "Fore and aft, no vocals, thank God!" I was thinking it then for the colonel. For the attendance file-in, Franny's soft, perfectly tempoed old folksy ballad, "Red River Valley," was exactly right; I, for one, felt the colonel's presence beside me, as I think each soul in the house did. The young minister had a bit of a time of it, and you felt for him, as I felt a squirm a time or two in the big frame next to me in our row.

At the conclusion of the service, Frances turned to the favorite composer, and I don't believe that I've ever heard "My Old Kentucky Home" so beautifully played. As we pallbearers waited at the side door there was not a murmur from any of us, but as the casket was wheeled between us, I felt a tickle of whiskers on my ear; turned it to the soft whisper:

"The sermon a bit off for the colonel . . . but the lady on that organ, Oofs! . . . we owe her a rare gold coin."

3

Very shortly afterward the date for my departure was set as March 8; I was pretty much in the clear, so I coasted along. Within himself, Papa cried in our loss, but only one time did I hear him voice it—an evening at our house. We stood looking out the window, a serene hour in the mountains when above the deep-shadowed slopes the alpenglow colors a high one here and there. He said that he hated the thought of Miss Till rattling around in the house all by herself, even if it would only be for a couple of months. Then:

"Well, Mr. Pappy, it hurts when your old friends die off and you can't dodge it that as you go along, some move away . . . we've lost a few in our time . . . we lost Gene in the worst hard luck, we lost Bud Hegstrom when he moved away while we were away so long, and now we've lost the colonel . . . with you two, he was of the beginning out here . . ."

He broke it off suddenly, apologized for "poking the gloom spook" but asked that as I went along on the new work during the summer and I gained an idea of the foreseeable future, I let them know. I promised. In the interim the subject of the house that I had photographed came up again, and my only act was obtaining the keys from a local who looked after it, let it be known that I had them, suggesting to Papa that if he was interested after he saw it, he talk to Chuck Atkinson who'd have an idea of price due to his business connections with the local lawyer for whom I'd done the picture job. He said he might. That was on Saturday, March 7, when Till and I spent the afternoon and evening at the Wisher house, loafing, talking, having a good time a week ahead of the Hemingways' departure, their lease up on March 15. I took down a number of small photographs that I'd made, to be inscribed and mailed to Hemingway friends everywhere—that little act no less than a circus. And of course the whole thing was a phony cover-up, but we helped it by finding by telephone a home for the cotsies, Papa and I walking up to the Heiss garage at dusk to feed Owlny who could fly well. Spring was on the way, came early that year; the owl would be freed to follow the cottonwoods down the creek to the river, and on down that to his old haunts thirty miles south. He had not suffered the indignity of his intended role because in so many ways it was a mixed-up winter.

From the Lodge at noon on Sunday I left on the bus for my train. When Papa embraced me in his usual way for such occasions and said: "Give Coop a ring when you get in down there," I had a bit of a time answering him. I gave Tillie the keys that I had and Papa told me they would look at the house with Chuck during the coming week. His sincerity was obvious, anything further than that, fully in my doubt. Since something did come of it—that I didn't learn about for two months—I'll take it on out.

For the drive to Key West he rented a Hertz car and Hotch, then finished with his teleplay "For Whom the Bell Tolls," came out a day or two ahead to help with the driving. The route was by way of Las Vegas, across Arizona and Texas to New Orleans.

About the same time they departed Las Vegas, Chuck Atkinson and George Kneeland, the local lawyer, left Phoenix where they had played a little golf with Bob Topping, the owner of the house and acreage around it on the west bank of Big Wood River a short way north of Ketchum. Bob built the house back in the early fifties when he married a local girl, an ice-skating employee at Sun Valley; lived in it a few years and quit Idaho for an easier climate. The house was furnished, ready for occupancy—then.

The two parties met about halfway—at Kingman, Arizona—stopped for a talk, then went on their ways. A short time into April, Chuck got through to the Finca by phone. Papa told him that he'd put a check for the house into the mail to him that day. Then Chuck mentioned that a Hailey merchant had a claim against certain small items like dishes, a few portable appliances and the like, and that he'd been instructed to allow their pickup by the claimant. Oh, hell, that stuff did not amount to anything, Papa said, but don't let them cart away that big stock of several thousand clay targets stacked in the basement garage (true, Topping dallied in trapshooting, had a regulation trap installed on the downriver flat near the main entrance gate to the property).

So, the Hemingway Idaho "hunting lodge"—"chalet"—"retreat" and what have you, came into being. In truth it was a fine home, for part-time or permanent living, its interior arrangement ideal for two people like the Hemingways. On the outside the house was not so pretty: cast in solid concrete, a borrow from the construction method used on Sun Valley's Lodge to almost exactly duplicate rough-hewn timber walls; the concrete was not yet stained in autumn brown imparting the weathered look; the house a two-story square with a hip roof that made it resemble "a blockhouse, a Fort Dearborn, like the pictures in our history books in school." Built to last indefinitely, however, its inside a classic in lovely wood paneling throughout, huge double-glazed windows bringing outdoors inside, the river sparkling along below, a hundred yards out from the broad sun deck along the east-fronting forty-foot-long living room. Some of the furnishings were a bit on the bizarre side, however, and not exactly to tastes of the new owners—which I damn well knew long before. Using a quote, they gave it a sort of "vulgar" look. The first thing Chuck had done was the staining of the exterior walls, making it a different house altogether to the eye.

4

In my short seven weeks in California I was on the road a great deal with Vince, working on two films of the state. Ready to head north on April 20, I got Mary's long letter—a carbon copy of her original to Till in Ketchum. Its surprises were reason for me to read it, I think several times at least, on our way to San Francisco. The first one was typed above the letter head:

"Our European address to be used from now on: Care Guaranty Trust Co. of New York—Place de la Concorde, Paris."

I recalled not even so much as a hint of a European summer, and one paragraph convinced me that their route home might have inspired thoughts of Spain in Papa's head. A wonderfully newsy letter, too.

Your fine letter, Pappy, about the job and your whereabouts, the good news that you'll be working in Idaho this summer came just this morning and I want to answer it quick before we get into the final whirligig of packing. I slipped a carbon in, so you don't have to forward or quote from this wacky epistle. Before anything else, Till darling that was the cutest birthday card I've ever had (description for me in parentheses, their birthdays a "thing" between them, just one day apart)—so gay you must have designed it yourself, had it custom made. My birthday was fine—it was a wild day on the "oceany" and after so long away from it, we had to work to keep our balance; but the sun was bright and the breeze perfumed and sweet, and Gregorio made fish with a favorite green sauce for lunch, and the sea produced a small present—one shining green and blue and gold dorado. How sweet the boys [Duke and Don] were to give you a shirt, Till.

Looking back on it, seems to me we were all stirred up emotionally for quite a while this year, with Taylor and then Pappy's leave-taking—that last night at our place was the kissingest and huggingest session I can recall ever. We were still limp and exhausted when we got to Elko, and Dan Bilbao and his wife gave us a fine time and a fine dinner and I was too tired to appreciate.

But in general our trip down was just great—gay and lucky too—no snowstorms, no rain, only very strong winds. Total mileage, 4,091.9—of which we spent 1,156.6 in Texas alone. Went across the Rio Grande first at El Paso, to Juarez on Palm Sunday—nice town without much character; next at Eagle Pass to Piedras Negras which is an adorable town with charming people, a gay, sparkling center square, fine market, pretty baroque church; finally at Laredo, with Nuevo Laredo dusty and hot and unattractive. Papa had a great reunion with Waldo Pierce, the artist, in Tucson and I fell in love with him—he's a true genius, with the sparkliest, gayest, widest-ranging enchanting mind we've met in a long time (awfully nice, pleasant wife) and a down-east accent, had me translating, as from a foreign language for the first hour.

We left Hotch at the airport in New Orleans to fly to the coast and came on in fine style, Papa driving very well and my nerves—you know how active they are in cars—gradually calming down. We saw the second half of FWTBT in Phoenix and I was moved to great admiration for Hotch's script and the directing and acting. Papa not wholly in favor—but largely so—his criticisms, of course, very acute.

Good news here, we had the usual blood tests etc. And Papa's things are all good, ie. all negative, which is just great. And my blood count up to over four million for the first time in years. Oh, Idaho! Other good news—the Finca is just lovely—scores of flowering trees and vines and shrubs—the planting around the pool lusher than ever and the pool divine, just cool enough to be stimulating and the water sparkling blue.

Pappy darling, I haven't answered your letter at all; but you know we're both delighted and excited that things are working out so well for you. It's rough on Till now but we have great faith in her capacity to survive rough stuff and you have the summer to look forward to, so we take off feeling just fine about you two.

We go to N.Y. next week (CONFIDENTIAL) and sail for Algeciras, Spain (confidential). Papa told me to take my fur coat, so who knows when we'll be back, either here or Idaho. But it wouldn't surprise me if we leave Europe before fur coat weather and turn up in Ketchum for at least part of the bird season. But we'll keep in touch. Dearest fellas—the greatest of luck to youse and the jobs and the house—and your healths—and also funwise."

Love and kisses—MARY

Scrawled across the bottom of Till's original:

"Best love, SIR TILL—I miss you very much—hope everything going okay."

PAPA

The "Sir Till" was the result of a "knighting" for something she did that for the life of us we can't remember what it was, lost it in the hilarity, no doubt; but do recall the ceremony, the flat of a butcher knife blade on her head at the Wisher house one night. One thing that she does not forget occurred during the week after I left. Down at the house that evening, all the change got to her; butterflies in her stomach, losing the bit of food she tried to eat. Papa drove her home and walked back. Early the next morning she heard him calling from out in the backyard where he could see her upstairs window. He hadn't used the phone since ours was downstairs, fearing she was too ill to answer it. She assured him she was much better and asked him in for coffee; no, he just wanted to be sure—thought she might need a doctor. A day or two into the following week the telephone man came and installed an upstairs extension. Pretty thoughtful, that, for a gal alone who would often be called at night, by me; and the instrument matched the color scheme of the room. 'Nuf said.

5

Back home in Idaho on April 30, I hit the road at once—the program working out almost exactly as planned. A first direct word was from Mary, dated June 7, Malaga, Spain. It seemed they were headquartering at the palatial home of an old friend, Bill Davis, her list of familiar place names to be taken in for the bullfights indicating that the summer over there was only a pup! Instinct said it was a binge in preparation—surprising in one way, considering the austerity theme we knew, and yet it was not. In her note was the first mention of the Topping house, confirming certain matters I'd warned about, she not getting anywhere in having a few interior changes made through the offers of Chuck to oversee.

One weekend in early July I bumped into George Saviers and was delighted to hear that he and Pat were going on a vacation to Spain right away, would meet up with the Papa entourage. It instantly struck me that it was his birthday month—they might run into a party. George said they just might, at that. The sixtieth year seems to be significant, observation of others told me. They ran into the party, indeed, and we got Mary's mailed description of it while it was tapering off the following evening of July 22—at the Davis home in Malaga. Well and good, but it had a purpose, her build-up to the true point:

". . . a crazy letter, but had to get this off my chest before I try to get down to business. No room in this zany life we lead of constant celebrations, and I'm getting awfully hungry for a day Papa and I might share, with absolutely nobody else at all around."

My busy summer naturally required above-normal concentration, but I had lots of time to think on long drives to and from distant work areas. Sensitive to a fault, perhaps, I often felt guilt probing the reasons that were "none of your damn business, tend to your own knitting, for what can you do about it, anyway?" But after all, it was my business, and I had stuck my nose into it before—voluntarily and by request—and how else would I know a little of what was going on, a continent and an ocean away? So often I would think of that long-ago time when Papa showed me the source—John Donne's writing—of his title for FWTBT, and when I'd read it, he said:

"Christ, if a man could write like that!"

He made quite a thing of it, was especially attracted with the latter lines:

Any mans death diminishes me, because I am involved in Mankinde; And therefore never send to know for whom the bell tolls; it tolls for thee.

For I finally had to come clean with myself, as I finally have to do here: I was intensely worried about my friend, and I had been for a long time. Somehow, to me, it was man's business, I'd even be reluctant to speak about it at home. As to doubt in my mind as to what was happening to Papa's there was none, whatsoever. You can walk through thick timber and all trees have a tendency to look alike, but a big one—a great one—stands out from the others, a thing apart, calling attention to itself; and when you don't live in the timber, but observe it from a middle distance, liking the tree for what it is and not its name over a long period of time, you hardly can fail to come up with a fairly good image on the ground glass of overall perspective. True, for ten years I had observed through the eyes and ears of another. But the second hand, I was quite sure, prepared me for the introduction to the image that alarmed me—the first glimpse of it in a hand-written letter. I said that it took the wind out of my sails. It did, but the great '58 fall brightened the picture so much that at times you just knew it was the old days coming back. In the background, of course, was the mounting Cuban thing; a waiting trigger, and when tripped, the process, the turmoil within, came to the surface in all too frequent intervals throughout the winter of '59. It was, quote not mine, a "problem winter" but I could easily, truthfully, underline it—uncontrollable other events, notwithstanding.

Yet, as the summer advanced, there came some brightening signs: Chuck commenced to receive interior things for the house from Spain, requests to have a few major changes made. In early September when I was in town he showed me what he'd had done to the long living room, and I hardly knew it. Gone was the glaring red wall-to-wall carpet, in its place, warm colored tile; the big distasteful bar, looking like a refined hogshead, gone from one outside corner opposite the stairs. The one room alone made it a different house inside, so you could speculate that perhaps Mary was right about no fur-coat weather in Spain—even a guy who'd only read about them knew that they couldn't fight bulls all winter!

I kept a promise when my summer work was finished and my fall program was slowed a bit before the bustling far-flung harvests. In a meeting with him on further increases in my schedule, the boss flatly told me that I could forget any possibility of having to change place of residence for a very long time. I at once fired away an airmail letter to the Paris address, and we heard no more until one October weekend when I stopped at home but a few hours. Tillie had received two identical color postcards, addressed and written to her, of the ship, Liberte that brought Papa home from Europe. Both said he was lonely, for there was no one aboard he knew; both mentioned a "secret" of his and Till's of the previous fall; both were written in mid-Atlantic, and mailed together in New York two days hence. We could not know why he was all by himself, or what was going on, and what was coming up. I drove 'way down into Colorado that trip, and I'm not a bit certain of remembering any other than a deep and sickening feeling much of the way.

I finished my outside work in early November and scheduled my vacation for the balance of the month. Tillie had her replacement trained by then and we took a long week to fly with Pete and Dorothy Hill to New Orleans—his a business trip, with time for all of us to have fun. We checked in at the Hotel Monteleone a bit past noon on Sunday, November 15, and landed back at Idaho Falls on Monday, November 23. Resting after lunch, we made a Christmas date with the Hills, leaving it open as to where—their house or ours—depending. We drove into Ketchum about six o'clock, me with a quick errand to run. Back shortly, I found Tillie on the phone with Mary Hemingway. They'd been back but a few days, had a date for the evening; there was plenty of time, though, so run out and say hello. Tillie had enough so that on our way out she gave me a fair sketch.

Mary had flown back from Europe in October to organize at the Finca, Papa came by boat—as per his postcards. While they were in Cuba, the great Spanish matador, Antonio Ordonez, with a Mexican itinerary ahead of him, stopped by with his pretty wife, Carmen. Papa talked the bullfighter into coming out to Idaho for some hunting. They got in a little, then a sudden change in the Ordonez plans was sending them on their way to Mexico the following day. Papa was quite upset about it, she said. Mary had flown up to Chicago to shop for some essentials for the house, then flew on out while the others came by car—Roberto Herraras, the chauffeur.

Roberto met us at the front door, Mary on the run behind him. Volubly glad to see us, she looked a bit fagged, too. Which she promptly said that she was—having to feed her visitors on paper plates before her dishes came from Chicago!

"Never a dull moment, you know, I hardly knew my way about the house—couldn't remember it."

As we chatted there by the step up into the hall, Papa's back was to us as he talked with the handsome couple by the fireplace—totally unaware of our arrival. Over his shoulder I saw Ordonez's eyes shift from his toward us, his head nodding. Papa went on talking, palms upward in the familiar emphasis spread. Mary took over, our chatter increasing as we approached.

"Hi, Miss Till, Mr. Pappy. Heard you went to New Orleans, thought you never would get back."

He graciously introduced us to the couple, made a clever amusing production of the seesaw translations about given names—right in the old groove—then abruptly reverted to all-out Spanish in taking on the one-sided intent conversation. I was surprised that neither of the couple spoke much English—our impression, anyway. Then we eased away toward the kitchen to pour a short one and do a fast shakedown with Mary and Roberto—and to know the pleasant dusky Jamaican girl, Lola, whom Mary flew out from the Finca with her, and whose full British accent made this mountain boy say to himself: Well, ah'll be damned!

With an eye on the time we eased back to the living room, our coats on, my hat in hand. Rather abruptly, the Ordonez couple offered their excuses to go upstairs to change, and he spoke our names perfectly. I don't believe it was my imagination that saw a faint shrug of his shoulders, an accompanying slight cock of his head, as if Ordonez conveyed his: Sorry, I guess you can see how it is. Nor can I recall a more awkward minute or so after their leave-taking, than trying to find something to say or do while a lonely Papa stared silently down into the fireplace, fingers hovering about his lower lip.

Suddenly he was back to reality, radiant as molten metal. He folded Sir Till in his arms, asked his first question: "Where did you stay in New Orleans?"

"At the Monteleone, Papa . . . had a great time, too."

His surprise widened his eyes, split his beard, then it all froze.

"What day did you get in down there?"

She told him and he said: "Well, I'll be damned, we waited for Carmen to come from church, got a late start, checked out about an hour before you came . . . what a shame that we didn't let you know, and you might have come a day early. . . ."

Did we get into the Famous Door on Bourbon Street, hear Al Hirt split that trumpet, did we eat at the Veux Carre—and so on? Yes, we probably got into too many doors on old Bourbon Street, and we had a couple of good stories, but we had to go—and we did not want to leave because it was going good. Mary said that she would call us tomorrow and Papa came outside with us, down the steps to our car. He was forthright and open about the disappointment of his friends leaving so suddenly, without notice; said that he didn't mind the dough he spent gearing them up, just thought that we could all have a fine time, a few more days; he could spare the time from going to work—the stuff he'd gathered over there during the summer.

"And don't you think they're really fine people?"

His "going to work" was an opening, so I hinted that it wouldn't do to try to jack up the fine big walnut dresser up in his room, scar up its top with a makeshift where he could write. No, he guessed it wouldn't but it was a fine place to write, that big window looking up the river, the Boulder Mountains for a background. I didn't merely offer—I said right out that with lumber scraps I had, I'd make a high-topped stand for him, do it tomorrow, and it wouldn't be very pretty, made in a hurry.

"Pretty don't write." He grinned. "As I was once told."

"Yeah, I know," I said. "But I can't remember her name."

"The hell you can't." He laughed. "And say, there are a few northern ducks down. . . ."

"I'm behind in that work, Papa. Long gun or short one?"

"Oh, they're a little wild, and so what?"

The evening air was right nippy, and as we drove out the main gate a couple of hundred yards from the house, my rear-view mirror showed him silhouetted in the wide front door, just standing there in his shirt-sleeves. Physically, Papa looked fine, and he *was* himself in the last ten minutes or so that we were there; but there is only one word for that other: obsession—and we wondered what he'd been searching for all summer. Certainly it was an old well-worn subject—as to "the stuff" that he said he'd gathered.

Entirely from scraps and plenty of tools in my basement shop, I whipped together an "old-fashioned bookkeeper's" affair that would do the job very well, and we took it out to the house in midafternoon. We shoved the heavy dresser to one side in the tasteful "man's" bedroom so beautifully panelled in solid walnut. I was ashamed of the scrubby thing we marred it with, and said so.

"Yeah, a hog in a parlor," was his hearty, laughing response. "But I tell you, kid, I'll boot a hog in the butt if we haven't done worse in our time."

The day was the indescribable kind that makes the mountain country falls what they are—good to be alive, wrapped in something that you vow you'll never allow to escape you. Down in the sun-flooded kitchen our gals were at it like farmwives catching up on the doings—"any takers, gentlemen, we're not budging for a while." You bet, there were takers—the time was exactly right for talk. I think we expected a "confession" report of the summer, and we got it—straight, all-out, told with laughs, as good as if you were there, and:

". . . it wasn't exactly what you'd call tourist class, I can tell you that, kids!"

It was perfect time for a bit of kidding, too, which I did by taking up the indifference over essentials claimed, but concern over the stock of clay targets in the basement.

"Yes, fine thing." Mary laughed. "To hell with what the housekeeping department has to do with, just so there's essentials for shooting." Sure, you're damned right, gotta have those—and the place would've been a better bargain with a hand-trap thrown in—good place straight out from the back door where the drive curves up the hill, good background, over the trees along the winding river to the north—a low rail fence to set your stack of targets and shells on. How much vacation time did I have left? A week, too broke for anything but hunt ducks; then a trip to California for reviewing work, then back on December 7—for certain. Did I have absolute faith in the no-moving business?

"Absolutely, Papa. I'm halfway through two films, and I'm slated for all winter right here in Idaho, filming in processing plants, glorifying the lowly potato, home weekends, and did you get my letter about it?"

Yes, but they couldn't remember where they were, and the best news, ever: "A gone spook that's bothered us since back in the spring. And did you get home for your birthday, kid?"

Yes, I had, close to home, made it on the nose, a Friday night, and we just finished celebrating it, and other things.

"Well, that makes us even then." He grinned.

Tillie and I subtly fished for an idea of how long in the west this time—a futile fishing—and dodged by a little rundown that indicated it wasn't so bad in Cuba. Dodged again by reminding Sir Till that she had a New Orleans story or two. She did, a fitting one, a smash hit: It was cold at night, and on one of them we waited for our friends to finish business—in a Bourbon Street bar where a top-billing stripper playing to an early scant house bought us two hillbilly kids a drink (which hit you $3.00 per round). Probably a part of her act, and so what; but the kick was the between-acts come-on gal, dressed in a powder puff and goose pimples due to the barker holding open the front door for passersby to get a peek of the raw inside. We sat at the bar, our backs to the door, and I could reach out and almost touch the goose pimples. Tillie showed her sympathy and the gal said, "Yes, ma'am, it's cold, and I hope the suckers get out and in quick so loud-mouth there can shut that goddamn door!"

"A fine story, Miss Till . . . it rhymes perfectly with 'roll up that goddamn window!' "

"On one leg of our flight down we flew over the Oklahoma-Texas panhandle country, and Pete edged over a few miles so that I could get a good look at my grandfather's old ranch; I hadn't seen it in forty years, but I recognized it miles away by the durable old white gypsum stone house that stuck out like a sore thumb, in country changed so much that I wouldn't have known it otherwise—except for certain scattered features. I was the kid all over again, open-mouthed, as Pete did me a circle, everyone amused, which I doubt I heard.

"And why not?" Papa said as warmly as if it had been he. "Those things nothing can ever take from you . . . that part of Pappy's young life I always envied . . . imagine me having such fun if after forty years I was flown over Oak Park, Illinois . . . Michigan, yes, the part I know."

Though he was casual about it, Papa was pleased with the few changes made since they were only lukewarm at the first look at the house. They had "borrowed back" the two cotsies from our neighbors who kept them; the hides were scattered about as throw rugs; the gun rack in the living room corner by the front hall step, "makes it even smell like you guys, the gun oil, and leather," as I put it. Papa laughed.

"I hope so. When we first looked in that room I thought we were in the western branch of the old Everleigh Sisters' Club in Chicago . . . only I wasn't that old in those days."

Mary wanted another change made; in a couple of big upholstered pieces: remove the bulging "bosoms" of the back cushions. Hell, they were all right—that kind of work cost a little dough! He lost that round—to a female army of two, and Mary teased him: "We don't mind a little extravagance—just on occasions, do we, lamb?"

"Naw, Kitner . . . I guess we don't, at that."

As a bonus? She got a hi-fi set, too, installed in a high-vertical antique cabinet that she found in Spain and shipped it well ahead. Of course that might have evened the score—the fine swivel-mounted TV sets in the house were a must for the weekly prizefight shows—to one who also loved good music.

6

We rustled about and borrowed a handtrap to do the first backyard trapshooting on Thanksgiving afternoon; shot well into dusk, wearing yellow glasses for contrast, the muzzles of our guns stabbing the gloom with pencils of flame; an old "shooting machine" breaking them neat as ever out over bare cottonwood limbs, good for judging the range. On Friday, Roberto returned to Cuba, and I stayed home from a duck hunt, a few things to do ahead of our trip. Bad luck hit hard.

On a stalk, a hidden snaky willow root on rough ground tripped Mary for a nasty fall. She obeyed the first law of the hunter—save your precious weapon first. She did, taking the jolt on her left elbow, going down so fast that she could not straighten out to take it with her hand. It was a bone-shattering, excruciatingly painful break. George Saviers was along, saw the gravity of it at once. They broke all records for the Sun Valley hospital. At the house that evening he had no choice but to say that it was like putting together a crushed eggshell, and that it would be touch-and-go to bring Mary out of it with a bendable elbow—even partially so. We saw her a few minutes Saturday afternoon, in a cumbersome boomerang-shaped cast, gritting her teeth. I called her a tough Minnesota Indian, and she said, "I hope I'm one, and keep the show going while I'm here, will you?"

We did our best, and it worked quite well, when Papa had us out for dinner with him Sunday evening. The gloom button was hit but once. "It's hell, rattling around in this big strange house all by yourself." Till took it fast.

"Yes, Papa, I know all about it; don't we old farmers say that we take the water for granted until the well goes dry?"

He gave her a frowning stare that slowly softened. Yes, he guessed that was the way of it; he was pretty demanding of his well, too, and, "Don't say that you know it because I know you do, Miss Till."

They let Mary come home on Monday, and rarely for me to lead off, I did that time: suggested to Papa we take a run down to Silver Creek. He readily agreed, and we had a fair take on a couple of bends on the main stream, handy to the road. Ours was not a very talkative two hours or so, and since Tillie and I were leaving the next day around noon, the happy thought came to me that in our freezer was something to lift his spirits, a little anyway: he'd gone for quite a while without some good fresh fish—I had them. While working in east Idaho at the end of the season, I took a weekend day to fish Palisades Reservoir on the upper Snake River with friends—who saw that I had "plenty" over my own catch. They were no less than dream fish; cutthroat trout averaging a half yard long, quick-frozen with all of their fresh good in them. I rolled newspapers around four of the biggest ones, and Till phoned that I was on my way. If I had taken a few gold ingots I doubt they'd have made half the hit. He bounded up into the kitchen as I walked in the opposite door: "Hi, Mr. Pappy. Hey, watcha got kid?" As in rapid-fire, for that long package did not look usual with me, nor was I ever associated with fish. Papers flew as leaves before a wind. Hearing the commotion, Mary came, wincing at every jarring step:

"Kitner, at one sitting can you work your way around one beauty trout as long as from your good elbow to your fingertips?"

"Well! . . . I'll bet I can get up one side of one, anyway."

"Hmph! There'll be no cotsy scraps from these, old Pelican Papa will see to that . . . tails, heads and gill plates look good enough to eat . . . you couldn't have timed them better, kid, but you're not . . ."

"No, not emptying the box just for a few days, Papa, we have more."

The old file box dished up the fact that the first fish feed we ever sat down to were cutthroats, "but not ball bats like these." He came out to the car with "the stranger dressed up in city clothes" to send his best regards to the man he'd never met, but had heard so many fine things about, and to whom he owed a drink, if I ever managed to get him up to Idaho at the right time.

"I will, Papa. See you Saturday, for sure. Old man Hunter is going on vacation, so I know we won't get stuck."

We were not—bumped into Mary and Papa at the market, saw his Buick station wagon there when we drove into town. Nothing would do but that we come out to the house when finished with our shopping—the boys were coming to shoot a round of targets. But one real purpose was to know that there was no change in my working plans. Second, to let us know, since attention to Mary's arm required it, they would be in Idaho for some time—meaning Christmas. The subject opened after we'd shot, over a short one in the kitchen, Papa only lukewarm at first. As the pace increased, so did his, and shortly he was leading it, going all-out over Mary's ebullience. She had a good cook in Lola—even he could roast the turkey, if necessary—Duke was assigned to "traditionally run down another goose" and since they now had a roof of their own over them, it was only right that Christmas dinner be at the house of Hemingway! Any arguments?

How the hell do you go against an order of the general—General? That's what the general thought all along! And as I would be working at Idaho Falls right up near to Christmas, would I be so good as to bear the invitation to Dort and old pilot Hill to join the fun? Yes, indeed, I would do that, but wondered how I'd squeeze in time to sneak out for the Christmas trees. Oh, just bring your thirst and a hunger as your contribution, but if you run into a real delicacy, it'll be as welcome as you.

Which is just about the way it was for the preliminary, for truth is, the buildup was cover-up of keen disappointment that Christmas could not be at their own home in Cuba. Though there was no open talk of it, the evidence was very obvious—and why not? My point is that, shaken, troubled as he was, I can only credit the outward show of exuberant anticipation to a discipline beyond the likes of me. In another way of putting it: there would be a best-substitute Christmas—somewhere —come hell and high snowbanks.

He worried about me driving the tricky road, in a questionable weather time of year, through the Craters of the Moon lava to and from Idaho Falls—four trips I'd have:

"Take that hell's frozen-over son of a bitch easy now, kid, won't you?"

He was right, and didn't need to tell me (it had become second nature to me by then), so I made it a point to call home by company line when I'd arrive. A laughable parallel of the past and present came up in my first week there. I was out to the Hill house one evening, wishing that I had been with Pete that morning. Normally not good so late in season, luck smiled on him—a pair of small Canada geese. Papa had asked "no presents," stressing it a bit, and none amounting to anything was planned at all. So, naturally, Pete's geese would grace the table, his contribution; Till would roast them, knocking out the need of "His Highness the Duke's" domestic bird. I put in a phone call, got Mary, heard the chatter in the kitchen —Papa and Duke just in from hunting, Tillie there, the lineup just right. Pete talked to Mary in thanks, then asked for the man of the house.

"This is the old coyote speaking, what service might he render you, Mr. Pete?"

Mr. P. wished to know about all the old guff of no presents. Well, if it was a brand that he hadn't tried—but he thought he knew them all. Oh, yes, he knew the brand well enough, and they'd come high, but not quite high enough—right over the pit that morning. There was complete silence for all of about three seconds, then: Over the "pit"—had he heard it? Yes, about forty yards over it—withdraw now?

"Why, hell yes, I withdraw it, they sound like Canucks to me, Pete, and say, the old dog's on scent of a turkey, saw him a day or two ago—tied to a leg of the butcher's block!"

One thing spurs another, so a gag present for "the pot" in order that Duke and I could hold up tradition: I'd heard of a butcher in Jackson, Wyoming, who made heavenly salami, his base, pure wild elk meat—common as dudes in summer in that area—so Pete saw that we got a "wagon-tongue" of it—meaning, for true, that it was put up in "gut" as big around as a man's fist and as long as his arm—out-of-this-world stuff, and a bite of it sent your sense somewhere else. That package took a back seat for nothing, went well into the new year—in several places. But, as to the pre-Christmas:

My working places shut down, I drove home on December 23, in bright weather, the road good. By noon of the twenty-fourth snow was coming down with a vengeance, and in a short while Papa rapped on our window with his alpenstock—snow water dripping off his whiskers, the mood good, but worrying about how it might be howling down out there in "Mr.Dante's country" that the Hills would have to drive across. He'd walked into town, to the market, and thought he'd better come up and we'd call Arco—midway to Idaho Falls.

"I've already talked to Pete, Papa. It's coming down out there, all right—if a single flake of snow looks about for a place to fall in Idaho, that's the place it picks, as you damn well know; but it's young yet, they're on their way."

Then, purely on impulse, I laughed outright, said that if we merely touched on a subject, damned if it didn't happen, even though I had beaten the weather and the lousy road. He gave me the one-sided owlish grin.

"You mean ol' Papa's spooks are rubbing off on you after listening to them so long?"

In rarity for such stops on his frequent walks, he doffed his parka to talk a while; the picture on Mary's arm was brighter by then, though plenty of attention was given it in whirlpool and other treatments made possible by a split, removable cast. He merely mentioned it, preferred to talk the subject at hand: Mary's pretty tree, her old-fashioned touch in lighting it with genuine tallow candles; and if Sir Till, who had never roasted a wild goose in her life, would stuff them with apple as the old-timers used to do. When he got up to go, you couldn't see two blocks toward town center, but:

"It's warm, not under thirty, walking in a good snow is the best there is . . . but check in with us when the kids get in, will you?"

They made it at a crawling pace, the storm still at it. Mary and Papa went to the Saviers' house on Christmas Eve, the little sister of their three young boys thinking Santa came early that year and didn't have much to do! The Hills and we went out for dinner, at the new Christiania Restaurant a mere three blocks from the house on the Sun Valley road. Afterward, the sky was star-studded, the streets not plowed in our neighborhood; we got stuck coming up the hill, a low-bellied car entirely at fault?—then sat around a good half the night listening to good music that the *same* Santa had a hand in 365 days before.

The weatherman stayed friendly, we shot some clay targets in midafternoon when Duke got off shift; and if your score was a dozen or more broken of a stack of fifteen you got a tongue-wetting nip from the bottle of Tavel sitting in a hole in the snow under the rail bordering the drive. Our dinner party was small: three couples of us, bachelor Duke, and Lola—far from home in a snowy white world sharply contrasting with her own. Mary's lovely table was set for eight.

I took a Rolleiflex out with me, flashbulbs for one roll of film; the truly fine time recorded by it is better than any words of mine.

The hilarity here: Duke MacMullen was taking a ribbing while trying to focus my camera. He almost got it!

Pete and "pint of soap" Dorothy Hill

Christmas, 1959. Adjusting the thermostat. "What'll it be, citizens, lovin' heat or eatin' heat?"

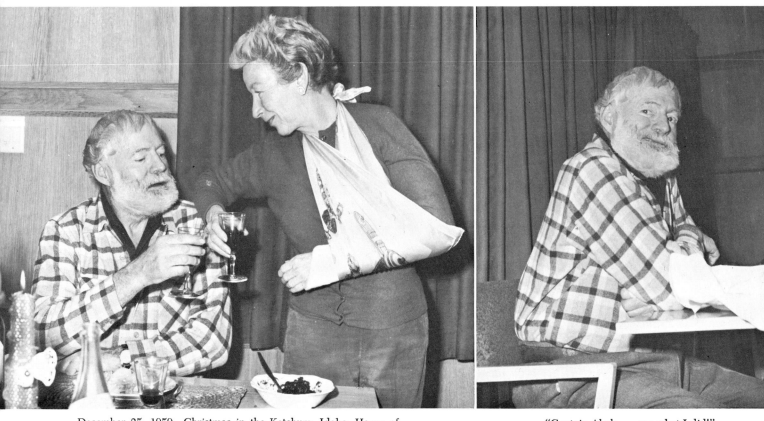

December 25, 1959. Christmas in the Ketchum, Idaho, House of Hemingway.

"Captain Ahab . . . see what I did!"

Christmas, 1959. Old pilot (Pete Hill) and old Ernie, the coyote (so self-named).

Christmas, 1959. Of the latter years, this is my favorite picture of the most interesting friends, ever.

The '59 Yule. "And furthermore. . . ." Pete Hill and Forrest "Duke" MacMullen getting a good one.

11.

1960 --- a Stormy Beginning . . .

1

By prearrangement I worked the first half of January right at home, and in nearby high-country snowfields, filming water sources for my irrigation documentary. By an odd quirk it was both ideal subject matter and the most miserable period of weather I could remember in my mountain experience—above-normal snowfall with emphasis on cold. I also had quite a bit of idle time for these very reasons, a trying yet easy period. I did experience one unheard-of thing: I had rough "work prints" of both my major films on hand, sent up by our studio for reviewing purposes, and on one stormy day, Papa Hemingway sat with me for an hour in our dining room "theater" looking at subject matter that I figured would bore him silly—well, he stayed, anyway, a comment being: "You get around an awful lot of country, and now I know how to irrigate and grow potatoes."

In sharp contrast, I drove down out of the Boulder Mountains one "dry blizzard" day so cold that when I pulled up behind Papa walking back toward town on the highway, opened the door for him, he hopped right in with no questions—except what in hell was either of us doing out on such a day? When you saw him wearing gloves while out for a walk you knew it was cold. He had brought his car into town for some minor thing, got a little exercise while waiting for it—half of it sitting by our fire after I picked him up. Need I say that such conditions brought on that restless, what-do-I-do-next disease called shack-happy? There was no covering up and denying it; he wasn't writing worth a goddamn, nothing sounded right when he got it down. He again opened up the subject of incorporating, one he'd made quite a to-do of the winter before; would we come in with our names? Sure we will, Papa, just as before, to satisfy the requirement of corporate law. Oh, hell, he wouldn't go for that—no "dollar-a-year name" in an outfit of his, just as he'd said— the taxes saved would do everybody some good. Well, he got off that one some way, maybe in his acceptance of a bite of salami and a small glass of wine—just looking at the blowing snow outside would suggest that. It went from one thing to another so fast that you wondered which to answer.

One blessing in that interim was the trapshooting; somehow, a session was managed nearly every day—for one special reason besides the obvious one. Doc Saviers would stop on his way home to lunch, check in with Mary, check his other patient's blood pressure—not upon George's insistence, by a long way. It got to be a sort of daily routine, when we were available—out came the guns, a case of targets, then everything was great, and you loved it. The kick the gals got out of our antics, watching from Mary's big upstairs window, was as good a spur as our own competitive efforts—and they were just that, no mistake.

One afternoon around four o'clock we saw Mary and Papa at the market, she doing the shopping, pushing her cart by one hand, Papa just standing by himself up front near the door—dejected, morose, way off somewhere. At whatever our greeting was, he said, oh, he wasn't up to much of anything, he was just the chauffeur, the errand boy around his establishment. In my clumsy way I said, weren't we all erranders in one way or another as we went along. Yeah, but I was an adaptable boy, he was just an old dog incapable of learning new tricks. He grinned as his sentence died, said, "Come on, Mr. Pappy, we're no good here. Let's go across the street . . . join us, Miss Till, when you and Miss Mary finish, huh?"

Across the street was the Christiania Restaurant's bar, a bar that Papa liked before the after-ski hour crowded it too much. It was the sort of weather to start such an hour a little early, but it wasn't bad yet and we sat alone at the end of the bar, talking to an old skiing friend of mine to whom I introduced Papa; they were hitting it off good, an empty stool between them—and that was too bad. A stranger strode up, paid no attention to any of us, and sat down on it, loudly called for himself a drink. A blind man could tell that he did not know who he sat beside, but a deaf man could hear him—any talk was his talk. Well, we were just about to get out of there when our gals came in, stopping at a table of some locals. At that precise moment the loud man turned and asked Papa if he had high-altitude, dry-air skin trouble, or did he wear the beard for effect?

Good God, sailors, I thought, clear the decks! My back was to the wall—the end stool—and a whole mountain of suede leather vest, Papa's back, rose up in front of me. I shook in my ski boots as he put his parka down on the bar, his old stocking cap on it. But he controlled himself, got the man told off in no uncertain terms—a very soft, deadly voice—then turned to tell me he'd go out to order drinks for the girls. He hoped it would be more pleasant when he came back. Surprisingly, his expression was quite calm, a cold glitter in his eye, however, nor could I wonder. The beard was a touchy subject, especially in the ski-crowded community where, likely as not, you could see a purple beard on an elephant. The man paid no attention to me, nor to my friend, while we tried to exchange a little talk in which he asked how long I'd known Mr. Hemingway—a long time, as he recalled—and he addressed me as Pappy. The loud-mouth spoke up, said, "So that's who he is, and you use a form of his name, huh?"

He was big enough to chew me up and spit me out, but I saw so much red in the atmosphere as I came off my stool that I didn't see Papa appear behind our charming company as it got up from its perch. It felt a forefinger jab hard on its shoulder, a cold voice say:

"Listen, my friend pirates nothing from nobody, his name long before I knew him, which is a hell of a long time; but you pirated this little privacy of ours at the end of this bar . . . come on, Mr. Pappy, it's not a good end any more."

He apologized to my friend. We worked our way to the open entrance to the room to wait for the girls. I'll give the intruder credit, though: while I held Papa's parka for him, the man caught my eye, plainly signaling that he'd come to apologize. I shook my head because I feared for him. Needlessly, perhaps, but—I'd seen the temper before.

Papa said in a moment, "Jesus, kid, I've never seen you so hot. You had me scared."

"So was I scared, Papa," and he replied with a disgusted half-grin, "The son of a bitch. . . . What was it your dad said . . . funny how there's so many more in the world than horses to go with 'em?" That was the end of it—for a while.

The intent was to come back to the Christiania for dinner; Papa had mentioned it when we left the market, said he felt the need, and he knew Mary did—her frequent, nerve-wracking treatments, worse than the discomfiture of a healing break itself. She'd come from one that afternoon, so instead of going out, we had a simple pickup evening meal at their house. I went up to Papa's room to help him flatten a bit too much tilt on his writing stand. He was talkative, as we did a temporary job with no tools, openly said he'd be so glad when the doctors released Miss Mary so they could get back to the Finca where he always wrote well. And there were people to do the menial jobs he was saddled with now.

"But we hate to leave, Mr. Pappy, truly we do . . . can you remember a time when I didn't hate to leave this country?"

Tired from her treatment, Mary went up to bed early, Till with her to help "unbutton me." There was half a bottle of wine left, the fire burning low. I was asked to toss another log on it—only ten o'clock. When I sat down at the table again, Papa's clenched fist was grinding the palm of his other hand, saying to himself more than to me: "So, he wanted to know if I wear the beard for effect, the son of a. . . ."

"Aw, Papa . . . that was more booze talking than sense. Probably had a bad skiing day. . . ."

He glared a hole in me while I plowed right on that the man wanted to apologize, but that I had headed him off because I was in the mood to take him on myself, once safely out, my back away from a wall. I got a feeble grin for the quick footwork, but it faded on sight of Tillie coming back. She knew nothing of the incident, got a full account of it; so obviously the long simmering had greased the skids, skid being a mild term for what flowed forth: Everything was going wrong, against his efforts at work; the doctors he knew were dragging their feet; Mary was dragging hers, it all costing a fortune; she wanted to wait until her cast was off, which he knew would be a long time; he could go by himself, but he'd not leave her behind—hell, anything could develop when a man deserts his wife when she's in trouble. Why, a gal just might tell a man to go to hell for that sort of thing.

I was about to try a tack, but the signs said no, it was woman's work, keep out. Had I done so, my head might be in orbit yet—in pieces, no doubt. Tillie waited for an opening, very patiently, and when she got it she held on stubbornly, simply telling him that he was being most unfair in belaboring a scapegoat. Scapegoat? —that was a mighty rough term for Miss Till to be using. Yes, indeed, and so was his attitude a rough one; accidents happened to everyone, he put a slant of deliberateness on it; wasn't it worth some mutual patience toward his Miss Mary having a good and usable arm instead of a stiff one? And just where did he get such ideas of the situation developing into anything as drastic as he hinted?

"Nothing is further from the truth, Papa, I know it and so do you."

She had no choice but to be her honest and loyal self—or risk being labelled a phony in appeasing him. He didn't slow up easily, but slow up he did, eventually, and thanked her for her fairness. And, God's miracle, she got a little chuckle from him when he remembered once asking her if she truly thought he was no angel to live with. She said, yes, in exactly the way he expected her to. When we left he went outside with us for a check on the weather—"cold enough to make a coyote howl off key."

But the evening shook us to our foundations, nonetheless; we were not total strangers to occasional evidence of hallucinatory amblings, small inventions on this and that; nor of magnifications, overly-severe criticism. Well, you say to yourself, it can't be too long until a letup of tension is due, and it wasn't long.

On Monday, January 11, her arm in a removable cast, the doctors released Mary. At once train reservations were applied for, came through for Sunday, the seventeenth, meaning a late Saturday night departure to catch the Union Pacific's crack "City of Portland" at the beastly hour of 2:00 A.M. in Shoshone. Preparations commenced immediately, spirits high; the show was about to get on the road again; the weather was miserable that week, but no matter—we shot traps daily in it, as if it were going out of style for keeps. I wound up my local work, and for Thursday night Tillie suggested a favorite dinner menu at our house. Great.

It was a warm night, a heavy snowstorm moving in when we drove out to get Mary and Papa about seven. There were about two inches of new fall down, and it did look as if we were in for a dilly. The first thing noticed on my car were chains on over my snow tires—for the drive, curving sharply upward around the house to the back-door parking, was often quite tricky just below where we shot traps. No worries now about getting home, or that the windshield wipers were hard put in keeping ahead of the sticky wet snow on our way into town, Papa joking about hoping we didn't wolf down all the rare roast beef—then Miss Till could slip him a nice thick slice for his breakfast. In town it was the hour of much traffic, stores closing, the late shoppers, so a block off the main intersection on Sun Valley road, we were slowed to a mere crawl as we went by the popular ski shop in the Sports Center building. In the smaller room next door the lights were full on in the local branch of the First Security Bank. A janitor took care of both establishments, but he was nowhere in sight. It was quite natural to glance toward the bank. Its manager was a mutual friend on whose old home place we often hunted down Silver Creek way; and Papa used the bank as a tap, stopped there often on errands about town to pass the time of day with R. G. Price whom everybody addressed by his initials—a good talker, a great kidder. My car was just gaining momentum again when Papa's elbow nudged me quite hard.

"Pappy, they're checking our accounts in there. . . ."

"Not mine, Papa, don't have one, as you know."

I said it with a small laugh, for that was true, and of course he was kidding. There was a stunned silence then, a moment of the rest of us realizing that his tone of voice, the familiar low one of alarm, was positively not a joking tone. Oh, it was the janitor, Till said, working in a back room; Mary said they were not involved enough there for a check of any sort. Well, goddamn it, he guessed he knew better than that, he had suspected it for some time, and now he knew it for sure. I can't begin to remember how we tried to cut it off in the few minutes up to the house. Once inside, I reached for his parka, and for a moment couldn't tell if he intended letting me hang it up, or not. He couldn't keep his eyes off that square of light showing dimly through several blocks of storm, stood silently by our big living room window. He did tear himself away from it to go to inspect the fine piece of meat that caught his keen nose.

Though he always conducted himself in our house like it were his own, he never was in a hurry to get to the niche-in-the-wall bar out in the dining room; but straight to it he went now, for just beyond the angling wall was the big under-the-porch window through which the view out over the town was the same except for peering between bare branches of a large shrub just off the porch, snow measuring stick just beyond it. And of course the drapes were open for observing it during the storm. He peered, all right, during our brief gathering there, called attention to the especially good red wine he'd brought. I went in to throw a log on the fire, then into the sitting room to put on music, where Papa made a pretense of searching the bookcase, idling humming a little tune so low you barely heard it. In a moment he was back at the big front window.

"See, I told you so, kid, they're still at it, and they won't stop until they know everything about you. . . ."

"Aw, Papa, R. G. may be doing a little overtime; he often does, and besides, your business is his to protect. . . ."

"Yeah, but you don't know how the big outfits work, absolutely none of it your own any more, no matter how hard you try to play it straight with 'em . . . you can't win, they won't let you."

You feel pretty awful when you have to resort to small tricks in a case of that sort, but I had one handy, and I used it. Nor could I have been more surprised. It worked. Papa always carved for our table. He liked to do it, was a whiz with a knife, could hone one to shave Paul Bunyan. I had given him a hand-forged carbon steel beauty of a knife when Mary discovered the year before that there was not so much as a paring blade in the new house. We didn't need it, our drawers full of heirloom knives, and he prized it highly, had really accepted it on a "while-in-residence basis." We had a fair old substitute of the heavy hunting type he preferred instead of a carver, so I got it out, the stone, and fortunately the roast was half done when we got to the house. He went to work on the honing, so the worry on monetary stuff seemed to have gone thataway. The big end window's drapes were closed, with my movie screen rolled and hanging on its cornice, where I had worked that afternoon. It goes without saying that the other curtain got closed. There was no intent of a long evening, for I had a date in the lower country the following day, to make arrangements at a processing plant for a job the next week. The weather a· factor governing the roads, I'd have to start early. The meal was a dream, highly complimented, and you wondered how much of the perfectly done beef was actually savored. Hardly before we were finished:

"Wonder how much snow we got down, it was coming awfully hard when last I looked."

I switched on the yard lights and pulled the curtain—on the identical lovely fairyland scene of a January night just a year before. Greatly admired then, now each one of the dime-sized flakes falling so thickly was a mountain of resistance between here and home. "We'd better get going soon or we'll never make it up our hill." He was the first to leave the table, with a dish in each hand. It was an unheard hour for such—a little past nine o'clock!

As we donned our wraps, a glance out the window showed but a dim night-light in the bank, and I drove right by it; not a word said. We sailed up the drive in seven or eight inches of fresh snow and the storm was fizzling out, a dim moon cutting a silver hole in spent wispy clouds—a bite in the air, plainly forecasting a clear-up. We'd better come in for a nightcap, figure what to do with the mallard ducks hanging over the woodpile by the back door. We did, cut them down for a slow thawing in the basement garage, so on Saturday night, if Till would supervise the cooking of filleted breast of duck, we'd round up enough of us to finish them off while the final packing and other chores were being done.

Tillie and I were in bed a little after ten, not exactly drifting off the minute our heads hit the pillows. Now we knew the real meaning of the word, jolt—spelled with tall letters. For the first time in our experience with a relentless thing we'd met fairly well so far—so we thought—I saw tears in Tillie's eyes.

My Friday trip was to a Snake River town that I normally drove to in a couple of hours; but, as said, the weather broke all the rules that month, the snow reaching down into all the lower country—not heavy, but enough that the roads were a glare of ice-hard, packed snow, driving a hazard. That, and my errand, detained me overnight, and I got home Saturday noon, having taken the full morning to drive the distance, the stretch from Timmerman Hill up to Ketchum quite enough to fray the nerves of a wooden Indian. As if that were not enough, it was clear as a bell, and *cold,* when even your winter tires felt like slick treads.

While she fed us some lunch, I asked Tillie how the departure preparations were going, and she said, fine; she'd been out that morning, and she had me dated up for a number of things that I could help with. Good, and we took off, a lightness in our steps, looking ahead to witness the feeling of "going home" that we knew was in charge. It was, indeed. His good knife keen-edged, Papa was waiting for me; fillet out the ducks first thing—a fast operation with two pairs of hands. We joked and laughed at everything, tramped forty trips to the basement storeroom; shot our last go at clay targets when Duke came out. I didn't tumble at all when, as he always did, Papa asked me about my trip; and I remember his surprised look when I told him in truth that where I'd seen the very wide Snake River at the Burley plants, a heavy truck could easily be driven across its frozen surface—a rarity, one for the book.

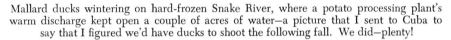

Mallard ducks wintering on hard-frozen Snake River, where a potato processing plant's warm discharge kept open a couple of acres of water—a picture that I sent to Cuba to say that I figured we'd have ducks to shoot the following fall. We did—plenty!

"And would you believe, Papa, that at twenty below zero down there this morning there were thousands of ducks feeding on the waste potato sludge, the warm discharge keeping the ice open for several acres—all big ducks, mallards—and I didn't have a still camera with me?"

"Those I would like to see," he said. "A hell of a note for the river, but at least they're wintering our ducks."

He scarcely believed that it was that cold in the lower country, but had vigorously complained of it when we cut the shooting short, and of when he'd walked to town earlier, then back. The Buick was in mothballs, covered in snow where it was usually parked near the back door; it was some sort of "courtesy thing" to Papa, in connection with sponsorship of his televised works. We intended to warm it up and clean it of snow, and put it in the garage for the local dealer to pick up for the turnback when called for—Duke and I would do it the next day.

An only low point in the very pleasant afternoon: farewell to the cotsies that Till and I took back to our neighbors on our way to do our small evening chores. Mary did it in a hurry and fled, but you know who just could not do it thus—and damned if I didn't come close to dampening a bit of fur as we held them in our arms for the small, touching ceremony at the back door. In my pocket was Papa's check in an amount to buy kitty food for at least six months!

From then on the evening—and night—just sort of grew into what it was: the judgment of a bunch of children, kindergarten age, at that—around the easy, but complex-sounding way of leaving the country by train. Being a railroad-owned and operated resort, Sun Valley was origin-point for service to its guests as well as the whole upper valley community; in short, its main-line busses were the train to and from Shoshone. If you wished to walk it or ride a horse, go to it, the bus would haul your luggage on your ticket. The Hemingways' were three first-class Pullman fares into Chicago, end-of-line for their crack train; the bus's departure from Sun Valley at 11:30 P.M. But that was not to be, and we did not know, but may have had a hunch.

Tillie and I picked up neighbor Clara Spiegel and drove out to the house about seven—Till all fixed up to help Lola with the cooking. It was a brilliant full-moon night, you could read a newspaper by it, and the thermometer on our back porch read an even twenty degrees below zero! The steady breeze off the mountains was a solid force almost impossible to face with your bare face. But no matter—it was the going-away shindig, simple, casual clothes, everyone pitch in and make it so. You had to, the exuberance rubbed off on you, enshrouded you in no time. It was Duke's dress—like for hunting, or cutting wood—that tipped me off, so I asked him about it, in an aside. Yes, Doc Saviers was set to drive the travelers to Shoshone in his old Chevy station wagon, and Duke was going along, just in case. Not at all enthused over it, he said, "Once we get past the eighteen miles to Bellevue, and the tricky turns between there and Timmerman Hill, the road the rest of the way could be all ours on this night; but it is Saturday, and it might be rough, to Bellevue, anyway." When George came I only suggested that they start in ample time, and that I would take the luggage to the Lodge and have it checked. That seemed to be the deal—then.

The meal was a delight, the lingering at the table like a rubber band stretching on and on. Papa got going on those hilariously funny singsong chants, parodies, or what-have-you, around personal history. At them, he was a master of ad lib, the stuff flowing out of him like water in tuneless tunes that you recognized part of the time. We watched the time, but, Papa was off in another era, the present out of the picture—as if he were singing: hell, we're having fun, we're not going anywhere. Mary's things were packed, Lola's ready, a part of Papa's "unimportant things" as he put it; some twenty-odd pieces piled near the living-room stairs. Suddenly it was ten-thirty, or thereabouts; I went outside to warm up my engine. Back in the house I got the news: not like Till, she suggested it to me because she figured it good for the cause; Papa fretted about his luggage; I said, "You mean I'll take it down to Shoshone, for it's far too much load for Doc's Chevy?" She said, yes, she'd go with me, Clara too. "Okay," I said. "It's nuts to even think about anyone driving," and I took off for home and some warmest clothes—suggesting a sensible alternative for her to try on the assemblage: We button up the party at the house, and do the finale up at the Lodge Duchin Room, then that big, warm dual-tired vehicle would take the travelers right from the front door; a safe, comfortable, unfailing fifty-six-mile ride.

However the suggestion was collectively received, it was no deal; the gayety going great when I got back about eleven o'clock. Doc agreed with me that we should be on our way at bus time, which regulations in winter allowed well over two hours for the connection. I at once started loading the packed luggage into my car, hating being a killjoy, ear cocked for the good licks in the show. Mary finally convinced Papa that he should get with the packing of his "vitals" and his clothes. An experienced and very fast packer, Clara went up with him and hastened the job. Now it was the opposite: organize and get going! It was agreed I lead the way, and our time was ample: the bus was but minutes ahead of me as I drove into town.

Between Ketchum and Hailey we expected to see cars off the road, half buried in the five-feet-high snowbanks; we did, a wrecker pulling one out, to go on to the next. The bitter cold had frosted the road to greased ice, the wheel in your hands like mush, your brakes worthless; you found a practical safe speed by feel—thirty-plus, no more, and no less—and we got along fine, until. . . .

Just a mile beyond Hailey at the end of the airstrip, a Saturday night driver, or an inconsiderate one, came at me, hugging the near center of the road, high lights on. I had no choice but to ease over as far as I could or suffer the side-swipe or half head-on. The soft "foot" snow sucked my right front wheel into it and I'd had it—period! The sudden, soft, spongy stop woke Clara from her nap and she said, "What happened, I can't see a thing?" No, I said, nor would I be going anywhere but back to town for a wrecker, if and when I could find one, some way.

George pulled up and I spoke my well-thought-out idea—take me back to the edge of town; I'd find a phone and call the station in Shoshone—I knew every man there. Ask them to consider three first-class fares on their way; in winter the crack train normally had a fair work stop—Sun Valley customers from the northwest—and there was a fair load of departees on the bus. And the facts I've mentioned were in their favor. Well, it didn't work, ten minutes at the very most could not be spared. I didn't mind that too much, even if the walk to town would be an ordeal, should I not flag a lift. It was the manner, and the way it was said. The show was on the road, and nothing was going to stop it. Nothing to do but try to squeeze thirty-odd pieces of luggage into Doc's small wagon, and I thought of that big roomy Buick— boy, that would do it! Somehow we got it all in, half-enveloping Mary and Lola on their seat, forcing the tailgate to lock. George was loaded to the guards, but his traction was better; then Duke spoke up that it was risky leaving the gals alone while I went to town—maybe he should stay with us. I wouldn't listen to that but had no chance to say so. One car refused to stop when I tried to flag him.

Hasty so-longs were said, and I told Papa that I had every faith in them getting along fine with a clear road all the way—just caution until over the hill. He agreed with me, and his bare hand whumped my shoulders as he turned to climb in the car.

"So long, kid, you'll make it."

"So long, Papa."

I kicked the snow away from my radiator to prevent over-heating the engine, checked the exhaust for clearance, and had every confidence that Tillie knew what to do in spite of my precautions, mainly: "If your engine quits, whatever you do, don't get out of this car!" She had her windows opened a crack as I started up the road, turning in a dozen paces to see headlights coming 'way off from Bellevue. The car was an aging one, having a time of it, the driver an elderly kind man who offered anything he could. I said, just a lift to his house—and a telephone? Sure, he said, and his engine quit as he started up, his battery refusing to turn it over.

In a mile plus a few blocks to his house, we'd walk a dozen paces, then turn our backs and walk backward another dozen to catch our breath from the icy blast that took it away. Even with crepe soles I could do a job of skating as easily as on an ice rink. I hoped the old man would not fall. There was coffee on his stove, we downed a quart while he finally got a promise of a wrecker. I waited for it until the jitters started me back afoot. Halfway, it picked me up, and the man asked if I knew that it was thirty-six below zero. I surely said, "You don't have to tell me, Mac!" My gals were okay and by two o'clock we were on our way. Fighting sleep, Clara said, "We ought to all have our heads examined." I wanted to blurt out exact- ly what I inwardly muttered while "leaning" up that windy road a couple of hours before—"to hell with it, to hell with all of it. . . . Who are you, anyway, Buster?"

The following afternoon, when Duke and I swept the Buick clean and put it away, I was ashamed of myself, and a little sick. Chuck Atkinson came out with the keys to the garage, and to check the house that he would see was looked after. The remembrance had been persistent for days, of the exhausting night a week before, when we'd heard a frightening remark of the house we now were closing up:

"It's a fine place, now that I'm a little used to it . . . but I bought it as a nest egg for Miss Mary."

Papa's, "So long, kid, you'll make it," kept ringing in my head.

2

In mid-July came Mary's long letter—typewritten—by the grateful "one-armed paperhanger" who wrote:

Thanks both of you for the sweet interest in my broken wing. The bloody thing still aches and aches and still requires hours of pushing and pulling every single day, such a bore, but thanks to Doctors George and Scott Earle, it's not made of aluminum.

Indeed, more credit was (and is) due the concerned doctors, understanding a situation, too, and meeting it, than perhaps meets the eye in these words.

Other items of significance in her letter:

Papa is fine, has worked prodigiously on his bullfight thing from last summer, which *Life* will publish and then will go into a book by Scribners.

Now we're getting ready for a vacation from here—Papa going to Spain to collect the final dope for his book, a comparatively short journey he now thinks, about six weeks. I will go up to New York and spend the time more or less fixing up our apartment there. Then going out to Ketchum, either with a detour to here, or straight from New York.

Thinking about this, it occurred to me that Miss Till has never seen New York, she might like to, and with our apartment more or less liveable it would cost neither you nor us anything more than the train fare if she'd like to come.

She went on to say they planned to leave Cuba between the twenty-sixth and thirtieth of July, and asked Till's reply before then, or awaiting them in New York. She wrote to the latter address, advising that we had problems and: "Will come if at all possible." That, she meant—the deterrent being an extremely dry summer, heavy demands on water being our local picture; us with a big yard of grass and flowers, and Tillie handling all of "the farming" which she could not find anyone to do for her. She was still on the fence when on August 16, Mary wrote from New York, her letter opening with this:

They had a lot of nonsense on the radio last Monday—August 8, about Papa being very ill in Spain—it took me 9 hours to find out the truth, every minute agony—all false.

Papa got off for Spain (by air) on August 4, to finish up all the dirty little chores that he has to do before he can finish either the *Life* piece or his book. . . .

It was something of a sweat getting away from Cuba, and we don't know what will happen to our stuff there, our whole both lives' treasures, actually. I'll tell you about it when I see you. There's nothing we can do about it at the moment.

I intended to go back to Cuba for a week or two in September, but now they make the entering and leaving so complicated that I think I'll stay here—waiting to hear from Papa.

She did not return to Cuba, which we learned in her disappointed, understanding reply to Tillie's word that going east was impossible for some time. Conjecture on our part, yes, but it was quite obvious from the limited news of the day that their Finca might as well be written off. Sensing that Papa himself had left it for the last time, Till said of herself: "I should say to hell with my yard full of work and at least go and help Mary cry—in our own way."

12.

The Short, Bright, Dark Fall of '60 . . .

1

While doing a few winter preparation jobs at home on a Sunday, October 16, I got careless with the power saw I had used a dozen years and came within an ace of losing a joint or two of my right forefinger—my "shootin' finger." The same Dr. Scott Earle, who did so much in saving Mary's arm, saved it for me. He kept me at home a few days, then immobilized it in a metal stall, fixed me up with dressing materials to be my own doctor daily, and to report back to him as often as my work permitted. Fortunately, my season was quite wound up; I was on a light program of picking up odds-and-ends filming on my oldest subjects, some research on a new major subject to be started the following spring. Oddly, I was due in Hollywood on November 21, then back at home, for vacation the last three weeks of December. Time-wise, it was necessary to the job; we had no plans. With a mangled finger it was about certain that I would do no late season duck shooting. Being a southpaw, basically, ambidexterous in some things, I couldn't hit a tightly closed barn from its inside with a gun at my left shoulder.

So, when Doc turned me loose in a few days, the boss's orders by phone were to concentrate on lining up locations and making arrangements for spring. My new picture was the story of Western beef—from a calf to the steaks—vital freight business to the railroad, and again so much of the material was close to home.

It was the weekend following my first short trip after my accident that the Hemingways arrived by train. Doc Saviers met the "City of Portland" in Shoshone and we waited at their house when they arrived at ten that night. I should liken it to a reunion, for the ten long months had seemed like so many years—and it was a soul-warming year, too.

Mary's arm was good for hugging—and shooting; Papa's, like those on an octopus. As ebullient as ever, the faint traces of travel weariness were hardly noticed. When presence of mind finally got us inside the house he took hold of my hand like it was an object of reverence, likened its metallic protuberance to a 20mm anti-aircraft shell, wanted to know how I worked with it.

"Don't have too much of that kind to do, Papa, but I'm a fair bird dog."

He was full of questions of things local, of our plans, asking of them right down to dates—all satisfactory. An amusing exchange was his in-person thanks for a letter I'd written back in the spring and of which Mary had written about later. In it I sent a picture of those hordes of wintering ducks on Snake River, made in the week I worked at the plant, following when I'd seen them last. Neatly encased in his comments on the nearly unbelievable photograph was his apology for that cold night on the road. I said:

"Maybe come December I'll have enough of this iron off so that I can trigger a gun."

"The old doctor says you might, but he doubts it. How about it, George?"

"If he wants to keep it all, he damn well better mind Scott Earle," George said.

"Sure, kid, I've never backed you up in my whole life, but for a modest fee, ol' Papa can keep us in birds, won't we, citizens?"

In the few days I was home, we knew it was going to be good: Papa got his fingers into the organizing; was pleased to get the familiar old rented Chevy he'd once had; got into the marketing up to his chin, and a very first renewal of the old was a picnic, hardly ahead of fully stocking the pantry. Pheasant season was not yet open, it was overly warm for ducks, and for a change, perhaps inspired over the view from his "working window," he steered it north by the river at the foot of the Boulder Range. The dry season made for a "beauty fall" of color, some departing, but the aspen still a flaming gold, sumac the deep hue of pigeon's blood, the willows rimming the river a shimmering, coppery green in the mountain breeze.

It was good to see Papa take the wheel because he wanted to, joking of the day so nice that for once he was not catching hell for freezing his back-seat passengers with a rolled-down window; hearing him say: "Let's go on over Galena Summit to the lookout place, just to feast our eyes on the Salmon River headwaters country, the Sawtooth Valley, the one to end all mountain valleys . . . anywhere that I have seen, anyway . . . we haven't been over for two years, Kitner, when we brought the Bruces, remember?"

While taking in the magnificent vista that can stir you to the depths, I mentioned that I had some scouting to do, when the big cattle herds moved out of the summer range in the lower valley and Stanley Basin to the winter range downriver around Challis; hinted that a trip or two with me be considered. Papa said, "Great, we'll put in our order that this weather stays so good." In late spring, when the wild flowers turned much of the valley and the lower basin into an unbelievable carpet of color, it was definitely planned that I make the opening of my new subject there —which I also mentioned only as a matter of course. Papa said, "We've heard so much about it, and in all the years, we've never seen it in summer. I wonder why. Well, we will." Then with the I-told-you-so look, he offered to bet that I would propose to use what we could of Bud Purdy's fine cattle operation at Silver Creek. I said that I certainly did intend to, and he replied:

"It figures, Bud is so damn loyal to friends . . . how would we have gotten along so well for so long without him?"

Back on Wood River at a little Forest Service place, we singed our fingers on the baked beans can, ate ash-sprinkled, fire-charred hot dogs skewered on green willow sticks; we had small beers chilled in the fringe-iced river, Papa tippled from a small bottle of red. He wouldn't let me help put out our fire but he hauled enough glass-thin sheets of ice from the stream "to put out the Chicago fire . . . we burn up no country with our litter-bugging."

Very soon there was an unprecedented little surprise. I missed him, being away a few days, but Coop came to town unannounced by any means. He had his old friend, Pat De Sica, with him, and said they were "just prowling all over hell's half acre." They had guns along, so timed it with the opening of bird season, got in a couple of hunting days with Papa. I, quite by chance, got a clue as to the winter. From Duke, I knew a little of the Valley's reservations, that the Coopers had theirs for the latter two weeks of January. Which meant that barring an earthquake, you could set your calendar, and your watch, by Coop's systematic way in such. Papa told me that he'd set a tentative date with Coop, and that he just might fix it up with Bud Purdy to trap magpies for a shoot or two. Because of things already said that indicated the opposite, I looked pleasingly surprised, and he caught it.

"Sure, why not? . . . even if it's a seven-foot-deep one, I would rather spend the winter here than in a two-bit apartment in the Big Town."

As usual, the weekly prizefights around the big swiveling TV set in their living room were "command performance" deals, and on election night we sat up until two o'clock—watching the incredibly close cat's-whisker contest for the White House between Kennedy and Nixon. Also, as usual, button-lipped on politics, the vigil ended with:

"It'll be a lot more fun tomorrow night, when we can see our bets in a pair of dark trunks versus the light ones."

Not long after their return, Mary rode to Twin Falls to do a bit of shopping with friends, and, finishing up work in her yard, Tillie called Papa and asked him to come to a simple lunch with her. He said, no, come and eat with him, there was some delicious cold turkey for sandwiches; he'd be getting it ready while she came. She told me all about it when she came by train to meet and ride back home with me on a monotonous long drive. She said that she didn't at all mind listening to Papa unwind considerably on a familiar old tack, nor was she particularly alarmed at a couple of high points—because they mutually got it squared off on the humorous angle. She got the idea that he'd had mail, a phone call, or had read something about himself, for out of the blue he led it off with: "Miss Till, you don't believe all the stuff that's put out about me, do you?" She responded by reminding him about the old one he had "skied with for so many years at Sun Valley," so naturally she had her own ideas about the truth of what she read.

"Well, I never wanted to be a celebrity, Miss Till, you know that, don't you? . . . and what can a guy do about so much swill? If he raises hell he's a bastard who's jealous of himself, truth or false, and he can't do a damn thing if he isn't around to protect himself. . . ."

"Well, Papa, you were a celebrity when we first knew you, and don't you think that we rejoiced in it as much as you, at that time?"

To me, Till said, "It got a good laugh out of him, and I went on to remind him about the guest who said that he had loved coming to our community for so long because the natives didn't pay a damn bit of attention to him or how much he was worth—to us he was just another old boot."

"In a word," I said, "you came within an ace, accidentally, of calling Papa one to his face."

"You might say that, I guess," she said. "And at the moment I probably could have gotten by with it if I had, for he said that he didn't want to be treated any other way."

"So you had a clean bill of health, when you left?" I said.

"Yes, after he said he guessed he wouldn't have his damned phones yanked out —he couldn't call his local friends, and they couldn't call him. Riding into town with me to get his mail, he said, 'Come out at the usual time, Sir Till, Miss Mary won't be late, and Mr. Pappy's gone . . .'"

"And so you did?" I said.

"Sure, and the shooting was at the usual high level, Papa having as much fun ejecting his empty shells into the carton as breaking the targets that came in it."

"He hits that carton, ten feet back, damn consistently," I said. "Because, honey, some basic things never change, do they?"

"No, they don't," she said. "And you get a bit confused at times, I guess I don't have to remind us of that."

Just as later, when I was ready to go on them, I was reminded of the one-day trips of scouting when we'd easily go by, or into, some old familiar country. No, there was too much work to do, better stay and get it done. Then, when I came in on Friday, November 11, and we went out to "check in" for the weekend, I mentioned that I had called Bud Purdy about coming down Saturday morning to talk about his future operations, Papa said, "Include me in, I'll get us a duck or two."

Driving down was a revelation, the talk of the "good old days," talk flowing like the sparkling water in the old creek itself. Feeling, with no gun, like a man in church without his pants, I took a camera along to make a few shots around Bud's place to take to California with me. We found Bud and his boys working a penful of young stock; I got my business with him out of the way while Papa perched on a fence, talking with a neighboring rancher. The duck gen was that several bunches were scattered up along the old south canal. We went after them, starting in at the far upper end that very seldom produced because of an open approach—hence our going along not too quietly, Papa stuffing shells in his old stubby W.D. pump gun. The sharp click of the action homing one in the chamber spooked a triple of mallard drakes hugging the low near bank of the sluggish water—all nicely in range. Papa exploded into action, as fast as I had ever seen him go. He nailed a double neatly, tried for a triple, the lead bird a wee bit out of range. It was flawless gun-handling, and pure luck that I happened to be a few paces behind him, the angle the ducks took exactly right for me to snap off a shot midway in the split-second action, by sighting over the closed reflex cover of the Rolleiflex I just happened to have hanging on me by its neckstrap. Two shots were left on the roll of film and I shot them off of the group after Bud's dog brought in the ducks. When winding off the film I told Papa that I just might have a shot of the action, and he said:

"Did you trigger it, kid, with your ten-gauge finger or a good one?"

"I couldn't answer that one, Papa, if my life depended on it."

I spoke the truth, wondering if my ten-gauge finger happened to cover half the

Like the early fishing picture, this might be a one and only, too. My own comment, echoing the shootin' man: "There are some things that nothing can take from you."

At left, rancher Bud Purdy, with whom we had a priceless "in."

lens, while we worked the rest of the canal for a fair haul of birds. It hadn't, I learned later—the negative showed the action as the eyes saw it. I did not know that the three negative envelopes would one day be marked "final." Their date was November 12, 1960.

2

The following week was a real bender, and at the end of it I was sure the "omens" really had meaning—starting on the thirteenth day of the month. Very calmly, smoothly. On Sunday I saw Papa at the market, picking up his newspapers. He grinned and asked me to "referee and scorekeep" a little trapshooting session in late day. I did, and tried to shoot with my second finger and felt the effects of recoil clear to my shoulder, Papa seconding the motion as George gave me a bit of hell. On Monday I left town in late forenoon, feeling sure that I would be back Wednesday night. I gassed up on my way through town; Papa drove in behind me for the same. In the way he asked me if I was sure of getting back then, I knew there was something on his mind, but my subtle tries failed to learn what. It turned out that my return was on Thursday, in midforenoon. Over a cup of coffee I got the first news from Tillie:

"The break finally came for Duke, at least I think it'll be good; he's going to Las Vegas next week to see about a job his friend has fairly well lined up."

"Does Papa know it?" I asked.

"He didn't last night, anyway," she said. "I was out for dinner, and if he had known, I'd have heard about it."

As we talked I happened to glance across the street and saw a familiar figure sauntering around in Clara's yard. I said, "Isn't that Hotch over there?" Till said yes, he had come in Monday night and checked in at Chuck's motel, but stayed a night or two with Don Anderson who looked after Clara's place in her off-season absences. Then I got what had been on Papa's mind; Till said:

"He wanted to know when you'd be back because Hotch has his finished teleplay with him—*The Killers*—on 16mm film, and there's to be a showing out at the house tonight or maybe tomorrow night. You, of course, he looks to for the projection equipment."

The machine I kept at home was one of two belonging to my old outfit at Sun

Valley, so I asked her why she hadn't simply arranged for both of them for Hotch. She said:

"I offered to, but Papa said he'd wait for you, sensitive about asking you, fretting that you'd hurt your finger lugging the heavy stuff around."

She went on to say that there seemed to be some difficulty in Papa's writing, for Hotch had a Dictaphone with him, suggested that Papa use it, play his stuff back to himself.

"Hotch turned it on at the table last night, Mary dictated a ditty to it, so did I, and Hotch played it back."

"And just what tall tale did you have?" I teased.

"I told the old one about the duck that Papa pointed his finger right onto her beak and told her he'd know her voice anywhere—remember?—and he said, 'Miss Till, you told it perfectly, except that I called her a bitch, instead of the son of one, remember?' Hotch said he would leave it with Papa, but I would bet he won't even try to use it, I could tell it by his manner—like it was a spook, or a snake, as he once called our old disc recorder when we tried to get him to read a sleeping-bag scene in the *Bell*."

Indeed he had, said it was as dangerous as a black mamba.

I went out and called to Hotch, told him that when they were ready for his show there would be no projection problems; I'd have both of them there, eliminating reel changing. Fine, he said. He was not long on time, had to leave the coming Sunday. Walking back to the house it struck me as rather ironical that just fourteen years before, I had a hand in rigging up a makeshift in projecting Hellinger's *The Killers* and Papa had fretted about that one, said that we should rent the movie house in Hailey.

I drove out to the house to check in around noon—the showing was set for that night. I took the machines, with Doc Saviers' help, when I went out to kibitz the shooting. It was then that Papa learned from Duke himself about his Las Vegas trip; his blessings were moving to hear, but a close look showed that it disturbed him deep inside, though he'd known for a year that it might come up. To me in an aside, he said: "He'll make it . . . won't it be a kick, though, if he gets wound up with one of them pretty gals." His laugh was good, but short.

With a big pull-down screen concealed in the ceiling at one end of the living room, we set the machines on the dining table at the opposite end—a good setup, with ample image size. With the Hemingways and Hotch, there were Doc and Pat Saviers, Duke, Tillie, and me. The sponsor for the nationwide network distribution was the Buick Motor Car Company, the credit to them the opening on the screen. Then the startler that was the credit to the author, who sat within arm's reach of me by the machines. On a slowly revolving base it was a sculpture of the Hemingway head, ruggedly done in the "thumb-dab" style (my term for it), against a low key background; a void, lighted by a narrow "pencil" spot hitting the high points of the work. Had it not been for background music and commentary, the machine muffled to silence, I'm sure that one could have heard a feather falling in the darkened room. Like in telepathy I could feel George wincing beside me. My own instant impulse was to jerk the power cord, stop the show, bring the room back to the light of reality. The effect was fitting, true, dramatically done with all good intent. But, in this opinion, soon borne out, not for the eyes that saw it.

When the show was over there was the usual stand-around commentary on it that I remember little of. I covered, or I guess I did, my feeling by taking down the machines, rolling up the screen, like the unconcerned in to do a job. I had my car at the back door to haul the equipment, so I picked up the lightweight speaker cases and went through the kitchen where I saw Papa standing alone by the window, staring out into the night. I expected something like that, so it was not alarm that caused me to bump a table leg with a case as I turned sidewise to make the narrow aisle between the table and the fireplace. At the small sound it made, Papa jerked his head around, eyes wide, said in a low hoarse voice, "I'll open the door for you, kid." In the narrow back hall I again had to turn sidewise to go past him, our faces little more than a couple of feet apart; and never will I live down the expression on poor old Papa's face, especially his frightened eyes. His right hand came up off the doorknob, his upturned fingers making a basket, a turning motion, and he said in the low half-whisper we'd heard so much of late:

"Fair show, as shows go . . . but Pappy, that awful head!"

He turned as he said it, just vanished back into the house. In the line of coats hanging there in front of me, well, I didn't see them; in their place I saw that fine sculpture—now detached, far out in space, by itself; yes, a head, and I could only interpret the fear in Papa's eyes that it was the thing that was destroying him an inch at a time, and the inches were steadily shortening. I repeat, that was my interpretation, coupled with something else—a morbid fear that left me trembling as I lifted the gear into the car.

Friday was an unsettled weather day, holding a promise of snow in the occasional spurts of cold rain. Papa called to ask if I'd like to go with him and Hotch for some ducks. By all means, I said, and I took my double gun with single trigger, determined that at least I would look the part I always had, whether I even loaded it, or not. It wasn't a fruitful hunt of about an hour in late afternoon; Papa did the business on a few, shooting well; I made a ragged kill and a tyro's miss on an easy one. Dropping me off at home, sniffing the snow in the air, Papa said, "How about tomorrow, looks like it might be good." I said, fine, and holding up the second finger of his right hand, he grinned the kind of grin you liked to see.

"You don't point with this one, Mr. Pappy, but it was a good try."

Saturday afternoon was bright and snappy cold, with several inches of new snow on the ground. Our guess wasn't an optimistic one out at the house, Papa breaking out of their cases a pair of matched double guns that he'd brought from Spain that last trip. To me there was an odd twist to that one: always a utilitarian, Papa did not go around spending his dough for semi-fancy guns, which these were; when first showing them to me, he was actually embarrassed, or apologetic. He never fired a shot from either of them, abhorred their "spongy" tandem triggers, and greatly admired their fine English trunk-style leather cases. Now he was getting them out for Hotch to again take the open-bored short one, offering me the long-range one since I insisted on taking a gun. His reason was sound enough: my single-trigger gun was Taylor's fine old $85.00 Browning over-under that Bob had given me. Not a hunting man himself, he did not have to urge it upon me, need I say. Papa was immensely pleased about it, joked me that no man on earth could shoot it like the colonel had, but on my rack, in his view, was where it belonged. Stocked "straight" for traps, it was a little slow for me in the field, but I could lay my crippled finger along the deep receiver and at least get off a shot. In his offer of the lighter-weight Spanish double, there was simply his understanding of my "useless" feeling. I tried the gun for swing and feel; he said: "No good, Mr. Pappy, better stick with the Browning, but don't get sore at yourself."

Hotch drove the old Chevy, the talk was good, and nary a duck did we see in the air going down. Pulling up at the gate to the big pasture of the old south canal, Papa wouldn't let me get out to unlock and open it. The car's nose, as he drove it through the gate, pointed straight toward the big cup in the hills beyond Coyote Bend, so Hotch said:

"Come to think about it, this is exactly the kind of day that it was two falls back when he gave you and me the royal one, remember?"

"Yes, it is, Hotch, and the way it looks now, either he or his brother has been there ahead of us, or maybe we can lay it to this cold wind."

We drove to our parking place a short walk from the canal, set up our guns, and waited for Papa to gear up. Never had I wanted so badly to give him a hand with the old Rube Goldberg affair that was his bird carrier and shell vest of the open suspender type. Only he could get into the thing that probably had carried a ton of birds in its time; and to me he'd be a stranger without it. His bare hands half-blue with the cold, he fumbled with this buckle, the horse blanket safety pin that served some mysterious purpose. A right pair of glasses was a must against the glare off the snow. He tried at least five pair that he had in as many pockets.

It took us close to an hour to work the canal—not so much as a feather did we put up; and had I been a prayin' man, I think I'd gone along on my knees. Then on our hunch, we took a different way out in the car, to pass by a small lateral drainage ditch that often produced ducks, if worked cautiously. We did, and a single mallard susie squawked out beyond the willows and Papa nailed her neat.

I assumed that we'd go on down to the ranch to check in with Bud, maybe hunt the inner canals near the creek. Papa doubted that it was worth it, so told Hotch to turn around and leave by way of the gate. As Hotch turned up the highway, Papa turned and looked back at me, his small grin sort of forlorn, but a grin just the same:

"Well, Mr. Pappy, we're not skunked, anyway . . . the northerners should really be down when you get back."

I avoided mention of that being two and a half weeks away, but did say that I might trigger a gun by then, probably with a short guard on my finger. He turned again, his grin a better one, reminded me what he'd said about it earlier: "Before you try, better soak it in a tumbler of hundred proof, kid." Now he added that he hoped that I could.

Those are the fleeting moments that make you put aside a forlorn grin but seconds before, think nothing about the lone lady duck on the old carrier lying on the seat beside you. But I thought ahead to the evening, and wondered what it would be like—because I couldn't help it. The ride on home was pleasant enough.

The evening was for Miss Mary's well-planned dinner party—a casual buffet sort of thing—for about a dozen of us locals and Hotch. Since I was committed for Monday morning in California, Tillie and I had to take the night train, went to the party all ready for travel but closing our luggage; we'd drive to Shoshone, leaving by midnight at the latest. Duke was set to leave for Las Vegas Sunday afternoon, stopping in Twin Falls where his parents lived; Hotch hitching a ride to Shoshone with him, to catch his train east. This whole departure business must have been the trigger.

Papa couldn't keep it on file that during the year past the through-car service to California was removed from the afternoon train—hell, I'd always taken it before because it was so fast and convenient, and it went through Las Vegas, too; why didn't we all go together, tomorrow, it would be daytime and he might drive us down for a small fee, and maybe shoot a pheasant in the bargain? He got Duke and me in a corner about it, George Saviers listening in, and who did more than we to get him off it eventually, satisfied, apparently. The pre-meal interim seemed all right—not a long one—Papa having a little wine, well cut with soda—his alcohol consumption practically nil those days.

For the delicious meal, the table handled ten, and the mental picture of it is very clear: Papa, Till, and Hotch; Dr. John and Mary Ellen Moritz; George and Pat Saviers; Chuck and Floss Atkinson, and Ruth Purdy. The rest of us, including Mary and Bud Purdy, were comfortably sitting around a long low coffee table by the fire, the floor our chairs. During most of the entire meal, Papa fretted because Bud was being slighted. (Bud, whom Papa liked from the first day he knew him, was the only old-timer who always called him Ernie). So to Till he said several times, "Why isn't Bud at old Ernie's table, with the rest of us?" Each time she reminded him that we were talking about me working with Bud come spring. Oh, sure, he knew that, but he should be at the table, anyway.

Till and I were the first to leave the party. I told Papa so long, I'd see him soon, and he kidded about my mountain legs when we'd sail with Vince in the harbor off Long Beach—all just fine. I went out to warm my engine, then talked with Mary in the kitchen while waiting for Till. When she came I saw that she struggled within herself to keep calm. She did, because Mary and I talked about Christmas, which was all set for our house again, and there was some small item we were to get for the occasion. Indeed, Mary had not been overlooked in the "slighting" business, but we naturally avoided that, more or less because we had "been there before." Instead, ours was, "We'll definitely be back on the seventh of December, the same date as last year," which I had assured Papa at least four times in as many days. So Tillie kept it to herself until we were well on our way, and when she let it come I knew why:

She put on her coat, sort of lingered close by Papa as he talked with Dr. John—quite intensely, she saw—then he saw her, and it was the usual; he remembered to send his best to her sister whom we'd see much of, and mentioned kidding her so much in the old days. Tillie turned to go then, but his hands on her shoulders stopped her, turned her around, his long arms folding her to him as if she would not come back, ever:

"Oh, my Miss Till, my good Miss Till!"

Till said that to her, his was a voice like an anguished sob, and, "I don't know how I kept from coming apart; I can hear his heartbeat, like a drum, in my ear now. Honey, I wish we weren't going, and yet I feel like I want to run. I tell you, something's going to give, soon."

In that, she was wrong—it was already giving, fast!

Our absence, we confessed to ourselves *was* "running" from it, because we got lost in our busy time, leaning, I suppose, on that old one: no news is good news. Several times I was on the verge of calling George Saviers or Chuck, but didn't, and the only news that we had was the promised note from Duke if his trip was successful. Yes, it was, he wrote, and he would be gone when we were home again. When reading it, we kept hearing the words that we had let bother us for a long time, ". . . it hurts when your old friends die off and you can't dodge it as you go along, some move away. . . ."

Accentuated, of course, by conditions, Papa Hemingway was reacting naturally; it just seemed to us that his mind kept telling him that the little tribe he'd come to lean on in the things that he loved so much, was diminishing in the only place that he could call home "any more"—as he would put it. Humanly selfish, yes, as we all are; but if you were a friend, he wished you well. Sure, other Indians were around, but some had been around a little more than others. How else could we figure it?

Coming home, on schedule, the staccato of wheels on the rails we rode wasn't nearly fast enough to suit us; and we could hardly resist picking up the phone when we got into the house—too late that night of the seventh.

In the morning I went down to market for something with our coffee for breakfast. Forgetting that we'd been away, Don Atkinson asked me if I knew when the Hemingways would be back. Back? Where were they? His dad could tell me more about it, he said. I was sort of glad I got the gen in two installments, but had I got it in one, the floor under me wouldn't have shaken too much. Chuck told me that Papa had registered in at the Mayo Clinic in Rochester, Minnesota—as Mr. George Saviers—on November 30. Larry Johnson had flown him, Mary, and Doc

Saviers, he said. Mary was there and Chuck gave me the name of her hotel; we talked but a few seconds about it, because the less we talked, the better. When I walked into the house, Tillie looked intently at me.

"Well . . . it's something about Papa, isn't it?"

Not fancying ourselves as even crude amateur analysts of the situation, we tried to creep inside Papa's head—came up with the logic that Mayo's was mainly thought of as for the *physically* sick; so wouldn't Mr. Saviers' difficulty be cloaked in something like hypertension? Which is what we soon learned as correct analysis. Surely, his own actions led us to be certain that Papa knew something had to be done.

In answer to my immediate letter, Mary called us not so long afterward, her first word that they would not be back by Christmas. Was it all right to write directly to Papa? By all means, please do, she said, and did we have any morsels at the moment —she was on her way to see him then—something they could share? I hesitated to say that I had been hunting a couple of times, and had done well, fairly normal again. She would not sort that out, she said, Papa would be delighted. An item in my schedule, that she knew of, had matured: I was to be home much of the winter, making a ski technique film for Sun Valley promotion, and a short specialty subject for television use. It was lucky, a "tuck-in" that I could do in the otherwise slow time in my regular program. So Mary said, "Great," and went on to say, "Shoot us a duck or two, and eat them for us, because I can't tell you more now, except that I have hopes of us getting out of here some time in January." When she wrote later that they were having Christmas dinner at the home of one of Papa's doctors, well—that more than matched the simple Christmas that we had with the Hills. Like a small boy, I had the warmness of knowing that in our own "cool, well ventilated place" there were ducks curing and some put away. Mary was correspondent, and the news was increasingly good, but by mid-January there still was nothing definite as to their return.

13.

1961...

1

Of the Coopers' visit to Idaho that winter, I can only say that I recall it with feelings almost beyond words—in spite of the fact that I considered myself capable of facing such issues as being tagged as company for a doomed man. For Coop was just that, and he knew—little doubt about it—that I knew it too. It came to me forcibly when I drove up behind Rocky and daughter Maria on their first morning in camp.

I ran down my off-window, but with a plainly beseeching look in her eyes, Rocky came around to my side, and when our simple greeting was finished, she said, "I hope that you'll find some time to go places with my Gary." I assured her that I would, one way or another, and thought back in time to two winters before when the Hemingways lived in the Wisher house. On a dreary storm-threatening day, Rocky had taken a few color pictures of Papa and Coop—close-ups out-of-doors in light that a pro would avoid if possible. Later she brought them to me—transparencies so dense, and unprintable—and she asked me if we could make passable black-and-white copies of them. I had to sorrowfully say no to her—for they were remarkably good likenesses, truly studies in character of both men. That's why I write "sorrowfully"—and I wondered why I hadn't done the job under good conditions myself. But, the point is, Rocky's manner plainly said: I doubt I'll ever get another chance. She didn't, so now I asked her where old Podner might be at the moment; I was committed for a couple of days, but I had a tip for him—one a local had passed on to me, knowing I'd be on the lookout. She directed me to the Lodge lobby, where most likely I'd find him on the phone—after me.

He was, talking to Tillie at home. All at once, my indescribable feeling left me—for this was like it had always been: just happen upon him, the way he liked it, the casualness of the man himself, old take-it-easy, so to speak. He asked at once, "How's the shootin' and seein' eye, Podner?" and I said, "Anxious, and ready as ever, I hope." I gave him the tip and took him to the man—over at the Inn—who gave it to me: a downed critter on the man's cattle-feeding setup down near Silver Creek, where magpies and perhaps a coyote or two might be hanging around, as targets. This was "excuse"—pure and simple—for Coop wasn't especially interested in shooting anything; he wanted to prowl, and company for such was scarce, always in skiing winters. I told him I'd get away in a couple of days—he was pleased with that—so, in my fixin' to do some shootin' I came in early that afternoon, got out my favorite old light rifle, found some aging ammunition, and took it up the highway north of town, fired a few sighting-in shots to get it on the nose. In short, this had to be as it always was, too. In a couple of nights, Coop called me at home to tell me there was another "coyoty notch" on his .243 Winchester. Actually, in telling me, his voice sounded a bit apologetic; but I was prepared for some time with him, and ours was, "Goodnight, see ya in the morning." Yes, I was filling in for someone else, too, and I didn't fret about any unpleasantness that would be present if there was talk about it—it was not, ever, that way with Coop.

Coop looked well, indeed, until you looked twice, and knew what to look for. He'd drive his little rented car, say, for an hour, then out of the corner of my eye I'd see him commence to flex his shoulders, twist his neck, like a too tall man who'd slept a cold night in a too short bunk. Hang on as long as he could, then:

"Pappy, ol' kid, wouldja mind takin' 'er a while, when we pull up an' stretch ar legs, ya know?"

Which meant that I would take her, generally, for most of the remaining day, and the first one out, it was as obvious as the long nose on my face what he was doing. We'd poke into places, "pockets of country" as he said, that we hadn't poked into in years, relive a time when he'd shot a handsome specimen of bobcat, made a whale of a shot here, and so on. We went out to the sage area by the old Frees farm, found to our surprise that we could still make a hit of three or four tries on running jacks with our rifles. On our last day out, we knew that Mary and Papa were on their way home; and I know that probably the forthcoming may be taken with a grain of salt; but happenstance, or no, here it is—a perfectly natural happening for the place we visited:

I described a coyote chase in a Buick convertible, back in the January of '48 part of this story. We went there, a day exactly like the one thirteen years before, dry and windy, the same old tall sage. We saw nothing of interest but "a iggle flyin' high 'n fancy" (Coop talk for eagle up high, and playing the thermals), in the cruise we made of short duration. Back at the drop-off of the mere trail to the river bridge far below, Coop saw a movement out some fifty yards in thin sage. We stopped and walked out to a fine specimen of a coyote that had succumbed to a poisoning—probably by cyanide often used where there is a menace to stock—in that case just down between us and the river. Rigor mortis had barely set in, to the back of our wrists the carcass was not even cold. The movement that caught Coop's sharp eye was the wind ruffling the bushy tail that had hung up in a little sage.

I would be lying if I put it down that we just laughed it off; but I will say that an

informed observer would hardly, if at all, have caught a trace of the telepathy going on, or a fleeting change in either expression. We made a bit of small talk, instead, of not skinning the carcass, its pelt in prime, as we had done so many times
down the long years. Coop took the wheel then—about two o'clock—and we crossed
the river and climbed out of the canyon to the little town of Bliss on the main stem
highway; a stop for truckers with an eatery or two, and we hadn't had any lunch.
In one of them I knew the waitress who had fed me in my travels; Coop waved
aside her menu and bet her that the cook might rustle up two orders of bacon
and eggs and fried spuds, if she'd twist his arm. She said:

"For this guy, sure, and for Mis . . . well, Gary Cooper . . . now don't tell me
you ain't him."

Just the sort of remark that Coop liked very much, from a friendly, being-her-
self, unflustered gal. Our in-from-the-plowing "dinner" went down very easy.

Up to then, in our brief scattered talks of our old huntin' pal, I had put off feeling
out Coop about tacking on a few extra days to their stay. On our way home I forthrightly said that if he could, and emphasizing that I was quite certain that Papa
would shy from an evening in public right off the bat, we might have a quiet dinner
at our house. He put on no act in speaking his appreciation for himself and Rocky;
he'd never acted for Till and me, so he just played himself. Slouched down and relaxed as I drove, he looked across, said: "Pappy, calendars are a damn nuisance, to
the things that you really wanta do, ya know." He leveled with it, so I had a good
hunch of what to expect. When I pulled up at the house, he uncoiled himself and
came in with me, without a word about it.

He doffed his hat, but declined a drink, said that they "have another little doin's
to go to" and chinned with us for perhaps ten minutes. He stood at the window
with an arm around Tillie, looking out over town, at the mountain looming black in
the deep dusk. Of my proposal, he said to her: "There's nothing that we'd like better,
Till gal, we'd have fun . . ." He trailed it off, recalled some "old" fun—quite rare
for him—one that had been laughed over a good many times: when one night in
our little postwar house he went to the bathroom—an afterthought built into a small
closet, with a low door and a shoehorn fit inside. We'd warned him about it, and
he ducked in fine, but the other way round he bumped his head, loud enough that
we heard it like a tree had fallen against the flimsy walls (there was about as much
"sound" privacy in the house as visual privacy in a fish bowl). He came into the
little sitting room, rubbing his forehead, mumbling about "a privy for a circus midget
and not for a long gink like me."

"Old Gable—don't see him much any more—sure poured it on me fer that stunt,
didn't he? . . . but at least I could get up from the table, Tillie, without having to
buckle up my pants first."

Coop always spent his last day in camp in leisurely preparing for the departure,
and he said that they would contact the Hemingways when they got in. When he
kissed Till "so long" he hoped that when I came down in the spring she would be

with me and, "give us a ring, you got our number . . . I'm sure we'll be in town." I went outside with him; a casual handshake, a few words, and my, "Be seein' ya, Coop" is about the only way I can put it. He wound himself in behind the wheel, tossed his familiar little salute, and off he went.

The following evening, he and Rocky drove out to Papa's house around cocktail hour. They had called and asked them out for dinner, which was declined—travel weariness—and they had a little visit, about an hour, I guess. Mary said that Coop was quietly fluent with his regrets, said he had business matters coming up that could not be put off. This, of course, in an aside to her. They left bright and early the following morning. January was at its end.

It was a tacit thing, then, that Mary called us, which she did that evening. We went out for a belated little Christmas exchange the following evening—also not more than an hour. We found Papa looking surprisingly good—we thought we would from the mail—a little gaunt, true, flat around his middle as a schoolboy, joking lightly about his weight hovering somewhere around the 180 mark. But the rest of his frame was just as staunch-looking as ever, his manner a little quieter, more subdued—a sort of mellowness, and very becoming—like it was built in. In short, pleasantly surprising. And as usual, he joked me about being back in my old groove, working a winter on skis.

When he told me of his short visit with Coop, he asked with a small grin if I minded old Papa thanking me for doing a few prowls with him. There was an old joke about anyone pinch-hitting, so I said, "Pay me the fifty cents now, Papa, and forget the thanks," and he laughed, said, "Is my credit still good, kid?" I looked for some signs of disappointment that Coop did not stay over, and I didn't see a trace of them. I believed then, as now, that Papa felt no hurt whatsoever; I think it would have embarrassed him to some extent, Coop also—both ways—nor do I believe they would have discussed their problems more than a skimming-over. Good friends, yes, but in the so-called record that has been a bit overdone. In my experience with these individualists, each was a phenomenon in his own right, entirely apart from the other, and certainly they respected and admired one another for such immeasurable gifts. But, as each was with a fellow like myself, there was an indescribable "line" that you did not cross, nor did any other man, or person, cross it with them—friendship-wise. As Papa himself once said: "It's more durable that way . . . and can't endure if you try to take it further." They had a particular arena in which they played their game, so the attitude of each that January evening of '61 leaves little doubt in my mind that theirs was a simple and sound case of: walk away from it while it's good. The pain in the inner depths, of course, we cannot see.

That is, I'm certain, what Papa said in expressing his pleasure that Coop didn't have to prowl about the country by himself, as he often had when no one could go with him. Which all says that Papa was much more in the groove than we had any reason to expect. As Tillie said to me later—you wanted to get up and dance, and added, but don't let him see you! True, even if the song in your soul was bursting for release, that was not the way friends could do.

Which was the reason that Tillie didn't make a change, but left a little card in his present as she wrote it when she bought it back in the fall. In Pete Lane's Inn store she saw "the shirt" for Papa (he suckered for them like picnics and fine leather stuff, to hell with the pants!), and its exquisitely subtle shadow-plaid pattern, and fine wool solved it on the spot. The top line of the makers, it was a "Sir Pendleton" if you please, but—she was hesitant of borrowing a thing of his, the "knighting" he honored her with. I stayed out of it, only that it was "our" present to him, so on second thought she left it as was. He slid it part way out of its wrapping and his voice was like the song of a little spring bubbling from a mountainside. He slowly pulled the card from the envelope, read it to himself, then in a soft but eloquent voice he read it aloud, as if it were a line from Shakespearean drama:

"For Sir Papa from Sir Till."

I said once before that Papa was capable of visible emotion, so this time he couldn't decide whether to cry or laugh, so he did both, and I guess you know which was more evident—that from which you don't blow your nose! Sliding it on out, he admired the shirt, looked again at the card, said softly:

"A musical line of poetry, better than a coat of arms, any day, Sir Till . . . this beauty Sir Papa will save to wear the first time to your house."

Being smothered, she told him to name the time, and paying his high compliments to both, he waved a hand and nodded his head to the gals who ran the arts culinary department in his favor—eye-to-eye, unfailingly. So he did save his shirt for an evening with us, followed his nose to the kitchen, found that the bosses there were doing all right for the now greatest-of-importance diet thing; then Till happened to think: preparing the salad vegetables, where he could see, casing the cookery instead, she said:

"Papa, can you still eat onion?"

He jerked around as if expecting to see her standing on her head.

"Miss Till . . . are you kiddin'?"

I said, things were looking up.

Papa had picked up his old favorite Chevy from Sun Valley's rentals, the long walks, almost daily, were underway, well north of town on the highway, where he'd drive for a good parking, then out for several miles afoot; the scenery magnificent, the traffic almost nothing, and February was a perfect winter month, weather-wise. Mary has often said that she walked more that winter than she'd even try to estimate in mileage and time—but that she has her own ideas of the value otherwise. She is not the only one—those walks did a job, and so did some personal discipline, plus wifely encouragement.

In that "good time" the trapshooting was about as usual—several times a week, mostly at midday. That was because it was "command" that George stop by to take Papa's blood pressure; my work was geared to the Ski School with its long noon hours, so we just left our guns in the rack at Papa's house. A long-time Sun Valley guest, who'd shot with us the winter before, Dave Pollak, from Cincinnati, a great "arm" with a handtrap and a fine shot, missed but a few of those half hours or so of fun. Though he kept it pretty much to himself, Papa missed Duke, and it was most evident then, for Duke's brand of humor seemed tailor-made for those occasions. When one of us would throw Papa a high-arching target, make him "reach" for it, and he'd break it to hell and gone out, he'd invariably chortle, "There's one for His Highness, goddamn it!" Duke had a good arm, too, and good medicine comes in many forms. The stacked cartons of targets steadily diminished, well up into March. Phony, fixed performances that they were, the weekly prizefight hours on TV were at least laughably entertaining, excuses for a get-together—keep the show going, and for the most part it went very well. Too, I broke a rule of my own, a self-imposed one. I asked Papa to inscribe a book for a friend.

Back in the fall I finally found in a Hollywood store a copy of the limited, illustrated, gift edition of *The Old Man and the Sea.* I had looked for one in my travels, then when I had it, I more or less gave up on the inscription idea when we learned that Papa was away. It was for my boss, Vince Hunter—a nut on anything pertaining to the sea, an avid reader and student, and a great admirer of Hemingway. Of course, having heard so much ever since he knew me, Papa felt that he knew Vince. Then when Mary's news was so good, I wrote Papa, and casually mentioned that Vince was due to come up in February for a crowded few days of work with me, and that I had a copy of the special edition. When I saw him next, we had talked but little when he brought the subject up, made quite a thing of it—stressing how he wished that the original edition had been made in such nice form. Our two witnesses were openly amused at us acting exactly as a pair of bashful boys over something that had never been done before.

The Hunters, and film technician Betty Cox, arrived about a week after Papa's return. We finished up our work first, then fooled around their last day, on which I made a date with Papa for us to come out around four that afternoon. About two I was on some errands, Priscilla Hunter with me, and drove up behind Papa walking toward Sun Valley. It was sharply cold and I asked if he wanted a lift. No, the walking was good, and when he had finished with his errand he'd hurry home, for he'd heard a rumor that old friends of old friends were coming out and he had to have a fire going under something. Don't hurry, Papa, I said, we had a number of things to do, could be a wee bit late. Great, he said, it could be that George might come if not tied up at the hospital, and we'd tuck in a round of trapshooting, too.

I drove on and Pris said quite excitedly:

"What a wonderful way to put it. Why, he fairly beamed. I had no idea that Ernest Hemingway is like that."

We got home just at four o'clock, and hearing his side of it I knew that Vince was talking to Papa on the phone. He chuckled to himself when he handed the receiver to me. Papa spoke very low.

"Gee, Mr. Pappy, I had to call you . . . every other place that I've called said that you had just left. I thought after you drove on, and I was out walking, you might have the idea that I was dodging you. I made it fine through the after-ski traffic, learning to do that real good . . . come anytime, you guys."

When I hung up, Vince said, "What a guy, he identified himself and I called him Mr. Hemingway, and there was silence for a second or so, then: 'You must be Vince . . . well Vince, Mister is a strange name to me, only people that I have to do business with, and few of those . . . will you tell Mr. Pappy for me that I'm home . . . oh, good, then I'll speak with the gentleman, please.'"

We went out at once, the Hunters and I, Tillie and Betty somewhere else, and they would follow. In a large mailer envelope I had the book that Vince knew nothing about, but the old sharpie may have had a hunch, for the name of the bookstore where we often browsed together was on the package. I laid it on a little pile of magazines always present on Mary's kitchen table, no one paying any attention—hah! It was just like old friends coming together after a long time. Papa had word that George could not make it, so since his targets were set out, we shot a short round anyway while waiting for the girls. As usual, he beat me a target or two, and I was shooting good then, using his stubby pump gun.

"Once in a while, Vince, he pitches me one he thinks I might leave for seed, down there in the chokecherry bushes . . . have to keep him honest, don't I!"

It was too damn cold for much of that and we cut it off—now Papa would buy the Scotsman that drink of Scotch he had owed him for so long. The only catch was, the Scot had long since confined his temperance to brandy and soda, but of course if the snakes were thick? . . .

"As noble a drink as any, Vince, nobler than most. Kitner, do we have some brandy?"

"No one here drinks it, Vince," Mary said. "But I keep a bottle for cooking," and she forthwith set out the bottle—Hennessy's!

"Why, I never drink anything but cooking brandy." Vince howled and Papa laughed. "Well, didn't I say I would have a fire going under something?"

We didn't plan to stay long, and didn't—in fact most of our time was spent in the kitchen, that room with something—cheer, at any hour of the day. Sitting at the table, Papa idly picked up the mailer and slid the book part way out, then shortly got up and went for a pen. Back in his chair, he thumbed through the pages, patiently waiting, but spicing the lively talk with those occasional synonyms and metaphors. Then:

"If the text of this was as good as the fine drawings, I would buy a copy of it myself so I can face the guy if and when I see him . . . Vince, I can spell easy, but how do I spell 'Priscilla'? . . . sure, with an *sc*. A pretty name, been with us a long time."

Ours was a warm, rewarding hour when you wanted to hug him; and in an aside to me as we prepared to leave he handed out one in a different wrapping.

"Fine people, Mr. Pappy, whom you work with, but you've been conservative, too much so . . . Vince is high number, truly high number."

Later, about an hour, he called me and neatly worked into his light talk how glad he was about it, so that I didn't have to revealingly reply. He was like talking to the Papa I knew twenty years before.

2

Like in seasons, March is the month of change—when, as the old almanac saying had it: March can come in like a lion and go out like a lamb. That one was pretty much the lamb all the way through. Spring signaled itself ahead of time, and on just such a day, bright, warm, when you feel the cocoon of winter deteriorating, I happened, quite by chance, upon a warning. It was just about noon, an odd time, when driving down Warm Springs Road I bumped into Papa walking up the narrow valley, its south-exposure slopes almost free of snow where hundreds of deer eagerly search out the browse of spring (it's an old preserve area), and on a nearby slope but a few hundred yards from Papa's house, a small band of elk were lying down in the sage. I slowed up and passed the time of day with him, and he said he guessed he'd ride into town with me—too many shuttling ski busses and other traffic. He made the familiar old comment of when we'd first known the country there were no elk in it, and these had wintered good, the deer, too, as anyone could see. We were almost in the middle of town, chatting amiably, when he said he wished to hell that he had wintered good, like the wildlife had. In snow country you can slide off one like that in reply quite easily, and I did, when letting him out at the drugstore and post-office corner. I hadn't seen him in two or three days, and I saw no other signs for alarm. Cheerful again, he wanted to know how I was coming with the work and I said that I was on the double to get it done while I had snow. Grinning broadly, he said, "Stay on it, kid, because the damn stuff can't go fast enough now to suit me"—and he added that a good picnic might soon be in order. I drove on my way, dismayed just the same, for the ring, or tone, of it was ominous.

A few nights later I could have done a turnabout. We went with some old-time friends to the Christiania for dinner, and there were Mary and Papa at a corner table, obviously enjoying themselves, quietly. It was midmonth, and probable that they privately celebrated their wedding anniversary. If we remembered, I can't recall; we made small greetings from our distance, and sat down. Near our table was a casual acquaintance who soon produced a pencil and paper, and Papa was about to be invaded to scribble his name. I no more than let the man—a nice chap—know that I saw his intentions and he made no move; but shortly asked if he thought my old friend would mind. I said that it embarrassed him in public, was all. So he asked me if I'd get the autograph for him, and I said, yes, when I saw it as the right time. So you knew who was enjoying the pantomime—but appreciating the setup, too. Pretty soon the waitress whispered in my ear: "Mr. Hemingway says that it is convenient for him if you care to see him now." Across several tables he was like I grinned back at a schoolboy who'd just got teacher with a spitball—Mary joining in. The man got his autograph, and a nice little wave-of-hand when the author went by his table. On our way to Sun Valley with our party we chatted a few seconds at the door, and as Till said later, it was like hearing Papa say when a situation was cleared up: "Everything's fine again, got it all fixed good."

Enhancing the good feeling about it was the fact that, as far as we knew, it was the first "night in public" after the return from Mayo's. But, as said, the small signs

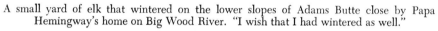

A small yard of elk that wintered on the lower slopes of Adams Butte close by Papa Hemingway's home on Big Wood River. "I wish that I had wintered as well."

had been seen, and to me a larger one soon showed up—as March was in its latter half.

It was a warm, almost hot day, on the flat at the foot of Ruud Mountain during the Harriman Cup ski races—the slalom events, on one of the world's best courses, from a spectator's point of view. Competing that day was also a field of some of the world's best skiers. I had finished filming what I needed—the first run of the event, working the finish gate—and with a tripoded camera on each shoulder, I picked my way across the soft corn snow, walking in boot holes a foot deep, head down, so that I almost stumbled right onto Papa and George Saviers. They stood above my level on a small patch of packed snow, and it surprised me in recognizing Papa's heavy leather birdshooter boots. My first thought was: Papa watching a ski race? —what the hell! That, because he never had watched one in Sun Valley—then the good, the wonderful, thought of seeing him there with George, and no matter whose idea it was—probably both—well, it was an ideal spring day, most of the throng of enthusiasts milling about the flat with sweaters tied around their middles, sleeves rolled, faces burned a coppery-brown in the brilliant light. Papa himself was in his shirt-sleeves and a light suede leather vest. George was on the job as one of two skiing doctors, in case of racing injuries.

Their eyes up in high-angle looking, neither man saw me, so our come-together was sudden all around. Apparently having trouble with the wrong kind of dark glasses, Papa had a time focusing his eyes down at me—in slow recognition. He said, "Hi, Mr. Pappy," in very soft, sort of farawayness; and to get back my breath I unburdened myself, planted my outfits upright in the snow. There wasn't much said while the first half of the event was finished, then Papa put his hand on my shoulder, about his belt-height, and said:

"Some great talent here, Mr. Pappy, haven't seen one of these in an awfully long time."

I told him that in my flounderings I knew he was among the spectators by the familiar boots. He grinned a little one, said he guessed I ought to know them, and that he supposed they had surprised me, among a jillion pair of ski boots! No, Papa, not too, I said, then impulsively I asked about his glasses, mentioned the murderous light; and, he said, yes, he just got the wrong pair, but he could do all right with his eyes shaded by the long green plastic-visored cap he wore (a fisherman's cap). But, oh, his poor eyes were taking a beating!

I walked out onto the flat to chat a few minutes with a few competitors I'd known some time, and I was probably a mechanical chatter while doing so. Again I had not seen Papa for several days, and though he was the physical man that we were accustomed to that winter, there was a tired, worn, and aged manner about him—an old, old man whom I definitely had not seen before. I tried to change my own mind; was my imagination running wild, at the eerie effect the green-filtered sunlight made on his bearded face? No, for his face was plainly pathetic in the apparent thoughts behind it: yearningly sad, warm in admiration of what he saw going on before him on the steep, twisting course: daring, speed, the skill and stamina of youth. As he had said, in other words. Seeing him from a little distance, I felt the sudden impact of years of realization; and I wished that I were a detached voice in his ear: Papa, you are *not* an old man, why have you worked at it so long and hard? Dammit to hell, Papa, you're just as big a kid as you've always been, when you let yourself. My mind's eye made a lap-dissolve back in time to my favorite image, that one of the fellow in blue jeans, rolled-up sleeves and a fringed vest, striding along like a big spring-legged cat, tossing me a "howdy" as I rode a horse across his path. The dissolve reversed itself to the present image—the old man standing with his loyal doctor and good friend on the small patch of hard-packed snow, elevated like an island in the thawing spring all around; the open bleachers full of spectators, their attention diverted to him in occasional glances; the chattering throng of youth cavorting and showing off around the flat on their skis, indifferent as youth always is in its own theater. I couldn't help recalling the deep impression that Ernest Hemingway had made on me when expressing his fascination and respect for the philosophical passage from which he chose the title of his most successful work —a passage that opens with these words:

"No man is an Iland, intire of it selfe."

And the old man had never wanted to be an island, or a celebrity—he wanted to be admired; he wanted to be loved by his friends, have them around, sort of handy; he loved attention, lapped it up like a cat laps cream; he dressed like and wanted to be just an old boot, and liked an ancient little town that had always treated him like one.

You wondered what had gone wrong in the long process of achieving monumental success at all of them, wrapped in a single package of himself, as few men could do.

3

By then I had my winter's work wrapped up, coasting at odds-and-ends work, so I wasn't pressed until April 4, my train space all set for my usual between-seasons trip for some studio work. So, acting on a hint that Papa had passed to Till, I took advantage and moved in on him. It was a bright afternoon near the end of March, and Till and I had gone out to Papa's house—just loafing and talking—for you couldn't walk on the highway without being drowned in the slush of melting snow, traffic coming alive in the bloom of the early spring. Out on the wide paved terrace on the south side of the house, Papa was quite sober in manner, but not indrawn, so the time seemed to be right. In words to this effect, I said, "Papa, it's a cinch that I'll be back by the middle of April, and I'll have quite a few close-in, one-day trips to make, on arrangements, like I have with Bud. . . ." He cut me off very pleasantly, said he had spoken to Till about it, and that he could put his work aside, a few days' neglect wouldn't matter one way or another; but was I sure that they wouldn't hamper my work in any way? "Hell, no, Papa, you can help me look, and it's all in country we know, Camas Prairie, the Salmon River country. . . ."

"Yes," he said. "Good to get out and around."

I asked him outright to promise that he would, for, the truth is, there was no better company on earth on such, yes, prowls of that sort. Warmly, Papa said that he had already promised himself, so it was dropped for some other casual talk—then the bombshell, in less than ten minutes. Papa started back into the house, stopped in the door and turned to look at me as if I had told him just what to do with his time; said he'd have to see how things worked out, he had so much to do and it wasn't going worth a damn. I was dismissed, just like that, feeling the stab of an icicle through me. Trying my best to make allowances, I waited a bit and went inside, saw Papa disappearing up the stairs at the opposite end of the living room. I joined Mary and Till in the kitchen where they were making small talk of a little event all set for within an evening or two. Again I was ready to say, "Oh, to hell with it." Fortunately my disturbance wasn't noticed.

The event was Till's and my wedding anniversary, on a Friday, March 31: a little dinner party of five of us at Clara Spiegel's house. Till and I never advertised any of our significant dates, so there was no production or fuss of any kind planned—just a get-together—in a splendid hostess' home. So, now at the point of reluctantly admitting that nothing would surprise us any more, Till and I were having a little private "here's how" in the warm sun on our back porch about four o'clock that Friday. Our back door was open and soon we heard the rap of a cane on our living-room window under the front porch. As I went for the front door, there was Papa, grinning as we hadn't seen him in some time. "Let me in, or am I interrupting anything?" Inside:

"Old Papa just had to stop and kiss the bride . . . anything wrong with that, Mr. Groom?"

There sure as hell wasn't; he did, and the groom enjoyed a hug, too, with all the old threat to his ribs with it. He didn't stay long, but long enough to ask if I minded him repeating an old one first spoken a long time ago.

"No, Papa, indeed I don't mind; it's your compliment to my good judgment, in at least one category."

The repeat was his "diamonds are indestructible" which more than once he had applied to his own bride with heavy emphasis—the fellow who also had once said to me with a glow in his voice:

"Mr. Pappy, we're lucky . . . from the first, our women have gotten along great, it can't be any good if they don't."

I asked him if he'd have a little one with us; no, he was "saving myself for the party" and asked if we'd mind coming out to get them. See you about seven, Papa, I said.

Watching him walk down the street, I said:

"Well, bride, I guess it might be a pretty fine evening after all."

"Now, you're talking," my bride happily replied. "Like you so often admit of yourself, don't cross a bridge until you get to it."

Close to seven o'clock our phone rang and Tillie got it. It was Papa telling her that they would be ready when we came. Then there was a short pause before he said in a low faraway voice:

"Miss Till . . . is Mr. Pappy going to wear a tie?"

She said that I was, and brightened it with the truth of my tying it at the moment. Good timing, he said, guessed that he should know I would, for such an occasion. Another pause, then:

"Miss Till . . . it's your thirty-third, isn't it?"

She said that was right, bracing herself—a long pause.

"Gee, Miss Till . . . I wish it were me."

"Well, Papa," she said instantly, "you and Miss Mary have a fine leg toward yours, and you know how happy we. . . ."

"Sure, Miss Till, and awfully good years, too . . . thanks ever so much . . . just come to the back door as usual, huh?"

It was a warm evening, enough that a jacket only would do, and Papa was slicked and combed to a fare-thee-well—talkative into town, bringing up the old joke of ours about choosing our wedding date so close to Tillie's birthday—for economical reasons: the money for her gift went for gas for the Model T Ford that took us on our two-day honeymoon. "Hell, I wished I had a Model T Ford, let alone the dough for a tank of gas for one." As the toastmaster at Clara's pretty table, he was at his best—not exuberant, but quietly dignified, and quite free with his follow-through on the good wine. Afterward, he was quieter, had to be nudged a bit now and then; but some amusing records on Clara's hi-fi produced some good laughs and personal paradoxes, too. When the talk inevitably got around to the natural topic—autumn reminiscences—Clara, with perfect timing, hit the jackpot in the laughs department—a favorite of her own, on herself.

Back in the early fifties there was some unbelievable dove shooting in a big fallowed field of sunflowers at exactly the right dryness for feeding; the birds as confused as we, who couldn't reload fast enough or know which bird to line up on. Clara reloaded from a bulging pocket of shells, got her lineup on a potential double, but only one barrel responded to her triggering—something that had not happened to her, and to few other gunners, I suspect.

"Papa," she said straight-faced, "have you ever tried to fire a tube of lipstick in your shotgun?"

"No," he fairly howled. "That's one I haven't tried . . . but say, for the sporting set, that might be a marketable item. Do you know a good patent lawyer?"

It was the good note that wound it up, and with a very warm good night out at the house, Papa looked at his watch.

"In a few minutes, now, it will be midnight, and you'll start on another good year."

Actually, Tillie told me only the "excuse" for Papa's call, and rounded it out for me the next morning at breakfast. She needn't have told me; we'd heard it before, put in different ways. Though he angled it in his direction, its basis was his lasting respect for our successful partnership. He was aware of some of its stormy passages, too, and I certainly never held it against him when he had once told me that Tillie deserved some sort of shiny medal, adding his favorite: ". . . you're a lucky dog." Well, I am; so was he.

On Sunday, April 2, I was sent to market, parked my car beside Papa's, and inside I said hello to him as he talked, intently, I noticed, with a mutual friend. When I came to the cashier with my purchases I didn't see him, but waiting there a few minutes in line I exchanged pleasantries with our friend who seemed a bit disturbed. In a moment I got it, in voluntary confidence from him. Resulting from excessive exposure to the sun, he'd had a small skin cancer removed from his face, said that Papa spotted the fresh scar and asked him about it, then:

"Been bothered with 'em ever since I can remember, now I got one of them inside of me, and that is plain hell." (It was not the case at all.)

I kept a calm exterior, for though I hadn't heard that one before, it figured. I thought: Oh, God, I'm glad I did no more than say "Hi" when I came in. When paid up, I headed for the door, and couldn't figure where Papa came from when he caught up with me outside. He rescued me from the search for something to say by kidding that we were operating on the one-meal-at-a-time basis ahead of our departure—did a good job of it, too—and he guessed that he'd fix it so that we could share their table with them, come Tuesday night. He had his Sunday papers, made a remark on the headline news, then got into his car while I waited for his door to close so I could open mine. Both engines were running when Papa looked across with that good, but shadowy, grin on his face.

"I wish, Mr. Pappy, that when you're through down there you could come up to San Francisco, and we could meet you and Miss Till, and you know what we'd do . . . what we've wanted to do for a long time. . . ."

I couldn't get out a reply to that one fast enough:

"Sure, Papa, we'd start with the Fisherman's Wharf and DiMaggio's place, and that might take the first week. . . ."

"All of that," he said, putting the car in gear and pulling away, not giving me a chance to say: "You name the day, Papa, I'll arrange it and we'll be there if we have to crawl." For that, I could and would have, one way or another; his wish was natural and one he had often spoken—the first time 'way back in the prewar days: ". . . go on a binge, where you can't eat your way through all of the good places in six months!" And not only "good-eating" town San Francisco, either, but of European countries that he knew so well; we'd take a long trip together sometime and spend the monies due him that he couldn't realize any other way; buy the gals sable coats, and hit all the good old places—and I think that he meant them all when said—as basically he'd meant it now. The irony of it was that it was all as easily attainable to him as the papers he'd just come for—and had been all along; but now there wasn't time, because Papa was broke—another way of saying that he couldn't write any more, he was done at that; and though he didn't say so directly you got the message that they had tampered with his think machine back there, and loused it up, so it was no good, what he labored to put on paper.

With my heart in my shoes I drove home, for poor old Papa could not help but know I was fully conscious of all of it—try as I had, we all had, to be our usual selves. So he couldn't give me a chance to say, "We'll be there if we have to crawl" —he was powerless within himself.

We were away exactly twelve days, returned home on a Sunday night, April 16. We hadn't been asked if we'd contact Coop when in Hollywood; we were in doubt because of grapevine word. I called old Cooper friends who said Coop was taking it easy at home, calls and callers screened, which meant the absolute minimum. On an errand we drove past his home in Holmby Hills one day—less than ten minutes from our studio—on the slim chance that we'd see him out-of-doors on the quite secluded property. We didn't, of course, and would not stop without notice, so Tillie spoke our thoughts perfectly: "Remember when we saw him last, he said, 'I'd like t'take off m'coat an' sit by the fire an' chin a while'? That was the Coop we knew, so why cloud it, make ourselves feel bad, and him?" So we left for home and hoped all the way that Papa Hemingway wouldn't ask if we'd at least called; nor could we have dreamed other than that the book was closed.

We were asked to come out to watch the telecast of the annual Motion Picture Academy Awards program with Mary and Papa on Monday evening, April 17. A quite disinterested, and, I may as well say it, frighteningly deteriorated Papa, surprisingly spoke up to say that he figured Master of Ceremony Bob Hope could make the slow spots in the long show go faster—would we come? His was more a plea than a question.

I fixed my affairs so we were there, and shockingly we witnessed what soon proved to be *the* turning point.

Just we four were present, the big living room set delivering a perfect picture and good sound (our local piped system often affected by weather, good at the time). The forever Bob Hope certainly did brighten the show, there were good laughs, one with: "Guess maybe I should've been a movie-goer—for the good ones, anyway." Naturally there was no clue whatsoever to the special honorary Oscar for Gary Cooper, a former two-time winner for his memorable *Sergeant York* and his classic Western of 1952, *High Noon.* Absentee himself, and watching the show at home, Coop's proxy was long-time friend Jimmy Stewart. What occurred when he accepted the award is Hollywood history: Jimmy's emotions surfaced in his faltering voice and expressive face before the microphones and tell-it-all cameras: "We're all very proud of you, Coop, tremendously proud."

There was a noticeable wincing in Papa, a squirming—in his chair at the moment —an odd little utterance, like an "mmmph!" But it was not particularly alarming, even when he got up, paced about, joining the normal comments about Coop before the set was switched off. Then, in all good intent, and thoughtfulness, based on seeing so little of him in the winter past, Mary suggested a call be put through to Coop —congratulate him, cheer him up. That, though how could she know, was the mistake. And to this day there is widespread belief through the printed word, in what we have sound reason to believe is a warpage of the truth; a twisting of the truth to make it more, shall I say, "earthily readable." All told, an inexcusable injustice to a nice guy like one Gary Cooper.

At Mary's suggestion, Papa resisted strongly: everybody he knew would be trying to call Coop; sure, already a pileup of calls; we wouldn't get one through until midnight; a Coop too harried by then to talk—was he right about that, he asked me. "No, Papa, I hardly think they'll pester him." He did not glare a hole through me, but asked his audience-at-large just what would *he* say to Coop, anyway; and he let us know with emphasis that long-distance phone calls cost a little dough! In persuasive, gentle tones, Mary eventually got his reluctant consent. As she lifted the phone, he hurried out to the kitchen phone for a pencil and a page torn from the pad, wandered back in deep thought, and Rocky Cooper was already talking to Mary—the call went through like a local. Sure, her Gary was right there, and she put him on. Mary talked to him for perhaps ten minutes—cheerful, both rising perfectly to the occasion, Coop, deeply appreciative, obviously pushing the talk more than his caller. Good, all of it, except. . . .

It was torture to poor Papa, intermittently checking the time ticking away on his watch; pencil poised, standing beside Till, glancing down at her, asking the walls and ceiling, or a chair: "What will I say to Coop, what can I say?" then write something on the paper cupped in his hand. Absorbed and yet conscious of it, Mary eventually came to a break and held the phone out to Papa. Gingerly reaching a hand, like it was the plague, his other hand stuffed the paper in his pocket.

"Hello . . . Coop?"

"--------------------------------------."

"Well it's good to talk to you."

"--------------------------------------."

"Well, how are ya Coop?"

"--------------------------------------."

"Well, Coop, I'm sick, too."

"---."

"Good ol' Coop."

"------------------------------."

"Good ol' Coop."

"------------------------------."

"Well, so long, Coop."

He passed the instrument down to Mary in the manner of—well, I got that over with in a hurry; sat down in a nearby chair. He'd been on the line all of thirty seconds! In but a few more seconds, Mary passed the phone to me, rather to my surprise in not knowing, now, what to say myself. Good old Coop was miles ahead of me; he asked me this:

"Pappy, ol' kid, did you have any more luck than we did in mouthing that lure to sound like a rabbit in trouble?"

"No, dammit, Coop, all I lured with it was Tillie."

"Was she on the prowl?"

"Yes, and on the howl, too," I said.

Coop's chuckle was a hearty one, he thanked me and I said, "Be seein' ya, Coop," and passed the phone back to Mary while Papa said to Till:

"Pappy's trying to compete with Bob Hope."

There were about ten minutes that things were quite normal; then, since I was leaving early in the morning, I got our coats and we had a chat and a small nightcap with Mary in the kitchen. Most of that was for the normal look; by then Papa's disturbance had run away with him. No caged lion ever matched his relentless pacing; if he answered our attempts at all, it was a mumbled something, or blank grin. In short, he disintegrated, eventually climbed the stairs to his room, left the three of us, just too plain scared to know what to say. I was on the verge of suggesting that I stick around somewhere for the night. Wouldn't that have been a hare-brained deed! On our way home, Tillie jarred herself and me further; she said:

"Do you suppose, while Papa was trying to say something to Coop, that he remembered their first acquaintance was by telephone, and now he knows that this was their last touch with each other?"

"More than likely it had a bearing . . . but then, how could we know?" I said, "The past has always been vivid to him."

Not so long later, when we read that Coop was supposed to have said to Papa: "I'll bet I'll beat you to the barn," we recalled that phone call so fresh in our minds, and asked ourselves: why would a guy like Coop, talking cheerfully to Mary and me, dip to that sort of "rub-in" to an old friend struggling to make sense. We simply felt that we knew Coop too well to believe that. Nor did we observe any indication that such a remark reached Papa's ear while on that phone. Tuned as he was to the wavering voice and manner of Jimmy Stewart, he'd have been jolted good had Coop said that to him—no mistake. We can easily believe, however, that after he'd hung up the phone, and in the privacy of his home, Coop naturally, and sadly, might well have said: "I bet I'll beat *him* to the barn."

Let the "right" reporter get hold of that, and what might he do with it? But I repeat, we were not on the phone.

As planned, I worked close to home, so we saw Papa during the rest of the week, and it was not good, not at all; then on Saturday, April 22, we felt the cold fingers of premonition. To me, at least, I was reminded of our little circle gripping the arms of our seats in the darkened theater of doom, before an ugly curtain that could open anytime—and, of course, we were, just that. You feel like crawling under anything at hand when trying to make talk, get nowhere, no matter what you say— thinking: My God, is this Papa, like a deaf man who sees the fun going on before him, joins in with a grin like on a mask? Then the fleeting moments of his efforts to make it good—like it once was. I'm sure that for myself, I recall it as the first time that I truly wanted to run—from a game that you can't win for losing; nor could I even wishfully think that anyone would win this one, unless something was done, and done fast. It was—on Sunday.

On his usual call at the house that forenoon, Doc Saviers saw at one glance that it was time to act. He did, calmly surfaced, and without resistance of any kind, got Papa to the Sun Valley hospital. Long later in the day we learned that arrangements were all set to fly Papa back to the Mayo Clinic in Rochester—Larry Johnson would be waiting at Hailey with his plane ready at eight o'clock Monday morning. Fully informed of the day's happenings, I shuddered in wondering if Papa would resist a return to what he surely must have known would be a nightmare to him. I resisted the thought that he would—but it was a persistent one, and it was still around when I left town the following morning, saw Larry warming up his plane as I drove past the Hailey airstrip about a quarter to eight.

I was on a short job that trip and returned around noon on Wednesday, and again I saw Larry on his hangar ramp, could not go on without stopping to ask him how their trip had been. He said, fine, except that he'd had minor engine trouble that was fixed at their one stop for fuel; then he added that they'd been home but a short while, the trip had been delayed until Tuesday morning. I knew that Mary was not slated to go that time, but I asked Larry no more and went on, wondering why the delay. I got it—voluntarily—from a friend who was asked at the last minute on Monday morning to go along. Thoughtfully, he stopped at our house that evening when he saw my road car out front.

It would be gracious not to put down the true facts of that crucial time; but I do because they've been publicly reported in distorted, magnified, and, in part, purely fabricated form. In short, dramatized, from information gained from a distance, so to speak, and not from eyewitnesses and participants. Such reporting is unjust, un- fair to Papa Hemingway—and God knows it's difficult enough to write the truth of an old friend on that sort of rough road. So, to set the record straight.

At the hospital that Monday morning, April 24, Doc Saviers and Papa were about to take off for Hailey; then George happened upon Don Anderson passing by, and with good reason asked him to make the trip. Taken by surprise, and not at all prepared for it, Don got the reason and agreed to go—time the factor, about a seven-hour flight to Rochester in normal conditions. George needed a few more minutes for other matters before leaving, so he asked Don to take his own car and drive Papa out home for some personal things that he refused to go without; George would follow within minutes in his car for their drive to Hailey, where he'd leave it. Nurse Joan Higgon went along to bring back Don's car.

Out at the house—at the back door—Don got out when Papa did, who said Don needn't come in, his things were upstairs where Mary was, he'd be down in minutes. Don was at his heels anyway, so close they practically went in as one; then Don was alone, for Papa took off like a shot. Don beckoned to Joan and followed him; at the corner gun rack in the living room, from behind him, Don pinned Papa's arms as he closed the breech on his double-barrel shotgun, and managed to get a thumb on the gun's opening lever. Joan pulled out the shells and the brief storm subsided immediately. The struggle was brisk but short, neither man off his feet or hurt in any way. George was there about as it ended, and Papa went quietly to the hospital again, for that day—the flight reset for a daylight takeoff Tuesday morning. That one went off on schedule, with no resistance of any kind evident—except a soft question: "Where are they taking me this time?"

Having flown the trip before, Larry's flight plan was simplicity itself, aided by geographical oddity. Lay a ruler on a map and see that it is a beeline from Hailey to Rochester, Minnesota, with Rapid City, South Dakota, almost exactly halfway of the distance and squarely on the ruler's edge. A busy airline stop, a port with facilities, this was the planned stop for fuel. Larry used his single-engine four-place Piper Apache airplane; the weather was good, a brisk tail wind an advantage. Ahead out of Idaho the high Tetons had to be climbed over, the plane heavily loaded, its cabin cramped. George rode "copilot" up front with Larry, Papa and Don in the rear seats—Don a smaller man, but husky, tipped the scales about at Papa's current weight. About an hour out, the old leather belt that Papa had clung to for more years than I can recall parted under its buckle, and Papa quietly asked if they might go back so he could get another. George turned to say it would be rough bucking the head wind over the Tetons, so Don appeased the situation by pulling off his own belt, and Papa accepted it—managed somehow in the tight confines to replace his old one with it.

The good pushing wind was luck, for farther along over Wyoming, Larry had to nurse his engine, but still managed the landing at Rapid City in good time. There it was discovered that a coil on one magneto was burned out, so the re-fueling stop for both passengers and plane stretched to something over an hour. Repairs were about finished when a twin-engine Aero Commander landed and taxied to a parking place on the transient aircraft apron where Larry's plane was parked nearby. As many of us might do, Papa stood at a wingtip of the Piper, appearing fascinated with the spinning props as the pilot revved the Commander's engines in clearing them for the cutoff. Both George and Don noticed it, and so Don moved over to say they were about ready to go. They were; the engine satisfied Larry, and the balance of the trip was smooth and easy.

At Rochester, Papa greeted his doctors warmly, even jocularly; George phoned Mary back in Ketchum that all was well, and the Piper got the men as far toward home as Rapid City, where they spent the night, completing the second leg the next morning.

So, it was natural that Larry told me their trip was fine, and passed off lightly their delay for minor repairs at Rapid City—there was nothing else for him to say. If there had been anything unusual, Larry would have told me—quietly. That weekend I ran into George Saviers, and talked but a couple of minutes with him. I invaded his realm only to say that I couldn't envy his role as both doctor and friend; his reply was a shake of his head, in man-to-man feeling.

4

Not long afterward, in one of my routine calls to California, I asked for the going word on Coop. It was going, all right, in respectful whispers; the window was closed, so I was told, the finale not far off. My informant was right.

I was driving home, across a stretch of open lonely country, on Saturday, May 13, my car radio turned on, something I very seldom did in driving alone. Paying little attention to its low drone, I was suddenly alerted, realized that I'd heard Gary Cooper's name, that I was listening to a Los Angeles newscast. Coop had died quietly in sleep early that morning, at his home in Holmby Hills. Expecting it, yes, but shock came, nonetheless, and like in dreams, countless hours and as many miles in Coop's company down the long years went by me in seconds. I said aloud:

"Good-bye, Coop, it's been fun, all of it."

Indeed, it had, and still a couple of hours from home, I wondered for most of it how that news might have been received elsewhere. As to that, I never heard.

5

From latter May on, following Mary's departure for Rochester, we had infrequent news from there—mainly good. The best news from that second sojourn there came from Papa himself—in the form of a letter. He wrote it to the second of the Saviers boys, a lad not yet in his teens, plagued with a chronic illness. It was a masterpiece in Papa's own handwriting, and so typically him, so touchingly appealing, that eventually it was reproduced in full in a summer issue of *Life* magazine.

There had been, however, some words a time or two that were not exactly encouraging. From mid-June on was a blank—and understandable, as we later learned. It was at month's end, a Friday evening, June 30, that I came home and we went to a big noisy cocktail party; heard in an aside almost at once that the Hemingways had arrived unannounced, but a short while before. Surprised no end, a first thought was to sneak back home to our telephone; but of course it was too soon for that, and there was a bonus with the good news, too. A Hertz car was rented back in Minnesota, and to do the driving to Idaho, Papa's old friend, retired gymnasium operator George Brown, had come out from New York. We considered that a good sign —for over many years we had heard such fine things about George—the genius in a boxing ring of whom Papa always said he was never allowed to so much as touch George's perfect nose with a glove, let alone hurt it; so naturally it was good to know that he'd called on this respected friend.

At the time I was just starting to work close to home, coming in each night from the Salmon River country, the Sawtooth Valley, and down farther around Stanley Basin. It was a good "water" year and never had I seen the country as verdantly beautiful. On Saturday morning I had a short job to do over there, and of course I recalled us talking about this very same country the fall before—when Papa wished that he'd known it in summer. Now I was sure that he would—and I would nudge that a bit with a natural: propose an outing over there for the weekend. My enthusiasm was dampened somewhat when I returned home for a late lunch, Tillie almost in tears.

Shortly before, she had pulled in at the market, saw a strange car pull in a few spaces from hers, and saw that its passenger was Papa. Fine, she thought, just right, happening upon him like this. She was just opening her door to greet him when he went hurrying into the store—a dozen feet from her car—looking neither left nor right, tensed in manner, and so shockingly thin and gaunt that to her he appeared several inches taller. Her voice was shaky when she told me, "I was a coward, I know, but if I had gone in that store and come face to face with Papa, I'm sure I'd have burst out in tears, and wouldn't that have been a fine thing to do?"

She backed out and drove up home, went back a bit later, when she had a few minutes with Chuck. He was a bit disturbed also; Papa had been so jittery in the few words he had with him, then went back farther in the store when George Brown came in. Chuck asked him about their trip out, and George said it was fine, until they got into old familiar country well out in Wyoming, then it couldn't go fast enough—checking progress by the road map and watch, concern for tires, impatience over stops for gas, and the like. But, there was a good note in George's chat with Chuck: he and Papa had been to the lumberyard that morning, had a heavy panel of plywood cut for rigging up a table to be out on the sunny south terrace at Papa's house; George was to stay on a while, and use his physiotherapy skill on his old friend. In hearing that, well, it was the best word yet. I had some month's-end paper work, some phoning to do that afternoon, and I threatened several times to interrupt it, and we'd drive out to say hello. I didn't interrupt myself, for in all of this —especially Tillie's one look at Papa—a thought kept nagging at me. If Papa was like this, why was he home? Had he talked himself out of the place back there? I had a suspicion that it was something like that, and in spite of all factors, I know that I never once underestimated the "force" that was Papa himself. Those ebbs and flows I remembered too well. Later, it was more than a mild hint that I got in confirmation of that fact.

Be that as it may, we didn't go out to the house, or call—we thought it best to wait, then in good time Sunday forenoon, we'd call Mary and suggest taking a drive over the summit, maybe take along a picnic basket. That idea at least had merit, the weather was absolutely perfect. We were dated for the evening with old friends from out of town, and our foursome ended up at the Christiania Bar not far from midnight, for a nightcap on our way home. There we learned that Mary, Papa, and George Brown had been there for a quietly pleasant dinner, Papa quite jovial, had a fine wine with his meal, had even chided a waitress when she poured him a refill from a near empty bottle, allowing a bit of the dregs to reach his glass. They had left for home but a short while before we dropped in.

With that word, ours was now less the on-the-fence view—as we turned off our light that night the over-all scene was brighter. Alas, it was but a flash of brightness. . . .

Epilogue . . .

In those last tense weeks when Papa was away, I so often thought of his remark:

"The truly good and wonderful things, you can know but once in a life."

He tried for quite a long time to know as many more as he could, and settled for picking up some pieces of the old ones. He frankly told me that at the end of the last truly good fall he knew here in Idaho—the 1958 fall. It was the night I found him sitting on the floor in our sitting room—when the mood was good, if a bit pensive.

No one will ever know—nor does it matter, really—when Papa decided that it wasn't any good. The awesome twin blast of his favorite shotgun was his announcement that it was not. It was Sunday morning, July 2, 1961—nineteen days short of his sixty-second year. Some reporter wrote that it was a shot heard round the world. An old phrase, but how true. I needn't dwell on that time—it's Hemingway history, some theory—but I have a thought or two about it that I want to leave for what they are worth; they are strictly my own, and from a man's point of view.

Papa's dilemma was many-sided, but I do know that paramount among them was deep humiliation, piano-wire sensitive man that he was. Observation tells me that he fought with all he had against doing what he did—he was against it, and wrote so in his own works, albeit as fiction. I did not know Papa as a man without God, so I'm sure that he did not *want* to kill himself. I pass on these views, not in biased defense of him, but because I feel it his due. He did care what would be thought about it, as he cared all his life what he was thought of—and expressed it countless times, in spite of how he lived it as his own man. I figure that he was certain he wasn't his own man any more and he was not about to face the *living* death. I did not live behind those lovable brown eyes, eyes that saw the view in true perspective, I'm quite sure. If it wasn't some courage at work that fateful Sunday morning, then I don't know what else it was.

We buried Papa Hemingway in the rather quaint but pretty little cemetery here in Ketchum on July 6. As a pallbearer with mutual local friends, I felt again that strange indescribable loneliness that I'd known twice before in the same small area —the first time twenty-two years back, when we were both pallbearers, and a beautiful tribute was read; then twenty years went by and we buried the colonel beside Gene Van Guilder. Yes, I was lonely, but I cannot truly say that I mourned. "That was the way of the Plan, and we can't tamper with it." Destiny does indeed write some strange scripts.

Five summers later a simple close-to-nature memorial to Papa was dedicated in public ceremony a short way out of Ketchum overlooking Trail Creek. Someone said: "A memorial to Ernest Hemingway? Who ever left more of a memorial than he did to himself—his legacy to us all?" He was looking at the ample bronze base plaque on the simple rocky footing supporting a pedestaled sculptured Hemingway head, and he added in a soft voice:

"But, he unknowingly contributed a bit to this one."

The words on the plaque are excerpts from the Gene Van Guilder eulogy, chosen by writers, then edited to finality by one of them—Miss Mary. Who, I wonder, would approve of them more than the man who wrote them?

> BEST OF ALL HE LOVED THE FALL
> THE LEAVES YELLOW ON THE COTTONWOODS
> LEAVES FLOATING ON THE TROUT STREAMS
> AND ABOVE THE HILLS
>   THE HIGH BLUE WINDLESS SKIES
> . . . NOW HE WILL BE A PART OF THEM FOREVER

The good, great, fun-loving guy I miss—and always will—and I miss him the most in the falls. But I do not mourn him because he's close by, his presence always felt, and I might hear a voice calling me a jerk. The guy I knew only here in the West, beating the paths to the fields, the marshes and the sloughs; and I'll never cease to wonder that I trod them well enough to keep some sort of pace. The guy who called himself a big "Batiste with the teeth" bending a canoe paddle to breaking point catching a downed mallard in the current ahead; cussing to high heaven, bawling for help, tearing his clothes in willows where a downed one chose to fall; the guy crawling beside me on his belly in wet marsh so we could get a look at a clutch of lovely little cinnamon teal that neither of us had ever seen before, and we could have gotten half of them with our guns, but only admired them "so that we'll never lose them this way"; the guy who winged a pintail drake, cradled the bird in his arms like a hurt child, and we bound his wing and took him home—to fly again the following fall migration; the guy who ate potluck with you; never complained if the birds did not fly that day, took it all in stride as hunters' luck because there would always be better days—there weren't any bad days when he was around.

It's an old truth that when you hunt with a man there has to be something that jells or it doesn't last. I think that we of our little tribe who are still around fully agree that in those wonderful falls with Papa, we just might have known him at his shining best—just as it might have been if we could have kept the same pace with him on the Gulf Stream, or, say, as safari men figuring how to make a sure shot on a kudu or a Cape buffalo. A pretty good way to know a man who knew how to check in with you, right down to the roots of it all; the simple, basic life in what he called in his writing, and spoke of so often: "I know a good country when I see one."

Quite a different sort of guy from the hair-on-the-chest, hell-raising, loud-talking, long-talking, wisecracking, boozing citizen of the world we had heard so much about when Gene and I first talked to him that morning back in 1939. I said that I liked the big kid I saw, examining us thoroughly and shrewdly; for in that big-barrel, grizzly-bear chest of a man there beat more often than not the heart of a playful, mischievous boy; a boy who could play rough and for keeps; and the only boy I ever knew to put a new roof on tennis-playing Father Dougherty's church—conned a friend of means out of a "C note" to help him with the job—and send a dead owl as a bouquet of flowers.

So often I wish that the vast community of interest could have known *that* Papa Hemingway, in this small, big-breathing corner of his world—the place of which he said in his last fall: If, when his time came, his real home was lost to him, Idaho was his only other choice.